PENGUIN BOOKS

500 GREAT BOOKS BY WOMEN: A READER'S GUIDE

Erica Bauermeister received her undergraduate degree in English from Occidental College and a master's and Ph.D. in English and American literature from the University of Washington. She currently lives in Seattle, Washington, where she spends her time writing, teaching, and watching her two children grow up.

Jesse Larsen is a working-class feminist artist, scholar, and educator who finished her B.A. in writing, got her first book contract (this one), and moved to Vermont in 1992, the year she turned fifty. She is currently finishing her first novel, *Shifting Sideways*, and her M.F.A. in writing at Goddard College.

Holly Smith, born in 1952, has had nearly as many jobs as her years. For the past seven years she has had the pleasure of managing a woman-owned bookstore. One of her joys in life is traveling; she has visited much of the United States and taken extended trips in the South Pacific and Southeast Asia. Throughout it all, she has read.

Erica Bauermeister,
Jesse Larsen, and
Holly Smith

Penguin Books

500 Great Books by Women

A Reader's Guide

PENGUIN BOOKS
Published by the Penguin Group
Penguin Books USA Inc., 375 Hudson Street,
New York, New York 10014, U.S.A.
Penguin Books Ltd, 27 Wrights Lane,
London W8 5TZ, England
Penguin Books Australia Ltd, Ringwood,
Victoria, Australia
Penguin Books Canada Ltd, 10 Alcorn Avenue,
Toronto, Ontario, Canada M4V 3B2
Penguin Books (N.Z.) Ltd, 182–190 Wairau Road,
Auckland 10, New Zealand

Penguin Books Ltd, Registered Offices:
Harmondsworth, Middlesex, England

First published in simultaneous hardcover and paperback editions by
Viking Penguin and Penguin Books, divisions of Penguin Books USA Inc. 1994

10 9 8 7 6 5

Copyright © Erica Bauermeister, Jesse Larsen,
and Holly Smith, 1994
All rights reserved

THE LIBRARY OF CONGRESS HAS CATALOGUED THE HARDCOVER AS FOLLOWS:
Bauermeister, Erica.
500 great books by women : a reader's guide / Erica Bauermeister,
Jesse Larsen, and Holly Smith.
p. cm.
Includes indexes.
ISBN 0-670-84829-8 (hc.)
ISBN 0 14 01.7590 3 (pbk.)
1. Women—Bibliography. 2. Literature—Women authors—
Bibliography. I. Larsen, Jesse. II. Smith, Holly.
III. Title. IV. Title: Five hundred great books by women.
Z7961.B35 1994
[HQ1150]
016.3054—dc20 94-15989

Printed in the United States of America
Set in Bembo
Designed by Kathryn Parise

Except in the United States of America,
this book is sold subject to the condition that it
shall not, by way of trade or otherwise, be lent, re-sold,
hired out, or otherwise circulated without the publisher's
prior consent in any form of binding or cover other
than that in which it is published and without a similar
condition including this condition being imposed
on the subsequent purchaser.

To Christine Bostrack Hoffman—Gram—
born in 1894 and still reading.
—H.S.

To my sisters, Anne Rusk and Karen Sue Greenup,
with love and respect.
—J.L.

To Caitlin Sarah Bauermeister,
who loves words.
—E.B.

Preface

> 'Tis woman's strongest vindication for speaking that *the world needs to hear her voice.* It would be subversive for every human interest that the cry of one half of the human family be stifled. . . . The world has had to limp along with the wobbling gait and one-sided hesitancy of a man with one eye. Suddenly the bandage is removed from the other eye and the whole body is filled with light. It sees a circle where before it saw a segment. The darkened eye restored, every member rejoices with it.
>
> —Anna Julia Cooper,
> *A Voice From the South*, 1892

We read to learn, to feel, to stretch beyond our own lives, to escape, and to understand. A book has the power to reach back toward us and let us know we are not alone. Up from a flat page of type comes joy or anger or sadness, a sentence that soars, or an image that surprises like a photograph long forgotten. For a few hundred pages we can feel new rhythms, see new images, learn about ourselves, become someone else.

But how often are we immersed in the rhythms and images of women? Women of all cultures still comprise a frustratingly small percentage of the authors represented in classrooms, reviews, and reader's guides. In the past, finding books by women authors has taken more persistence and time than many readers had. For years, those of us involved in this project wished there was a guide to books by women we could take with us when we went to bookstores and libraries. We wanted a guide that was personable and articulate, a guide that not only gave us titles and authors' names, but a sense of a book's content and style. Finally, we decided the only way to get such a guide was to write it ourselves.

We three editors are book-loving European-American women—a bookseller, a working-class writer, and an academic—committed to finding a multitude of voices. Some of the research for this guide has involved plowing our way through libraries and squinting over *Books in Print.* But there has been another kind of research—the kind that has been around as long as women have shared ideas. We wanted to include books that readers have loved, so we asked for suggestions from readers of all ages and backgrounds. Their responses were warm and enthusiastic, full of the kind of passion and excitement that books inspire. We have included many of their voices here so that you could experience their words directly. The diversity the contributors brought was inspiring, and reinforced for us, again and again, the pleasure and importance of individual opinion and style.

Our goal has been to create a guide that presents a wide variety of genres, cultures, and eras. To be considered, a work had to be (1) written by a woman, (2) written in or translated into English, (3) written in prose, and (4) in print as of January 1994. Of these considerations, it was the last that caused the most frustration. It is appalling how many books by women are no longer in print. Because we wanted this to be a guide that readers could use to find copies of the books, we kept the "in print" rule.

It is not our intent to present a "greatest books" list or a "female canon"—there are no must-reads, for every reader's tastes and needs are different and constantly changing. Rather, we have chosen to present a collection of books we love, which represent a myriad of opinions on a multitude of subjects. There are novels, essays, autobiographies and biographies, histories, short stories, letters, interviews, journals, sociological and philosophical studies, oral histories, and diaries. Roughly half the books are from the United States; the other half come from seventy other countries, and represent every continent except Antarctica. We have made a conscious effort to find works by women of color from around the world and books by and about working-class people—literature that all too often has not received attention or acknowledgment. Our commitment to women of color and international books in translation, as well as our requirement that all books be currently in print, has by necessity meant that the majority of books are from the twentieth century, with a large number having been published in the last forty-five years. But women have been writing for a long time, and while many of their books are no longer in print, the works included here go back as far as the thirteenth century. Together these authors create a chorus of astonishing power and beauty.

In an effort to make such a large mass of material accessible, we have organized these books by theme. In so doing, we are aware of the divisive and arbitrary nature of such categorizations, and we also understand that any one book could fit under several thematic categories. Looking at these books in groups, however, reinforces the notion that, while these authors share a common identification as women, each of these women has her own opinions about the world and her own sense of artistic presentation. So that you can use the guide in many ways, we have included indexes by title, author, date, and genre, as well as by country (based on the content of each book). We also have included indexes for books about people of color in the United States and books about lesbian and gay people, literature that has been traditionally underrepresented and thus difficult to find.

The books we have featured are ones we have found to be thought-provoking, beautiful, and satisfying. We make no claim to objectivity; reading is, after all, a personal process. We each brought our favorites, books that captured us through the power of the characters, the depth of introspection, the ability to create a mood, use words, or open our minds. Here are women who speak about their lives or make us see our own—authors who through the sheer beauty of their words can make us forget how to breathe. At times, discovering these books has meant suddenly understanding that writing is possible—or our lives are worthwhile—or perhaps simply that we aren't crazy.

It is our hope that you will experience the joy, the wisdom, the love that comes with finding these authors and their books. What we present here is a beginning—long overdue. Welcome.

How to Use This Book

This book is designed to be used by theme. If you wish to locate a book by its title, author, genre, date written or first published, or country of book content, or if you are interested in finding books about people of color in the United States or books about lesbian and gay people, the cross-reference indexes at the end of this guide can help you.

In the text, each entry's heading provides most of this information as well:

Title, Author, *original date of publication**, *Country of Book Content***, GENRE

*If the original date of publication differs significantly from the date the book was written, the date written will come first, with date of publication following in parentheses.

**If the author's country is different from that of the book content, information on the author's country will follow in parentheses.

Acknowledgments

Our thanks and appreciation go to Elizabeth and Ed Knappman, who helped shape a wish into a book; Caroline White, who believed in our idea and has done so much to make it a reality; and our contributors, who poured their hours and enthusiasm into this project. The librarians of the Wallingford-Wilmont Library of the Seattle Public Library system provided invaluable assistance; the Eliot Pratt Center at Goddard College and Carol Santoro of Second Story Bookstore in Seattle gave us access to a computerized Books in Print; Ben Bauermeister was a source of endless computer assistance and support. Our in-print restriction has caused us to treasure those publishers who take risks on lesser-known authors, keep books in print, and make translated copies of non-English books available: in particular, we are grateful to Rutgers University Press, The Feminist Press, Ayer Company, Milkweed Press, The Longman Group, Aunt Lute Books, Seal Press, Beacon Press, Arte Publico, University of Arizona Press, University of Texas Press, Serpent's Tail, Reader's International, Kitchen Table, Firebrand, Latin American Literary Review Press, South End Press, and Viking Penguin. A special note of thanks to Annette Windhorn at University of Nebraska, Elizabeth Valway at Heineman Educational Books, Paul Bennett at Academy Chicago, and Jeanne Dufour of Dufour Editions, for their time and support.

A long time ago, my parents gave me the gift of a childhood where I was allowed to read as much as I wanted, indiscriminately and voraciously. Through this project and the support of many people, I have had the luxury of recreating that experience as an adult. Bill Meierding and Elizabeth Knappman got me started; Rebecca Sullivan always listened and often brought my family dinner; Gloria Bauermeister, Colleen McQueen, and Nina Meierding provided solidity in a world of words. My love and admiration go to Ben, Caitlin, and Rylan Bauermeister, who in so many beautiful and patient ways have made this book their own, and to Holly and Jesse, who teach me so much.

—*Erica Bauermeister*

I hope Erica Bauermeister and Holly Smith already know how respectfully grateful I am to them for putting up, getting down, and keeping on. For graceful, intelligent, and reliable advice and encouragement, and for the life-saving constancy of their warm, smart, and artful love, I thank my mother, Hazel Loretta Tinsley; my daughters, Patricia Renee and Sonja Anne Larsen; and my friends Stephanie Rae Dickie, April Richardson, Nelle Christensen, Nancy Katz, Hank Bradley, Heather Downey, Linda Wiley, Suzanne Sowinska, Chris Kellett, Margaret Svec, Jane Keefer, Tom and Dee Barth, Erin Shrader, Andrea Freud Lowenstein, Paij Wadley-Bailey, Dagmar Nickerson, and Kae Bostrom. For the models of inspiration, endurance, enrichment, and excellence they continue to provide, I am grateful to bell hooks, Toni Morrison, Chrystos, Lucille Clifton, Irena Klepfisz, Alice Walker, Adrienne Rich, Patricia Hill Collins, Sandra Cisneros, Dorothy Allison, Tillie Olsen, and Lynda Barry. And for her financial support during the summer of 1993, when I had to read about a million books, I thank Anne Stokes.

—*Jesse Larsen*

I want to express my gratitude to the many people who, through their support, made this book a reality. Nancy Nordhoff and the staff at the Cottages at Hedgebrook, and the other writers there, provided me with a slice of heaven while on earth. Carol Santoro was always interested in the project and flexible with my work schedule. Gerry and Cubby Smith generously gave me a place away from the day-to-day, to read, write, and walk. Marie Ciliberto let me laugh, cry, and brag whenever it was necessary, and offered hugs and questions that enhanced my view of the individual and group project. Erica Bauermeister and Jesse Larsen, through their distinctive styles, taught me life lessons I was ready to learn. My large and extended family and full circle of friends have always provided a solid foundation for me. Thank you to all.

—*Holly Smith*

Contents

500 Great Books by Women

Art

What drives, pushes, pulls, and plagues people to make art? For some, the quest starts early. Hayden Herrera and Laurie Lisle describe the maturation of the astonishing talents of Frida Kahlo and Georgia O'Keeffe. Elizabeth Bishop, Eudora Welty, and Grazia Deledda remember their childhoods: a natural affinity toward the physical beauty of numbers, but not their function; a house where any room could be a reading room; a moment when it became important to write about reality and not myth. Being a woman artist can create frustrating, sometimes nearly overwhelming obstacles: Vicki Goldberg traces Margaret Bourke-White's determination to succeed in the male-dominated profession of photography. Elizabeth Stuart Phelps creates a painfully recognizable portrait of one woman's struggle to balance her life as wife, mother, and painter; more than one hundred years later, Anne Truitt writes of trying to find time and inspiration in the midst of her daily life as a single mother/sculptor/painter/grandmother. With research and formidable passion, Tillie Olsen demonstrates that art is work that takes time, tools, and training, and that the issues of what is called art and of what artists' work is rewarded and made profitable are deeply influenced by the biases that permeate our society. The essays collected by Janet Sternburg in *The Writer on Her Work, Volume II*, as well as the journal entries of Diane Glancy, consider art as a cultural expression, a history of a people. In these works, art emerges as passionate self-definition, a need that clamors to be met, and a fulfillment that cannot be found elsewhere.

Artemisia	Anna Banti
The Autobiography of Alice B. Toklas	Gertrude Stein
Black Women Writers at Work	Claudia Tate, ed.
Claiming Breath	Diane Glancy
Cosima	Grazia Deledda
Cry to Heaven	Anne Rice
Dancing on the Edge of the World	Ursula K. Le Guin
Daybook	Anne Truitt
Elizabeth Bishop: The Collected Prose	Elizabeth Bishop
Frida	Hayden Herrera
Margaret Bourke-White	Vicki Goldberg
One Writer's Beginnings	Eudora Welty
Portrait of an Artist	Laurie Lisle
The Road Through Miyama	Leila Philip
Silences	Tillie Olsen
The Story of Avis	Elizabeth Stuart Phelps
The Ultraviolet Sky	Alma Luz Villanueva
The Writer on Her Work, Volume II	Janet Sternburg, ed.

Artemisia, Anna Banti, *translated from Italian by Shirley d'Ardia Caracciolo, 1947, Italy,* NOVEL

Artemisia is a work of love and devotion. The known facts concerning the seventeenth-century Italian painter Artemisia Gentileschi are few and easily contained in a short paragraph in the introduction. Art historian and writer Anna Banti (Lucia Lopresti) became intrigued by Artemisia, invented what she did not know, then saw her manuscript destroyed in World War II. When she began the manuscript again, her own experience entered in and challenged the boundaries of traditional biography. Across time, without time, author and subject speak to each other; as the author speculates, Artemisia is fleshed out. Neither true biography nor historical fiction, *Artemisia* floats on the surface of the seventeenth century, diving down for brief bursts of detail as if to capture pictures and feelings rather than pin down facts. Moments, meetings, and thought processes are described in lush, vivid detail—a woman pulling a bucket up from a well, a curl falling unrestrained, an encounter with a servant, a body run over by a carriage—did any of them happen? Are they any more true than the portraits Artemisia paints of the aristocracy, or than her misattributed "self-portrait"? Is the insecurity and self-doubt described here Artemisia's or the author's? All of these questions, implied and explicit, make for a rich, complex, thought-provoking book that requires and deserves careful attention on the part of the reader. Take it slow, and maybe twice.

E.B.

The Autobiography of Alice B. Toklas, Gertrude Stein, *1933, France (United States)*, NONFICTION

The Autobiography of Alice B. Toklas is actually the autobiography of Gertrude Stein. With complete self-assurance and audacity, speaking through the unassuming persona of her companion Alice B. Toklas, Gertrude Stein indulged herself delightfully in this ode to herself and her literary/artistic circle. Perhaps she was quoting Alice's actual words when she wrote, "I may say that only three times in my life have I met a genius and each time a bell within me rang and I was not mistaken." One of the geniuses referred to is, of course, Gertrude Stein. Fortunately, conceit is leavened with irony and wordplay, and the gossip is elevated to the level of myth by the stature of its subjects. Gertrude Stein wrote, and apparently lived, with self-conscious sensitivity to her role among a generation of writers and artists in Paris who were engaged in becoming legends. Although her characters were "giants" of art and literature whose contributions she considered with a discerning eye, her anecdotes of their behavior could be small talk taken to the point of farce. The *Autobiography* offers glimpses of the dazzling and often baffling experimental style for which the author is famous, but the guileless, conversational tone of this book makes it one of her most easily accessible works.

K.B.

Black Women Writers at Work, Claudia Tate, editor, *1989, United States,* INTERVIEWS

The tone and spirit of this splendid volume of conversations with fourteen black women writers is eloquently captured in Claudia Tate's introduction: "With one penetrating glance they cut through layers of institutionalized racism and sexism and uncover a core of social contradictions and intimate dilemmas which plague all of us, regardless of our race or gender." Responding to basic questions on the themes of why and for whom they write, and how they perceive their responsibility to their work, to others, and to society, these well-known playwrights, poets, novelists, and essayists talk about the connections between their lives and their art. Toni Morrison notes that the longing for commercial success "is a substitute for value in your life." Kristin Hunter is "interested in the enormous and varied adaptations of black people to the distorting, terrifying restrictions of society." Toni Cade Bambara wants readers to understand why women need to keep writing their "anger, dismay, disappointment, or just sheer bewilderment" about the woman-man thing: "Women are not going to shut up. We care too much . . . about the development of ourselves and our brothers, fathers, lovers, sons to negotiate a bogus peace." Nikki Giovanni speaks of alienation as a force that can produce vigor: "Our strength is that we are not comfortable any place; therefore, we're comfortable *every place.*" In this superb collection, the answers, asides, and truth-telling are as diverse, dazzling, and large-spirited as the writers themselves.

J.L.

Claiming Breath, Diane Glancy, *1992, United States,* MEMOIR

Claiming Breath is a collage composed of notes, poems, and thoughts written over the course of a year in Diane Glancy's life. It is a year in which she reflects on her marriage and divorce, confronts her mother's death after a three-year battle with cancer, and explores the conflicts and similarities between her Cherokee heritage and her Christian beliefs. As a representative for the Oklahoma State Art Council, she spends long hours driving to schools to "teach" poetry to the children, and as she drives, many thoughts occur to her. Diane Glancy's art is her poetry, words are her palette: "The word is important in Native American tradition. You speak the path on which you walk. Your words make the trail." This multifaceted woman allows you to peer over her shoulder as she explores her "memories & their relational aspects to the present." With insights that are engaging and thought-provoking, she questions what it is to be a Native American, a poet, a Christian, and a woman, and she challenges her readers: "Aren't all of us made up of paradox and diversity, anger, hurt, hope, guilt, endurance?" *Claiming Breath* is a free flow of thoughts, written in a note-taking style very similar to that of a personal journal, which includes incomplete sentences and occasional lack of punctuation. It is a style that suits and illuminates Diane Glancy's own curiosities and opinions and can open new visions and reinforce personal philosophies for readers.

H.S.

Cosima, Grazia Deledda, *translated from Italian by Martha King, 1937, Italy,* NOVEL

Cosima is the fictionalized autobiography of Grazia Deledda, the first Italian woman to win a Nobel Prize for literature (1926). Focusing on her early life in rural Sardinia, the novel mixes realism with the perceptions of young Cosima to show a world both terrible and wonderful. Cosima is part of a large family full of tragedy: her scholarly eldest brother becomes an alcoholic, her father dies, another brother manages the family interests but keeps most of the income for himself. Cosima carries on, finding beauty and learning about life. Her first story is published in a fashion magazine; encouraged, she steals a liter of oil from the cellar to pay the postage on her first novel manuscript, which is accepted for publication. Her payment is a hundred copies, "and the big package plummeted into the house like a meteorite. Her mother was frightened by it, walking around it evenings with the fearful distrust of a dog that sees a strange animal." As Cosima oversees the family oil-pressing mill, she hears the stories of the peasants: "genuine people, hard-working and gentle who, even if they could get their claws on the little bit belonging to their neighbors . . . would do it sparingly and then go to confession." She stops writing romances and concentrates on Sardinia—a place where myth melds with grinding reality, where a woman can fall in love with a sheep, where bandits come to your door, and where everyone gossips about that strange little Cosima, who writes.

E.B.

Cry to Heaven, Anne Rice, *1982, Italy* (*United States*), NOVEL

The stage is Rome, the music is the opera, and the soprano is the castrato. In her historically accurate novel, *Cry to Heaven*, Anne Rice retells the composer's dilemma of who will sing the soprano arias—the most popular songs—when there is a papal ban against women performing: "and Guido perceived that when the woman is taken out of an entire realm of life that must needs imitate the world itself, then some substitute for that woman is inevitable. Something must rise to take the place of that which is feminine." That inevitable substitute is the castrato, the surgically altered boy whose voice will never change to that of a man. Anne Rice sets the stage by explaining who and what the castrato is. We are privy to the daily life and work of the castrato student, which begins two hours before dawn: the vocal exercises, the instrumental lessons, the endless technical exercises in composition and notation, the wearing of the black tunic with the red sash and the black ribbon at the "nape of the neck" which identifies one as a castrato. And finally, the performance in the role of a woman, in complete feminine attire, on the operatic stage. Immersed in an era of European music and awed by the power of the castrato, we become the audience as the beauty and majesty of his performances come alive.

D.N.-W.

Dancing on the Edge of the World: Thoughts on Words, Women, Places, Ursula K. Le Guin, *1989, United States,* ESSAYS

This collection of lucid, witty, warm, and intelligent "talks, essays, occasional pieces and reviews" was written with the goal "to subvert as much as possible without hurting anybody's feelings" on matters about which she says "I think I ought to stand up and be counted, lest silence collude with injustice." Her subjects, which she categorizes (and even codes for the reader) as Feminism, Social Responsibility, Literature, and Travel, offer astute observations on a variety of timely topics. What do women recently graduated from college need to know? Where do ideas come from? What are the prospects for women in writing? "No matter how successful, beloved, influential her work was, when a woman author dies, nine times out of ten, she gets dropped from the lists, the courses, the anthologies, while the men get kept. . . . If she had the nerve to have children, her chances of getting dropped are higher still. . . . So if you want your writing to be taken seriously, don't marry and have kids, and above all, don't die. But if you have to die, commit suicide. They approve of that." This collection offers both nutritious food for thought and excellent examples of a variety of writing styles: well-researched essays, whimsical and imaginative anecdotes, reflective personal memory. It is spiced to perfection with Ursula Le Guin's great sense of humor; she takes herself and her subject matter just seriously enough.

J.L.

Daybook: The Journal of an Artist, Anne Truitt, *1982, United States,* JOURNAL

Anne Truitt is a sculptor, painter, mother, and grandmother. *Daybook*, her first published journal, is illuminating and nourishing: "It is as if there are external equivalents for truths which I already in some mysterious way know. In order to catch these equivalents, I have to stay 'turned on' all the time, to keep my receptivity to what is around me totally open. Preconception is fatal to this process. Vulnerability is implicit in it; pain, inevitable." For Anne Truitt, art is life. While refusing "the inflated definition of artists as special people with special prerogatives and special excuses," she recognizes special difficulties and differences between artists and other professionals. The work of doctors and lawyers involves a clearly defined practice, the skills needed by plumbers and carpenters are obvious. Artists, however, must "spin their work out of themselves, discover its law, and then present themselves turned inside out to the public gaze." The mother of three children abandoned by a husband who never looked back, she is harried by everyday concerns: "I feel a little pulled at the seams. Too much is happening too fast for me to integrate. Life unrolls like a Mack Sennett comedy. The film is so speeded up that events threaten to splinter into nonsense." In a consistently tender and down-to-earth voice, Anne Truitt explores her life and work, gently guiding herself—and her fortunate readers—through a growing woman's life.

J.L.

Elizabeth Bishop: The Collected Prose 1937–1970, Elizabeth Bishop, *United States/Canada/Brazil,* MEMOIRS/ESSAYS/SHORT STORIES

This wonderful collection of prose pieces by a Pulitzer Prize–winning poet consists of seventeen essays, memoirs, and short stories written between 1937 and 1970. When Elizabeth Bishop was still an infant, her father died and her mother returned home to her parents in Nova Scotia, Canada. "Primer Class" tells how Elizabeth, as a first-grader who cannot fathom long columns of figures, finds "drawing numbers enjoyable—I mean 'artistically' enjoyable." The poignancy is palpable in "The Country Mouse," an account of the day her unknown, wealthy, and quite stuffy paternal grandparents appear in Nova Scotia to take six-year-old Elizabeth to Worcester, Massachusetts: "It was a day that seemed to include months in it, or even years, a whole unknown past I was made to feel I should have known about, and a strange, unpredictable future." Elizabeth's first job after graduating from Vassar is hilariously recounted in "The U.S.A. School of Writing," where she is hired to teach in the name of "Fred G. Margolies" until all Mr. Margolies's students graduate. The author's personal and literary friendship with the poet Marianne Moore is depicted in an elegantly witty and tender memoir entitled "Efforts of Affection." Readers who love precise language and ingenious thinking will enjoy this sumptuous and stunning collection.

J.L.

Frida: A Biography of Frida Kahlo, Hayden Herrera, *1983, Mexico* (*United States*), BIOGRAPHY

In *Frida*, art historian Hayden Herrera vividly portrays a woman of strength, talent, humor, and endurance. Frida Kahlo (1907–1954) was born in Mexico City, the child of a Mexican mother and a German father. Her early years were influenced by the turmoil of the Mexican revolution and a bout with polio, but she remained spirited, resilient, and mischievous. Her father, a photographer, encouraged her artistic interests, and her education at an elite school drew her to new ideas and to a group of irreverent radicals who would become some of Mexico's most respected intellectuals. When she was nineteen, Frida Kahlo's life was transformed when a bus in which she was riding was hit by a trolley car. Pierced by a steel handrail and broken in many places, she entered a long period of convalescence during which she began to paint self-portraits. In 1928, at twenty-one, she joined the Communist party and came to know Diego Rivera. The forty-one-year-old Rivera, Mexico's most famous painter, was impressed by the force of her personality and by the authenticity of her art, and the two soon married. Though they were devoted to each other, intermittent affairs on both sides, Frida Kahlo's grief over her inability to bear a child, and her frequent illnesses made the marriage tumultuous. Hayden Herrera—combining biographical research, Frida Kahlo's own letters, and analyses of her paintings—illuminates and amplifies the painter's life story, her importance as an artist, and her ultimate triumph over tragedy.

L.A.

Margaret Bourke-White: A Biography, Vicki Goldberg, *1987, United States,* BIOGRAPHY

Art historian and photography critic Vicki Goldberg gives us a perceptive portrait of Margaret Bourke-White (1904–1971), a woman who witnessed and interpreted many of the major events of the 1930s through the 1950s. As a child, Margaret White wanted to do "all the things women never do," and her nonconformist parents encouraged her. After a brief marriage at nineteen, she combined her parents' surnames to rechristen herself Bourke-White. This began a process of self-definition that is documented throughout the book. Margaret Bourke-White soon found the vehicle for her ambition: photography. Single-minded hard work, an avid interest in the world, vigorous self-promotion, and a total lack of fear allowed her to succeed in an overwhelmingly male-dominated profession, and to become one of the most famous and sought-after photographer-journalists of her day. Her photographs have become icons of this century: Fort Peck Dam on the first cover of *Life* magazine, flood victims during the Depression, Moscow under fire during World War II, survivors of Buchenwald concentration camp, Gandhi at his spinning wheel. In 1939, Margaret Bourke-White married writer Erskine Caldwell. Although the marriage was short-lived, it produced a collaboration of words and photographs comprising several books that chronicled the changes taking place in Russia, Europe, and the United States. For the last twenty years of her life, Margaret Bourke-White battled Parkinson's disease and the loneliness that increased isolation and inability to work imposed upon her. Yet she remained an optimist, writing her autobiography and living as full a life as possible with her characteristic passion and fearlessness.

L.A.

One Writer's Beginnings, Eudora Welty, *1983, United States,* MEMOIR

Eudora Welty's many awards for her writings include the 1973 Pulitzer Prize for the novel *The Optimist's Daughter.* In *One Writer's Beginnings* she explores the path that led her to become a writer. In her seventies when she wrote this memoir, she looks back fondly on a happy childhood with her family. Her father, a man who looks to the future, instills in his children a broad view of life; her mother makes every room a reading room at any time of day. Family trips to visit out-of-state relatives are journeys with "direction, movement, development, change" that plant the seeds for her first novel, and from these seeds her words grow, watered and tended by imagination and curiosity. Eudora Welty knows, loves, and appreciates her family for the firm foundation they have provided, a foundation she has built on throughout her life. As her mother, "lying helpless and nearly blind, in her bed, an old lady," recites poetry, the author is aware: "She was teaching me one more, almost her last, lesson: emotions do not grow old. I knew that I would feel as she did, and I do." Filled with tenderness and honesty, this is but one of the many reflections that comes through, a reminder to us not to dismiss the importance of our pasts or our emotions.

H.S.

Portrait of an Artist: A Biography of Georgia O'Keeffe, Laurie Lisle, *1980, United States,* BIOGRAPHY

This honest and admiring biography relates the story of Georgia O'Keeffe (1887–1986). Raised on a Wisconsin farm in a family of "irrepressible individualists," Georgia O'Keeffe was a self-reliant child who decided early to become an artist. She worked steadily toward that goal, attending art schools and teaching when family misfortunes dictate. In 1916, a friend sent some of her drawings to Alfred Stieglitz, renowned photographer and champion of avant-garde art. He promptly exhibited them, proclaiming that they revealed "a woman on paper." Furious at his presumption, Georgia O'Keeffe confronted him. They became lovers and later married, beginning an energetic collaboration that lasted until his death. When she wanted to have a baby, he insisted that she chose between motherhood and art. He promoted her work, which immediately became famous for its sexually suggestive imagery, an interpretation she resolutely denied. Finding it increasingly difficult to live in his orbit, she gradually established a pattern of spending six months with him in New York followed by six months in New Mexico, her "spiritual home." By the time Alfred Stieglitz died in 1946, Georgia O'Keeffe had firmly established herself as an artist. "Besides having a rich talent, ambition, assistance, and virtually no doubt about the validity of her vision, O'Keeffe had the brains to match her artistic gift and guide its flowering." As she examines Georgia O'Keeffe's complex personality, her choices and her reactions to the social and physical landscape around her, Laurie Lisle succeeds in drawing an inspiring portrait of a truly original, courageous woman.

L.A.

The Road Through Miyama, Leila Philip, *1989, Japan* (*United States*), NONFICTION

Leila Philip—blond, blue-eyed American—spent from 1983 to 1985 as a potter's apprentice in the small Japanese village of Miyama. There she learned pottery through observation and painstaking repetition; using this same attention to detail she learned about people and traditions. *The Road Through Miyama* is full of the history and personalities of this small town originally settled by Korean potters captured and brought to Japan at the beginning of the seventeenth century. Pottery remains the industry of this village of six hundred, as well as its signature: "Everywhere in the weeds are ancient black pots. Bits of black pottery crunch underfoot on all the pathways; the earth itself is potshards." In her daily walks, conversations with villagers, and research, Leila Philip comes to learn about life and art in this country where "even the [potter's] wheel spins in the opposite direction from wheels at home." Through her mesmerizing prose she gives us history lessons, takes us to the site of an ancient abandoned communal kiln, tells us about the harvesting of rice and *takenoko* (bamboo), describes the firing process that lasts many hours. On every subject, the language is beautiful—smooth, elegant, and full of substance. *The Road Through Miyama* speaks much about Leila Philip's experience as a potter, yet it moves far beyond the individual to become a testament to a way of life.

E.B.

Silences, Tillie Olsen, *1978, United States,* NONFICTION

"This book is about silences. It is concerned with the relationship of circumstances—including class, color, sex; the times, climate into which one is born—to the creation of literature." In the United States, why are there so many more male authors than female authors listed in literary course offerings, reviews, and anthologies? Why, especially, when as far back as 1971, one out of every four or five books published were written by women? Is this more proof, "in this so much more favorable century," that women are innately incapable of artistic literary achievement? With poetic language and painstaking thoroughness, Tillie Olsen articulates the obstacles, difficulties, frustrations, and imperatives faced when nonprivileged people—women especially—are driven to write: How do working people get sustained periods of time not devoted to wage labor or corrupted by economic pressures? Where do women writers find sufficient space and encouragement to keep writing? Written over a period of fifteen years in time squeezed between wage work and mothering, *Silences* continues to serve as a model of inviting and accessible scholarship: "A passion and purpose inform its pages: love for my incomparable medium, literature; hatred for all that, societally rooted, unnecessarily lessens and denies it; slows, impairs, silences writers. It is written to rededicate and encourage."

J.L.

The Story of Avis, Elizabeth Stuart Phelps, *1877, United States,* NOVEL

Avis is a nineteenth-century painter who strives to keep herself free of marriage and entanglements. As a child, Avis decides that, given a woman's options of marriage or being a "lady," "I think I'd rather keep dogs." She is caught all the same, by a "modern man." Although Avis declares, and her fiancé agrees, that she must not "resign my profession as an artist," the reality greets her with their first house: "It was not quite clear where the studio was to be, unless in the attic." But the house is near the college, where her husband teaches, and that, "in the view of the New England winters, and the delicate health of the young professor, was decisive." She returns from an hour in her studio to clogged drains and unexpected company, descending "from the sphinx to the drainpipe in one fell swoop." Truly, she does hate housekeeping, and while she loves her baby, "sometimes, sitting burdened with the child upon her arms, she looked out and off upon the summer sky with a strangling desolation like that of a forgotten diver, who sees the clouds flit, from the bottom of the sea." And so it goes. How modern is the "modern man" and how much do women's roles ever change? This book, written more than one hundred years ago, will still seem very real to many women today.

E.B.

The Ultraviolet Sky, Alma Luz Villanueva, *1988, United States,* NOVEL

When, at thirty-four, teacher and painter Rosa decides to make changes in her life, she has to contend with those who do not agree or understand. Rosa's seventeen-year-old son, Sean, feels slighted; Sierra, Rosa's best friend, is threatened; and Rosa's second husband, Julio, is angry at Rosa and himself. How can she do this to him? he demands. The intensity of the love and hate she feels for Julio confuses Rosa. When they are in sync, conversation flows and making love is a powerful pleasure, but more often their simmering anger erupts. So she buys the house revealed to her in her dreams and lives by herself for the first time. When she finds out she is pregnant and decides to have Julio's baby, alone, everyone is—again—full of questions and accusations. Staring at her paintings and her belly, she, too, wonders what she is doing. Rosa is far from perfect—she drinks lots of wine, loves to flirt, and falls into bed with Julio when she tells herself she won't. She also has a strong and curious spirit, listens to her dreams, and fondly remembers the grandmother who raised her. Rosa is aware of her own "powerful softness" and realizes that "it takes all the strength I've got to push down through my fear, and you never really know if you're going to make it." Still she bravely questions, without knowing the answers, the roles and values she is expected to live by.

H.S.

The Writer on Her Work, Volume II: New Essays in New Territory, Janet Sternburg, editor, *1991, United States,* ESSAYS

In the 1970s, Janet Sternburg wanted to read a book about how various writers came to write, but, in order to read that book, she had to make it happen. The first volume of *The Writer on Her Work* was published in 1980. Volume two, spanning a broader range of geography and generations than its predecessor, explores women's perceptions of their engagement with the world through their art. "I write in order to belong," explains Elena Poniatowska, a woman of Polish ancestry born in France and raised in Mexico, a woman whose language is Spanish, who knows she is a Mexican writer. Bharati Mukherjee insists that she is an American writer, "in the American mainstream, trying to extend it"; she is an immigrant whose "investment is in the American reality, not the Indian." Jan Morris, a writer who used to be a male named James, continues to try to believe "the fount of art to be beyond gender." Rita Dove wants to know "How far can a Greek Goddess lead a Black poet?" Margaret Atwood says, "It never gets any easier." This book, like volume one, belongs in the library of every woman who wants to make art.

J.L.

Choices

Throughout our lives, we make choices and live with their repercussions, both anticipated and unexpected. The books and authors here explore a vast variety of decisions that face women, and how these decisions are affected not only by our individual personalities, but by the cultures we live in. Bahiah Shaheen shocks Egyptian society when she starts to wear pants in *Two Women in One*; in the United States, Eleanor Roosevelt carves out her own life in the midst of social and political expectations. Nella Larsen portrays two light-skinned African-American women who have the option of passing for white; one chooses to, the other doesn't. Joyce Carol Oates shows what happens when two teenagers silently agree not to confess to a murder; Elizabeth Robins's *The Convert* portrays one woman's decision to become actively involved in feminist politics in early-twentieth-century Britain. Kate Chopin's heroine leaves her husband's house; *The Dollmaker*'s Gertie Nevells gives up her dream of owning a farm, in order to keep her family together; Tomo of *The Waiting Years* is allowed to choose her husband's mistress. Mariama Ba writes of two Senegalese women's reactions when their husbands take second wives. Anita Brookner, Miles Franklin, May Sarton, Camilla Collett, and Sylvia Townsend Warner explore five different women's choices about marriage. Jean Rhys describes Julia Martin's conflict between personal dignity and financial survival. These women must decide for themselves, often in opposition to society's expectations. Their choices—clear, complicated, or confusing—make for thought-provoking reading.

After Leaving Mr. McKenzie	Jean Rhys
Aquamarine	Carol Anshaw
The Awakening	Kate Chopin
Because It Is Bitter, and Because It Is My Heart	Joyce Carol Oates
The Convert	Elizabeth Robins
The District Governor's Daughters	Camilla Collett
The Dollmaker	Harriet Arnow
Eleanor Roosevelt, Volume One	Blanche Wiesen Cook
From the Lanai and Other Hawaii Stories	Jessica K. Saki
The Garden Party and Other Stories	Katherine Mansfield
Hotel du Lac	Anita Brookner
Lolly Willowes	Sylvia Townsend Warner
The Magnificent Spinster	May Sarton
Miss Sophie's Diary	Ding Ling
My Brilliant Career	Miles Franklin
Passing	Nella Larsen
So Long a Letter	Mariama Ba
Testament of Youth	Vera Brittain
Three	Lillian Hellman
Three Guineas	Virginia Woolf
Two Women in One	Nawal El Saadawi
The Waiting Years	Fumiko Enchi

After Leaving Mr. McKenzie, Jean Rhys, *1931, England,* NOVEL

Julia Martin wants more than the usual woman's lot, but the only thing she knows how to do is please men. When she was young, it was easy to find glamour and adventure in affairs with respectable married men. Always willing to be cunning enough to start an affair with the kind of man she could wangle a living out of, she was never willing—or able—to make all the compromises necessary to keep an affair going. Now living in a dingy hotel, alienated by her past from family and friends, she faces a lonely and wanting middle age. Her affair with Mr. McKenzie is over, the last in a string of affairs with men whose respect she cannot earn and whose money she desperately needs; there are no likely new prospects. The last time Julia meets Mr. McKenzie, she is angrily proud: " 'Oh, yes, look here, this check . . . This check I got today. I don't want it.' 'Good,' said Mr. McKenzie. 'Just as you like, of course.' She picked up her glove and hit his cheek with it. 'I despise you,' she said. 'Quite,' said Mr. McKenzie." Called "terrible and superb" by Rebecca West, *After Leaving Mr. McKenzie* is an intense and penetrating picture of the sinking of a woman who only wanted to live a little.

J.L.

Aquamarine, Carol Anshaw, *1992, United States,* NOVEL

It's the 1968 Summer Olympics and seventeen-year-old Jesse, a gold medal contender in swimming, falls in love for the first time with Marty, her main competitor. Jesse comes in second and Marty wins the gold—but is Marty the better swimmer? The novel then shifts to 1990 and portrays three paths Jesse could have chosen, each with Marty's lingering influence. On one trail Jesse is married, having her first child late in life, living in the town where she grew up. In the back of her mind she feels "she missed the one fast chance she had to slip out." Down another path she is bringing her current lover home for a visit with her mother, trying to decide if she will admit to her that she is a lesbian. Before visiting home, "she tries to prepare herself, get the issues lined up, sorted out, internally addressed so she doesn't get ambushed by them when she's there. This, of course, doesn't work." On the third road she is divorced with two adolescent children. "She worries she's replicating her own mother's brand of parenting, leaving the strong child to fend for herself while fighting a lifetime of battles on behalf of the weak one." Throughout *Aquamarine* Jesse wonders "what if?" An interesting, entertaining, warm-hearted novel, it may leave the reader wondering about her own life paths as well.

H.S.

The Awakening, Kate Chopin, *1899, United States,* NOVEL

Edna Pontellier, the heroine of *The Awakening,* shocked readers in 1899, and the scandal created by the book haunted Kate Chopin for the rest of her life. *The Awakening* begins at a crisis point in twenty-eight-year-old Edna Pontellier's life. Edna is a passionate and artistic woman who finds few acceptable outlets for her desires in her role as wife and mother of two sons living in conventional Creole society. Unlike the married women around her, whose sensuality seems to flow naturally into maternity, Edna finds herself wanting her own emotional and sexual identity. During one summer while her husband is out of town, her frustrations find an outlet in an affair with a younger man. Energized and filled with a desire to define her own life, she sends her children to the country and removes herself to a small house of her own: "Every step she took toward relieving herself from obligations added to her strength and expansion as an individual. She began to look with her own eyes; to see and apprehend the deeper undercurrents of life. No longer was she content to 'feed upon the opinion' when her own soul had invited her." Her triumph is short-lived, however, destroyed by a society that has no place for a self-determined, unattached woman. Her story is a tragedy, and it was one of many clarion calls in its day to examine the institution of marriage and women's opportunities in an oppressive world.

E.B.

Because It Is Bitter, and Because It Is My Heart, Joyce Carol Oates, *1990, United States,* NOVEL

In 1956 in upstate New York, a murder committed in rage binds the lives of a fifteen-year-old white woman and a seventeen-year-old black man forever. Their casual school acquaintance takes on another dimension as they decide, without words, not to confess to the crime. It's a decision that takes a toll on each: for one it means an erosion of self-esteem, for the other it creates a smug but false confidence that they got away with it. Depicting children who come from homes that are struggling financially and emotionally to get by, Joyce Carol Oates explores, through voices of black and white, male and female, and parent and child, the impact that parents' decisions have on their children and that children's choices have on their future lives. In this small, industrial town before the civil rights movement of the 1960s, the issue of race both confuses and defines many of the characters' actions. *Because It Is Bitter, and Because It Is My Heart* looks closely into the lives of these young people: why they remained silent about the murder, why they felt they had no other options, and what it cost them. At times the reader may want to reach through the pages and shake these people, tell them to see a bigger picture; at the same time, it's hard not to feel absorbed in the characters' lives, as though we are making their choices with them.

H.S.

The Convert, Elizabeth Robins, *1907, England* (*United States*), NOVEL

Although Elizabeth Robins was American by birth, she spent a good portion of her life in England as an actress and feminist activist. *The Convert* is about the British suffrage movement, which the author knew well. Part witty and scathing commentary on the upper classes, part political rhetoric quoted directly from open-air meetings, and part muckraking realism, *The Convert* moves back and forth between the personal and the political until the two can no longer be distinguished. The novel uses as its frame the political "conversion" of Vida Levering, a beautiful upper-middle-class woman. We follow Vida's growing discontent with "country weekend" society and her increasing awareness of the common lot of women. Forthright and direct, Elizabeth Robins discusses issues that must have been shocking in 1907: unwed motherhood, the effects of the inequality of women, and the essential disrespect that underlies chivalry. Reminiscent of Jane Austen and foreshadowing the work of Virginia Woolf, *The Convert* is a fascinating novel. It provides us with a sense of history and a feeling of pride in what women could and did accomplish. It is also disturbing because far too many of the issues are still relevant.

E.B.

The District Governor's Daughters, Camilla Collett, *translated from Norwegian by Kirsten Seaver, 1854–55, Norway,* NOVEL

Although its main plot line follows the course of a romantic entanglement, *The District Governor's Daughters* is marked by the characters' many long speeches and the narrator's equally long philosophical addresses to the reader—all of which can make the book slow going. So why read it? For many reasons. This was the first book to address directly social problems in Norway (in particular the inequities of marriage and the treatment of women) and was a major force in the creation of the Norwegian feminist movement. It is the discussions, not the action, that make this a vehement, powerful book. Sometimes Camilla Collett is brutal: "Weddings were invented for the happy [brides]. No doubt they serve the same function as cymbals and kettledrums during the sacrifices performed by savages: they stun the victims and drown out their screams." Sometimes she is sly and ironic, as on ballroom dancing: "None of the partners seemed to take any real pleasure in the business, and I did not know what to think. I wonder if the reason is that the ladies are not allowed to dance with whom they want?" At other moments, as when the young protagonist Sophie is writing in her diary, the novel is poignant, sad, and almost hopeful. Should Sophie choose a life of independence, a lover she cannot completely trust, or the older man who loves and admires her? And does she really have a choice at all?

E.B.

The Dollmaker, Harriet Arnow, *1954, United States,* NOVEL

In the opening scene of *The Dollmaker,* a rough-hewn, uneducated woman performs a tracheotomy on her dying son, guided only by her love for her child and rural common sense. Thus we are introduced to Gertie Nevells, one of the most amazing women in literature. Gertie is a powerful, compassionate woman, a wood sculptor, a mother who talks to her daughter's imaginary playmates. Her one dream is to buy her own farm in the backwoods of the South and live there with her husband and children. But World War II intervenes, and as a good wife she must take her children and follow her husband to Detroit, where he has been put to work in a war factory. In the city, Gertie fights desperately to keep her family together and maintain their rural values, but it's a hard fight and even her flowers seem to know it: "There was something frantic in their blooming, as if they knew that frost was near and then the bitter cold. They'd lived through all the heat and noise and stench of summertime, and now each widely opened flower was like a triumphant cry, 'We will, we will make seed before we die.' " A big book, full of vividly drawn characters and masterful scenes, *The Dollmaker* is both a passionate denunciation of industrialization and war, and a tribute to a woman's love for her children and the land.

E.B.

Eleanor Roosevelt, Volume One: 1884–1933, Blanche Wiesen Cook, *1992, United States,* BIOGRAPHY

Eleanor Roosevelt is an extensively researched, revisionist text that sings praises of one of this century's most revered and least understood women. Eleanor Roosevelt was born in 1884 into a prominent American family, but her childhood was often bitter. Her parents could not offer her the love and security she needed, and they died when she was very young. Raised by maternal relatives, she studied for a time in England, then fell in love with her cousin, Franklin Roosevelt. She seemed destined to be the socialite wife of a wealthy politician, and that is how her life has most often been interpreted. But Blanche Cook chronicles Eleanor Roosevelt's real life: her political agenda—often refreshingly at odds with that of the powerful politicians surrounding her husband—and her lifelong efforts on behalf of women, children, and workers. Equally compelling is the author's compassionate and revealing study of this remarkable woman's personal life. Although her abiding respect and love for her husband and children were central to her life, it was Eleanor Roosevelt's passionate friendships with the independent and sometimes radical women intellectuals of her time, and in particular her intense relationship with Lorena Hickock, that underscored her deep commitment and her struggle to create a separate and fulfilling life for herself.

We are left in awe of this woman, this freethinking iconoclast who bucks tradition, and of Blanche Cook's inspired telling of Eleanor Roosevelt's first fifty years.

R.S.

From the Lanai and Other Hawaii Stories, Jessica K. Saki, *1991, United States,* SHORT STORIES

There is a special beauty in an artist's pencil sketches that form the basis for the later, heavier oil paintings. The slightness of the lines carry implications; an arm outstretched, yet unfinished, conveys its own emotion. So it is with Jessica Saki's stories. Brief and elusive, their meanings are contained in what is suggested but seldom explained. Style mirrors content in this collection of seventeen stories about the people of the Japanese-American community in Hawaii. Alienated from the white-skinned haoles that occasionally enter their lives, they teeter between old Japan and new Hawaiian America, as they search for self in the midst of contradictory options. Young people and old maids cross the lines of convention, quietly or in full rebellion; old men search for meanings they have lost; haoles attempt with only occasional success to reach beyond their own circumscribed points of view. Through brief conversations packed with meaning and descriptions that touch down and lift off as deftly as dragonflies, Jessica Saki shows us unexpected mavericks, small pains, sudden realizations, and the sometimes complete misunderstanding that can exist between human beings and across cultures.

E.B.

The Garden Party and Other Stories, Katherine Mansfield, *1922, England,* SHORT STORIES

In the title story of this collection, an extravagant garden party coincides with the accidental death of a local working-class man, and the daughter of the party's hostess is touched by a newborn social conscience: "Just for a moment she had another glimpse of that poor woman and those children, and the body being carried into the house. But it all seemed blurred, unreal, like a picture in the newspaper. I'll remember it again after the party's over, she decided." The irony is eloquent as she later intrudes upon the funeral with an afterthought gift, is shocked at the genuine grief and poverty of her neighbors, and leaves with her sense of romantic tragedy intact. Katherine Mansfield's stories tend to be laced with such irony. While at times she can be heavy-handed and marked by the prejudices of her time and class, at her best she is insightful and wry, conveying complicated relationships and difficult ideas through deceptively simple language. Her characters include couples who embark upon marriage compromises or endure marriage's charades; people disdaining, deceiving, envying one another; people desperately and persistently misunderstanding each other and themselves. Many of these characters have outlived their dreams and cling to illusions of their own usefulness and happiness. The stories in *The Garden Party* are morality plays that dramatize significant moments in shallow lives and show how tragedy can transcend the trivial.

K.B.

Hotel du Lac, Anita Brookner, *1985, Switzerland* (*England*), NOVEL

In the beginning of this novel, we know only that Edith Hope, "a writer of romantic fiction under a more thrusting name," has been banished to the Hotel du Lac, a "quiet hotel . . . in which she could be counted upon to retrieve her serious and hard-working personality and to forget the unfortunate lapse which had led to this brief exile." Penelope, the friend and neighbor responsible for sending Edith away for her as-yet-unexplained act is prepared to forgive only when Edith becomes "properly apologetic." Slowly, through luxurious prose narrated by way of Edith's thoughts, unsent letters, and conversations with hotel residents, Edith's transgression emerges. Not surprisingly, this is a story of love: the love between women friends who have differing values, the love of a man who needs a woman now that his mother is dead, the love of a single woman who everyone thinks needs a faithful man. Edith struggles to understand and articulate her own truths while she lives in the overly proper and ostentatious hotel, takes long walks, eats excellent cuisine, retires early, and tries to write romantic fiction. She ponders accepting the proposal of a man she doesn't love: "I shall settle down now. I shall have to, for I doubt if I have anything more to look forward to." But can she? Or will she, as she fears, "turn to stone" if she settles for less than her kind of love?

J.L.

Lolly Willowes; or The Loving Huntsman, Sylvia Townsend Warner, *1926, England,* NOVEL

In this intriguing story, a middle-aged woman finally escapes her role as spinster when she decides to have a life of her own, "not an existence doled out to you by others." Laura Willowes—Lolly to her family—is twenty-eight when her father dies and she is taken in by her elder brother, Henry, and his family in London. While Lolly has no desire to leave Lady Place, her childhood country home, she proffers no argument to her family's assumption that she must live with someone. Henry and his family live a well-regulated and comfortable life into which Laura settles herself with quiet, nearly unconscious discomfort. Henry is a lawyer—a profession which, in Laura's mind, "had changed his natural sturdy stupidity into a browbeating indifference to other people's point of view." Although Laura tries her best to like London, she cannot. There are no fields to roam, no herbs to gather; there is no quiet to comfort her and feed her dreams. When Laura can no longer hide her feelings that the jaws of her potential suitors "were like so many mousetraps, baited with commonplaces," Henry and his wife stop inviting eligible bachelors to their home. Rendered in wry and piercingly lovely prose, *Lolly Willowes* posits a realistic and still relevant social dilemma that Sylvia Townsend Warner resolves with surprising élan.

J.L.

The Magnificent Spinster, May Sarton, *1985, United States,* NOVEL

In *The Magnificent Spinster,* the life story of Jane Reid is told by Cam, a seventy-year-old retired historian and Jane's friend for fifty years. Born before World War I and raised on an island off the Maine coast, Jane grows up with her extended family—her parents, five sisters, aunts, uncles, cousins, close family friends—in a world of rustic white Anglo-Saxon Protestant elegance. The children's main excitements center around "escaping the grown-ups," especially their nanny, Snooker: "Jane's world was running off with her sister Alix to pick blueberries, lying for hours in the soft warm grass, filling their baskets, or simply sneaking off to explore, if possible get lost, and frighten themselves with imaginary dangers, and frighten Snooker by being late for lunch." As Jane becomes an adult, her gentle persistence and intelligent strength steer her clear of conventional expectations. She remains single, becomes a well-loved teacher, does what she can for the war-wounded world, and moves easily into the role of family mentor as the elders pass on. Written in lovely and compelling prose, this is a long and spacious novel about a kind of life and love rarely acknowledged.

J.L.

Miss Sophie's Diary, Ding Ling, *translated by W. J. F. Jenner, 1927–1941, China,* SHORT STORIES

In the title story, twenty-year-old Sophie, sick with tuberculosis, spends her days languishing in a small hostel room in Beijing, penning letters to friends and writing in her diary. When friends come to visit, they bring with them an attractive Chinese man named Ling. Sophie becomes obsessed with Ling, despite the loyal courting of another man and Ling's own preoccupation with material success and dalliances at brothels. She writes, "At a time like this language and words seem so useless. My heart feels as if it's being gnawed by hordes of mice, or as if a brazier were burning inside it." Ding Ling's frankness about the power of emotions and sexual desire are refreshing, coming from a country where the existence of women's feelings has been largely denied for centuries, and at a time (the late 1920s to early 1940s) when foreign invasion and mass economic deprivation were constant. The other eight stories in the collection depict choices made by young Chinese people struggling with their emotions and with the violent events of modern China. Ding Ling writes from experience; in 1933, at the age of twenty-nine, she was imprisoned by the nationalist government for three years. An ardent Communist, she created stories that reflected her beliefs without sacrificing memorable characters. The translated stories occasionally have awkward expressions, and standard punctuation is noticeably absent; still, the stories captivate with their insight into the human conditions of prerevolutionary China.

C.C.-L.

My Brilliant Career, Miles Franklin, *Australia, 1901,* NOVEL

Strong-headed, competent Sybylla has lived her sixteen years in and out of poverty in the Australian outback. She happily remembers her early years, including her mother's concern that she is too much of a tomboy, and her father's response that "the curse of her sex will bother her soon enough." When she is ten, Sybylla's life changes drastically as her family moves, her father's businesses fail, and years of drought blight their land: "We felt the full force of the heavy hand of poverty . . . the wounded pride and humiliation which attacked us." At fifteen, with no visions of escape from her difficult life, Sybylla is invited to her grandmother's estate and there tastes some of the pleasures she longs for—music, books, art. She also falls in love and feels the joy and sorrow love can bring. Sybylla's story provides a vivid portrait of youth, as she fights the conventions of her time and pays a high price to be true to her heart. Under the pen name Miles Franklin, Stella Marie Sarah Miles Franklin wrote *My Brilliant Career* at the age of sixteen. Many contemporary readers saw the novel as purely autobiographical, and the negative reaction to her portrayal of people in the outback made her stop further publication of the book. She continued to write throughout her life, but *My Brilliant Career,* an exploration and celebration of life and its choices, was not reprinted until 1966, twelve years after her death.

H.S.

Passing, Nella Larsen, *1929, United States,* NOVEL

Beautiful, ambitious Clare Kendry, tired of accepting the narrow lot of black life when she looks white, has chosen to pass for white and cut herself off from her past relationships. Her childhood friend, Irene Redfield, can also pass, but has chosen not to, and is now married to a black man and has two sons. Each woman faces a dilemma: How much of her heritage can she keep or ignore without destroying her life? Clare, married to a white bigot who does not know about her black blood, desperately misses her old ties and traditions. Irene, living in New York with her successful doctor/husband, wants to ignore the negative parts of her heritage: she refuses to let her husband explain about lynching to their boys, and rejects his desire to move to Brazil where he hopes to escape the racism he has seen in the United States. A chance encounter brings Clare and Irene together once again. As elegant, hypnotic, relentless Clare moves increasingly into Irene's life, Irene senses the danger Clare poses to her own safe existence. Although on the surface a story of passing, hypocrisy, and adultery, *Passing* is far more complex than it might first appear, and compels us to ask ourselves where we draw our own lines.

E.B.

So Long a Letter, Mariama Ba, *translated from French by Modupe Bode-Thomas, 1980, Senegal,* NOVEL

So Long a Letter is a landmark book—a sensation in its own country and an education for outsiders. Mariama Ba, a longtime women's activist, set out to expose the double standard between men and women in Africa. The result, *So Long a Letter*, won the first Noma Award for Publishing in Africa. The book takes the form of a long letter written by a widow, Ramatoulaye, to her friend, over the mandatory forty-day mourning period following the death of a husband. Both women had married for love and had happy, productive marriages; both were educated, had work they loved, and were intellectually alive. During their lives, both of these women's husbands chose to take a second wife—and each woman then made a different choice. Ramatoulaye decided to stay married, although it meant rarely seeing her husband and knowing that he was squandering money on a young girl, a friend of her own daughter. Ramatoulaye's friend divorced her husband and eventually left the country, settling in the United States. In her letter, Ramatoulaye examines her life and that of other women of Senegal—their upbringing and training and the cultural restrictions placed upon them. It is a devastating attack, made all the more powerful because of the intelligence and maturity of the narrator and the ability of Mariama Ba to honor two very different choices within one framework.

E.B.

Testament of Youth, Vera Brittain, *1933, England,*
AUTOBIOGRAPHY

It would seem enough that Vera Brittain's autobiography is an honestly gut-wrenching love story, a haunting account of her romance with a brilliant young soldier who died at the front in World War I. *Testament of Youth* is her tribute to her beloved warrior, but it is also an insightful and beautifully written record of her world before, during, and after the war. As the book begins, Vera Brittain is a young woman determined to free herself from the constraints placed upon females in England. She longs for "a more eventful existence and a less restricted horizon." Ironically, soon after her hard-won acceptance at mostly male Oxford, war begins, and the repressive English society is altered at its core. While the war cruelly robs Vera Brittain of her lover, her brother, her dearest friends, and her academic work, it also opens a new world for her, allowing her to leave her previously cloistered and chaperoned female enclave and to go alone to various foreign fronts as a nurse for wounded soldiers. She is a shrewd and intelligent observer of all aspects of the war, and her liberal use of passages from letters, diaries, and the poetry of her wartime contemporaries gives her story a directness and an emotional impact that obliterates the decades between then and now. In the end, this is a testament to a fiercely independent spirit and a strong, wise feminist who was not afraid.

R.S.

Three: An Unfinished Woman, Pentimento and Scoundrel Time, Lillian Hellman, *1969/1973/1976, United States,*
MEMOIR

Lillian Hellman (1907–1984) became America's best-known and probably most notorious female playwright of the 1930s and 1940s after the enthusiastic response to her first play, *The Children's Hour,* which tells the tale of two schoolteachers whose lives are destroyed after they are accused of being lesbians. The success of her plays made her a natural for the flourishing Hollywood film industry, while her left-leaning political beliefs and world travel placed her in Spain during the Civil War, in Paris and Germany just as fascism began to sweep Europe, and in Moscow and Leningrad during World War II.

In 1969, Lillian Hellman published the first of three separate collections of her intensely personal, passionate, and painful memoirs, in which she describes her extraordinary life, including her thirty-year love affair with Dashiell Hammett, her close friendship with Dorothy Parker, her blacklisting during the McCarthy era, and her refusal to name other people before the House Un-American Activities Committee: "I cannot and will not cut my conscience to fit this year's fashions." Lillian Hellman's *An Unfinished Woman* won the National Book Award; the memoir "Julia" from *Pentimento* was made into an Oscar-winning film; and *Scoundrel Time* became an acclaimed best-seller. *Three* brings these memoirs together in one volume. Although historical fact is sometimes at odds with Lillian Hellman's memories, she writes with eloquence and grace, re-creating the fear, suspicion, and hope of an era.

S.S.

Three Guineas, Virginia Woolf, *1938, England,* ESSAY

Like Virginia Woolf's better-known *A Room of One's Own, Three Guineas* is still timely and well worth the effort required to read it. In this book-length essay, an English writer responds to a letter—from a society for preventing war and protecting culture and intellectual liberty—which asks, "How in your opinion are we to prevent war?" and requests a one-guinea donation. Her response examines this and two similar requests, one from a women's college building fund, and the other from a society promoting the employment of professional women. Each request for a guinea is seriously and thoroughly considered by questioning, in detail, why each of the needs exists: Why doesn't the English government support education for women? Why are women in England barred from professional work? And why is World War II imminent? With scathing humor, boundless dignity, and engaging detail, Virginia Woolf finds the answers to all three questions in the same source: "We can best help you to prevent war not by repeating your words and following your methods but by finding new words and creating new methods . . . to assert 'the rights of all—all men and women—to the respect in their persons of the great principles of Justice and Equality and Liberty.' "

J.L.

Two Women in One, Nawal El Saadawi, *translated from Arabic by Osman Nushri and Jana Gough, 1975, Egypt,* NOVEL

In contemporary Egypt, eighteen-year-old Bahiah Shaheen struggles to fulfill her inner need for independence. Her world consists of her family home and medical school, but she yearns for a freedom of which neither her mother nor her female classmates seem to be aware. As she looks at the women around her she is struck with despair by the falseness she feels about their lives. In her culture, where women's skirts bind their legs together by narrowing at the knees, she wears pants, which causes people to wonder: "Was she a woman or a man? . . . But since she was a woman, it was legitimate to stare." Her involvement in a student uprising further defies her family and cultural expectations; it is a decision that changes her life. She notes: "We never know the reality of things: we see only what we are aware of. It is our consciousness that determines the shape of the world around us—its size, motion and meaning." Much of this story is told through Bahiah's thoughts, which infuse a dreamlike quality into the reality of her life. With her awareness, drive, and action, Bahiah Shaheen's search for a life different from the expected provides insight into the power of ancient and traditional Egyptian culture over women's lives.

H.S.

The Waiting Years, Fumiko Enchi, *translated from Japanese by John Bester, 1957, Japan,* NOVEL

Tomo is buying a mistress for her husband, an act that bewilders many people: not the fact that her husband should have a mistress, but that Tomo is acquiring her. Tomo did not choose this course in her life, but she swallows her pain and personal humiliation and rationalizes how lucky she is to select the woman. Her choice, Suga, believes she is to be Tomo's maid and, with the honest innocence of her protected fifteen years, moves into Tomo's home. In time, Suga too begins to repress her feelings: "Inside the self that achieved expression neither in actions nor in words, that seemed so ineffectual, the feelings that could find no relief lay dark, cold, and silent, like snow settled by night." Ten years later there is another mistress, another humiliation for Tomo. Tomo spends her whole life denying herself for the sake of her family and of what she perceives as a greater good. A remarkable woman, she manages the family household, oversees various land holdings without the aid of her husband or an education, and provides for many, in spite of the restrictions of her life. Beautiful and thought-provoking, *The Waiting Years* was awarded the Japanese Noma Literary Prize, Japan's highest literary honor.

H.S.

Conflicting Cultures

Two billiard balls clash together and spin apart. Red wine vinegar is poured onto a plate of oil; one flavors the other, but they will not mix without help. Cultures meet, clash, intermingle, blend, recoil. Sometimes the conflict is between an immigrant and a new land and way of thinking. The title character in *Jasmine* emigrates to North America from India, Eva Hoffman from Poland, *Clay Walls*'s Haesu from Korea. Simi Bedford's Remi is six when she leaves Nigeria to go to school in England; Elspeth Huxley is the same age when she moves with her parents from England to Kenya. Other authors describe the ebb and flow, the screech and clash of cultural groups that share space within a single country. Anne Moody remembers being young and black, growing up in the southern United States before and during the civil rights movement. *Scent of the Gods* describes how one girl learns the personal impact of the struggle between Malaysians and Chinese in Singapore, while Elizabeth Cook-Lynn's stories portray the attack on Native American culture by white "civilization." Katherine S. Prichard describes the thwarted love between Coonardoo, an Aboriginal native, and the rich, white Australian son of a land owner. When cultures collide, traditions can disappear like loose feathers in the wind; they can also be clung to with a tenacity that is nothing short of miraculous. Languages are learned, or lost. Laws are challenged. Books are written. And sometimes minds are opened.

The Abandoned Baobab	Ken Bugul
American Indian Stories	Zitkala-Ša
Blue Taxis	Eileen Drew
Castle Rackrent	Maria Edgeworth
The Clay That Breathes	Catherine Browder
Clay Walls	Kim Ronyoung
Cleaned Out	Annie Ernaux
Coming Home and Other Stories	Farida Karodia
Coming of Age in Mississippi	Anne Moody
Coonardoo	Katherine S. Prichard
Crick Crack, Monkey	Merle Hodge
The Flame Trees of Thika	Elspeth Huxley
The Gates of Ivory	Margaret Drabble
The Getting of Wisdom	Henry Handel Richardson
Halfbreed	Maria Campbell
Jasmine	Bharati Mukherjee
Juletane	Myriam Warner-Vieyra
The Land of Look Behind	Michelle Cliff
Letters of a Javanese Princess	Raden Adjeng Kartini
Lost in Translation	Eva Hoffman
Moccasin Maker	E. Pauline Johnson
Nisei Daughter	Monica Sone
The Power of Horses and Other Stories	Elizabeth Cook-Lynn
Sans Souci and Other Stories	Dionne Brand
The Scent of the Gods	Fiona Cheong
Seventh Heaven	Alice Hoffman
Veils	Nahid Rachlin
Yoruba Girl Dancing	Simi Bedford

The Abandoned Baobab, Ken Bugul, *translated from French by Marjolijn de Jager, 1984, Senegal,* AUTOBIOGRAPHY

In Wolof, a language of Senegal, Ken Bugul means "the person no one wants." It's an appropriate pseudonym for this bright, angry young woman who continually feels like an outsider. Ken Bugul fondly remembers her early years in her village until, when she is five, her mother leaves her for one year; the sense of abandonment that this instills in her won't go away. She refers to her family as "the mother," "the father," "the sister," or "the brother"; to Ken Bugul, these people remain nameless. Her feelings of abandonment and isolation intensify when she attends a missionary school, becoming the only woman in her family to receive an education, and then is granted a scholarship to a university in Brussels. While in Brussels she begins to recognize and then reject her family's indifference, her colonial education, the racism in Europe, and the men who want her because of her exotic beauty. Her response leads her down a road of self-destruction. Told in an almost staccato style, Ken Bugul's struggle is painful and all-encompassing: "I, who had dreamed of a home, of a father, of a mother, of ancestors, I who wanted to be recognized! I was thrown into the cage of unfulfilled fantasies and was taking wild rides into the world of surreal dream." Reading her attempts to reconcile her destructive feelings can be challenging, but it is ultimately rewarding for the insights she gives into her culture, religion, and way of understanding how people learn, know, and grow.

H.S.

American Indian Stories, Zitkala-Ša, *1921, United States,* SHORT STORIES

Zitkala-Ša, renamed Gertrude Simmons by Catholic missionaries, was one of the first Sioux women to write the stories and traditions of her people. The first set of stories in this collection is autobiographical. Zitkala-Ša describes living in her mother's wigwam on the Yankton Reservation at the edge of the Missouri River, where she is "as free as the wind that blew my hair, and no less spirited than a bounding deer." Until she is eight years old, Zitkala-Ša's only fear is "that of intruding myself upon others." Then, despite her mother's objections, she is enticed by visions of endless apple trees and the excitement of riding on "the iron horse," and leaves her mother for school in the East. Although Zitkala-Ša goes on to become a teacher, she never stops questioning "whether real life or long-lasting death lies beneath this semblance of [white] civilization." The second half of the book contains stories based on her family's tradition of oral history. "The Trial Path" describes the course of tribal justice after a murder. Tusee, in "A Warrior's Daughter," is the courageous and shrewd woman who risks everything for her husband-to-be. The son in "The Sioux" must kill twice to save his father from starvation. Written with elegant simplicity more than seventy years ago, Zitkala-Ša's *American Indian Stories* remains a powerful plea for justice.

J.L.

Blue Taxis: Stories About Africa, Eileen Drew, *1989, Africa (United States)*, SHORT STORIES

Blue Taxis draws from Eileen Drew's experiences as the daughter of a diplomat and as a Peace Corps volunteer in Africa to create stories about Westerners and Africans and the tremendous cultural differences between them. One story focuses on young Ruzi, who calls her new teacher, the one sent from AfricEd, "a one year missionary without a church" and encourages her to find a man to make her happy. In another, a white diplomat's daughter is accosted by a native black Ghanaian: "You think nothing can happen here because you are white. White people can't be poor in Africa. You never get our problems, there's nothing that can touch that watery skin." Then there's Little Zola, who covets a pair of glasses so he can see like white people: "Colors must be different, everything would sparkle. What if buildings were like the bolts of cloth standing on end in the market—rows and rows of print so different the flowers from one jumped into the trees of the next?" Each of these characters is confronted by a world that is different from what he or she expected—sometimes better, sometimes worse, always presenting another reality. With understanding and insight, Eileen Drew enters their minds and shows us how "foreign" each of us is to one another, whether we are crossing cultural boundaries or simply trying to talk within our own families.

E.B.

Castle Rackrent, Maria Edgeworth, *1800, England,* NOVEL

Having lived on the estate of Castle Rackrent for most of his long life, Thady Quirk—or "honest Thady"—takes it upon himself to "publish the MEMOIRS of the RACKRENT FAMILY." Speaking in Irish vernacular, he describes the masters he and his family have served under: Sir Patrick, who fills his house with guests and drinks himself to death; Sir Murtagh, his heir, a "great lawyer," who refuses—"out of honor"—to pay Sir Patrick's debts; and Sir Kit, who gambles and eventually sells his estate to Thady's son. Through Thady's memories of these landowners (and the tenants who all too often had to pay for the landowners' indulgences) we gain a picture of feudal life in Ireland before the Irish revolution. Thady is an unreliable narrator who, it appears, cannot—or does not—tell the whole story. Which leaves a question. Is Thady a naïve and loyal servant, or is he a clever and self-serving man who understands how to get his point across and his plans accomplished without seeming to know what he is saying or doing? Adding to the underlying irony of the narrative is the contrast between Thady's voice and the anonymous, condescending British tone of the mock glossary of terms. Humorous and biting, *Castle Rackrent* is a largely unrecognized jewel of social satire.

E.B.

The Clay That Breathes: A Novella and Stories, Catherine Browder, *1991, Japan/United States* (*United States*), NOVELLA/ SHORT STORIES

The stories and novella included in this collection move back and forth between the United States and Japan, examining the lives of foreigners—Americans traveling, studying, and working in Japan; Cambodian, Japanese, and Lao-Hmong immigrants attempting to adjust to life in the United States. Dara's Ma now lives in the United States, never telling her new, American husband the horror of what the Khmer Rouge did to Dara's father and Uncle Sothea. Barbara Spratt, with her "voice as plump as a feather pillow," tries to teach Hmong refugees "life skills," "until she thought she had more to learn than teach, and her heart grew heavy in her chest." Heitman, renting an ancestral farm house in Osaka, lovingly refinishes the family altar, and then just as lovingly fills it with two rows of his books. Eve goes to Japan to learn about pottery, but finds that is only the beginning, or perhaps the end, of the lessons. Tomura, now widowed and elderly, comes to the United States to live with his son, and prays to return home. Subtly and beautifully written, deep in compassion and understanding, these stories cross cultures and enter minds, looking at the differences between American and Asian ways of thinking and living, and at the pain, confusion, and discoveries that occur when these cultures come together.

E.B.

Clay Walls, Kim Ronyoung, *1987, United States,* NOVEL

At one point in *Clay Walls*, Faye, a second-generation Korean-American, comments that reading is "just a way for me to see how other people live. I haven't found a book yet written about the people I know." *Clay Walls* begins to fill that gap, giving a clear-eyed view of two generations of Korean-Americans in pre– and post–World War II Los Angeles. The novel starts with recently immigrated Haesu, who is being "taught" how to clean a toilet by Mrs. Randolph: Haesu "did not know the English equivalent for 'low woman' but she did know how to say, 'I quit' and later said it to Mrs. Randolph." Born a *yangban*, or an aristocrat, Haesu is determined never to work for anyone else. Her husband, Chun, starts a successful produce business and eventually buys them a house, but Haesu always dreams of going home. Her hatred of anything Japanese is unwavering, especially after she visits Korea and sees that a permanent return is impossible as long as the Japanese are present. Her children grow up under the influence of their mother's fierce pride; when Chun loses their savings and eventually leaves them, Haesu refuses charity and spends endless hours doing piecework embroidery at their table because a *yangban* would never work outside the home. As one generation gives over to the next, the focus of *Clay Walls* shifts to Haesu's daughter, Faye, who must find her place between her mother's world and the United States outside her front door.

E.B.

Cleaned Out, Annie Ernaux, *translated from French by Carol Sanders, 1974, France,* NOVEL

Twenty-year-old Denise has just had an illegal abortion and is wondering if she will die because of it. Born into the working class, now part of the educated elite, Denise is cleaned out physically and emotionally. She wants to "Find out where the whole mess began. I don't believe it, I didn't hate them from birth, I didn't always hate my parents, the customers, the store . . . I hate the others too now, those with an education, the professors, respectable people." She fondly remembers her early years, at her parents' French neighborhood store and tavern, but when she is sent to a private school—where "the children turn out better"—her life of distancing begins. To deal with the prejudices and contradictions she encounters, she keeps each aspect of her life separate; as a result, she becomes an angry elitist in both worlds. *Cleaned Out* inspires empathy, frustration, and anger: toward Denise's parents, who want only the best but cannot comprehend the position their daughter is in; toward her classmates with their smug attitudes; and toward Denise, who hurts herself the most with her refusal to be honest. Annie Ernaux's intense and impassioned writing creates a draining yet mesmerizing story.

H.S.

Coming Home and Other Stories, Farida Karodia, *1988, South Africa* (*South Africa/Canada*), SHORT STORIES

The nine stories in this collection present a chorus of voices—black, white, east Indian; horrifically poor, offensively rich; angry, oblivious, beaten—that rise up off the page until each story seems to have its own sound. One can almost hear the groan that is the life of Burns Mpangela, who drinks away the grocery money and whose wife's most extravagant dream is "a wooden bed with a mattress, and maybe a table, and some plates." Or the shrill pitch of Angela Ramsbotham, whose life revolves around perfect dinner parties, elegant antiques, and making sure her "houseboy" wears white gloves, because "It's their skin color. It just never looks clean." Then there is Henny, who passes for white only to learn it means a lifetime of listening silently to racist remarks; and Kathleen Stewart, who finally learns in her middle-class middle age that "there are no innocent bystanders." Behind and through each story, like an undercurrent, is an unexpressed violence simmering in the *tsotsi* who roam the suburban streets looking for trouble and in the frustration that mounts through the stench and poverty of a township or behind the locked gates of a mansion. Each story stands alone, yet together they become something more, a complicated mix of cacophony and harmony that is Farida Karodia's South Africa.

E.B.

Coming of Age in Mississippi, Anne Moody, *1968, United States,* AUTOBIOGRAPHY

Blunt, powerful, and angry, *Coming of Age in Mississippi* dares the reader to find anything poetic in the lives of black people living in rural Mississippi in the 1940s and 1950s, "where they knew, as I knew, the price you pay daily for being black." Anne Moody begins by describing her childhood: rooms papered with newspaper, children left alone because parents had to work, her own after-school housecleaning jobs that she began when she was nine so she could help her family eat. Smart and athletic, she earns college scholarships, but her thoughts are increasingly consumed by the racism that surrounds her. She is one of the original protesters at the Woolworth's counter in Jackson; after college she helps lead a voter registration drive in rural Canton, Mississippi, "where Negroes frequently turned up dead." She describes finding her own name on a Ku Klux Klan "wanted" list, seeing a boy beaten as FBI agents watch from across the street, hearing of murders—of Emmett Till, Medgar Evers, John F. Kennedy, and her own uncle. She lives her life knowing she can no longer return safely to her hometown, and feeling estranged from family members who do not share her passionate commitment to fighting racism. She is easy on no one, not even Martin Luther King, whose nonviolent stance she eventually questions. Anne Moody's book, written when she was twenty-eight, is both proof of her convictions and a forthright testament to the sacrifices, terror, and courage that made up the U.S. civil rights movement of the 1960s.

E.B.

Coonardoo, Katherine S. Prichard, *1929, Australia,* NOVEL

Katherine Prichard's family saga *Coonardoo* is set in the vast expanse of northwestern Australia. Coonardoo, an Aborigine native, and her extended family work at Wytaliba, the million-acre station owned by Hugh, the white man who inherits the land where he and Coonardoo grew up together. Cattle ranching and horse-breaking provide the station's income, and Hugh cannot run Wytaliba without Coonardoo and the native people. "Through his love of the country and of Wytaliba, Hugh realized, was woven regard for the people who had grown in and were bound to it." The novel is full of descriptions of the land, of native people treated "well," and of an unspoken love between Coonardoo—who can—and Hugh—who can't—accept it. Both Coonardoo and Hugh, influenced by society's attitudes, experience torments from love denied. The years unfold: there is happiness with rain and children, sadness because of people's cunning, blackmail, and the always-present threat of drought. The lack of respect shown people of color by so many of the characters can make reading *Coonardoo* painful, but Katherine Prichard was mirroring her world. She was also ahead of her time in her portrayal of Coonardoo and Hugh's relationship, which created a controversy when the book was published. Ultimately, *Coonardoo* is a rich, rewarding life tale, full of the spirit of the people and the land.

H.S.

Crick Crack, Monkey, Merle Hodge, *1970, Caribbean,* NOVEL

Young Tee and her younger brother Toddan are taken home by Tantie, their father's sister, when their mother dies in childbirth. Shortly thereafter, their father goes to England and Tee concludes that he left "to see whether he could find Mammy and the baby." The life Tantie offers Tee and Toddan is full of fiercely raucous love; when Tantie is crossed, "the neighbors for six houses on every side of us were generally aware of this fact." Throughout Tee's early years, Mammy's sister Beatrice—a woman with a voice that sounds "like high-heels and stockings"—attempts to get custody of Tee and Toddan. Tee's love and loyalty to Tantie are strained as she grows up and begins to want the pretty clothes and tidy life Beatrice offers.

Tantie's bellowing resistance to Tee's desire to live with Beatrice finally dissolves when Tee wins a scholarship and must move in with Auntie Beatrice's family in order to continue her education. To her dismay, everything about living with Auntie Beatrice makes Tee feel bad, and she begins to blame Tantie: "If Auntie Beatrice had whisked us away from the very beginning and brought us here, then I would have been nice . . . and the front door would not have been forbidding nor the armchairs in the living room disapproving." In rollicking and poignant prose, *Crick Crack, Monkey* tells the story of a young girl caught between two worlds, neither of which feels like hers.

J.L.

The Flame Trees of Thika, Elspeth Huxley, *1959, Kenya,* MEMOIR

In 1913, at the age of six, Elspeth Huxley accompanied her parents from England to their recently acquired land in Kenya, "a bit of El Dorado my father had been fortunate enough to buy in the bar of the Norfolk hotel from a man wearing an Old Etonian tie." The land is not nearly what its seller claimed, but Elspeth's parents are undaunted and begin their coffee plantation. Her mother, a resourceful, adventurous woman, "eager always to extract from every moment its last drop of interest or pleasure," keeps an eye on Elspeth's education but also allows her extensive freedom. Through Elspeth Huxley's marvelous gift for description, early-twentieth-century Kenya comes alive with all the excitement and naïve insight of a child who watches with eyes wide open as coffee trees are planted, buffalo are skinned, pythons are disemboweled, and cultures collide with all the grace of runaway trains. With a freewheeling imagination and a dry wit, she describes the interactions of Kikuyus, Masais, Dutch Boers, Britons, and Scots, mixing rapid-fire descriptions with philosophical musings. It is a mixture that suits her land of contrasts and unknowns, where vastly different peoples live and work side by side but rarely come together, like the arms of an egg beater that "whirled independently and never touched, so that perhaps one arm never knew the other was there; yet they were together, turned by the same handle, and the cake was mixed by both."

E.B.

The Gates of Ivory, Margaret Drabble, *1991, England/ Cambodia* (*England*), NOVEL

The Gates of Ivory examines people's need to make sense of history, both personal and public, by creating a world in which small comforts and big questions struggle to achieve their balance between "Good Time" and "Bad Time." Good Time is the security of friends, lovers, and the wisdom of small epiphanies and reduced expectation. Bad Time is the world of atrocity and terror, both the world we witness on the nightly news and the land we enter when we are touched by random death or sickness. For Margaret Drabble's middle-aged characters, put in a position of advantage by education and circumstance, it is also the realization that the idealism they grapple with is itself a product of privilege. Exiles, refugees, and tourists cross the bridge between the worlds of Good Time and Bad Time in England and the Far East, struggling to understand their connection. When psychiatrist Liz Headeland receives a package from Cambodia containing the possessions of her friend Stephen Cox, she must question not only his fate, but the nature of his quest. Has Cox traveled into bad time, as he claimed, to write a play about the death of communism, the death of a nation? Or is he evading his life in England? Combining mystery and philosophy, the domestic and the unknown, *The Gates of Ivory* is intimate in tone and expansive in scope.

S.L.

The Getting of Wisdom, Henry Handel Richardson (Ethel Florence Lindsay Richardson), *1910, Australia* (*Australia / England*), NOVEL

Laura Tweedle Rambotham was raised in a tiny coastal village in Australia at the beginning of the twentieth century. The natural beauty and spaciousness of her rural first home softened many of the harsh realities caused by the meager income of her widowed mother, who worked as a seamstress. Laura—called "disobedient and self-willed" by her mother and "Wondrous Fair" by her younger sister and brothers in honor of the many happy hours they've spent acting out Laura's favorite stories—is sent off to Melbourne to attend boarding school at age twelve. Wearing a dress she is sure is too short and a hat her mother lined with embarrassingly vivid red velvet, and carrying only one small suitcase of clothing, Laura finds her self-confidence diminishing with each mile of her train ride. Within a week of her arrival at school, she knows "You might regulate your outward habit to the last button of what you were expected to wear; you might conceal the tiny flaws and shuffle over the big improprieties in your home life . . . yet of what use were all your pains, if you could not marshal your thoughts and feelings—the very realest part of you—in rank and file as well?" *The Getting of Wisdom* is a poignantly hilarious account of a young woman's desperate attempts to control her feelings and survive her education.

J.L.

Halfbreed, Maria Campbell, *1973, Canada,* MEMOIR

After the Halfbreed people's losing struggle with the Canadian government to keep their land in the 1860s, many Halfbreed families homesteaded in northern Saskatchewan. Maria Campbell's family, a mixture of "Scottish, French, Cree, English, Irish" who "spoke a language completely different" from the people around them, was "a combination of everything: hunters, trappers and ak-ee-top [pretend] farmers." Born in 1940 in a home where ancient Cree rituals were practiced alongside Catholic ceremony, Maria writes this story "for all of you, to tell you what it is like to be a Halfbreed woman in our country. I want to tell you about the joys and sorrows, the oppressing poverty, the frustrations and the dreams." Raised by a hardworking, hard-drinking father, a "very beautiful, tiny, blue-eyed" mother who loved books, and Cheechum, her father's Cree grandmother, Maria grows up strengthened by the Cree traditions and Cheechum's wisdom and weakened by the burdens and shame wrought by her family's steadily growing poverty. When Maria moves to Vancouver, British Columbia, she is confronted with the brutal realities of urban racism and poverty: drugs, prostitution, alcoholism, violence. After many years of hardship and struggle, Maria makes new friends who help her remember her Cheechum's lessons, and "years of searching, loneliness and pain" end. Through her work with organizations of Native people—"brothers and sisters, all over the country"—Maria

Campbell shares her steeled strength and gentle wisdom about what it means to be *Halfbreed.*

J.L.

Jasmine, Bharati Mukherjee, *1989, United States,* NOVEL

"Fates are so intertwined in the modern world, how can a god keep them straight?" At the start of this novel we meet Jane, a twenty-four-year-old woman, pregnant and living on an Iowa farm with an adopted son, Du, a teenager from Southeast Asia. Jane began life as Jyoti, born in a village in India. As a teenage bride, then a teenage widow, she was known as Jasmine. With illegal documents she arrived in Florida with the name Jyoti Vijh; while working as an au pair she was Jace. How did she become all these people? Who is the real person? As the novel moves back and forth in time, Jasmine lives in villages in India, travels aboard a boat overflowing with illegal immigrants, and resides in apartments in New York City. Now in Iowa, Jane introduces Indian foods to the local people and heats leftovers in the microwave. Some of the lands Jasmine inhabits are familiar, but, through her eyes, they seem new. *Jasmine* is ultimately a tale of identity, loss, courage, and hope. "Jyoti of Hasnapur was not Jasmine . . . that Jasmine isn't this Jane Ripplemeyer . . . And which of us is the undetected murderer of a half-faced monster, which of us held a dying husband, which of us was raped and raped and raped in boats and cars and motel rooms?" Bharati Mukherjee invites the reader in to explore and learn with them all.

H.S.

Juletane, Myriam Warner-Vieyra, *translated from French by Betty Wilson, 1982, West Africa/France* (*Senegal*), NOVEL

While packing to move, Helene comes across Juletane's forgotten journal. Helene, a social worker, was given this journal to gain insights into Juletane's suffering and withdrawal from life. Helene didn't read it before; now she can't put it down. Juletane was born in the French West Indies; both her parents died before she was ten, and she was sent to Paris to live with a strict godmother, whose death when Juletane was nineteen finally left her free and alone. Soon she met and married a West African, only to learn when she arrived in his homeland that she was his second wife. In France she and her husband shared the experience of being people of color in a predominantly white society, but in West Africa, although she is the same color as those around her, Juletane can find nothing in common with the people or their customs. As she pours out her unhappiness in her journal—her village life, her interactions with the co-wives, her memories of the past—she discovers "that my life is not in pieces, that it had only been coiled deep down inside of me and now comes back in huge raging waves." Helene, who has a geographic background similar to Juletane's, is a woman who feels very much in control of her life. Reading Juletane's journal forces her to reconsider who she is and how she lives.

H.S.

The Land of Look Behind: Prose and Poetry, Michelle Cliff, *1985, United States/West Indies,* ESSAYS/SHORT STORIES

Michelle Cliff is a light-skinned woman from Jamaica who could not help but "pass." She was educated in England and once believed firmly that only the king's English could produce real literature: all else was folklore and not art. Her earlier published works, "Notes on Speechlessness" and "Claiming an Identity They Taught Me to Despise," form the foundation for *The Land of Look Behind.* Each dream, poem, prose poem, imaginary conversation, essay, and observation in this book carves new shapes and forms for subjects the king's English resists: "The Laughing Mulatto (Formerly a Statue) Speaks," "If I Could Write This in Fire, I Would Write This in Fire," "Europe Becomes Blacker." Each is colored by memories of her life as a Caribbean woman with African roots; each piece speaks its truth through patois—her mother tongue—with the king's English gracefully, pungently, and purposefully strip-mined for meaning. With conscience, care, and precision, Michelle Cliff delivers up rich imagery, giving these English words meaning no king has the power to claim.

J.L.

Letters of a Javanese Princess, Raden Adjeng Kartini, *translated from Dutch by Agnes Louise Symmers, 1899–1904, Indonesia,* LETTERS

Through these letters, written between 1899 and 1904, the compassion, growth, humility, and pride of a young Indonesian woman, Raden Adjeng Kartini, reach out for the reader to embrace and hold dear. Raden Kartini wrote these letters between the ages of twenty and twenty-five, when she suddenly died after childbirth. Her formal education, rare for girls of her time, stopped at adolescence. At fifteen, she and her sisters were tutored in "feminine" handicrafts by a young Dutch woman, Mevrouw Ovink-Soer, an ardent feminist and socialist who articulated and nurtured the seeds of independence already planted in Kartini. Kartini's goal was education for Javanese girls, a radical thought at the time and at odds with tenets of her Muslim religion. But as envisioned by Kartini, education was the way to "set the rice upon the table for every Javanese." Indonesia, a Dutch colony for more than two hundred years, had a small but vocal Dutch group concerned with the treatment of the Indonesian people. Through her father's position in local government, Kartini met and corresponded with many Dutch people sympathetic to their plight. A childlike innocence permeates her letters, and while we read her changing thoughts about the Dutch and follow her growth as she comes to a more developed understanding of her culture and religion, we are pulled into her struggles for a greater good and filled with sorrow at her early death.

H.S.

Lost in Translation, Eva Hoffman, *1989, United States,* AUTOBIOGRAPHY

Lost in Translation traces the struggle of a musically gifted, passionate, and thoughtful adolescent who is painfully uprooted when her Polish family emigrates to Canada. Eva Hoffman describes her early years as defined by marginality and dislocation, first as a member of a Jewish family in Catholic Poland, then as an immigrant in Canada, "stuffed into a false persona" and pitched headlong into a strange language. Re-creating her frustration at being unable to express wit and irony, and her confusion and distress over her loss of verbal spontaneity, she articulates her personal experience of the idea that linguistic dispossession is "close to dispossession of oneself." Above all, *Lost in Translation* is a deeply felt meditation on the nature of language and its crucial connections to personal identity. Eva Hoffman explores the agony of learning to articulate her thoughts in a new voice that can encompass all the tongues we must speak in our lives: the language of dreams and intimacy, of political discourse and academic argument, of memory and gossip. Her journey takes her from her childhood in Poland to her adult life as a professional New York writer, and from the nostalgia, rage, and alienation of internal exile to the fully fledged "invention of another me."

P.H.

Moccasin Maker, E. Pauline Johnson, *1913, Canada,* SHORT STORIES

E. Pauline Johnson, the daughter of a Mohawk Chief and an English woman, was born in Canada in 1861. *Moccasin Maker* opens with the life story of the author's mother, Lydia. The stories that follow concern what it means to be Indian in a country conquered by the British. "The Tenas Klootchman" (girl-baby in Chinook) is the touching, true story of Maarda, an Indian woman whose beautifully woven baby basket sits empty after her infant dies, and a sick white widow whom Maarda finds carrying a strong, healthy infant girl "rolled in a shawl." While Maarda cares for the woman and child, the empty basket haunts her: "she seemed to see a wee flower face looking up at her like the blossom of a russet-brown pansy." In addition to its lovely prose and elegant plot twists, this collection is particularly stunning for the honor and respect it pays to the birth cultures of the author.

J.L.

Nisei Daughter, Monica Sone, *1953, United States,* AUTOBIOGRAPHY

Monica Sone spent her childhood in pre–World War II Seattle, in a part-Japanese, part-American world. Dinner might be steak and pumpkin pie or pickled daikon, rice, and soy sauce; there was American public school during the day and the strict formality of Japanese school in the late afternoons. "I found myself switching my personality back and forth daily like a chameleon. At Bailey Gatzert School I was a jumping, screaming, roustabout Yankee, but at the stroke of three . . . I suddenly became a modest, faltering, earnest little Japanese girl with a small timid voice." Her memories of growing up are vivid and full of marvelous stories that show the confusion, frustration, and enrichment of living within two cultures. These elements come together when Japan bombs Pearl Harbor and Monica and her family are sent to an internment camp in Topaz, Idaho. *Nisei Daughter* describes the loss of property and the personal insults, the barbed wire and armed guards, the dust storms, horrible food, unfinished barracks, and barren land—and the efforts of the Japanese-Americans to maintain their ethics, family life, and belief in the United States. Monica Sone is furious at the blatant disregard of her civil rights, and yet ironically, it is during her time in the camps and afterward in the Midwest that she finally brings together the various aspects of her heritage. Straightforward, searching, often funny, this is a highly readable account of one woman's experience living in several worlds.

E.B.

The Power of Horses and Other Stories, Elizabeth Cook-Lynn, *1990, United States,* SHORT STORIES

Elizabeth Cook-Lynn, a member of the Crow Creek Sioux tribe, was born and raised on a reservation in Fort Thompson, South Dakota. The fifteen stories in this collection are delicately drawn pictures of lives rent by violent change and held together by the strong and living traditions passed down through countless generations of people living in the "Dakotapi of the Upper Plains." "Loss of the Sky," which takes place right before the United States enters World War I, tells of Joseph Shields, "a fifty-year-old Sioux Indian who in his own way knew something of the rise of brutal doctrines, something of the destruction of ancient civilizations, something of a change of worlds." In "A Visit from Reverend Tileston," the reverend and two female missionaries make an unannounced home visit to pray and sing. Grandmother and Mother politely stop their work, kneel and bow their heads, but their dogs are not so well-behaved. "La Deaux" is a story about a "breed" no one knew too well, a man with a face that "looked like 'twenty miles of bad road.'" Gentle, poetic, and humorous, *The Power of Horses* portrays moments of grief, tragedy, joy, and beauty in the lives of some of North America's original people.

J.L.

Sans Souci and Other Stories, Dionne Brand, *1989, Trinidad/ Canada,* SHORT STORIES

Dionne Brand was born and raised in Trinidad, then moved to Canada, where she has spent most of her adult life. Many of the characters in this collection of stories set in the Caribbean and Canada deal with issues pervasive in both cultures, including alienation, sexism, and racism. Often the stories lend themselves to being read aloud, as Dionne Brand creates stories within stories: "But truthfully, what makes a good story if not for the indiscretions we reveal, the admissions of being human. In this way, I will tell you some of my life; though I must admit that some of it is fiction, not much mind you, but what is lie, I do not live through with any less tragedy." She explores her two worlds, with their physical variation—one with the "snow, icy through the gray air," the other where "there wasn't one good reason why flowers should be so red and leaves so green." Her characters struggle with injustice and develop the skills they need in order to survive; through their lives, Dionne Brand examines the costs of survival.

H.S.

The Scent of the Gods, Fiona Cheong, *1991, Singapore (Singapore/United States),* NOVEL

The conflicts of family, heritage, and national identity are explored through the voice of eleven-year-old Su Yen shortly after Singapore's independence in 1965. Su Yen and two boy cousins, all parentless, live in their great-grandfather's home amid a large extended family. Their grandmother, who came to Singapore from China, believes "if you want to preserve the customs of your ancestors, you must teach them to your children in the home." Su Yen is aware that differences between Malay and Chinese citizens have caused demonstrations and riots; she knows that her uncle disappeared because of his political beliefs and that Grandmother offers prayers reserved for the dead for him at the altar in the kitchen. She also knows that her duty as a girl "is to watch and listen," yet she questions her cousins, especially seventeen-year-old Li Yuen, about Singapore and China. Su Yen listens to her grandmother's stories and wonders about the Malaysian Muslims and the beliefs of the nuns at the Catholic school she attends. Mixed among her musings are vivid descriptions of the sky before a rain, food cooking in the kitchen, the smell of frangipani flowers. Young Su Yen, who loves the security of the family compound with its dilapidated fence and trees planted for ancestors, comes to understand that life beyond the compound has a direct and lasting impact on her.

H.S.

Seventh Heaven, Alice Hoffman, *1990, United States,* NOVEL

It is 1959, in a Long Island suburb. Hemlock Street consists of identical houses, all six years old. Everyone is married, has the same values, thinks the same thoughts. Into this community comes Nora Silk—wearing black stretch pants when all the mothers wear Bermuda shorts, bringing with her a son who reads people's minds, a baby, and no husband. Maybe she is a witch; certainly she is not a regular mother. Her idea of cooking revolves around Twinkies and food coloring, even if she does love her children. As the reality of Nora slowly but irresistibly opens the eyes of her neighbors to the limitations of their own lives and values, marriages begins to show their cracks and hidden strains become visible for the first time. Potentially, *Seventh Heaven* could have been a horribly depressing book. Abused children kill their parents; teenagers die in accidents; mothers walk out the door in the middle of the night and do not return. Yet Alice Hoffman makes the opening of eyes a good and worthwhile thing. Not everyone survives, not everyone is happy. But there is a feeling—embodied in Nora—that happiness, and even unhappiness, is better than marriages with no love, or houses that all look alike.

E.B.

Veils, Nahid Rachlin, *1992, United States/Iran,* SHORT STORIES

Nahid Rachlin highlights the details of the everyday life of Iranians and people whose paths have crossed with Iranians. The commonalities of life, wherever it's lived, shine through in these tales of family, friendship, love, and war; the stories offer perspectives on how cultural influences create different expectations of life. The characters and narrators include teenagers, single and remarried women, mothers who don't want to lose their sons to wars, and older women, widowed and wise, still learning from life. "The Calling" tells of Mohtaram, a widow who moved to the United States to be near her children, and Narghes, her sister, who is finally visiting from Iran. With this visit Mohtaram sees her life through her sister's eyes and comes to unexpected decisions: "Memories hit her again, more strongly and vividly in the dark. . . . She wished she could break out of the prison of this new self, and be reborn into the old one." These are rarely stories of great hope or laughter; the pain in them is palpable and universal. They are stories of strength and endurance that continually remind us how fragile our outer shells can be, how deeply love can be felt, and how strong the influence of home is, wherever home may be.

H.S.

Yoruba Girl Dancing, Simi Bedford, *1992, Nigeria/England,* NOVEL

Remi lives with her grandparents in Nigeria in a huge house full of servants and extended family who speak "four languages, and two of them were English." Remi's early life is one of exuberance and warm embraces, feasts, celebrations, and laughter. When she turns six, however, her father decides it is time for her to go to school in England, in order to prepare her to help "build Nigeria." Accompanied by her white British stepgrandmother, Remi travels to England and encounters a country that is cold, austere, and hopelessly alien. Remi's initial innocence concerning racism provides Simi Bedford with multiple opportunities to deflate the myth of English superiority. Upon arrival, Remi's grandmother requests that Remi now call her Aunty, not Bigmama; on the street people stare at the "darkie." Soon Remi learns to banish her "towering Nigerian vowels" and to tell the other girls at school stories from Tarzan movies in place of her own experiences. She succeeds in becoming properly English; yet while her father wonders if "the transformation is too complete," it is obvious to Remi after more than a decade in England that she will never be regarded as English by the British. Remi is quick, brave, proud, and blunt; her retorts and asides throughout the novel are hilarious and devastating. A character far funnier, wiser, and more alive than her surroundings, she captures you early and doesn't let go.

E.B.

Ethics

"But what can any individual do? . . . There is one thing that every individual can do,—they can see to it that *they feel right.*" Writing in 1851, Harriet Beecher Stowe entreated her readers to acknowledge and act upon the evils of slavery. The authors in this section consider issues of what is right, fair, or just, for individuals and society as a whole. Rebecca Harding Davis and Rachel Carson appeal directly to readers to change business and social practices that treat laborers and nature as exploitable resources. Using a stunning array of voices and points of view, Alice Walker challenges us to understand the personal and global impact of female genital mutilation. Shirley Jackson's eerie, chilling stories explore the horrors of racism and scapegoating. Hope Leslie rebels against the restrictions of her Puritan tradition. In England, pure and beautiful Evelina lives without parents amidst the lax morals of the eighteenth-century landed gentry, while Mary Barton must decide her place amid the revolutionary politics of the nineteenth-century working class. Olive Schreiner and Françoise Sagan explore the complicated and confusing searches for truth, sexual identity, and honor of two very different young women living in nineteenth-century South Africa and twentieth-century France. Drawing from their own experiences, Irina Ratushinskaya describes the daily moral decisions involved in living in a Soviet prison camp, while Pearl Cleage speaks out on issues of sexism and racism that face African-American women. In a multitude of countries, in a variety of genres, these authors explore their societies and their souls to determine a path toward fairness and justice, and call upon us to do the same.

The Bell	Iris Murdoch
Bonjour Tristesse	Françoise Sagan
Deals with the Devil and Other Reasons to Riot	Pearl Cleage
Evelina	Fanny Burney
Grey Is the Color of Hope	Irina Ratushinskaya
Hope Leslie	Catharine Sedgwick
Life in the Iron Mills and Other Stories	Rebecca Harding Davis
The Lottery and Other Stories	Shirley Jackson
Mary Barton	Elizabeth Gaskell
Possessing the Secret of Joy	Alice Walker
The Potter's Field	Ellis Peters
Requiem	Shizuko Go
Silent Spring	Rachel Carson
A Small Place	Jamaica Kincaid
The Story of an African Farm	Olive Schreiner
Strange Fruit	Lillian Smith
To Kill a Mockingbird	Harper Lee
Uncle Tom's Cabin	Harriet Beecher Stowe
A Voice from the South	Anna Julia Cooper
Walls	Hiltgunt Zassenhaus

The Bell, Iris Murdoch, *1958, England,* NOVEL

Outside of Imber Abbey, the home of an enclosed order of nuns, lies Michael Meade's ancestral home, Imber Court. Michael's homosexuality has in the past complicated his desire to become an ordained priest, and he has decided to make Imber Court a lay community of the abbey. To the court comes a small group of more and less "pure" people, "whose desire for God makes them unsatisfactory citizens of an ordinary life, but whose strength or temperament fails them to surrender the world completely." Added to them are the visitors: Toby Gashe, a handsome and earnest young man, soon to attend Oxford; Nick Fawley, with whom Michael had a disastrous affair several years previously; Paul Greenfield, an egotistical art historian; and Paul's bohemian wife Dora, who "had begun to suspect that Paul thought her the tiniest bit vulgar." Iris Murdoch combines rarefied philosophy, intellectual introspection, and a terrifically dry humor as she takes us into the minds of troubled people seeking a good and satisfying life in the midst of their religion, their culture, and the natural tendencies of their own personalities. The force and tension of repressed contemplation grows until it is released by a series of stunning events. These characters want to be saved; *The Bell* asks us to consider what it is that saves us.

E.B.

Bonjour Tristesse, Françoise Sagan, *translated from French by Irene Ash, 1955, France,* NOVEL

Cecile is seventeen. Most of her youth was spent in a convent school, but for the past two years she has lived with her widowed father, a hedonistic forty-year-old with a wandering eye. Cecile has accepted the constantly changing women of their household and cherishes the free-spirited life she shares with her father, including, most recently, a two-month summer vacation at a villa with her father's new mistress, Elsa. The villa is beautiful, Elsa is "rather simple-minded and unpretentious," and Cecile has her own plans for sexual exploration with a "tall and almost beautiful" law student. To Cecile's surprise, however, Anne comes from Paris to join them. Anne, her late mother's friend, is cool, intelligent, and restrained; Cecile and her father are exuberant and careless. Cecile expects complications when she realizes that Anne is in love with her father: "All the elements of a drama were to hand—a libertine, a demimondaine, and a strong-minded woman." What unfolds is far from what she imagines. Sympathetic and unsparing, Françoise Sagan takes us into the mind of a precocious seventeen-year-old as she attempts to understand and control a world beyond her years.

E.B.

Deals with the Devil and Other Reasons to Riot, Pearl Cleage, *1993, United States,* ESSAYS

"I am writing to expose and explore the point where racism and sexism meet. . . . I am writing to allow myself to feel the anger. I am writing to keep from running toward it or away from it or into anybody's arms. I am writing to find solutions and pass them on. I am writing to find a language and pass it on. I am writing, writing, writing for my life. *Think of this as a workbook.*" Pearl Cleage is outspoken, thought-provoking, determined, and down-to-earth; she can take a sentence and make it sing like a saxophone. Her essays are often on contemporary celebrities and subjects—Magic Johnson and "floozies," Miles Davis's confessed abuse of women, *Driving Miss Daisy, Daughters of the Dust*, Anita Hill and Clarence Thomas—but Pearl Cleage uncovers the deeper and often undiscussed social issues operating behind the stories and personalities. Her essays range in style from gentle confessions about the beauty of solitude, to frustrated denunciations of local politicians, to sad and angry descriptions of physical abuse of women, to a list of rules regarding sex, violence, and safety that should be required reading for every young girl and woman. Pearl Cleage writes what many are barely willing to think; her essays can be a hand pulling you out of deep water or shaking you awake.

E.B.

Evelina; or the History of a Young Lady's Entrance Into the World, Fanny Burney, *1778, England,* NOVEL

In many ways, novels in the eighteenth century occupied the same position as today's soap operas. In *Evelina* there are rakes and heroes, farcical episodes, romantic misunderstandings, and serious social commentary—all described through the eighteenth-century convention of a series of letters to and from sweet, pure, beautiful Evelina Anville. Evelina has grown up in seclusion, her sole source of education the elderly pastor who is her guardian. Her mother died soon after giving birth to Evelina; her father deserted her mother and has refused to acknowledge their marriage or their child. As the story begins, Evelina leaves her isolated life in the country and goes to London with friends. Once there, she tours the sights, encounters more potential lovers and husbands than seems possible, and meets long-lost relations who demonstrate such a lack of good breeding that poor Evelina is continually on the verge of physical collapse (although morally she stays as constant as Big Ben). This book has something for those who want to know more about London and England in the eighteenth century; something for those who love a good plot twist; and something for those who wish for sharply drawn characters and social satire.

E.B.

Grey Is the Color of Hope, Irina Ratushinskaya, *translated from Russian by Alyona Kojevnikov, 1988, Russia,* MEMOIR

In 1983 in the Soviet Union, twenty-eight-year-old poet and human rights activist Irina Ratushinskaya was sentenced to seven years of hard labor and five years of internal exile. *Grey Is the Color of Hope* is her story of four years spent among a small group of female political prisoners, isolated from other "criminals" because they were considered "especially dangerous." From her first moment among these five women, Irina senses their commitment to ideals and to each other. Irina is told she will be required to wear an identity tag. Refusing may cost Irina her one "long" meeting per year with her husband and her visits to the camp kiosk; it may even mean confinement in SHIZO—a place of deprivation and torture that can mean death. Refusing also means claiming herself as a human being: "Yes, we are behind barbed wire, they have stripped us of everything they could, they have torn us away from our friends and families, but unless we acknowledge this as their right, we remain free." Time and again, these women go on hunger strikes and survive the freezing temperatures of SHIZO to stake their claim to dignity and identity, for themselves and for each other. Their strength is awe-inspiring, their ingenuity and sense of humor beautiful. Do they confiscate your poetry? Write it on a bar of soap, memorize it, tap it through the pipes to the other prisoners in SHIZO. Above all, remember: "Back to freedom with a clear conscience."

E.B.

Hope Leslie; or Early Times in Massachusetts, Catharine Sedgwick, *1827, United States,* NOVEL

During the 1800s, Catharine Sedgwick was considered one of the founding authors of American literature; unfortunately she was relegated to obscurity in our century and only recently rediscovered. But there's more to Catharine Sedgwick than historical interest; she was a writer who considered political and ethical questions through marketable, often fast-paced literature, and who produced some of the most spirited women in fiction. Hope Leslie whirls off the pages like a combination of Pippi Longstocking, Laura Ingalls Wilder, and Gloria Steinem. A free-thinker in the midst of a repressive eighteenth-century Puritan tradition, Hope is determined to follow her own conscience, and she repeatedly rebels in ingenious, dangerous, and often humorous ways. She frees imprisoned Indians, challenges the restrictions placed upon women by Puritan leaders, refuses a suitor she does not want—and that is just the beginning. Surrounding Hope are three very different women: articulate, angry Magawisca, one of the few Pequod survivors of a massacre by white men; Esther, Hope's close friend, a meek and subservient Puritan woman; and Rosa, who dresses as a boy to follow her lover to America and then exacts a powerful revenge when he rejects her. This is a story packed with romantic misunderstandings, politics, and philosophy, set in a potentially dark world whose hope is the democracy symbolized in its adventurous, quick-thinking heroine.

E.B.

Life in the Iron Mills and Other Stories, Rebecca Harding Davis, *1861, United States,* NOVELLA

"Stop a moment. I am going to be honest. This is what I want you to do. I want you to hide your disgust, take no heed to your clean clothes, and come right down with me—here, into the thickest of the fog and mud and foul effluvia. I want you to hear a story." "Life in the Iron Mills" shocked the *Atlantic Monthly* readership when it was published in 1861. It tells the story of Hugh Wolfe, a desperately poor worker in the iron mills, and his cousin Deb, who steals money so that Hugh might have a chance to become an artist. The anonymous narrator of the story is merciless, intent upon showing her readers life at the bottom, complete with drunkenness, rotten food, and slimy hovels. Hugh Wolfe's life is a daily as well as an archetypal tragedy, captured in prose imbued with outrage, spirituality, and nightmare. Again and again, Rebecca Harding Davis demands compassion and action; the solution she sees lies not only in working-class leadership but in the need for businessmen to see their workers as human beings with hearts and souls. This is a courageous, hypnotic story; appropriately enough, its republication in 1972, the first title in the Feminist Press rediscovered classics reprint series, helped mobilize a movement toward the republication of neglected works by American women.

E.B.

The Lottery and Other Stories, Shirley Jackson, *1948, United States,* SHORT STORIES

Shirley Jackson's "The Lottery" is a memorable and terrifying masterpiece, fueled by a tension that creeps up on you slowly without any clear indication of why. This is just a townful of people, after all, choosing their numbers for the annual lottery. What's there to be scared of? The ending is all the more stunning for the social commentary that comes like the slap of a hand and is gone. While "The Lottery" is probably the darkest story in this collection, the twist, the dig, and the unrelenting insights into human prejudices and frailties are present throughout. Prime targets are self-satisfied matrons, whose racism and elitism are glaringly exposed. Other tales are gentler yet often eerie: a woman waits expectantly for the man she is to marry that morning, only to find he has disappeared as completely as if he had never existed; mild Emily Johnson faces down her kleptomaniac neighbor; Margaret's dream vacation in New York City begins to feel like a nightmare. Sometimes the stories are downright funny, including a hilarious description of working at Macy's, yet even in the humorous pieces, there is an unsettling feeling; it's like looking into a fun-house mirror, where nothing is quite as you expected. This is a collection that will make you think while sending big and little chills down your spine.

E.B.

Mary Barton: A Tale From Manchester Life, Elizabeth Gaskell, *1848, England,* NOVEL

While *Mary Barton* is literally a murder mystery, it is also an abundantly detailed and sympathetic view of the nineteenth-century English weaving village of Manchester and some of its people. Mary Barton is young, kind, and beautiful—perhaps dangerously so. John Barton, her hearty and intelligent but grievously uneducated father who "could never abide the gentlefolk," pours fierce love and courage into his family and work. When Mary's beautiful Aunt Esther disappears, her beauty is blamed: "Not but what beauty is a sad snare. Here was Esther so puffed up, that there was no holding her in." Mary's love—for her father, her friends, her charming rich suitor (the son of a factory owner) and his rival, her faithful childhood friend Jem who "loves her above life itself"—provides rich texture and suspense in this finely spun tale: Will Mary's pride be her ruin? Will Jem pay with his life for his love for Mary? Occasionally punctuated with authorial observation, scenes of family life, work, and love in a nineteenth-century industrial village come alive.

J.L.

Possessing the Secret of Joy, Alice Walker, *1992, Africa/ United States* (*United States*), NOVEL

Through intense character development, innovative plot structure, and dazzling manipulation of point of view, *Possessing the Secret of Joy* attacks the practice of female genital mutilation and the mythologies various cultures use to sustain this horrific practice. Well into her adolescence, Tashi chooses to have a clitorectomy—"the only remaining definitive stamp of Olinka tradition"—to help ensure the solidarity and preservation of her African tribe. She almost dies, but she survives and marries. It is only later that she comprehends the full implications of what has happened to her, and is filled with a desire for revenge. While the action she takes may be abhorrent to some, it ultimately frees her. In Tashi's living room and bedroom, with medical doctors and on psychiatrists' couches, in tribal villages and in an African jail and courtroom, Tashi works to understand and overcome her pain and rage. The novel is witnessed through the eyes of Tashi, her husband, her son, other family members, acquaintances, friends, and enemies. Tashi's suffering is neither silent nor singular; that "mutilation," "enslavement," "the domination of women," and "the collaboration of our mothers" constitute the unholiest of alliances can no longer be denied after one experiences Alice Walker's telling of Tashi's tale. This "magical journey" is an initiation into ways of knowing, and an indictment of all that is cruel.

M.H.W.L./H.S.

The Potter's Field, Ellis Peters, *1990, England,* NOVEL

The Potter's Field is Ellis Peters's seventeenth mystery about Brother Cadfael, the gentle and gracefully aging confidant of the abbot, who carefully balances his religious duties with the often more satisfying work of solving mysteries. Set in England in 1143, the tale commences when the abbey ploughman finds, "lying along the furrow for almost the length of a man's forearm, black and wavy and fine, a long, thick tress of dark hair" on a newly traded piece of land. The plowing stops, a body—now only bones—is uncovered. From the hair, they know it is a woman. But who? And why was she buried with care—her hands carefully arranged to hold a cross made of sticks—but without consecration? Brother Rauld, who only recently took his final monastic vows, owned the field for many years before he abandoned it—and his wife—for his calling. His wife then disappeared without a trace shortly after he entered the monastery. Can there be any doubt about who the dead woman is? Or who killed her? Yes, there certainly can be, and there is. In this delicately beautiful and infinitely patient portrayal of a time, a place, and a populace, Brother Cadfael's tenderly shrewd investigative methods shine an intriguingly feminine light on the end of a period of history usually called dark.

J.L.

Requiem, Shizuko Go, *translated from Japanese by Geraldine Harcourt, 1973, Japan,* NOVEL

The end of World War II in the city of Yokohama, Japan, is portrayed through the heartfelt conversations and letters of two young women. Setsuko and Naomi, classmates and friends living in a bombed-out city, sort through their individual beliefs: "two girls, seventeen and fifteen at their next birthday, and though their real lives had yet to begin they were talking like old folk lost in reminiscences. Or perhaps this was their old age, for the hour of their death was near, as they well knew." Everyone close to Setsuko is dead as a result of the war, yet she believes in the war unquestioningly and writes letters to soldiers on the front urging them to fight to the finish. Naomi's father is imprisoned because of his antiwar beliefs and she struggles to find justification for war. Over the course of the novel, through flashbacks that occur within sentences or paragraphs, the horrors of the war are brought painfully to life, and each young woman questions her own stand. Who is more patriotic? What are the rules of war when it is in your front yard? Shizuko Go, herself a survivor of the bombing of Yokohama, has written a devastating and important novel.

H.S.

Silent Spring, Rachel Carson, *1962, United States,* NONFICTION

Silent Spring, one of the first calls for public awareness and environmental action and a seminal work of the 1960s, examines the way dangerous chemicals have been used without sufficient research or regard for their potential to harm wildlife, water, soil, and humans, creating a sinister chain of poisoning and death. *Silent Spring* is meticulously researched and accessible to the lay reader, and its message is as clear as it is devastating: Humans have willfully disturbed the whole web of life, the "intimate and essential relations" between the earth and all its passengers, animate and inanimate. Rachel Carson's work is informed by an appreciation of the intricate beauty of a flourishing environment, her sorrow over what has already been irrevocably changed or lost, and her sense that humankind is immeasurably diminished by heedlessness and aggression. Thirty years after it was first published, this landmark study is still eloquent, chilling, and, regrettably, timely. Also a portrait of corporate greed and the arrogance and irresponsibility of control agencies and individual specialists, *Silent Spring* speaks out against the way in which a single species, gifted with ingenuity and intelligence, has misused its power to assault the integrity of the environment. An elegy to a world once perfectly in balance, it is a heartfelt call for imagination, care, and humility, as we move to preempt our own destruction and find a way to live harmoniously in our natural world.

P.H.

A Small Place, Jamaica Kincaid, *1988, Antigua* (*Antigua / United States*), ESSAY

Born and raised in Antigua, Jamaica Kincaid is angry and frustrated with the white people who dominated the land and nonwhite people of her birthplace. In this thought-provoking essay, she appeals to the reader/tourist to look beyond the beautiful blues of the ocean and into the local people's lives, to question why Antigua does not have a decent library or hospital or sewer or school system. She believes the corruption of the government is a direct result of the power of money, and of examples set by the British. She asks: "Have you ever wondered why it is that all we seemed to have learned from you is how to corrupt our society and how to be tyrants? . . . You came. You took things that were not yours, and you did not even, for appearance's sake, ask first." When you take the time to look into this small, beautiful place you eventually have to look inside yourself, to think about Western colonialism and standards and their impact on non-Western people. And as you look, Jamaica Kincaid invites you to see our common humanity and the benefits such broadening of vision can bring.

H.S.

The Story of an African Farm, Olive Schreiner, *1883, South Africa,* NOVEL

Renowned as a pioneering effort of South African literature, *The Story of an African Farm* was a work strongly influenced by nineteenth-century British traditions, filled with extended philosophical discussions, characters reminiscent of Charles Dickens, and an almost complete silence on the issue of race relations. But for all its Victorian attributes, the novel is a landmark in many ways. First is the setting in the rural South African landscape which Olive Schreiner evokes in all its bleakness and beauty, a fitting backdrop for the spiritual and philosophical development of Lyndall and Waldo, two soulmates who search for truth throughout their lives. Their quest is frustrated—in Lyndall's case by gender restrictions and in Waldo's by social position. The novel is also significant for Lyndall's character. Her forthright feminism, her refusal to alter her principles, and her determination not to marry her lover despite her pregnancy make her a noteworthy female character in nineteenth-century literature. In the end, the book has an uneven quality, but it is important both for its place in literary history and for the moments when it soars in its descriptions and philosophical revelations.

E.B.

Strange Fruit, Lillian Smith, *1944, United States,* NOVEL

It's August, it's hot, it's revival time in Maxwell, Georgia. Tracy Deen, the rebel child who always disappoints his self-sacrificing mother, returns home from World War I. It is clear as day, once he is able to put his feelings into words, that he loves Nonnie Anderson. But Tracy Deen is white and Nonnie Anderson isn't. She's from one of the best "colored" families in Maxwell, even college-educated, but she isn't white; and now she's pregnant with Tracy's child and she's glad. Nonnie's brother and sister try to make Nonnie see the problems they all now face. Maxwell is a town where, on the surface, people know their place. But after a white man is murdered in the black part of town, fear takes over and a vigilante group soon appears. A young man laments: "Right now, I have some ideas. . . . If I stay here twenty years, I won't have them. Now I see things without color getting in the way—I won't be able to, then. It'll get me. It gets us all. Like quicksand. The more you struggle, the deeper you sink in it—I'm damned scared to stay." Written fifty years ago, *Strange Fruit* confronts problems that have yet to be resolved, that still need to be read about and acted upon.

H.S.

To Kill a Mockingbird, Harper Lee, *1960, United States,* NOVEL

In 1960, *To Kill a Mockingbird* won the Pulitzer Prize; thirty years later shopping malls may have replaced the main street of Maycomb, Alabama, but not even thirty years of civil rights laws render this book an anachronism. Harper Lee combines two of the most common themes of Southern writing—a child's recollection of life among eccentrics in a small town seemingly untouched by the twentieth century, and the glaring injustice of racial prejudice—to create a contemporary American classic. *To Kill a Mockingbird* has two main threads that carry the plot. The first involves the role of Atticus Finch, who is appointed to defend a shy black man accused of raping the oldest daughter of the town's least respected citizen. The second is the mythology surrounding the reclusive Boo Radley, about whom it was said, "when people's azaleas froze in a cold snap, it was because he had breathed on them." But what saves the novel from cliché are the irreverent perceptions of the story's narrator, Atticus Finch's nine-year-old daughter, Scout, who depicts mean racist aspects of Southern life as well as humorous and quite often satirical vignettes. *To Kill a Mockingbird* only gets better with rereading; each time the streets of Maycomb become more real and alive, each time Scout is more insightful, Atticus more heroic, and Boo Radley more tragically human.

M.M.

Uncle Tom's Cabin, Harriet Beecher Stowe, *1851, United States,* NOVEL

This is one of those books that everybody has heard about but few people these days have actually read. It deserves to be read—not simply because it is the basis for symbols so deeply ingrained in American culture that we no longer realize their source, nor because it is one of the best-selling books of all time. This is a book that changed history. Harriet Beecher Stowe was appalled by slavery, and she took one of the few options open to nineteenth-century women who wanted to affect public opinion: she wrote a novel, a huge, enthralling narrative that claimed the heart, soul, and politics of pre–Civil War Americans. It is unabashed propaganda and overtly moralistic, an attempt to make whites—North and South—see slaves as mothers, fathers, and people with (Christian) souls. In a time when women might see the majority of their children die, Harriet Beecher Stowe portrayed beautiful Eliza fleeing slavery to protect her son. In a time when many whites claimed slavery had "good effects" on blacks, *Uncle Tom's Cabin* painted pictures of three plantations, each worse than the other, where even the "best" plantation leaves a slave at the mercy of fate or debt. By twentieth-century standards, her propaganda verges on melodrama, and it is clear that even while arguing for the abolition of slavery she did not rise above her own racism. Yet her questions remain penetrating even today: "Is *man* ever a creature to be trusted with wholly irresponsible power?"

E.B.

A Voice from the South, Anna Julia Cooper, *1892, United States,* ESSAYS

Anna Julia Cooper was an extraordinary woman—a high school principal, the fourth African-American woman to receive a doctorate, a woman who spoke her mind eloquently and forcefully. Writing more than one hundred years ago, she argued that just as white men cannot fully understand the consciousness of black men, neither can black men completely comprehend black women's experience—and that it is black women who mark the progression of society: "Only when the BLACK WOMAN can say 'when and where I enter, in the quiet, undisputed dignity of my womanhood, without violence and without suing or special patronage, then and there the whole *Negro race enters with me.*' " At times her feminism seems conservative, as when she discusses women as a background moral force. Yet more often she is far ahead of her (and sometimes our) time, and unafraid of delivering scathing commentary. Addressing the concern she has heard from Southern men that education will limit a woman's "chawnces" for marriage, she writes, "The question is not now with the woman 'How shall I so cramp, stunt, simplify and nullify myself as to make me eligible to the honor of being swallowed up into some little man?' but . . . how [man] can so develop his God-given powers as to reach the ideal of a generation of women who demand the noblest, grandest and best achievements of which he is capable."

Sharp and passionate, *A Voice from the South* is full of relevant, eye-opening questions and insights.

E.B.

Walls: Resisting the Third Reich, One Woman's Story,
Hiltgunt Zassenhaus, *1974, Germany,* MEMOIR

Hiltgunt Zassenhaus is a schoolgirl in 1933 when she defiantly refuses to join the rest of the class in proclaiming "Heil, Hitler" each morning. A summer vacation in Denmark provokes her interest in Scandinavian languages, which later forms the foundation for her resistance work. Assigned by the Germans as an official interpreter, she is to censor the letters from Scandinavian political prisoners and oversee visits between the prisoners and a Norwegian minister. Secretly, she begins to keep files on "her" prisoners. During visits, she smuggles in vitamins, food, paper, books, anything she can fit in a purse or suitcase. Three times she is called in for questioning by the Gestapo. Her friends repeatedly urge her to flee, but she refuses, and it is her secret files that allow the Swedish Red Cross to locate Scandinavian prisoners and get them out of Germany before the massive killings of political prisoners at the end of the war. Philosophical by nature, Hiltgunt Zassenhaus intends her book to serve not only as a memoir but as a warning across time, a reminder to people that the conditions that created Hitler are still present. Mixed with nerve-wracking episodes of deaths and near-misses are moments of reflection on human nature, evil, the importance of assisting others, and of never taking freedom for granted.

E.B.

Families

Single-parent. Extended. Nuclear. Multigenerational. Dysfunctional. Happy. Nonexistent. A label may describe a family structure or a mode of behavior, but it will never hold the feelings you carry with you all your life. *Cantora*'s Ampora remembers afternoon embroidery lessons with her grandmother; Natalie Kusz describes the first time she stuck up for her little brother on the playground; the title character of *Maud Martha* recognizes her older sister's beauty and tries to find her own. *Housekeeping* presents the reactions of two sisters when they discover their mother has left. *Paradise of the Blind* describes a country and a family engaged in civil war; *Dreaming in Cuban* and *Singing Softly* portray the bond felt by family members separated by miles and countries. The mother in *The Last of the Menu Girls* reminds her daughter that the stories she has to tell are from the streets where she grew up. In *Little Altars Everywhere*, Baylor recalls the cabin that meant summer and rope swings and no bedtimes, ever; his brother remembers the times his mother got into his bed. Chuang Hua re-creates the sensations of eating crabs with your hands, while R. A. Sasaki's *The Loom* explores the language that was only spoken at home. Our families never leave us. They are incredibly, gloriously complicated, and like blood or food or that scar right under your chin, they sustain and mark us.

Bastard Out of Carolina	Dorothy Allison
Bone	Fae Myenne Ng
Cantora	Sylvia López-Medina
Clear Light of Day	Anita Desai
Cold Comfort Farm	Stella Gibbons
Crossings	Chuang Hua
Dreaming in Cuban	Cristina Garcia
Family Pictures	Sue Miller
Fortunate Lives	Robb Forman Dew
Housekeeping	Marilynne Robinson
Jubilee	Margaret Walker
The Last of the Menu Girls	Denise Chávez
Little Altars Everywhere	Rebecca Wells
Little Women	Louisa May Alcott
The Loom and Other Stories	R. A. Sasaki
Maud Martha	Gwendolyn Brooks
Owls Do Cry	Janet Frame
Paradise of the Blind	Duong Thu Huong
Princess	Jean P. Sasson
Queen Lear	Molly Keane
The Rector's Daughter	F. M. Mayor
The Revolution of Little Girls	Blanche Boyd
Rituals of Survival	Nicholasa Mohr
Road Song	Natalie Kusz
Singing Softly/Cantando Bajito	Carmen de Monteflores
Six of One	Rita Mae Brown
A Thousand Acres	Jane Smiley

Bastard Out of Carolina, Dorothy Allison, *1992, United States,* NOVEL

At her birth in Greenville, South Carolina, Ruth Anne Boatwright is nicknamed Bone because she is so long and skinny. Because her Mama is fifteen and single when Bone is born, a stamp in "oversized red-inked block letters" reading "Illegitimate" blots the bottom of Bone's birth certificate, and Bone's Mama never gives up her efforts to have this stamp removed. The Boatwright family is large and stormy, especially Bone's talented, handsome, hard-drinking, womanizing uncles. Granny Boatwright and her daughters are known for how beautiful they used to be, before too many children and not enough money carved deep lines into their faces and bent their backs. Bone understands and supports her Mama's desperate need for love until it leaves Bone with scars that won't go away. *Bastard Out of Carolina* is an emotionally stunning story of criminally familiar pain; of the strength and struggle it takes to survive it; and of the importance of having at least one person smart enough to tell you to "get out there and do things, girl. Make people nervous and make your old aunt glad."

J.L.

Bone, Fae Myenne Ng, *1993, United States,* NOVEL

"I believe that the secrets we hold in our hearts are our anchors, that even the unspoken between us is a measure of our every promise to the living and the dead. And all our promises, like all our hopes, move us through life with the power of an ocean liner pushing us through the sea." So speaks Leila, oldest of three Chinese-American daughters. *Bone* follows Leila's search as she looks back on her life in an attempt to understand her family and her sister Ona's suicide. The memories wander without any chronological order; there is rarely a linear pattern to thoughts released by pain and confusion. Leila remembers moments of celebration, when her stepfather Leon would come home from the sea; and times of conflict and disappointment. There was her mother's affair, the friends that cheated them of five months of labor and their life savings, the fights between Leon and her mother. And Ona, loving Leon, always trying to get him to come home again. Although it's easy to approach this book as a mystery

—Why did Ona kill herself?—Fae Myenne Ng soon makes clear that explanation and understanding may be two different things. There are no clear answers, and no pure joy or sorrow. The artistry of this book is Fae Myenne Ng's ability to capture this complexity and make it real.

E.B.

Cantora, Sylvia López-Medina, *1992, United States,* NOVEL

Born and raised in the United States and now an adult, Ampora seeks to unravel her family's history—the lives of her mother Teresita, her Aunt Pilar, and her grandmothers Rosario from Mexico and Isobel from Spain. Ampora's probing curiosity about details of family stories that have been alluded to breaks into full song as histories are revealed. Ampora fondly remembers Grandmother Rosario's private altar, where she "would bless me in Spanish, chanting benedictions, filling the room with magic"; Aunt Pilar, who always treated Ampora with a special tenderness and was so different from the other relatives; the tension between her parents and her mother's unwavering defense of Ampora. She remembers meeting with Grandmother Isobel every Saturday morning for the much-dreaded embroidery lessons, made easier by her grandmother's love and determination. But when Ampora marries a man not of her grandmother's choosing, Grandmother Isobel tells her: "Today you will break faith with your ancestors. . . . I cannot witness this destruction. Never forget who you are! Never forget where you come from!" Through Ampora's memories, her quest for answers about her family past, and her questions about how she lives her own life, she begins to understand how history can repeat itself and at the same time to learn the chorus of her song.

H.S.

Clear Light of Day, Anita Desai, *1980, India,* NOVEL

Clear Light of Day is at once an examination of contemporary India and a family history in which two sisters, Bim and Tara, learn that although there will always be family scars, the ability to forgive and forget is a powerful ally against life's sorrows. Twenty years ago, when Tara married, she left Old Delhi and a home full of sickness and death, while Bim continued to live in the family home, taking care of their autistic brother, Baba. Now Tara has returned, for the first time in ten years, to attend their niece's wedding. Bim refuses to attend; she can't visit their brother Raja, who, like Tara, left her many years ago. Instead Bim dwells bitterly on her feelings of abandonment and the impact on her of her country's recent history: the violent conflicts between Hindus and Muslims, the death of Gandhi and the ensuing struggle for political power, and the malaria epidemic that killed so many. In Bim's presence, Tara once again feels "herself shrink into that small miserable wretch of twenty years ago, both admiring and resenting her tall striding sister," while "Bim was calmly unaware of any of her sister's agonies, past or present." Describing the harshness and beauty of the family and the land, Anita Desai takes the reader with Tara and Bim on their struggle to confront and heal old wounds.

H.S.

Cold Comfort Farm, Stella Gibbons, *1932, England,* NOVEL

Winner of the 1933 Femina Vie Heureuse Prize, *Cold Comfort Farm* is a witty, irreverent parody of the works of Thomas Hardy and D. H. Lawrence. Flora Poste, left an orphan at the end of her "expensive, athletic, and prolonged" education, sets off for her relatives at Cold Comfort Farm, despite dire warnings of doom and damnation. Once there she encounters Seth, full of rampant sexuality; Elfine, who flits in and out in a cloak that is decidedly the wrong color; Meriam, the hired girl who gets pregnant every year when the "sukebind is in bloom"; and Aunt Ada Doom, the aging, reclusive matriarch who once "saw something nasty in the woodshed." Flora decides to "tidy up life at Cold Comfort Farm." Mocking Hardy's and Lawrence's melodrama, sensuality, and use of symbolism, Stella Gibbons has Flora, with her no-nonsense attitude, give Elfine a good haircut, teach Meriam some elementary lessons in birth control, and send various morose, rural relatives off to happier fates. *Cold Comfort Farm* is funny even without a background in Hardy or Lawrence, but for those readers who have been frustrated attempting to find exactly where in *Tess of the D'Urbervilles* Tess is "seduced," or who have plowed through the intensity of *Sons and Lovers, Cold Comfort Farm* is sweet, hilarious revenge.

E.B.

Crossings, Chuang Hua, *1968, United States,* NOVEL

There is no straightforward plot line in *Crossings*: details, memories, images, parts of conversations, rituals of cooking, planting, and cleaning float toward the reader like brightly colored confetti thrown to the sky. A reader can put the pieces together like a puzzle and learn the story of Fourth Jane Chuang Hua, devoted middle daughter in a traditional upper-class Chinese-American family, "not sure who I am on the outside of the old context and . . . afraid I might not survive the new." Or you can allow *Crossings* to come to you in images, through your senses. Listen as grandmother responds to her grandchildren's birthday salutations with "machine gun"—"the only word she could remember now in English." Feel the coldness of dying Dyada's feet as his daughter Fourth Jane places them near her heart. Get ready to eat crabs: "cracking and tearing shells apart, chewing, sucking . . . Of a hundred different ways to eat crabs this is the best, stirs the heart and is the most basic." Watch Ngmah clean a room with four pieces of cheese cloth, from top to bottom; come to know what it means for Fourth Jane to reject her brother's wife because she is a "barbarian." By the end, you realize that many things, novels included, cannot be contained in a straightforward and linear form.

E.B.

Dreaming in Cuban, Cristina Garcia, *1992, Cuba/United States* (*United States*), NOVEL

The matriarch Celia, equipped with binoculars, is honored to guard the north coast of Cuba dressed in her best housedress and drop pearl earrings. She believes in the revolution: it's helped the people in the past and they must work for a common good. Because of her disagreement with the revolution, Celia's eldest child, Lourdes, moved to Brooklyn many years ago and opened the Yankee Doodle Bakery, with plans of eventually owning hundreds across the nation. Lourdes's daughter, Pilar, has spiritual ties with her grandmother in

Cuba, though the power has weakened over their years of separation. Celia's youngest child, Felicia, still lives in Cuba with her three children, but her delusions and visions further separate the family. This is a story, told through many voices, of loyalties that provide the threads of love woven with diversities that pull at the seams. Come and dream with Felicia as spirits call only to her, dream with Lourdes as her deceased father "talks" only to her, dream with Celia as she "talks" to her granddaughter in Brooklyn, and dream with Pilar as she dreams, for the first time, in Cuban.

H.S.

Family Pictures, Sue Miller, *1990, United States,* NOVEL

Family Pictures is a book that doesn't let go. You may want to read it twice: the first time to allow yourself to be swept up in caring and aching for this family, then again to savor Sue Miller's words and grasp their full impact. The story is told through the eyes of four different family members, and the complexity of family relationships is brought home through the various ways different characters interpret and react to the same events. The catalyst for this family's dysfunction is an autistic child, and each family member deals with Randall's mute power in his or her own way. The psychiatrist father withdraws emotionally and physically, unable to bear his family's pain as he does his patients'. The mother manifests her love, guilt, and shame through compulsive achievements, from wallpapering to having three more "perfect" children to compensate for Randall. The children foray into rebellious acts of teens in the 1960s. Each character comes to realize with varying degrees of poignancy "that each child represents such risk, such blind daring on its parents' parts—such possibility for anguish and pain—that each one's existence was kind of a miracle." This warm, gritty, realistic tale is about such daring.

S.L.S.

Fortunate Lives, Robb Forman Dew, *1991, United States,* NOVEL

Fortunate Lives is a quiet and exceptionally honest book, a remarkable rendering of a not terribly remarkable family. Robb Forman Dew has beautifully captured a small, privileged segment of American society in the characters of Dinah and Martin Howells, who live in the established, intellectual New England milieu that sends its daughters and sons to Harvard. They are accomplished, self-satisfied, and discreet, but their lives are not without sorrow; the tragic death of a young son five years earlier has infused the Howells' lives with a persistent and often painful introspection. The story focuses on Dinah, Martin, and their two teenage children, though it is Dinah who is the most prominent. It is her strength that promises to keep her family together even as they are attempting to survive the loss of their son, the impending departure of another son to college, and the challenges of growing older. Watching her son out of the window, she realizes that "eventually his absence would seem a natural condition of the world to her. She could even anticipate that eventually his homecomings, although always longed for, might be disruptive, even intrusive in her life. . . . What she couldn't imagine, looking out of the blurred, moisture-beaded window, was the way in which she and Martin would lead their lives after the departure of their children."

R.S.

Housekeeping, Marilynne Robinson, *1981, United States,* NOVEL

Housekeeping begins, "My name is Ruth." It ends with Ruth remarking that she had "never distinguished readily between thinking and dreaming" and realizing that her "life would be much different if I could ever say, This I have learned from my senses, while that I have merely imagined." Although Ruth and her sister Lucille spend most of their childhood in one house near a lake in Idaho—terrain described at length through poignant and radiant prose—Ruth never loses the feeling of being a homeless woman, a person who, with her sister, "had spent our lives watching and listening with the constant sharp attention of children lost in the dark. It seemed that we were bewilderingly lost in a landscape that, with any light at all, would be wholly unfamiliar." In *Housekeeping,* lives change drastically just when nothing seems to be happening. Marilynne Robinson's vibrant and visual language floats and flows out of Ruth's most secret self, only to remind us how impossible it is ever to really get under another person's skin.

J.L.

Jubilee, Margaret Walker, *1966, United States,* NOVEL

Jubilee tells the life story of Vyry, daughter of the house slave and the "master," from "slavery-time" through the Civil War. Dr. Margaret Walker, respected African-American poet and scholar, heard this story as a child from her own grandmother, Vyry's daughter, and vowed to write it so the world could know. Vyry is intelligent, strong, honest, brave, enduring: heroic qualities common to many "ordinary" African-American women but still painfully scarce in literature. Dr. Walker spent thirty years researching *Jubilee,* and the result is a factual book that reads like a good friend talking. We see and feel the details of Vyry's daily life: the foods she grew and ate, the colors and textures of the quilts she made, the grotesque realities of slavery, the joys and sorrows of love. And in the moments of Vyry's life—her early girlhood, the death of her mother, the sale of her "other-mother," her first love, the births and lives of her children, the war and resettlement, Ku Klux Klan violence, and, finally, a home of her own—we see a big picture of this part of American history from an urgently caring and essential perspective.

J.L.

The Last of the Menu Girls, Denise Chávez, *1986, United States,* SHORT STORIES

The lyrical, delicate writing of Denise Chávez in these seven connected short stories holds the impressions of Rocio Esquibel's life—her vision of youth, her schoolteacher mother, her relatives in Texas, her often absent father. The title story recalls Rocio's first job in a local hospital, portraying the staff, the patients, and her Great Aunt Eutilia, whose death was the first one seventeen-year-old Rocio experienced. Childhood memories are brought to life in "Willow Game," as Rocio pays tribute to a tree in her neighborhood that has provided much comfort and shade and is destroyed by a neighborhood boy. Looking at her mother's shoes in "The Closet," Rocio thinks: "They are the shoes of a woman with big feet, tired legs, furious bitter hopes." In "Shooting Star," she sees the faces of the women from her family in the plaster walls of her home and wonders if beauty is "a physical or spiritual thing." Will she be beautiful like her sister, or have soft skin like her grandmother when she is old? And when Rocio decides to become a writer, her mother reminds her that all the stories she has to tell are from the street where she grew up.

H.S.

Little Altars Everywhere, Rebecca Wells, *1992, United States,* NOVEL

Little Altars Everywhere is a book that stuns—aesthetically, emotionally, psychologically. At its core is Siddalee's dysfunctional Southern family. Now thirty-eight, Siddalee lives in New York and tries to understand a childhood dominated by her beautiful, dramatic mother, Viviane, who drank and then beat and sexually abused her children. Then there's Siddalee's father, Big Shep, an alcoholic as well, a sensitive Louisiana farmer who can never quite say what he wants, unless it's to yell at his wife. Siddalee's siblings have their own problems, and Willetta and Chaney, the black "help," have no power to save them. Chaney remarks: "Only thing my Letta done lost sleep over is those children. . . . You hand-wash a family's underthings and you learn more about them than you ever want to." All of them tell their stories, packing full lives into anecdotes and scenes. Rebecca Wells takes those stories, so filled with pain, and makes beauty. After Siddalee allows her long, red hair to be cut on one of her mother's binge days, Siddalee lies out on the grass: "My heart starts pounding, my breath gets real tight, and I get all afraid. But I can feel the ground underneath me. And I tell myself: The earth is holding me up. I am lighter than I was before. My hair is like grass planted on the top of my head. If I can just wait long enough, maybe it will grow back in some other season."

E.B.

Little Women, Louisa May Alcott, *1868, United States,* NOVEL

Louisa May Alcott was a successful writer of sensational fiction before she produced a "girl's story" at the request of her publisher. Her book, *Little Women,* has always had a following among young readers, yet this story of four girls growing up at the time of the Civil War provides much for twentieth-century adult readers as well, not only as a straightforward and affecting narrative, but as a feminist primer on female relationships and the values of nineteenth-century New England society. Louisa May Alcott drew from her own memories to create the adventures and trials of the four sisters—domestic Meg, tomboyish Jo, gentle Beth, and artistic Amy—who are helped by their beloved Marmee to conquer their minor faults and disappointments and reach their "castles in the air." Many readers will identify with Jo, who longs for independence; cry when Beth dies; and happily follow Amy on her extended European tour. Although Victorian in sensibility, the novel escapes being cloying. Rich in love, Meg, Jo, and Amy ultimately learn their lessons and end up happily married, as convention would dictate. But the differences in their personalities and in the paths they take to attain their goals offer a critique of a society that would place women within a single mold.

A.C.

The Loom and Other Stories, R. A. Sasaki, *1991, United States,* SHORT STORIES

In *The Loom,* R. A. Sasaki, a native of California and a third-generation Japanese-American, draws on the traditions, confusions, conflicts, and joys that are a part of her heritage. Throughout the nine loosely connected stories, the narrator shifts; sometimes it is the wonderfully blunt voice of a young girl: "I was an ugly child. I had a long horse face, not much of a nose, and two front teeth that got in the way no matter what I tried to do." In other stories, the voice changes to third person and the mood is quiet and reflective, describing the colors in a weaving: "white, the color of five sets of sheets, which she had washed, hung out, and ironed each week—also the color of the bathroom sink and the lather of shampoo against four small black heads"; or the language spoken at home: "Theirs was a comfortable language, like a comfortable old sweater that had been well washed and rendered shapeless by wear. . . . It was a personal thing, like a hole in one's sock, which was perfectly all right at home but would be a horrible embarrassment if seen by *yoso no hito*." The various voices play off and move between each other, illuminating at yet another level these stories about people living between cultures, about parents and children, about death and the vibrant life of childhood memories.

E.B.

Maud Martha, Gwendolyn Brooks, *1953, United States,* NOVELLA

When Maud Martha Brown is seven years old, what she likes even better than "candy buttons, and books, . . . and the west sky" are dandelions: "Yellow jewels for everyday studding the patched green dress of her back yard." Maud Martha's nine-year-old sister, Helen, is heart-catchingly beautiful; Maud Martha comforts herself with knowing that what is common—like the demurely pretty dandelion with "only ordinary allurements"—is also a flower. Through pithy and poetic chapter-moments—"spring landscape: detail," "death of grandmother," "first beau," "low yellow," "everybody will be surprised"—Maud Martha grows up, gets married, and gives birth to a daughter. *Maud Martha,* a gentle woman with "scraps of baffled hate in her, hate with no eyes, no smile," who knows "while people did live they would be grand, would be glorious and brave, would have nimble hearts that would beat and beat," is portrayed with exquisitely imaginative and tender detail by Gwendolyn Brooks, the first African-American to win a Pulitzer Prize.

J.L.

Owls Do Cry, Janet Frame, *1960, New Zealand,* NOVEL

Janet Frame's first novel, *Owls Do Cry,* draws on many details of her own life. Her childhood was shadowed by poverty, sickness, and accidental death, and shaped by the power of the spoken and written word. At twenty-one, she was institutionalized in a mental hospital and later saved from a threatened lobotomy only by her achievement as a writer. *Owls Do Cry* explores the life of the Withers family in a New Zealand town "halfway between the South Pole and the equator." Poverty and a reputation for strangeness exclude the Witherses from the hollow conventions and artifacts of suburban life. They do not possess revolving clotheslines, walkie talkie dolls, or uncomfortable chairs, yet the children's lives are rich in "wonder currency": rhymes and rituals, play and dreams. Twenty years later, this currency is subsumed for each of them into vivid, haunted inner lives. *Owls Do Cry* lyrically evokes "the private and lonely night, with a room of its own but no window," within which the characters are caught. The parents are worn down by worry and love; the children grow into baffled, damaged adults. Each has taken hold of "the wrong magic and the wrong fairy tale." The special quality of this novel lies in its poetic, hallucinatory, perceptive voice, imbued with the surreal visions of childhood and madness.

P.H.

Paradise of the Blind, Duong Thu Huong, *translated from Vietnamese by Phan Hut Duong and Nina McPherson, 1988, Vietnam,* NOVEL

The first Vietnamese novel translated and published in North America, *Paradise of the Blind* is a riveting and revealing view of one family's life over the past forty years. At its heart are twenty-year-old Hang, her mother Que, and her father's sister Aunt Tam. While on a long train ride, Hang, now an "exported worker" in Russia, recalls her family's history. Before her birth, the 1950s land-reform campaigns created a split in her family that has never been overcome. It forced Hang's mother to move to the slums of Hanoi—far away from the home of her ancestors—and work as a street vendor. Hang remembers the neighborhood with "seven different sticky-rice vendors. You could recognize each one immediately by the lilt of her voice. Their dawn cries were the first music of my childhood." Aunt Tam still lives in the hamlet where her family is from, unable to forget the past and determined that her hard work will benefit Hang. Hang is caught between her mother and her aunt, the government's past and present actions, and her own yearnings. The foods, flowers, heat, and rain of Vietnam are evoked to expose the broken world of Hang and her family. Duong Thu Huong, an advocate for democratic political reform and one of Vietnam's most popular writers, wrote *Paradise of the Blind* in response to a government call for writers to use their art to encourage traditional Vietnamese values. More than 40,000 copies were sold in her country before this book—along with her other novels—was banned by the government.

H.S.

Princess: A True Story of Life Behind the Veil in Saudi Arabia, Jean P. Sasson, *1992, Saudi Arabia* (*United States*), BIOGRAPHY

While living in Saudi Arabia, Jean Sasson befriended a woman named Sultana. Sultana wanted her life to be known and she gave Jean her diaries and notes, entrusting her to write her life story. Jean did so, changing names and places for Sultana's protection. The result is a vivid depiction of the restrictions of Saudi Arabian society and the raw, corrupt, and unquestionable power of the royal males and religious leaders. Born into the royal family in 1956, the independent-minded Sultana was the tenth daughter and the last of her mother's children to survive childhood. By age fifteen, Sultana had seen her brother participate in the rape of an eight-year-old, brought her seventeen-year-old sister home after an attempted suicide because of her forced marriage to a sadistic fifty-three-year-old man, and buried her mother. Sultana marries, and at home she dresses as she pleases and voices her opinions about the inequities she lives, though usually her views are ignored. Outside her home she must cover herself completely in black, and is expected to be subservient in every way. Conversations with Marci, a Filipina who has been her maid since birth, expose Sultana to the countless wrongs suffered by foreign workers in Saudi Arabia. Sultana's lifestyle—which includes four homes, shopping trips to Europe, and gardens in the desert—contrasts sharply with what she learns from Marci, and causes her further anguish and anger. *Princess* is an intimate look at one woman's struggle against the injustices of an extremely repressive society.

H.S.

Queen Lear, Molly Keane, *1988, Ireland,* NOVEL

At Deer Forest, an opulent but decaying estate in early twentieth-century Ireland, eight-year-old Nicandra wants only to love and be loved. Named after her father's favorite horse, she doesn't even try to win the love of this tiny, dandy man who can only really love his animals. To earn Maman's love is her fondest wish, a dream fed by rare but ever-so-lovely moments of tenderness. Nicandra's growing up is stewarded by Aunt Tossie, whose fawning affections are too available for Nicandra to value, and who is obsessed with Nicandra's chances of finding a suitable husband: "The list of sons of the right sort, still available in this country, was miserably short in comparison with that of the golden lads who had come to dust in Flanders and other places." When Nicandra does find a husband, she finds that love—the ways she has learned to know it—is indeed blind. Enmeshed in dying customs that demand thorough disregard for the humanity of servants and shopkeepers, Nicandra remains oblivious to the dangers facing her from those whose feelings she has trampled over as if they were part of the Irish landscape. Through penetrating and witty observation, sympathetic reflection, and a masterfully suspenseful plot, *Queen Lear* proves itself a shockingly good read.

J.L.

The Rector's Daughter, F. M. (Flora Macdonald) Mayor, *1924, England,* NOVEL

The rector's daughter, Mary Jocelyn, is "as much a part of her village as its homely hawthorns." Mary's mother is long dead, her brothers have both left England, and Ruth, her sick sister, requires constant care. Her father, Canon Jocelyn, "rather despise[s] the rest of Europe" and is "an austere critic of young women, demanding little of them in action, but everything in repose." Mary's few acquaintances are old family friends to whom she feels more obligation than true affection and, try as she might to deny it, she knows all tenderness in her father died with her mother. Now a middle-aged spinster, Mary is used to being lonely, but she cannot stop longing for love. Then Mr. Herbert, the son of her father's old friend, moves into the neighborhood. Slowly, surely, and without intention on either one's part, love blossoms—love so strong that Mary cannot speak of it or control her blissful fantasies. When Mr. Herbert leaves for the seashore to recover from a chill, they both believe he will return to ask for Mary's hand in marriage. An elegantly written and scathingly honest account of society, manners, and marriage, *The Rector's Daughter* is a passionate and tender story of love and loss.

J.L.

The Revolution of Little Girls, Blanche Boyd, *1991, United States,* NOVEL

The Revolution of Little Girls starts with a summary of the major events of Ellen Larraine Burns's life, then proceeds to reveal the details in a manner that reads like a narrative tour through a shoebox full of sharply focused but randomly tossed photographs. Here is Ellen at thirteen playing Tarzan, stealing fish, and learning to kiss with Hutch. Here is Ellen at age five before her father was killed in a car accident. The guy with the cigar hanging out of his mouth is Uncle Royce who was mean to them in ways they barely remember. This is Ellen at twenty getting ready to marry Nicky, the man who didn't let her drink or take drugs and who took care of her for a seven-year period she remembers as "like a long stay in a good hospital." That's Blacklock, the southern mansion—"a white island in a sea of black folks"—that felt haunted and attracted electrical storms. The man in front of the house with her mother is Dr. Post, Ellen's gynecologist when she was twelve and her stepfather when she was thirteen. The last picture is of Ellen's mother, a woman who used to embarrass Ellen by "speaking in italics." The shadows in the background might be Ellen's little-girl ghosts disappearing; Ellen doesn't need them anymore, now that she remembers why she loves her mother, can resist alcohol, and knows enough to honor her woman-loving, unstarved self.

J.L.

Rituals of Survival: A Woman's Portfolio, Nicholasa Mohr, *1985, United States,* SHORT STORIES

What can and can't a family provide? The short stories in this collection, set in present-day New York City, describe the lives of six Puerto Rican women without bitterness, but not without anger.

Carmela has to contend with her adult children's plans for her life after the death of her husband; in fact, it's about all she can do to tolerate them in her apartment; she needs time to be alone with her grief and relief. Inez, by her eighteenth birthday, realizes that her six-month-old marriage, an effort to escape from her aunt's house, is just another trap. Zoraida's husband has no understanding of his wife and forces her further into her own silent world. Amy finds a way to have a Thanksgiving Day celebration with her four young children, on the second Thanksgiving since her husband's sudden death. Lucia doesn't want her family, living in Puerto Rico, to know she's in a hospital awaiting death; instead, on her twentieth birthday, she waits in vain for a visit from her pimp/boyfriend. Virginia has returned to town after ten years and is living with Mateo and the children his wife left behind. Nicholasa Mohr shows each woman's resolve in the face of often difficult circumstances, and while each of these stories is unique, they are also universal in the ways they open our eyes to the many forms that strength needed to survive can take.

H.S.

Road Song, Natalie Kusz, *1990, United States,* AUTOBIOGRAPHY

Natalie Kusz's father was five years old and living in Poland when World War II started. He watched as people "turned into dogs" and his own family was splintered in an effort to survive; later he moved to the United States. Natalie's mother had no intention of marrying the young man with the heavy accent and cumbersome manners, yet she did, and together they created a family with four children. In 1968, when their oldest child, Natalie, is six years old, they move to Alaska, to escape the violence and artificiality of life in California. For the next eight years they live in a trailer with no running water or electricity, always planning the house they will build when they can afford it. The first winter, Natalie is mauled by a dog; she loses half her face and is expected to die. Over the years she and her family endure surgeries, poverty, heart attacks, and teenage pregnancy. Natalie Kusz's insights, won at great cost, are presented with a singular grace: "Hopes are white stones shining up from the bottoms of pools, and every clear day we reach in up to the shoulder, selecting a few and rearranging the others, drawing our arms smoothly back into air, leaving no scar on the water." A book of calm, solid wisdom and beauty, *Road Song* is her testament to her family and the traditions and beliefs that held them together.

E.B.

Singing Softly/Cantando Bajito, Carmen de Monteflores, *1989, Puerto Rico* (*United States*), NOVEL

Now a grown woman, Meli is still curious about her family. Her grandmother, *abuelita* Pilar—the person who told her stories, who made her feel safe, who sang softly to her as they walked—was a source of strength for Meli. But Pilar died many years ago, and that life feels so far away. *Singing Softly* centers on Pilar and her families, the one she was born into and the one she created with her own children and grandchildren. Pilar's white father works cutting sugar cane, barely making enough money to feed the family. Her Puerto Rican mother is fully occupied with raising the children, stretching the food, and making clothing last and last. Pilar knows that "Poverty had made her mother old. . . . Poverty was the worst kind of sickness." When Juan, the local shop owner's relative, falls in love with Pilar, it's a love her family doesn't trust. How could a wealthy white man love their daughter? Looking back, Meli tries to understand the effects of color and poverty on her grandmother, her mother, and herself. Though Meli's search uncovers painful lessons, Carmen de Monteflores gently exposes a bit of the story now, more later, swaying back and forth in time with language that is warm and inviting.

H.S.

Six of One, Rita Mae Brown, *1989, United States,* NOVEL

This hilarious family history of love, war, and sibling rivalry takes place in Runneymede, a town located "smack dab on the Mason Dixon line" half in Maryland, half in Pennsylvania. The story of two sisters, Juts and Wheezie, and their mother Cora is told in dated chapters; those in the present tense cover a five-month period in 1980; the past-tense chapters relate events that occurred between 1909 and 1961. Juts and the religious Wheezie have not stopped squabbling for seventy-five years. When Nickel, the daughter of Juts and narrator of the 1980 chapters, goes off to college, writes successful books about her family, and then—to top it all off—buys her mother a new car with some of her earnings . . . Well! Wheezie can barely stand it and doesn't let Juts forget for one minute that both Nickel's books and her bisexual lifestyle are completely unforgivable, unless of course Nickel might want to buy her something? Juts manages Wheezie's bitchy snoopiness by yelling out seventy-five-year-old insults: "Wheezie sucks green monkey dicks" gets rid of her in a minute; calling her a "piano fart" shuts her up instantly. Runneymede —past and present—is filled with colorful characters and lively stories. A fun, funny, and penetrating novel, *Six of One* sparkles with warm-spirited humor and keen perceptions about women, men, war, and social status.

J.L.

A Thousand Acres, Jane Smiley, *1991, United States,* NOVEL

The vast and beautiful landscape of a thousand-acre farm is where Jane Smiley begins her Pulitzer Prize–winning novel. Scanning the countryside through a fish-eye lens, the novel eventually focuses on a small barbecue party where a decision has been made that will break down the frail framework that has held together a seemingly idyllic and prosperous third-generation farm family. The focus narrows further as Jane Smiley delves into her complex, trapped characters, who are blindly leading themselves into unchangeable situations. Drawing on Shakespeare's *King Lear,* the story revolves around three daughters and their father, Larry, who sees them as one entity with no personality, whose only reason for existence is to serve him. Ginny, the indecisive protagonist, selflessly wants to please everyone. Rose, the witty, sarcastic middle sister, is at first the only person with whom Ginny can identify. The confident Caroline, who left the farm to become a lawyer, now drifts through Ginny's and Rose's lives like an outsider. Just when it seems that the reader knows everything about these characters, Jane Smiley exposes another layer of their lives. Vivid and unsettling, *A Thousand Acres* takes us to the edge of unbelievable desperation and makes us question whether anyone's life is what it seems.

G.B.

Friendships and Interactions

Few of us, no matter what our situation, can avoid the human interactions that color and shape our days. Sometimes these chance meetings take root, grow, and become so central to our sense of self that it is hard to remember what we were like before. *The Mixquiahila Letters* follows one half of a ten-year correspondence between two women; the author offers three different orders in which to read the letters, each portraying a different picture of the friendship. Lane von Herzen writes a powerful novel about the friendship between two young women, one black, one white; Margaret Atwood explores the sometimes destructive relationships that can occur among young females, while Nayantara Sahgal describes a long-term friendship between two very different women in India. Mary McCarthy writes a shimmering and sharply pointed satire of *The Group*—eight Vassar graduates, class of '33. The short story collections in particular focus on the brief meetings or the moments of revelation within long-term relationships that pierce our souls and make us see the world differently. Writing from Germany, Botswana, France, Finland, and the United States, authors take small encounters and examine their impact until they expand and bloom like paper flowers placed in water. All of these books explore the instances of reaching out and pulling away that make up the extraordinary and ordinary lives of human beings.

Cat's Eye	Margaret Atwood
Circe's Mountain	Marie Luise Kaschnitz
Collector of Treasures and Other Botswana Tales	Bessie Head
Copper Crown	Lane von Herzen
Cordelia and Other Stories	Françoise Maillet-Joris
The Country of the Pointed Firs	Sarah Orne Jewett
The Group	Mary McCarthy
Heartwork	Solveig von Schoultz
Hitchhiking	Gabriele Eckart
Later the Same Day	Grace Paley
The Lover of Horses	Tess Gallagher
Middlemarch	George Eliot
The Mixquiahila Letters	Ana Castillo
Rain of Scorpions and Other Stories	Estaela Portillo Trambley
Rich Like Us	Nayantara Sahgal
A River Sutra	Gita Mehta
Seventeen Syllables and Other Stories	Hisaye Yamamoto
Twilight and Other Stories	Shulamith Hareven
A Weave of Women	E. M. Broner

Cat's Eye, Margaret Atwood, *1988, Canada,* NOVEL

Through the character of Elaine Risley, an artist who returns to her home town of Toronto for a retrospective of her work, Margaret Atwood charts the psychological process from memory as compulsion to memory as a healing act. Elaine's visit triggers thoughts of her childhood with all the urgency of a bad rash. Dominating her reflections are her childhood "friends," three girls who wreak havoc on Elaine's self-esteem. Having spent her early childhood on the road with an entomologist father, a less than traditional mother, and a brother more concerned with snot and snakes than the intricate behavior codes of girls, the young Elaine is vulnerable to the indirect aggression of Cordelia, the ringleader of the group who seeks to improve her. Through Elaine's experiences, Margaret Atwood turns a keen and ironic eye on the training of females in North American culture: "All I have to do is sit on the floor and cut frying pans out of the Eaton's Catalogue with embroidery scissors, and say I've done it badly." The self-effacement of these girl-children barely masks a need for power that erupts all too often in cruel forms of play. This is a story in which the lines between victims and oppressors blur, in which forgiveness becomes an act of gaining power. Through humor, pain, and insight, she makes us see, with surprise and recognition, details from childhood we may well have forgotten.

C.K.

Circe's Mountain, Marie Luise Kaschnitz, *translated from German by Lisel Mueller, 1952–1966, Germany/Italy (Germany),* SHORT STORIES

Marie Luise Kaschnitz was one of Germany's most respected writers, the recipient of all of her country's major literary awards. The stories of *Circe's Mountain* display a wide range of styles, subjects, and locations, from "Long Distance," which evolves completely through one-sided conversations on the phone, to the highly descriptive evocations of mood and place that appear in other stories. There are tales that describe specific events and people in Germany during World War II, a confrontation between a young German tourist and a would-be twelve-year-old rapist, a poignant portrayal of a couple's silver wedding anniversary, and several eerily mystical, close encounters with death. The stories set in Italy carry a particular lush heaviness. One is a beautiful autobiographical exploration of a widow's grief and return from devastation after the death of her beloved husband: "Even after the most excruciating experience we obey the laws of gravity; our legs go down and our heads up; we wake up, put on our clothes and go out, remaining in the skin we wanted to jump out of, at least in spirit. We have become sadder and probably less curious but not new, and the pool of words to express the incredible is no greater than it was." Selected from volumes published between 1952 and 1966 and drawing from many different parts of Marie Kaschnitz's life, *Circe's Mountain* provides an eclectic reading experience, like looking back through a series of letters from a good friend who has grown and changed over the years.

E.B.

Collector of Treasures and Other Botswana Village Tales,
Bessie Head, *1977, Botswana,* SHORT STORIES

Collector of Treasures explores the lives of Botswana villagers, both before their colonization by the British and after their independence in 1966. Bessie Head tells tales of ancient leaders, of educated women trying to find their way between city and village life, of women who must suffer while men treat the independence of their country as an opportunity to throw away all restrictions, British or tribal. In these stories, it is the women who suffer most—who bear the children after the men have deserted them, who endure the village gossip, who raise the money for their children's school fees as their husbands support other women. But though they suffer, these are women of strength and inner beauty. Johannah, tall and striking, reminds the villagers that "the children of a real woman do not get lean or die." Dikeledi, in jail for killing her husband, still "had always found gold amidst the ash, deep loves that had joined her heart to the hearts of others." While men are often the villains of these stories, *Collector of Treasures* also creates a new hero, the kind of man Bessie Head calls "a poem of tenderness." The author's love for her characters is rich and glowing, as strong as her anger at those, British or African, who destroy traditions of empathy, hard work, and sharing. Her words flow through their "uncertain story of independence" like a great, golden river.

E.B.

Copper Crown, Lane von Herzen, *1991, United States,* NOVEL

Cass is fifteen: "I was going months without feeling any wiser in my blood, while a time was coming when, under the sky of a few days and nights, I'd get me an understanding I wouldn't ever let go of—an understanding of death and its workings that threw back a light on all living so it never appeared itself so beautiful." Cass and Allie are friends; the fact that Cass is white and Allie is black is something that their small, early-twentieth-century Texas town will never let them forget. But they are close friends, and together they leave their town, which has destroyed itself through racism. Cass gets a job cooking in a dining hall—she can't cook, but she is white. Allie takes over the cooking in secret, while in the night, Cass plants trees in the barren soil. Together they take care of Ruby, a baby neither of them bore but both of them love. Around them in the growing trees shimmer the spirits of those who have died, glowing blue in the night and talking to those who can hear. *Copper Crown* is a rich and magical book, as deep and generous as the best in human nature. While it never flinches in its presentation of the tragedy of ignorance and closed-heartedness, it soars in its descriptions of better ways of living.

E.B.

Cordelia and Other Stories, Françoise Maillet-Joris, *translated from French by Peter Green, 1956, France,* SHORT STORIES

Writing with the keen insight of a psychologist, Françoise Maillet-Joris explores in these twelve stories the minds and actions of those fragile, self-flattering, complicated animals called humans. Precisely and gracefully, she eviscerates their pretenses like an expert fisherman gutting his catch, or examines their fears with the calm determination of a mother cleaning the skinned knee of a beloved but clumsy child. Though few win her commendation, all are granted her understanding. There is Fanny, young and spoiled, who plans an affair only to learn that there is more than one way to deceive a husband; and Marie, who leaves her beautiful, blond husband because "something had come to a head in her that had never been there before, something which demanded unhappiness, imperfection, suffering, something which guaranteed that every minute she now lived was hers, completely and utterly." Nathan Oppheim runs a tragic race away from his fear of death; Verna uses self-denigration to hold onto a man just one night longer. At times the stories show moments of compassion and bravery, as when Sylvia defies the cruel, conceited host at a dinner party, or a young gypsy rejects the "charity" of a town and the expectations that accompany it. In every case, Françoise Maillet-Joris's insights are penetrating, portrayed through characters who naïvely reveal what they would never consciously acknowledge.

E.B.

The Country of the Pointed Firs, Sarah Orne Jewett, *1896, United States,* SHORT STORIES

Sarah Orne Jewett draws the reader into *The Country of the Pointed Firs* with scenic descriptions, honest characters, and conversations written with an ear for dialect and an instinct for emotional truth. While you'll find no adventure within these pages, the series of everyday events that are recounted create a warm and enchanting tale of simpler times. The narrator invites you to see through her eyes as she observes life in the New England seaside village where she spends a summer in the late 1800s. She develops friendships with her hostess and with her hostess's mother and brother, who live on a nearby island, and learns much about the history and dwellers of the town. Each person, including the narrator, seems to find satisfaction in his or her life's course, while never quite believing that neighbor or kin holds the same contentedness. At the reunion of a local family the narrator comments, "More than one face among the Bowdens showed that only opportunity and stimulus were lacking—a narrow set of circumstances had caged a fine character and held it captive." The bonds and love of community and kin are clear and strong, and it is difficult to leave these people at the end of the book, yet the narrator's words offer assurance and a final challenge: "Their counterparts are in every village in the world, thank heaven, and the gift to one's life is only in its discernment."

S.L.S.

The Group, Mary McCarthy, *1954, United States,* NOVEL

Mary McCarthy's *The Group* is a sharply pointed satire of upper-class New England society that follows the postcollege lives of eight

Vassar graduates, class of '33. Helena was registered for Vassar at birth; Pokey forged her mother's signature on her college application in defiance of the family tradition of "being dim-witted and vain of it." Out in the "real" world, Dottie loses her virginity to a "bad sort" but discovers that she enjoys sex, while Kay subsumes her own talent to the artistic "genius" of her egocentric and philandering husband. Libby writes book reviews that are almost as long as the original material, and Polly works as a nurse, while Priss is forced by her pediatrician-husband to go against "tradition" and her inclinations and breast-feed her baby, as proof of his theories. Elinor "Lakey" Eastlake, the sleek, rich leader of the group, travels about Europe and ultimately returns full of surprises. In a style that mimics the generally well-intentioned but hopelessly narrow-minded perspective that typifies the worst of the group, Mary McCarthy filets Ivy League society, socialism, 1930s child-rearing practices, sexual double-standards, psychoanalysis, and men in general.

E.B.

Heartwork, Solveig von Schoultz, *translated from Swedish by Marlaine Delargy and Joan Tate, 1951–1976, Finland,* SHORT STORIES

Solveig von Schoultz's ideal short story is "like a waterdrop that reflects the whole of human existence." Her insights are penetrating; often they recapture things we have forgotten, or portray feelings we would rather not acknowledge. What makes her stories exceptional, however, is the compassion that permeates them. The stories' focus moves from youth to old age. First there is young Ansa, forced to acknowledge that grown-ups can't hear the needs and voices of inanimate objects and don't know that "the slightest little dot on an *i* can beg to be fatter as you write, and your whole body feels wrong until you have obeyed." Then there is Eva, an adolescent who goes to see the father who deserted her and discovers a stranger. The title character of "The Girl" struggles with the baby she didn't expect, while the narrator of "Report" is a middle-aged wife and mother whose interactions with a homeless man cause her to realize that "even if I took all I had and shared it with Pulli, it would count for nothing . . . Not so long as I close my eyes at the door, so that I don't have to look at him." The last three stories describe women with adult children and difficult marriages, whose lives are filled with reconsideration and reflection and whose futures offer both hope and frustration. Even the painful stories carry a deep, calm beauty; there is a sense that these moments are miracles, if only because they are a part of life.

E.B.

Hitchhiking: Twelve German Tales, Gabriele Eckart, *translated from German by Wayne Kvam, 1987, Germany,* SHORT STORIES

The information shared between a hitchhiker and driver can be very personal, but the relationship is essentially anonymous and rarely extends beyond the hitchhiker's destination. While only two of these twelve stories involve actual instances of hitchhiking, a similar feeling permeates them all—a mixture of intimacy and purposeful distance. The narrator is usually a woman from East Germany, often in college, who steps beyond the boundaries of her life as she gets to know a poor, elderly woman on her street; works on a construction site or as a street sweeper; visits aging, eccentric relatives; learns of an uncle's past transgression; has an aborted relationship with a man from West Germany. While there are moments of true connection between individuals, each of the main characters remains isolated by an inability to trust or by the divisions of class, gender, or age. Even the ideas are separated into short paragraphs that stand out on a page like pickets on a fence, linked but separate, striking in their clarity. Although the emotions and situations will be familiar to many Western readers, Gabriele Eckart explicitly links the problems she sees to failed socialism and the East German government, which makes it all the more surprising that this book was published in East Germany several years before the dismantling of the Berlin Wall.

E.B.

Later the Same Day, Grace Paley, *1985, United States,* SHORT STORIES

Later the Same Day combines Grace Paley's talent for innovative short stories with her unwavering commitment to feminist peace activism. Her characters are heroic in ordinary ways—they talk, laugh, and think about the things that matter to them. They live normal lives yet remain awake and focused in their concern about the future; they emanate wisdom, humor, disappointment, hope, and fear. These stories center upon an appropriately named character, Faith, who tells and listens to the stories of friends, neighbors, lovers, and strangers struggling to find hope and meaning in their sometimes shattered lives. As the story titles suggest, Faith's endless confidence in her friends and in the ordinary powers of listening and of becoming a "story hearer" pave the way for radical transformation. In "Zagrowsky Tells," Faith runs into the old Jewish pharmacist whose drugstore she and her friends once picketed because he refused to sell to black patrons. Now, years later, she listens to how the ordinary act of learning to love his half-black, half-Jewish grandson has taught him to unlearn his racism. Throughout the collection, neighbors learn to listen to each other, husbands and lovers learn to hear women, women who are longtime friends and political allies validate each other's lives, and strangers tell stories that need to be heard. For Grace Paley, these important ties of love, faith, and language are what create community.

S.S.

The Lover of Horses, Tess Gallagher, *1982–1986, United States,* SHORT STORIES

Some storytellers are literary magicians who can capture a situation and spin it out, remembering details like pink hair curlers or the smell of the dark space under a back porch. They take the everyday and invest it with significance and life. Reading the stories in *The Lover of Horses* is like sitting at the feet of a kind, knowing woman whose hands are endlessly full of yarn, who knits something fantastic out of what is, after all, sheep hair. One story shows what happens when you bring together a woman, her Avon lady, and a fortune-teller. Then there is the wife who comes to understand the worth of her short, balding husband; the widow who realizes what her loveless marriage meant to her and to her husband; the daughter who comes home to her dying father. Tess Gallagher shows us people reaching across small and large spaces, bouncing off each other, meeting for moments, or living together for years. Through her stories they become fascinating and beautiful, as full of depth and texture as plain cotton cloth viewed through a microscope.

E.B.

Middlemarch, George Eliot, *1871, England,* NOVEL

Dorothea Brooke can find no acceptable outlet for her talents or energy, and few who share her ideals. As an upper-middle-class woman in Victorian England she can't learn Greek or Latin simply for herself; she certainly can't become an architect or have a career; and thus, Dorothea finds herself "Saint Theresa of nothing." Believing she will be happy and fulfilled as "the lampholder" for his great scholarly work, she marries the self-centered intellectual Casaubon, twenty-seven years her senior. Dorothea is not the only character caught by the expectations of British society in this huge, sprawling book. *Middlemarch* stands above its large and varied fictional community, picking up and examining characters like a jeweler observing stones. There is Lydgate, a struggling young doctor in love with the beautiful but unsuitable Rosamond Vincy; Rosamond's gambling brother Fred and his love, the plain-speaking Mary Garth; Will Ladislaw, Casaubon's attractive cousin; and the ever-curious Mrs. Cadwallader. The characters mingle and interact, bowing and turning in an intricate dance of social expectations and desires. Through them George Eliot creates a full, textured picture of life in provincial nineteenth-century England.

E.B.

The Mixquiahila Letters, Ana Castillo, *1986, United States,* NOVEL

The table of contents gives three options as to the order in which the forty letters in this epistolary novel may be read: one for the conformist, one for the cynic, and one for the quixotic. With each option a different and powerful story emerges; a book group could have a fascinating discussion about this book if each person chooses her own option. The letters are written by a Mexican Indian woman from Chicago to her Anglo friend. The two meet in Mexico when they are twenty years old, and over the next ten years correspond, visit, and travel together. Through these letters, the stories of their lives emerge, of their times with and without jobs, with and without husbands or boyfriends. These are stories of opposites: one is an artist who is always sketching and can't stand alcohol or cigarettes, the other a poet who likes to smoke and drink with the company at hand. One is a distant and standoffish woman whose world comes alive when she dances; the other is a believer in spirits and intangible forces. Each letter can be a story in itself, which delivers to the reader the power of a woman's words of relationship and life: "We needled, stabbed, manipulated, cut, and through it all we loved, driven to see the other improved in her own reflection."

H.S.

Rain of Scorpions and Other Stories, Estaela Portillo Trambley, *1975, United States,* SHORT STORIES

Estaela Trambley's nine short stories and the novella "Rain of Scorpions" mix magic, earth, and the realities of life to evoke heartfelt sadness for her characters or a smile at the twists a story takes. The title piece combines all these elements in a tale of the people of a mining town where Papa At is a source of wisdom and history to many, though his lack of Christian faith angers some. Inspired by his stories of Gotallama and the green valley, five young boys, hoping to save the village from the many dangers of the mines, set out in search of this enchanted place. In "The Paris Gown" a young woman meets her grandmother, Clo, for the first time. The granddaughter, who has heard many tales of Clo, never knew how her grandmother came to leave Mexico to live on her own in Paris; now she learns the truth from Clo herself. "The Burning" offers a painful yet compelling example of how the choices and expectations of differing religions dictate people's actions. In "Duende" we meet a gypsy "full of the duende spirit from the mountains of the old country" who knows that "passion [is] the main artery to the feel and freedom of the day." Often Estaela Trambly begins these stories with a vivid image that she expands upon throughout these exquisite tales of joy and sorrow.

H.S.

Rich Like Us, Nayantara Sahgal, *1985, India,* NOVEL

The setting is New Delhi shortly after Indira Gandhi declares a state of emergency; its impact is viewed through the lives of sixty-three-year-old Rose and thirty-eight-year-old Sonali. Born and raised in England, Rose moved to India more than forty years ago when she married Ram. Rose was wife number two; she shared a house with Ram's first wife and son, and struggled to adapt to a new country and culture. She freely voices her opinions about the state of emergency, the current business practices in India, and her husband's son, who now controls the family's wealth. Rose and Ram were friends with Sonali's family, and over the years a true friendship has developed between the two women. Sonali, a civil servant seeking to "Indianize India," feels that she and her co-workers must remain silent about the state of emergency in order to keep their jobs. Her dreams and ideals for her homeland evaporate with her sudden dismissal. Sorting through her deceased father's papers, learning much of her family's and her country's history, Sonali comes to realize the importance of her dreams. Through Rose and Sonali's lives we witness compassion, corruption, courage, and trust. In *Rich Like Us* "the present is the merest flicker between the long long time past and the things that haven't yet happened but most assuredly will."

H.S.

A River Sutra, Gita Mehta, *1993, India,* NOVEL/FOLK TALES

The Narmada River, one of the holiest rivers in India, flows west through central India, emptying into the Arabian Sea. The narrator of *A River Sutra* leaves his civil service job to manage a rest house situated on the banks of the Narmada River and to give himself time to reflect on his life. He is unprepared for the number of people who are drawn to the river, and those who come often surprise and confuse him. With Tariq Mia, a mullah living in a Muslim village near the narrator's rest house, he discusses spiritual and life issues. A Jain monk on a pilgrimage intrigues him; he feels this monk "might know some secret of the heart that could shatter the shell of numbness that enclose[s] me." An executive of a tea farm comes to the river to perform centuries-old rituals to recapture his lost soul. A mother arrives in search of her kidnapped daughter, certain she is being held in the jungles along the river's banks. Like the river's whirlpools, life circles around the narrator as Hindus, Sufis, musicians, ascetics, and archaeologists heed the river's call. Through them and the river itself, Gita Mehta explores India's history, religions, and mythologies.

H.S.

Seventeen Syllables and Other Stories, Hisaye Yamamoto, *1948–1987, United States,* SHORT STORIES

Written between 1948 and 1987, Hisaye Yamamoto's stories cover many subjects, from sexual harassment to the internment of Japanese-Americans during World War II to a simple, magical tale of growing up. A recurrent theme is the experience of Japanese-American women: women often living in isolation, caught between the traditional world of their husbands and the Western values and identities of their children. Always these stories are about the living of life, its movement and motion: "But reading is reading, talking is talking, thinking is thinking, and living is different." Hisaye Yamamoto's people carve out an existence on the fringes of American culture, compelling readers to think deeply about situations that may or may not be the same as their own. For her tender, revealing stories, Hisaye Yamamoto was awarded the 1986 American Book Award for Lifetime Achievement from the Before Columbus Foundation.

H.S.

Twilight and Other Stories, Shulamith Hareven, *translated from Hebrew by Miriam Arad, Hillel Halkin, J. M. Lask, and David Weber, 1992, Israel,* SHORT STORIES

Shulamith Hareven's short stories, set in and around contemporary Jerusalem, are mesmerizing; her ability to bring the reader into the lives and worlds of her characters is powerful and rewarding. "Twilight" takes place in a dream/nightmare world where the impossible seems probable: "In that one night's year I met a man, married, became pregnant, and gave birth to a murky child who grew fast, all without light." In "Loneliness" we feel the deep isolation of Dolly, a refugee with a past she can't fully remember and needs she cannot express. Out of this loneliness a passionate temptation arises: "A current of rare flame shot through Dolly's body and, with it, an indistinct fear." In "A Matter of Identity" we meet a woman who is "one of those women whose body is not important because her actual presence means more than her shape." Shulamith Hareven's stories create psychological tension and evoke a genuine concern for her characters, while Jerusalem, an ancient walled city with roofed alleys, newly constructed buildings, and many refugees, provides a fitting backdrop for the many lives she represents.

H.S.

A Weave of Women, E. M. Broner, *1978, Israel* (*United States*), NOVEL

"Women long ago unlearned the words that preceded weeping, the incantations, anagrams, curses, witchcraft. Now, instead of muttering these words, instead of chanting them, they weep." The importance of ritual, of life's spiritual path, is at the center of E. M. Broner's classic novel, *A Weave of Women.* An eclectic community of women living in and around Jerusalem, the characters are committed to each other by spiritual need. They range from teenagers to women in their fifties—an international mix who form a society within a society, and seek ecclesiastical guidance that their traditions do not provide. Each woman is an individual; each knows they must stand together. They learn a political lesson when they rally to save the Home for Jewish Wayward Girls: they change the name to Home for Jewish Future Homemakers and funds come pouring in. Life's contradictions live throughout this novel: "To love easily is a blessing. To be hurt easily is a curse." Laughing, crying, and struggling to make their lives complete, these women address issues of friendship, incest, love, abuse, loneliness, birth, and death, and perform rituals that cleanse, strengthen, and renew. Their rituals serve to empower them and the reader as well.

H.S.

Growing Old

Growing old is a process that begins at no set age and proceeds with no set pattern. The authors of these books write movingly about the realizations, adjustments, freedoms, and frustrations of growing older in many different societies. Karin Michaëlis and Pearl S. Buck portray two very different women who reach midlife and discover—one with pain, the other with exhilaration—that life has many beginnings. Barbara Macdonald speaks out against ageism from the perspective of a sixty-five-year-old lesbian. The title characters of *Two Old Women*, left behind by their tribe during a period of starvation, gain strength in the face of imminent death. Writing from Canada, England, Australia, and the United States, Margaret Laurence, Penelope Lively, Jessica Anderson, and Helen Hull create women characters who look back over long lives and ponder their meanings. *Memory Board* follows the loving relationship between two women as one of them slowly loses her mind to Alzheimer's disease. Akiko of *The Twilight Years*, facing her own middle age, must add the care of her elderly father-in-law to her already overwhelming duties of wife, mother, and paid worker. Mama King from *Frangipani House* and Carobeth Laird in *Limbo* struggle to retain dignity and control of their lives in nursing homes. Here are warm, strong, audacious, loving, and irascible women. Wise from experience, they give us unique and irreplaceable knowledge.

The Dangerous Age	Karin Michaëlis
Frangipani House	Beryl Gilroy
Islanders	Helen R. Hull
Limbo	Carobeth Laird
Look Me in the Eye	Barbara Macdonald with Cynthia Rich
Memory Board	Jane Rule
Moon Tiger	Penelope Lively
On the Golden Porch	Tatyana Tolstaya
The Pavilion of Women	Pearl S. Buck
Sister Age	M. F. K. Fisher
The Stone Angel	Margaret Laurence
The Summer of the Great-Grandmother	Madeleine L'Engle
Tirra Lirra by the River	Jessica Anderson
The Twilight Years	Sawako Ariyoshi
Two Old Women	Velma Wallis

The Dangerous Age: Letters and Fragments from a Woman's Diary, Karin Michaëlis, *translated from Danish (translator unknown), 1910, Denmark,* NOVEL

"As they grow older—when the summer comes and the days lengthen—women become more and more women. Their feminality goes on ripening into the depths of winter. Yet the world compels them to steer a false course. Their youth only counts so long as their complexions remain clear and their figures slim. . . . A woman who tries late in life to make good her claim to existence, is regarded with contempt. For her there is neither shelter nor sympathy." At forty-two, approaching that "dangerous age" and determined to eliminate the hypocrisy in her life, Elsie divorces her husband, leaves behind a young potential lover, and retreats to an isolated villa on an island. Through her letters and diary, *The Dangerous Age* takes us into Elsie's inner turmoil as she faces herself, her solitude, and an increasing desire for physical contact. Although Elsie can be unflinchingly blunt, she also can hide—and hide from—the truth, a trait she states is common to all women "corrupted by society." Her moods and desires constantly shift as she searches for self in the midst of societal expectations and physical changes; as a result, her letters and diary are complicated and contradictory. Does she want to live alone? Or should she see her lover again? Or should she take her husband back? Or . . . ? First published in 1910, *The Dangerous Age* is still a shockingly forthright and provocative book.

E.B.

Frangipani House, Beryl Gilroy, *1986, Caribbean (Guyana/ England),* NOVEL

Sixty-nine-year-old Mama King has been suffering from a series of ailments. Her daughters, both in the United States, send money to move Mama King to the Frangipani House, a place on the island for "aged old folk—black women . . . forty-three of them." As Mama King's health is restored, all she wants is to get away from the confinement and control of Miss Trask, the matron. Mama King, a strong woman who raised her daughters without a husband and her grandchildren without much help from their mothers, realizes that the boredom in this place will kill her before her health fails. Here at Frangipani House she misses "her faithful friends, work and hardship" and is heard mumbling to herself: "I am going lazy-handed to meet my Maker. Me mother dead with sod in her hair. Me father dead with rice grass underneath him. And me I sittin' till me bones get sore waitin'." So Mama King sits, knowing her clothes are disappearing, her letters to her daughters aren't being posted, and the injections the matron gives her are no good. Woven through the narrative are Mama King's memories, tales from the past that interconnect family and friends, and her plans for escape. Complete with births and deaths, confessions and dreams, *Frangipani House* is a warmly told story of the independence and spirit of an aging woman who demands a say in her own life.

H.S.

Islanders, Helen R. Hull, *1927, United States,* NOVEL

This full-bodied novel opens in the midwest in 1850, as Ellen Darcy says good-bye to her fiancé; he and some male members of Ellen's family are heading west to California with promises to return in a year, rich. Left behind are Ellen, her mother Martha, and a younger brother. Over the next eighteen years, Ellen and Martha work the land, and Martha, a sturdy, honest woman, instills in her daughter a strong sense of self while teaching her the skills of survival. Ellen's fiancé never returns and she never marries; instead she becomes the family caregiver. With age, she begins to conceive of women as islanders, economically and socially isolated, who watch their men leave—to hunt for gold, to fight wars, to get an education. To survive, women fill their lives with lace doilies, food, charities, and the never-ending task of making the islands comfortable for the men. At sixty-three she thinks, "I haven't a roof nor a penny. I'm too old to go out and work: folks wouldn't have me, strong as I am. Shame, more bitter than anything she had ever tasted, curled the tips of her nerves, choked in her throat . . . This has happened because I am a woman." During Ellen's largely unfulfilled life she confronts many issues—war, a woman's place in the world, the church, the "American dream"—issues which, more than sixty years later, are still relevant.

H.S.

Limbo: A Memoir About Life in a Nursing Home by a Survivor, Carobeth Laird, *1989, United States,* MEMOIR

Limbo recounts Carobeth Laird's "efforts to hold onto sanity and identity in an atmosphere which was, by its very nature, dehumanizing." In straightforward, wryly observant, and reflective prose, she describes her seventy-ninth year, the year her gall bladder burst. She winds up a resident of the Golden Mesa nursing home. Nearly paralyzed and hopeless, and feeling trapped by a "body, with its relentless unreasoning instinct for survival [that] was at cross-purposes with a mind that could see absolutely no future," she begins to articulate her experience. The Caucasian widow of a member of the Chemehuevis/Malki tribe, Carobeth Laird enhances her prose with acute observations and comments on race, and by her ability to maintain her sense of humor despite many humiliating and heartbreaking experiences. Several months after her arrival in Golden Mesa, her manuscripts *Encounter with an Angry God* and *The Chemehuevis*—both written after her seventy-fifth birthday—are accepted for publication, and Carobeth Laird remembers just why she wants to live again.

J.L.

Look Me in the Eye: Old Women, Aging and Ageism, Barbara Macdonald with Cynthia Rich, *1978–1983, United States,* ESSAYS

These thought-provoking essays—written primarily by Barbara Macdonald, with contributions by her lover and partner Cynthia Rich—challenge readers to consider society's and their own attitudes toward older women. Barbara Macdonald has "always been a lesbian—always loved women, gotten my strength and my sense of self from women." Because of her sexuality, her life has been that of an "other;" now in her sixties, she finds she has joined a second group of "others" in United States culture—she is an old woman. In the title piece, at a Take Back the Night march, she discovers that some people feel that she, at sixty-five, will slow down the march. She is enraged; not only was she not personally addressed, but she is sure people are judging her solely because of her gray hair and wrinkled skin. In the essay "An Open Letter to the Women's Movement," she challenges the notion that older people talk too much about their health; younger women, she notes, endlessly discuss "abortion, contraception, pre-menstrual syndromes, toxic shock or turkey basters." Each essay gives the reader a look at the existence of older women, many of whom are invisible, silenced by economic conditions, ignored by the women's movement, and too often not considered contributing members of society. These essays will make you question your own role in reinforcing or rebuking these ingrained attitudes.

H.S.

Memory Board, Jane Rule, *1987, Canada,* NOVEL

Memory Board is a multifaceted novel about aging, loss, and the redefinition of family. Diana and David are twins, now in their mid-sixties; Diana and Constance are longtime lovers. David is struggling to rebuild a connection with his sister after a long separation; Diana has settled into a private, monastic daily life arranged around Constance's progressive short-term memory loss. Jane Rule's emphasis is on people and their interactions, on dialogue and ideas. Her writing relies mostly on straightforward exposition, yet the central metaphor—the "memory board"—adds depth and complexity. Diana writes each day's prospects (work in the garden, dinner with her brother) on an erasable board to help Constance keep track of her life. Inevitably, Constance will forget even Diana, yet their lives are filled not only with the apprehension of loss but also with the immediate vitality that can only be experienced by those who must live for the present. "Constance was never overly concerned with the consequences, she assumed that what you learned from experience sometimes hurt without automatically assigning it moral significance." *Memory Board* is satisfying because it promises nothing beyond the connections that exist, right now, between people who know that they may lose each other at any time.

K.B.

Moon Tiger, Penelope Lively, *1987, England,* NOVEL

Aged seventy-six and on her deathbed, Claudia Hampton decides to write "The history of the world as selected by Claudia: fact and fiction, myth and evidence, images and documents." It's a history seen through a kaleidoscope: "Chronology irritates me. There is no chronology inside my head. I am composed of a myriad of Claudias who spin and mix and part like sparks of sunlight on water." We meet Claudia, a woman always willing to share her opinions, who has admirers and enemies, loves and losses; fatherless Claudia, who grew up almost too close to her brother and best friend Gordon; Claudia, who could never really be a mother to her child, Lisa, or marry Jasper, Lisa's father. And Claudia certainly wouldn't tell anyone about Tom, the one love of her life; he's her own private memory, how could they understand? An independent and competitive woman, Claudia worked as a reporter in Egypt during World War II and met Tom near the front. Their brief but intense love affair affirms the power and thrill of falling in love. As people visit Claudia on her deathbed, the kaleidoscope turns, to reveal, through changing speed, movement, and voice, each of them and Claudia's impact on their world.

H.S.

On the Golden Porch, Tatyana Tolstaya, *translated from Russian by Antonina W. Bouis, 1987, Russia,* SHORT STORIES

Some writers can make mud sing; Tatyana Tolstaya is one of these. *On the Golden Porch* takes moments in life that age us, and through words gives beauty to their very sadness, pain, or release. Here are stories of young children, single women, old men; each piece has a distinct voice, richly and fully explored. At times these stories become surreal—as when a man undergoes an operation to remove Life so he can be brash and successful. At other times they are painfully real and depressing—as in the story of the man set apart from society by his soft belly and restrictive upbringing. The sheer beauty of the writing sustains readers until we learn the lesson, or experience the moment of revelation waiting at the end. Tatyana Tolstaya takes this mud that is life and shows us that it is more than dirt and water; it can be soft and warm and used to build things like dreams: "Old Peters pushed the window frame—the blue glass rang, a thousand yellow birds flew up, and the naked golden spring cried, laughing: catch me, catch me! . . . And wanting nothing, regretting nothing, Peters smiled gratefully at life—running past, indifferent, ungrateful, treacherous, mocking, meaningless, alien—marvelous, marvelous, marvelous."

E.B.

The Pavilion of Women, Pearl S. Buck, *1946, China* (*United States*), NOVEL

On her fortieth birthday, Madame Wu takes a step she has been planning for a long time: she tells her husband that, after twenty-four years, their sexual life together is now over and she wishes him to take a second wife. The House of Wu, one of the oldest and most revered in China, is thrown into an uproar by her decision, but Madame Wu will not be dissuaded, and arranges for a young country girl to come take her place in bed. Elegant and detached, Madame Wu orchestrates this change as she manages everything in the extended household of more than sixty relatives and servants. Alone in her own quarters, she relishes her freedom and reads books she has never been allowed to touch. When her son begins English lessons, she listens, and is soon learning from the "foreigner," a freethinking priest named Brother André, who will change her life. *The Pavilion of Women* is a thought-provoking combination of Old China, unorthodox Christianity, and liberation, written by Pearl S. Buck, a Nobel Prize winner raised in China. Few books raise so many questions about the nature and roles of men and women, about self-discipline and happiness. At the center is the amazing Madame Wu —brilliant, beautiful, full of contradictions and authority.

E.B.

Sister Age, M. F. K. Fisher, *1984, United States,* SHORT STORIES/ESSAYS

M. F. K. Fisher is famous for her tantalizing food writing, but she's never been limited to the kitchen. *Sister Age* is a collection of stories—many apparently autobiographical, all drawn from the author's experience and encounters—that reflect a perspective on old age which transcends cliché. With a portrait of an elderly woman named Ursula Von Ott acting as her muse, M. F. K. Fisher "wrote fast, to compress and catch a lesson while I could still hear it," choosing stories containing clues about the true experience of aging. In the author's unique voice, even the most bizarre situations are described with matter-of-fact eloquence. The pieces in *Sister Age* include an unsentimental account of a stranger's sudden death, a story in which two girls attempt to match their young divorced mother with an old fisherman, a description of the social dynamics in a French boardinghouse, and even a couple of ghost stories. M. F. K. Fisher observes everything from the horrors of a bad oyster to the wonders of "an ancient oak flush toilet on a raised platform" with rigorous attention to detail, just as she observes and analyzes human emotions, especially her own, with unflinching honesty.

K.B.

The Stone Angel, Margaret Laurence, *1964, Canada,* NOVEL

The Stone Angel is a compelling journey seen through the eyes of a woman nearing the end of her life. At ninety, Hagar Shipley speaks movingly of the perils of growing old and reflects, with bitterness, humor, and a painful awareness of her own frailties, on the life she has led. From her childhood as the daughter of a respected merchant, to her marriage full of rebellion, Hagar has fought a long and sometimes misguided battle for independence and respect. In the course of examining and trying to understand the shape her life has taken, her divided feelings about her husband, her passionate attachment to one son, and her neglect of another, she is sometimes regretful, but rarely penitent. Asking forgiveness from neither God nor those around her, she must still wrestle with her own nature: "Pride was my wilderness, and the demon that led me there was fear." She has been afraid of being unrespectable, afraid of needing too much, afraid of giving too much, and her pride is both disturbing and inspiring. *The Stone Angel* is an excellent example of the realism and compassion present in all of Margaret Laurence's writing.

S.L.

The Summer of the Great-Grandmother, Madeleine L'Engle, *1974, United States,* JOURNAL

"This is the summer of the great-grandmother. . . . This is the summer after her ninetieth birthday, the summer of the swift descent." In "Summer's Beginning," during the fourth four-generation summer at Crosswicks, her family's "two-hundred-and-some-year-old farmhouse" in Connecticut, Madeleine L'Engle cares for and contemplates her mother's life. There is her mother now, the great-grandmother with atherosclerosis who is often anxious, can't remember where she is, and needs constantly increasing care. There is "The Mother I Knew," a woman who had miscarriages all over the world before her treasured first child, Madeleine, was born, the mother who never ran out of stories to tell, or classical music to play on her piano. There is "The Mother I Did Not Know," the young woman who was born during the American Civil War to a Southern family fresh with bitter memories of "lost fathers and brothers and homes and money." Throughout this touching journal, memory, pain, respect, fear, and the daily details of life in Crosswicks Lawns merge into a haunting and lovely chronicle of a lively home filled with pets, small children, visitors, helpers, and newlyweds, through "Summer's End."

J.L.

Tirra Lirra by the River, Jessica Anderson, *1978, Australia,* NOVEL

A woman of spirit and independence, Nora Porteous is still somewhat apprehensive about what the coming years hold. Now in her seventies, she has returned to the house she grew up in and the town she escaped from forty-five years ago when she got married and moved to Sydney. Initially her marriage had felt like love—she wanted her feelings to be love—but after ten years there was no denying that it wasn't. At thirty-five, for the first time in her life, she realizes she has options: they don't have to be escapes or decisions made to please others. "And that's how I came to go to London, not because I particularly wanted to go, but as an affirmation of the wonderful discovery that nobody could stop me." With high spirits and newfound independence, she leaves for London with plans to return to Australia in a year. Instead she establishes a life in London, gets a job, makes friends, and stays for more than thirty years. When she returns to Australia, floods of long-forgotten memories surface. As she looks back on her life, she slowly comes to an understanding of who she is and what her choices have been. *Tirra Lirra by the River* is about Nora's journey—to Sydney, to London, back home, and to herself.

H.S.

The Twilight Years, Sawako Ariyoshi, *translated from Japanese by Mildred Tahara, 1972, Japan,* NOVEL

Akiko's superwoman life takes an unexpected turn when her father-in-law, Shigezo, becomes senile. Because of Shigezo's rude and disrespectful treatment of Akiko over the years, she and her husband had a house built out back for her in-laws, physically close but emotionally distant. Now Akiko's mother-in-law is dead, and Shigezo is slipping further out of touch with reality, becoming childlike and dependent on Akiko, staying in her home and complicating her already full life. How can she work her full-time job, including half days on Saturday, clean house, cook meals, and provide a home for her husband and teenage son—as well as care for an aging, difficult man? She can't, and it causes her to wonder: "Was her husband about to tell her that she could not go to work and leave his father unattended? Would he also say that it was high time she stayed at home where she belonged?" Her struggles are compounded as she tries to reconcile her harsh feelings for Shigezo. *The Twilight Years* is Akiko's life in the kitchen, the bathroom, at work, and with herself, a portrait of a woman caught between traditions, expectations, and personal realities. The issues Akiko deals with are not uncommon, the solutions are not easy. But from her struggles, Akiko emerges a stronger, more defined woman.

H.S.

Two Old Women: An Alaska Legend of Betrayal, Courage and Survival, Velma Wallis, *1993, United States,* NOVEL

The Athabaskan people of Alaska have long told the legend of two old women intentionally left behind by their tribe during a winter of severe starvation. Velma Wallis takes this legend and gives it life, filling in the details of the survival of the women from her own experiences trapping and living in a remote area near Fort Yukon. In her vision, the two women, seventy-five-year-old Sa' and eighty-year-old Ch'idzigyaak, have grown old ungracefully. They still contribute to the tribe, but they tend to complain and believe they must rely upon their walking sticks. When they are deserted, however, their will to live asserts itself and they declare, "If we are going to die . . . let us die trying, not sitting." Leaving their walking sticks behind, they travel, make camps, and remember the skills of hunting and survival they learned as girls who shunned the traditional path for young women. When the tribe returns after a year and, out of guilt, seeks them out, they find strong, well-fed, and powerful women who save their tribe from starvation but insist upon maintaining their own hard-won autonomy. Their struggle is not easy; their victory is not simple. Velma Wallis tells their legend in clear, unadorned language, with insights about respect, aging, generosity, and love that will reach young and old.

E.B.

Growing Up

What is it we search for when we look back over our growing-up years? Our childhoods contain the beginnings of who we are now; they are sources of pain and well-springs of strength. For authors, childhood has special qualities: memories are sharp and distinct because they are fewer; naïveté and insight abound. The world is a newer place, which makes it both magical and ripe for destruction. Nathalie Sarraute tells of navigating her way between two sets of parents in France and Russia; Louise Meriwether describes the life of a twelve-year-old girl living in Harlem amidst violence, desperation, and hope. The title character of *Kristin Lavransdatter* grows up in fourteenth-century Scandinavia; a Chilean girl named Solita tries to find her place in *Paradise*. Wherever you grow up—a village in New Zealand, motels across the United States, a sugar plantation in Venezuela, a small town in Scotland or Arkansas, or the outback of Australia—you share certain childhood experiences. You learn about adults and how they can love and hurt you. You come to understand where your own strength is. You realize that there are many things to learn, and that a few are important. And if you are very lucky, you come out of growing up with some magic still in your eyes.

Allegra Maud Goldman	Edith Konecky
The Changelings	Jo Sinclair
Childhood	Nathalie Sarraute
Circle of Friends	Maeve Binchy
Cold Sassy Tree	Olive Ann Burns
Daddy was a Number Runner	Louise Meriwether
Early Spring	Tove Ditlevsen
Ellen Foster	Kaye Gibbons
Fifth Chinese Daughter	Jade Snow Wong
Floating in My Mother's Palm	Ursula Hegi
The Floating World	Cynthia Kadohata
Gorilla, My Love	Toni Cade Bambara
I Know Why the Caged Bird Sings	Maya Angelou
Kristin Lavransdatter	Sigrid Undset
The Lamplighter	Maria Susanna Cummins
Lives of Girls and Women	Alice Munro
The Lover	Marguerite Duras
Mama Blanca's Memoirs	Teresa de la Parra
The Member of the Wedding	Carson McCullers
My Friend Annie	Jane Duncan
Paradise	Elena Castedo
Rich in Love	Josephine Humphreys
The Road from Coorain	Jill Ker Conway
Silent Dancing	Judith Ortiz Cofer
Sweet Summer	Bebe Moore Campbell
Tahuri	Ngahuia Te Awekotuku
There Never Was a Once Upon a Time	Carmen Naranjo

Allegra Maud Goldman, Edith Konecky, *1976, United States,* NOVEL

"Allegra Maud Goldman. There's a whole plot in that name. . . . I knew from the beginning that I would never fit that name." For Allegra, growing up is challenging on every front. Her father is rarely happy, her mother is rarely home, and her older brother just wants to practice the piano. Grandma stays in the background, except at Passover—then she is in the kitchen. Allegra questions everything, coming up with her own answers to what she sees through her young eyes, and her observations are fun and refreshing. She is the kind of child who drives her parents and teachers crazy: she's not bad, she's not mean, people call her precocious. But as Allegra observes, "they never said it as though it were anything good to be." When she is forced to take home economics, she sees her teacher as "a large, jolly-looking woman with a heart of stone." Her friend Melanie wonders about the home economics course: "If they're preparing us to be housewives and mothers, why don't they teach us something really useful like sexual intercourse?" About which Allegra remarks: "That's the kind of girl she was. Brainy." By the end of the novel, through Allegra's laughter and tears, we feel excitement for her future and realize that she does indeed fit her name.

H.S.

The Changelings, Jo Sinclair (Ruth Seid), *1955, United States,* NOVEL

Twelve-year-old Judy Vincent—Judy to her family, Vincent to her friends—is a tomboy, and a gang leader in her 1950s all-white Midwestern urban neighborhood. Her favorite place is the gang's headquarters in the Gully, especially after dark: "In the darkness, fire music could be like an arch of tenderness over the Gully. Or it could be the gathering together in her of a thousand questions into one flame-colored core of feeling." Vincent and most of her friends are from first-generation Eastern European Jewish immigrant families struggling to make ends meet; their parents are bonded by language, religion, desperate economics, and their nearly hysterical fear of *Schwartze*—Yiddish for black people—moving onto their block. One of Vincent's friends calls Vincent a changeling, the kid in a family who "thinks entirely different" from the parents. When Vincent meets and falls in love with a young black girl, she knows "I'm the changeling in my house . . . I'm not scared. I'm not going to run around crying and hating people. Spying to see who's going to do me dirt. See? I'm not going to talk their language." *The Changelings* is a riveting and richly rewarding portrait of one summer and fall in the lives of Vincent and her friends, some of whom are changelings too.

J.L.

Childhood, Nathalie Sarraute, *translated from French by Barbara Wright, 1984, France,* MEMOIR

Reading *Childhood* is like watching a memory at work. Images and moments from Nathalie Sarraute's early years are presented in chronological order but without any attempt to fill in the gaps that are naturally present when a mind looks back ten, twenty, thirty years. What emerges is still a story: the childhood of a young girl living in the first half of the twentieth century, who divides her time between divorced parents in Russia and France. By dismissing the need for a cohesive narrative, Nathalie Sarraute gives her memories immediacy. Her search for truth brings in a second voice that interrupts—testing, reassuring, prompting, creating a dialogue. *Childhood* puts the reader in a child's place as she relives the ritual of cutting open the pages of a book, the love for a favorite doll, the pain of intentional and unintentional slights, the joy of creating a first story, and the confusion of being passed back and forth between two sets of parents.

E.B.

Circle of Friends, Maeve Binchy, *1989, Ireland,* NOVEL

This is the story of Benny's growing-up years, a story of family love, friendship, and Irish Catholic human nature, told in language full of gritty grace and warm humor. Living in a small town in Ireland, Benny is the pampered fat only child of local merchants. She's also a good-natured, stubborn, and lonely girl who finds love surprising, difficult, not always reasonable, and potentially dangerous. We meet her at the age of ten, when she tearfully learns that the tiny pink ballet slippers she wants won't make her size-ten feet look any smaller, and we follow her through adolescence and high school. Benny's circle of friends, her family and her community, are enlivened by Maeve Binchy's wickedly innocent knack for noticing the hilarious, often sweet, and sometimes tragic aspects of religious dogma and cultural tradition.

J.L.

Cold Sassy Tree, Olive Ann Burns, *1984, United States,* NOVEL

Cold Sassy Tree is a novel full of warm humor and honesty, told by Will Tweedy, a fourteen-year-old boy living in a small, turn-of-the-century Georgia town. Will's hero is Grandpa Rucker, who runs the town's general store, carrying all the power and privilege thereof. When Grandpa Rucker marries his store's young milliner barely three weeks after his wife's death, the town is set on its ear. Will Tweedy matures as he watches his family's reaction and adjustment to the news. He is trapped in the awkward phase of rising to adult expectations—driving the first cars in town—while still orchestrating wild pranks and starting scandalous gossip through his childish bragging. He seeks the wisdom of his grandpa and has his eyes opened to Southern "ways" under the tutelage of Grandpa's new Yankee wife, Miss Love. Still, Will "couldn't figure out . . . why in the heck she would marry the old man." But Miss Love's influence seems to be transforming Grandpa into a younger man, and the answer unfolds slowly and sweetly as Will Tweedy becomes the confidant and staunch defender of this unlikely couple. The lessons of life and death, of piousness and irreverence, shape the lives of the memorable characters and form the heart of a book that is both difficult to put down and hard to leave.

S.L.S.

Daddy Was a Number Runner, Louise Meriwether, *1970, United States,* NOVEL

For Francie, childhood in 1930s Harlem means having one brother in the gangs and another who gives up his dream of being a chemist because "How many firms gonna hire a black chemist?" It's having a big, beautiful father who can't find legal work and a mother who defies her husband and hires out as domestic labor in order to keep the family from starving. Childhood for Francie is having household chores such as attaching the jumper to get free electricity, and facing the disdain of Mrs. Burnett when she buys groceries from her on credit. It's avoiding the groping hands of the butcher, the baker, and the fat little white man who sits next to her in the theater—or maybe not avoiding them, for the extra meat, rolls, or dime they might offer. It means reading "smutty" comic books and walking down 118th Street where the prostitutes work, but not knowing what is happening when her period starts. Francie's Harlem is a powerful, pent-up place, where dreams and good people are changed and destroyed, a neighborhood where strength and beauty, love and friendship, all try to grow like plants without soil or water. And for Francie, during the year she turns from twelve to thirteen, living in Harlem means exchanging her longing for the white-hatted cowboy in the movies for a feeling of kinship with the Indians and a realization of what it means to be black and female in the United States.

E.B.

Early Spring, Tove Ditlevsen, *translated from Danish by Tiina Nunnally, 1967, Denmark,* AUTOBIOGRAPHY

For three years, Tove Ditlevsen, one of Denmark's favorite writers, was unable to write. Then six words appeared to her: "In the morning there was hope." These became the first words of her memoir, *Early Spring,* fitting for a book that spares the reader none of the squalid details of Tove Ditlevsen's first eighteen years, yet is filled with beauty and aspirations. Tove Ditlevsen grew up in a Danish working-class neighborhood, the child of constantly arguing and often impoverished parents. There was no physical privacy, and yet her way of thinking and love of words kept her apart from her harsh and domineering mother, her father who loved her yet told her that "girls can't be poets," and her friends who were mostly interested in sex and stealing. While the details of her life are sometimes harsh, Tove Ditlevsen portrays her neighborhood and family with well-considered love: "Down in the bottom of my childhood my father stands laughing. He's big and black and old like the stove, but there is nothing about him that I'm afraid of." Telling her story primarily through the consciousness of herself as a child and then as an adolescent, Tove Ditlevsen re-creates the naïve, touching egoism of her youth.

E.B.

Ellen Foster, Kaye Gibbons, *1988, United States,* NOVEL

Adolescent Ellen tells her first-person memory-narrative in two distinct time frames—now, while she is safe, and two years ago, when she was not. Now: "I live in a clean brick house. . . . When I start to carry an odor I take a bath and folks tell me how sweet I look." And then: "When I was little I would think of ways to kill my daddy." Ellen's father is an abusive drunk, her mother a beaten and defeated woman who finally deserts her only child by taking an overdose of drugs. Until her father dies of alcohol poisoning, Ellen continues to live with him near her only friend Starletta, the daughter of neighboring field workers who welcome Ellen anytime. Ellen's father's death precipitates a series of disastrous living situations, all described in detail that does not miss the humor possible in human relationships no matter how dismal. Although segregation prevents Ellen and Starletta from living close to each other, Ellen eventually comes to treasure Starletta's friendship above all others: "Sometimes I even think I was cut out to be colored and I got bleached and sent to the wrong bunch of folks." Stirring realism and the warmth of a lively spirit make *Ellen Foster* an outstanding novel.

J.L.

Fifth Chinese Daughter, Jade Snow Wong, *1945, United States,* AUTOBIOGRAPHY

Jade Snow Wong grew up in a traditional Chinese family in San Francisco's pre–World War II Chinatown. It was a world in which wives were introduced by their husbands as "my inferior woman," rules were taught with corporal punishment, and home life was literally connected to the family business: "As much a part of home as her bedroom were the sewing machines she passed before she came to her bedroom door. She talked above the din of a factory full of motors and machines in operation, and practically breathed in rhythm to the running stitches." A highly intelligent child who consistently skips grades throughout public school (while attending Chinese school at night and taking over much of the family housework), Jade Snow Wong becomes determined to go to college and gain more independence than she has been taught to expect. Her decision sets off a balancing process between cultures that Jade Snow Wong explores with humor, reverence, and philosophical insight. On one level a universal story of a child learning to assert her own identity, *Fifth Chinese Daughter* is also a marvelous source of information on Chinese cooking, festivals, and child-rearing techniques, as well as a portrait of Chinatown before and during World War II. Straightforward, honest, full of love, Jade Snow Wong's book is a wonderful and educational reading experience.

E.B.

Floating in My Mother's Palm, Ursula Hegi, *1990, Germany* (*United States*), NOVEL

Floating in My Mother's Palm is labeled a novel, but it reads more like a series of beautiful, luminous, interconnected stories about postwar life in the small German town where Hanna Malter grew up. Many of these stories are about painful issues—incest, death, illegitimacy—yet through Ursula Hegi's calm, loving eyes the stories become acts of faith. Young Hanna tells of Hannelore Beier, whose crippled hands become a thing of beauty; of Hanna's mother, a woman who loves to paint and to swim in the quarry during lightning storms; and of Hanna's father, a dentist, whose only reckless act in life was to marry the woman he loved. Hanna describes her friend, who has to go to "the baby mansion," and Frau Weiler, who watches silently, impassively, as her abusive husband threatens to kill himself. Ursula Hegi's descriptions are as filled with light as Hanna's mother's paintings; her philosophical musings are quietly striking. In one story, after Hanna has attempted to cure her friend's polio-crippled leg with stolen holy water, she notes: "Some acts of faith, I believe, have the power to grant us something infinitely wiser than what we imagine." Each story glows like a perfect seashell found on a rocky beach, and reminds us of the mysteries of everyday life and of the beauty and pain of unconventionality.

E.B.

The Floating World, Cynthia Kadohata, *1989, United States,* NOVEL

Olivia spends her childhood and adolescence in what her grandmother calls *ukiyo* or "floating world," traveling with her family across the United States as her father looks for jobs: "The floating world was the gas station attendants, restaurants and jobs we depended on, the motel towns floating in the middle of fields and mountains . . . but it also referred to change and the pleasures and loneliness change brings." One of the beauties of this novel is its ability to re-create a rhythm particular to both travel and adolescence, a stop-and-flow combination of heightened sensitivity and languid introspection mirrored in Olivia's observations, which are blunt, poetic, or philosophical, sometimes changing from one sentence to the next. The incidents and people are offbeat and colorful, events are both real and surreal. Olivia describes her grandmother's death, her job at the chicken-sexing factory, her brother who likes to hide places and sometimes gets left behind on trips, her first boyfriend, her second, her encounter with her father's ghost. It is a marvelous journey, filled with descriptions and ideas that make you almost believe that thoughts are separate, perfect things you can pick up and carry in your pocket like treasures. Holding it all together is Olivia, clear-headed and thoughtful, knowing her future has more potential freedom than her parents', but remembering what her grandmother used to say: "Watch out for life . . . It's harder than it looks."

E.B.

Gorilla, My Love, Toni Cade Bambara, *1981, United States,* SHORT STORIES

Starting with "A Sort of Preface," Toni Cade Bambara lets her readers know for sure that the fifteen superb stories that follow are not autobiographical fiction "cause the minute the book hits the stand here comes your mama screamin how could you and sighin death where is thy sting." Most of the stories are told in the resonant voices of young women with views. "My Man Bovanne" is an affectionate story about blind and aging love. "The Hammer Man" tells the girl's side of the story of her fight with Manny, who "was supposed to be crazy. That was his story. To say you were bad put some people off. But to say you were crazy, well you were officially not to be messed with." "Raymond's Run" tells how twelve-year-old Hazel Elizabeth Deborah Parker—a girl with "a big rep as the baddest thing around"—takes care of her big brother Raymond and beats Gretchen P. Lewis in the fifty-yard dash. In "Mississippi Ham Rider" an aspiring young reporter from New York—called, "in the third person absentular," a "high-yaller Northern bitch" trying "to hit on evil old Ham"—tries to interview and tape an old Southern blues guitar player. In resplendent and affectionate language, Toni Cade Bambara writes "straight-up fiction" with the powerful and lasting force of good strong love.

J.L.

I Know Why the Caged Bird Sings, Maya Angelou, *1969, United States,* AUTOBIOGRAPHY

I Know Why the Caged Bird Sings is the brilliant, sonorous story of Maya Angelou's early life in Arkansas and California. At the age of five, Maya and her brother Bailey are taken to St. Louis to visit their mother, but after Maya is raped they are returned to the rock-hard loving care of their grandmother in Stamps, Arkansas. Maya stops speaking for five years, but becomes a keen observer of everything around her, including the racial politics and divisions of her town. Mrs. Bertha Flowers, "aristocrat of Black Stamps," becomes the woman who throws Maya her "first life line." Mrs. Flowers tells the silent child: "Words mean more than what is set down on paper. It takes the human voice to infuse them with the shades of deeper meaning." So begins the reawakening of Maya's voice and her own music. She survives adolescence, breaks a racial barrier in seeking work, and becomes a mother in what is the beginning of a wondrous series of autobiographical works. A consummate poet, Maya Angelou creates phrases like "voices rubbed together," "Bailey looped his language around his tongue," and "knapsack of misery," as she writes of pain, self-discovery, and, most lovingly, of joy.

V.S.

Kristin Lavransdatter, Sigrid Undset, *translated from Norwegian by Charles Archer and J. S. Scott, 1923/1925/1927, Norway,* NOVEL

A landmark among historical novels, *Kristin Lavransdatter* is part of the body of work that won Sigrid Undset the Nobel Prize in 1928. This trilogy of more than one thousand pages (comprising *The Bridal Wreath, The Mistress of Husaby,* and *The Cross*) follows its title character through her life in fourteenth-century Scandinavia. It is a novel full of big and dramatic happenings: romantic intrigues, political schemes, and spiritual debates. It is also a novel about one woman's life. Sigrid Undset makes us understand Kristin's love for her sons and husband, the feeling of milk in her breasts, and the hard work of living in the fourteenth century. As with any good historical novel, *Kristin Lavransdatter* immerses us in its time through rich details concerning dress and manners as well as social and historical events. The multitude of character names is confusing at first, but if you stick with it, you will get a firsthand experience of another world.

E.B.

The Lamplighter, Maria Susanna Cummins, *1854, United States,* NOVEL

Second only to *Uncle Tom's Cabin* among the top-selling books of nineteenth-century America, *The Lamplighter* is almost completely unknown today, its very popularity having been used to condemn it in literary critical circles. It tells the story of the development of a young, orphaned girl into a resilient, capable young woman who gets her man—her childhood compatriot—but does just fine on her own, thank you, until he returns at the end of the book from his quest to make his fortune overseas. When the reader first meets Gerty she is an orphaned hellion, physically and mentally abused by the brutal and miserly Nan Grant: "No one loved her, and she loved no one; no one treated her kindly; no one tried to make her happy, or cared whether she were so. She was but eight years old and all alone in the world." Gerty is rescued by Trueman Flint, a kindly lamplighter who teaches her about love and respect. A second teacher enters in the form of saintly, blind Emily Graham, who brings a reverence for God into Gerty's life. But while both teachers attempt to tame Gerty's wildness, grown-up Gertrude still retains the backbone and energy that made her such an endearing character to nineteenth-century readers. Gertrude's willingness to defy male and female authority, her courage in emergencies, her rejection of suitors, her loyalty to female friends, and her resourcefulness during hard times make her a strong and inspiring woman in any century.

E.B.

Lives of Girls and Women, Alice Munro, *1971, Canada,* NOVEL

Alice Munro's novel, "autobiographical in form but not in fact," is full of piercing and detailed observations tempered, but never dulled, by tenderness. Del Jordan romps, stumbles, and races toward womanhood in her hometown of Jubilee, Ontario. She knows she will someday be a famous writer, and she keeps journals, memorizes poetry, and makes lists in preparation: "A list of all the stores and businesses going up and down the main street and who owned them, a list of family names, names on the tombstones in the cemetery and any inscriptions underneath. A list of the titles of movies that played at the Lyceum theater from 1938 to 1950, roughly speaking." When her mother, Ada, "goes on the road" alone to sell encyclopedias to farmers, Del is outwardly mortified and secretly proud. At first disgusted, then fascinated, and finally obsessed with sex, Del resents her growing breasts and tries to rationalize her sexual cravings; still, she can't make herself fall in love with the first boy who makes her want to wash her hair. Del Jordan is sharp, sexy, tender, and hilarious. Let the world beware: she's about to become a woman.

J.L.

The Lover, Marguerite Duras, *translated from French by Barbara Bray, 1985, Vietnam (France),* NOVEL

It is said old loves can haunt us. *The Lover* creates this feeling through an atmosphere of shadows, veils, floating memories that come from—was it this boat trip or the last one? From age eight or twelve or thirty? In the end it doesn't matter, for the experience is now embedded, a distinct yet inseparable part of the personality. Marguerite Duras mines her own past to tell the story of an adolescent girl growing up in Indochina during the 1930s. The girl is wayward, rebellious; one day, returning to school on the ferry, dressed in gold lamé shoes, a man's hat, and a silk dress, she encounters the son of a Chinese millionaire. Soon they are involved in the first affair of her life, one she claims has no basis in love for her. He can never marry her—his father has refused—and she says she will leave without regrets. But is that possible? Years later she looks back. By presenting ideas and memories in paragraphs that are literally isolated yet constantly overlapping, *The Lover* creates a misty world of connections made by emotion rather than logic or chronology, and a feeling that lingers after the book itself is closed.

E.B.

Mama Blanca's Memoirs, Teresa de la Parra, *translated from Spanish by Harriet de Onis, 1929, Venezuela,* NOVEL

Ostensibly the story of a much-loved old woman, *Mama Blanca's Memoirs* is the semifictional account of Teresa de la Parra's late-nineteenth-century childhood on a Venezuelan sugar plantation. Witnessed through the eyes of Blanca Nieves ("Snow White"), this is the story of six little girls who "formed a rising staircase stretching from seven months to seven years" and knew their plantation, Piedra Azul, "existed for the sole purpose of enfolding us in its bosom and displaying day after day new surprises to our admiring eyes." Despite the fact that Mama Blanca is dark-eyed, brown-skinned, and black-haired, she and her name became inseparable, "a walking absurdity that only habit, with its kindly indulgence, made acceptable." Besides stories about Blanca's sisters and mama, here are tales about Papa, who wanted sons; Evelyn, their English-speaking nanny who spoke Spanish without articles; Candelaria, the grumpy queen of their kitchen; Vincente, the medicine man, handyman, and revolutionary general; Cousin Juanacho, who "wore his noble, well-brushed poverty with quiet dignity"; and Daniel, the dairy man whose songs made the cows' milk flow. Teresa de la Parra's skilled mixture of sweet warmth and witty realism makes *Mama Blanca's Memoirs* an evocative and engrossing read.

J.L.

The Member of the Wedding, Carson McCullers, *1946, United States,* NOVEL

In Carson McCullers's writing, every word evokes the tragic and miraculous emotional truths of ordinary experience. Her characters are complex, even weird, but feel entirely genuine; her scenes are accessible even when they aren't familiar. In *The Member of the Wedding*, Frankie Adams is hungry for escape, hungry for belonging; it is her peculiar resolution to this classic adolescent paradox that makes her unique. Frankie finds a new identity in her determination to become an integral part of her brother's wedding: "At last she knew just who she was and understood where she was going. She loved her brother and the bride and she was a member of the wedding. The three of them would go into the world and they would always be together." This fantasy transforms Frankie's twelve-year-old perspective on herself, her relationships, and her small Southern hometown. Her inevitable disillusionment and ultimate survival seem almost mythical, yet the tale is told in the simplest terms. The ongoing conversations in the hot kitchen between Frankie, her cousin John Henry, and the cook Berenice resonate with social and personal authenticity. This is a story to be read and reread, to be heard and felt and trusted.

K.B.

My Friend Annie, Jane Duncan, *1965, Scotland,* NOVEL

Janet Sandison is a precocious, happy ten-year-old in Reachfar, Scotland. Her world is suddenly and drastically changed when her mother dies, and then, soon after, her father loses his position as grieve (farm manager) to the local baronet. Janet leaves her precious home and friends to begin her life as a brilliant—if slightly eccentric—student in Cairnshaw in the south of Scotland. Her "friend" Annie is the daughter of Cairnshaw neighbors, people Janet's stepmother, Jean, admires and extols Janet to emulate, but people for whom Janet feels complete contempt: Annie wears lace and keeps clean, Janet likes coveralls and dirt; Annie stays quiet and smiles, Janet speaks her mind and sometimes yells. *My Friend Annie* provides an affectionate glimpse of growing up in Scotland before World War II, with just enough spark in the relationship between Janet and Jean, and just enough mystery, to make for a memorable read.

J.L.

Paradise, Elena Castedo, *1990, Chile* (*United States*), NOVEL

"The best way to get where you want to be is to please those who own the road," Pilar warns Solita, her ten-year-old daughter. Pilar, a dispossessed aristocrat who escaped Franco's Spain with Julian, Solita's exciting labor-lawyer father, wants a change. Tired of living as an unemployed refugee in a run-down neighborhood in a crowded city in Chile, she is ecstatic when she finds people who do indeed own a road going where she wants to be: paradise. And paradise, an estate called El Topaz owned by "important people" with children Solita can make "lasting and lifelong friendship with," is where Solita, her younger brother, and their mother go. This paradise is full of bored aristocrats, quirky animals who "smell normal," servants with strong personalities, and children who endlessly measure everything about everybody. For Solita, used to hand-me-down clothes, one pair of panties with rotten elastic, and her mother's constant smiling reminder, "When in Rome . . . ," paradise is full of roadblocks, secrets, sometimes thrilling dangers, and an unending longing to return home to her father. We experience the world Solita experiences in colorful, sweet, and gory detail. And with her we learn about choosing the people and the roads we follow.

J.L.

Rich in Love, Josephine Humphreys, *1987, United States,* NOVEL

What is it about adolescence that draws us to relive its pain and turmoil through books, movies, and television? Perhaps it is the advantage or safety of hindsight, or the comfort in realizing that even those who seemed so confident were suffering, too. Seventeen-year-old Lucille Odom is one such seemingly mature teenager. She tries to hold her family together when her mother departs abruptly—leaving the ice cream melting in the grocery bag on the front seat of the car—and her twenty-five-year-old sister returns home with a new husband and a baby on the way. As life goes on without her mother, it becomes clear that Lucille is not as strong and mature as she portrays herself to be. Josephine Humphreys has created a fully believable portrait of an adolescent who eventually realizes that she does not have all the answers—nor do the adults around her. She is challenged to turn outward and to deal with the hard truth of why her mother left. As she moves beyond her own needs, she begins to understand the complexity of love in its many forms—parental, filial, fraternal, sexual, and self-love. Written in deceptively simple and direct language, this is a story of growing up—with all its pain and glory—and of a family becoming individuals in order to remain a family.

S.L.S.

The Road from Coorain, Jill Ker Conway, *1989, Australia,* AUTOBIOGRAPHY

Jill Ker Conway writes that as a child she sought refuge from the adult concerns and duties of her life by retiring to her swing in the eucalyptus grove. There she "would kick furiously in order to rise up higher and see a little farther beyond the horizon." *The Road from Coorain* describes Jill Ker Conway's life until the age of twenty-three, when she leaves Australia for graduate school at Harvard University and a life of academic honor, including her role as the first woman president of Smith College. Dr. Conway is a historian by training as well as by nature. With careful attention to each step of the journey, she chronicles her growth as she moves from an isolated childhood on a drought-ridden sheep ranch to her school years in the crowded, confusing urban life in Sydney. Her father dies when she is a still a child; her mother, unable to cope, suffers from alcoholism and depression. Raised with British attitudes that essentially ignored the reality of her native Australian culture, in college she comes to recognize the necessity of studying her country as an independent entity. Her personal evolution mirrors her academic life as she realizes that she, too, must claim her independence from her mother and from familial responsibilities.

K.B.-B.

Silent Dancing: A Partial Remembrance of a Puerto Rican Childhood, Judith Ortiz Cofer, *1990, United States/Puerto Rico,* MEMOIR

Judith Ortiz Cofer's talent for storytelling was learned at the knee of her grandmother, "Mama." In this entertaining and perceptive book, the author's life unfolds through tales set in Mama's room, in Puerto Rican pueblos, and in Paterson, New Jersey, apartments. Her father joins the U.S. Navy; when his ship is in port in New York City, the family lives in New Jersey and when he is at sea, they move back to Puerto Rico, to a life with family and many friends. After Judith starts school, the family spends summers in Puerto Rico and the school year in New Jersey. Life there is very restricted: her father leaves instructions not to mingle with neighbors; he has plans for a better life for his family, certainly one better than the near-poverty conditions of this neighborhood. Judith Cofer's mother takes her husband's words to heart and rarely interacts with her New Jersey acquaintances, leaving Judith to become her mother's voice in dealing with neighbors and shopkeepers while her father is away. Her father, a strong person, takes on much of Judith's responsibility when he is home. This relieves her, but also creates confusion about her role in the family. Growing up in two cultures, Judith identifies with and feels rejected by each. This memoir comprises essays that can stand alone, and also includes some of the author's poems, which further illuminate her experiences and add to our understanding of this child of two worlds.

H.S.

Sweet Summer: Growing Up With and Without My Dad, Bebe Moore Campbell, *1989, United States,* AUTOBIOGRAPHY

Sweet Summer reverberates with love—the idolatrous reverence of a young girl for the father she sees only during her summers in North Carolina, the complicated passions of an adolescent who becomes aware of her father's failings, the balanced love of a daughter with a husband and a child of her own. It is rich and glowing, full of portraits of Bebe Moore Campbell's father and of the men in her life who take his place during the falls, winters, and springs of her childhood in Philadelphia, when she fears she will be smothered by the teachings and closeness of "the Bosoms" in her grandmother and mother's house. *Sweet Summer* is a book about growing up, about new clothes and mosquito bites, about being one of too few black students in an integrated school, about family rituals and ties, about loving your parents and not understanding divorce. Thoughtful, poignant, humorous, it is full of details that make scenes burst open in front of your eyes. Bebe Moore Campbell's book strengthens like a good meal—through the languorous rhythms of North Carolina and the stop-start street talk of Philadelphia that take you home even if you never lived there, and through her ability to accept and love those around her, especially her father, the big, black, determined man in a wheelchair who used to sing out "BebebebebebeMoore."

E.B.

Tahuri, Ngahuia Te Awekotuku, *1989, New Zealand,*
SHORT STORIES

At the heart of this collection are two young Maori women, Tahuri and Whero, who struggle with their identities as Maoris and as individuals. Most of the tales revolve around daily life in the *pa* (village), where Tahuri and Whero laugh with the joy of community and cry at injustices often directed at them because of their color, sex, or choice of lovers. Adventurous and spirited, they also explore life away from the *pa*. Set on New Zealand's North Island in an area known for its thermal springs and sulfur baths, these stories of small, isolated incidents allow the reader a searing look into these lives. It's a world of aunties, girl cousins, and girlfriends; of grandmothers who are round and soft, with laps full of love and comfort. When Auntie Pani is storytelling in the baths, "all her chins waggled with excitement, and her left eye, slightly lopsided, winked wickedly at her niece, closest to her, head just above the surface of the water, ears glowing in the heat, hair slicked about her neck like leaves of long wet grass." These are also tales of pain and abuse. After Tahuri is raped, a young male friend refuses to believe her and "quietly insist[s] that the boys wouldn't treat a Maori girl, one of their own, like that." Throughout Ngahuia Te Awekotuku's stories, Tahuri and Whero find women whom they can emulate and who will guide them and help them discover the strength they need to carry the sometimes very weighty burdens of youth.

H.S.

There Never Was a Once Upon a Time, Carmen Naranjo, *translated from Spanish by Linda Britt, 1989, Costa Rica,* SHORT STORIES

Each of the ten short stories in this collection is told in the first person by a child narrator, usually but not always female; each is told in a rambling and magically inconsistent present tense, as characterized by the opening lines of the title story: "There never was a once upon a time, you told me that afternoon at nearly six o'clock, and I answered: you're a liar, there is always a once upon a time, today, yesterday, tomorrow, because time always has room for long agos." In another story, Carlos, who is sick, accepts his adored friend's challenge to discover eighteen ways to make a mental square. Carlos makes himself sicker as he works frantically to meet the deadline: "I'm confused and I can't tell the difference between mental and spiritual squares. 16. When you decide to believe in a God that has the face of authority and keeps marking your grades down in his notebook." Finally he finishes with a flourish and a number nineteen: "19. When you believe you are somebody for wanting to be like someone else." In "Everybody Loves Clowns," the narrator compares the camouflage of garlics and lizards to her inner and outer self, then decides she is a clown who must wear a disguise "like someone who doesn't realize that's what she is." Through the rich imaginations of children, these stories describe the problems of youth—primarily adults who barely understand and rarely respect them—with inventive and sophisticated vitality.

J.L.

Heritage

Heritage is the cultural identification from which we sprout and grow. It is our country, our neighborhood, the food we eat, the air we breathe; it structures our families and forms our languages. In Ticasuk's loving memories of six generations of her Eskimo family, heritage is a source of pride and strength. Writing in the fifteenth century, Christine de Pizan stoutly defends women by citing numerous historical examples of strong, intelligent, brave women. For some authors and characters, heritage is a strait-jacket: Maxine Hong Kingston, Anzia Yezierska, and Tsitsi Dangarembga protest against Chinese, Jewish, and African traditions that negate the value of women. Other authors and characters must find their heritage in order to understand themselves fully. In *Obasan* the search is a painful uncovering of the treatment of Japanese-Canadians during World War II. Paule Marshall and Flora Nwapa write beautiful, stirring novels about two different women's discovery of their spiritual roots. Marguerite Yourcenar and Pauli Murray both seek their genealogical histories; one creates an elegant, multilayered study of her Belgian family and culture, the other a moving and insightful memoir of a multiracial family in the southern United States. Whether restrictive or liberating, a source of strength or a curse, our heritages provide our foundations. In order to build, we must understand from what they are made.

Alicia: My Story	Alicia Appleman-Jurman
The Book of the City of Ladies	Christine de Pizan
The Book of Ruth	Jane Hamilton
Bread Givers	Anzia Yezierska
Burger's Daughter	Nadine Gordimer
Confessions of Lady Nijo	Lady Nijo
Dear Departed	Marguerite Yourcenar
The Dust Roads of Monferrato	Rosetta Loy
Efuru	Flora Nwapa
The Fountain Overflows	Rebecca West
Ganado Red	Susan Lowell
How the Garcia Girls Lost Their Accents	Julia Alvarez
The Keepers of the House	Shirley Ann Grau
Loving in the War Years	Cherríe Moraga
Moses, Man of the Mountain	Zora Neale Hurston
My Place	Sally Morgan
Nervous Conditions	Tsitsi Dangarembga
Obasan	Joy Kogawa
Once Upon an Eskimo Time	Edna Wilder
Praisesong for the Widow	Paule Marshall
Proud Shoes	Pauli Murray
The Roots of Ticasuk	Ticasuk
The Seventh Garment	Eugenia Fakinou
Spring Moon	Bette Bao Lord
Talking Indian	Anna Lee Walters
This Bridge Called My Back	Cherríe Moraga and Gloria Anzaldúa, eds.
Tracks	Louise Erdrich
The Woman Warrior	Maxine Hong Kingston

Alicia: My Story, Alicia Appleman-Jurman, *1988, Poland,* MEMOIR

Alicia Jurman was born in Buczacz, Poland, in 1930, the daughter of orthodox Jewish parents. Alicia's family had a long history in Poland; her father ran a successful mercantile business which supported the family comfortably, and the Jewish population was large and close enough to create culture, community, and a sense of security for Alicia and her three brothers. Racist anti-Semitism was a fact of life the family almost learned to ignore until 1938, when the Germans invaded Poland and occupied Buczacz, and one of Alicia's brothers was killed. In 1939, the Russians drove the Germans out; another brother died. In 1941, the Germans returned; within a year, Alicia Jurman was the last living member of her family. In compelling detail, she describes hiding in fields, finding food, narrowly escaping from prison and firing squads, helping others escape, searching for survivors of her family. Written as straightforward, nonpolitical, and graceful narrative, this is the story eleven-year-old Alicia swore she would someday tell: "Through the story of 'Alicia' I wish to reach out, not only to survivors like myself, but to all people. . . . I believe that the book will teach young people what enormous reserves of strength they possess within themselves."

J.L.

The Book of the City of Ladies, Christine de Pizan, *translated from French by Jeffrey Richards, 1405, France,* NONFICTION

The Book of the City of Ladies should be included on any comprehensive reading list, if only on the basis of historical interest. Christine de Pizan is known as the first woman to earn her living by writing; left a widow at twenty-five, with three children and no inheritance, she saw it as one of her few options. She is more than a historical curiosity, however; her books are literate, feminist, and thought-provoking, and cover a wide range of topics. *The Book of the City of Ladies* is a defense of women that strikes home even in the twentieth century. Using the narrative device of a dialogue between the author and several allegorical figures, the narrator first digs her foundation for a city by defending women against the allegations of lack of intelligence, virtue, strength, and bravery, then builds her walls with an astonishing number of examples of women who disprove all popular misconceptions. Readers whose primary aim is to find out about women figures from the past might prefer more straightforward women's history books; the repetitive style of *The Book of the City of Ladies* can become wearing. On the other hand, there is a thrill in reaching across almost six hundred years to Christine de Pizan, who discusses issues we still argue about today and introduces us to women we never knew existed.

E.B.

The Book of Ruth, Jane Hamilton, *1988, United States,* NOVEL

Ruth says right off: "I tell myself that it should be simple to see through to the past now that I'm set loose, now that I can invent my own words, but nothing much has come my way without a price." In Ruth's story, which takes place in a rural town in Illinois sometime in the mid–twentieth century, it's detail, not the big picture, that governs. There is her body, which refuses to be beautiful like those in the magazines, her mother's unrelenting anger and bitterness, her distant and disturbed father, her handsome and heartless brother, her friends no one else likes, her love for a crazy man who loves her back like no one else ever did, her correspondence with Aunt Sid who believes in her. Telling her story is a struggle: "We were the products of our limited vocabulary: we had no words for savory odors or the colors of the winter sky or the unexpected compulsion to sing." With Aunt Sid's help, Ruth survives to recount her amazingly ordinary life-story—with its relentless hours of unrewarding hard work, its painful and recurrent disappointments, and its vicious violence—with extraordinary dignity and daring.

J.L.

Bread Givers, Anzia Yezierska, *1925, United States,* NOVEL

Conscious of her outsider status—as Polish immigrant, writer in a foreign language, and Jewish female—Anzia Yezierska takes us inside an early-twentieth-century American immigrant Jewish family, a family without a son to lighten their load or brighten their lives. Sarah, the narrator of *Bread Givers*, describes with urgency and in detail the lives she, her sisters, and her mother live to support their revered, Torah-reading father: the crowded rooms they share so he can study undisturbed; the numerous jobs the women work to maintain the family and pay for his books, charities, and manner of dress; his constant and often impossible demands. Sarah struggles to remain loyal: "I began to feel I was different than my sisters. . . . If they ever had times they hated Father, they were too frightened of themselves to confess. . . . But could I help it what was inside me? I had to feel what I felt even if it killed me." Through profuse and perceptive dialogue, Anzia Yezierska brings to life a heritage whose strength, wisdom, and idiom continue, seventy years later, to enrich North American culture and language.

J.L.

Burger's Daughter, Nadine Gordimer, *1979, South Africa,* NOVEL

Rosa Burger grew up in a home under constant surveillance by the South African government. Her parents were detained for their political beliefs; her father died in prison. When her mother, whose health suffered from her time in jail, eventually dies as well, Rosa, a white South African in her early twenties, is left the only surviving member of her family. Yet even after her parents' deaths, the history of their anti-apartheid beliefs and practices have a daily impact on her life: it seems everyone has expectations of her, and the government is still watching. A quiet, private person, Rosa constantly searches her memories to find herself, to grasp this heritage that weighs her down. Over a period of several years, Rosa comes to understand the impact of the South African political climate on her and how she became who she is. Take time to read this novel; the political realities it describes are complicated. The narrative interweaves straightforward storytelling and Rosa's most personal thoughts. In *Burger's Daughter,* Nobel Prize–winner Nadine Gordimer takes a situation much read about in newspapers and makes it real, in a memorable story of coming to terms with circumstances over which we have little control, yet which directly affect our lives.

H.S.

Confessions of Lady Nijo, Lady Nijo, *translated from Japanese by Karen Brazell, circa 1300, Japan,* DIARY

One of the oldest books in print by a woman, *Confessions of Lady Nijo* comprises the thoughts, reflections, and poetry of an opinionated Japanese imperial court concubine, covering the years 1271 to 1306. Writing in diary form toward the end of her life, Lady Nijo chronicles her life in the Imperial court, where her strong personality and aspirations for a higher position provoked the jealousy of the empress and caused her dismissal; her travels throughout the country as a Buddhist nun; and her development into a mature and compassionate woman. Whether she is commenting on fashion and personalities at court, or coming to understand the lives of the lower caste, Lady Nijo's reflections show that while much may change in seven hundred years, there is much more that does not. There are births and deaths, marriages and affairs, richness and poverty. Her writing is beautiful and often touching: "The snow covered peaks glowing against the faintly dawning sky gave an unearthly aspect to the scene. Two or three attendants dressed in plain robes accompanied him. I was sad, unbearably sad, when he left." Read this book for its history and intimacy, its feelings of familiarity and difference, its joy and sadness that reach across centuries and continents.

H.S.

Dear Departed, Marguerite Yourcenar, *translated from French by Maria Louise Ascher, 1974, France,* BIOGRAPHY

In a note to her translator, Marguerite Yourcenar wrote, "It is *very important* that the reader *not* get the impression that the author is greatly or personally interested in her origins, since the whole quest is more sociological and historical than personal." It is this attitude that makes *Dear Departed* such an extraordinary work. Marguerite Yourcenar's mother died of puerperal fever when her daughter was only a few days old. Ostensibly a search into her mother's ancestors, about whom the author has few family stories or memories to rely on, the book is actually a luminous collage of historical anecdotes, visits to châteaus past and present, philosophical musings, angry denunciations of industrial practices, semifictional biographies, and marvelous recreations of life among the Belgian landed gentry of long ago. Marguerite Yourcenar's distance from her subjects, particularly those closest to her, can be disconcerting, as when she explains her various mundane uses of the few treasures of her mother's that her father saved: "Nothing shows better the insignificance of our human individuality, which we prize so highly, than the rapidity with which those objects that support it and sometimes symbolize it are, in their turn, outmoded, outworn or lost." Yet she can also delve into intimate aspects of those far removed, as when she muses about the sex life of her grandparents. The book moves in and out of historic events and individual lives, raising questions about love and loyalty, traditions and their consequences.

E.B.

The Dust Roads of Monferrato, Rosetta Loy, *translated from Italian by William Weaver, 1987, Italy,* NOVEL

Reading *The Dust Roads of Monferrato* is like standing alone before an ancient tapestry in an old museum. There is a hush; the story before you is muted but rich, full of glowing browns, faded oranges and greens. A best-seller and winner of numerous awards in Italy, *The Dust Roads of Monferrato* encompasses four generations of a rural nineteenth-century Italian family: the Great Masten, who builds a house and accumulates land; his two sons Giai and Pidren, who both love the same woman; and Pidren's children and grandchildren. The almost complete absence of dialogue, rather than distancing the reader, makes the book seem timeless. Pairs of brothers, sisters, and lovers come and go, form bonds and then gracefully or violently break them. There are floods and wars, childbirths and illnesses. Pidren's granddaughter and her half-brother fall in love; later she will marry someone else. At times you can hear the fiddle of the long-dead Giai along the halls; outside, the walnut tree spreads ever wider. In her room, a dying woman cries repeatedly, "Where has my sister gone?" and her young grandniece knows that "from afar, from its source, that chant dragged with it, like the magic piper, the formless characters of dreams. Things similar to the first years of life, or perhaps the same things." Within a view that is both sweeping and intimately detailed, the intensity and movement of these lives is covered and soothed by the dust of time.

E.B.

Efuru, Flora Nwapa, *1966, Nigeria,* NOVEL

It is rare to find a book by a native Nigerian woman in print in the United States. *Efuru* is even more noteworthy because with this book, in 1966, Flora Nwapa became the first native Nigerian woman to be published in Nigeria, and the first nonwhite African woman to be published in England. *Efuru* explores Nigerian village life and values, a world where spirits are a part of everyday life—as accepted, respected, and feared as one's own relatives. Efuru, a highly respected woman of her village, carries on the family tradition of treating others well, and is successful as a trader. Yet her personal life is mired in tragedy: she has two unsuccessful marriages, and her only child dies. In her village, a single, childless woman is a cause for fear, and the villagers begin to gossip—a favorite and powerful pastime. They question her good deeds and wonder what she has done to upset the spirits, whose influence and power are at the center of their lives. In her struggle to understand all that has happened to her, Efuru seeks the advice of the *dibias*—village doctors—and finds her spiritual guide and the path she must follow.

H.S.

The Fountain Overflows, Rebecca West, *1956, England,* NOVEL

Rose, the perceptive narrator of *The Fountain Overflows*, is a fictionalized version of the youthful Rebecca West. In early-1900s London, Papa, a misunderstood writer and never-successful politician, goes away—again—to earn money. The children stay very busy being young, trying hard to respect and live with Mamma's tradition of genteel Englishness and Papa's foolishness while their worrisome —and embarrassing—poverty deepens. Mamma is discouraged but brave, "a nerve-jerked woman" able to "straighten her shoulders and cock her hat and assume the character of a smart and undefeated woman." A concert pianist turned wife and mother, she makes music a constant for her children. Rose and Mary play the piano; Cordelia performs on the violin "with the air of somebody who is being photographed," determined to make it her road to fame and fortune. *The Fountain Overflows* is a reader's feast of subtle, penetrating, and hilarious observations on childhood, social posturing, and Anglo-Saxon heritage.

J.L.

Ganado Red: A Novella and Stories, Susan Lowell, *1988, United States,* SHORT STORIES

In the novella that accompanies the eight stories in this collection, Susan Lowell traces the ownership of an intricate Navajo rug—the Ganado Red of the title—over sixty years, from its Navajo creator through its various owners. With each owner, the story rests, collects itself, looks about to examine its surroundings, the characters, and the effect of the brilliant blood-red rug upon the people around it. It is the last owner who, at a turning point in her life, discovers the red thread that runs through the black border: "the spirit line. . . . Every Navajo design is supposed to be imperfect, with an opening so the spirits won't be trapped. Sometimes it's called the weaver's pathway—on to another rug. A better one, maybe." Susan Lowell's other stories follow a similar pattern: wild pigs, illegal aliens, nuclear bomb tests, a gun—each provides a continuing thread and symbol while the story spreads out around it. The majority of these stories are set in the southwestern United States, where the author lives, and they reflect the spare beauty of the country. The details, never many, are inserted almost cautiously in between the cool detachment of the characters' thoughts. The effect is clear and arid, sometimes sharp, at other times serene.

E.B.

How the Garcia Girls Lost Their Accents, Julia Alvarez, *1991, United States,* NOVEL

While visiting her relatives in the Dominican Republic, Yolanda reflects: "She and her sisters have led such turbulent lives—so many husbands, homes, jobs, wrong turns among them. But look at her cousins, women with households and authority in their voices. Let this turn out to be my home." Yolanda left this home in the early 1960s when, for political reasons, her parents immigrated to the United States with their four young daughters. Her parents made sure Yolanda and her sisters went to prep school to meet the "right kind" of Americans, and in time, when the political climate cooled down in the Dominican Republic, the girls were allowed to return to spend summers with their extended family. Now the daughters are grown. Carla is a child psychologist who believes her and her sisters' identities were weakened because they were dressed alike as children. Sandi is obsessed with her weight, never quite satisfied with her life. Sofia, always a rebel, has just given birth to the first male child in two generations and named him after his grandfather. Yolanda contemplates a move back to the Dominican Republic; perhaps there she can shed her uncomfortable identity as the family poet. With humor, grace, and insight, *How the Garcia Girls Lost Their Accents* looks back on the lives of the four Garcia sisters and their parents, blending family history and expectations with the realities of their adopted culture.

H.S.

The Keepers of the House, Shirley Ann Grau, *1964, United States,* NOVEL

What happens if a wealthy, white Southern man falls in love, marries, and has children with his black housekeeper after his white wife has died? If he lives in the country and is discreet, if his light-skinned children are sent off to school and he never tells anyone he is actually married, perhaps nothing. But what about his children and grandchildren? Winner of a 1964 Pulitzer Prize, *The Keepers of the House* attacks the hypocrisy of Southern racism and examines the consequences of rage and revenge among the members of the Howland family. The narrator is Abigail Howland, white granddaughter of William Howland and his first wife, the only one left to face the wrath of the town after the secret is exposed. Complex and defiant, enmeshed in racism and familial obligations, she is compelled to go back through her family history in order to understand herself, her father, and the South. Shirley Ann Grau is a masterful storyteller; we know something shocking is coming, but caught up in the emotions of the moment we sometimes forget where the memories and stories are leading, until suddenly we are confronted by Abigail's dramatic and electrifying revenge on the town which has risen up against her.

E.B.

Loving in the War Years, Cherríe Moraga, *1983, United States,* NONFICTION

"I am a Chicana lesbian. My own particular relationship to being a sexual person; and a radical stand in direct contradiction to, and in violation of, the women I was raised to be." In the poetry, prose, and personal stories in *Loving in the War Years*, Cherríe Moraga explores this contradiction, weaving her confusion and pain into the fabric of her eventual self-acceptance. She writes about prejudices she suffers because she is half-white and a lesbian born in a Catholic, Chicano culture. She tells of her frustrations with the importance men were given as she was growing up and with the exclusion of lesbian women of color from the women's movement. In her struggles, she has drawn from those parts of her upbringing that are necessary to sustain her physical, emotional, and spiritual well-being—the love of her mother's home, the sense of community among Chicana women, the smell of the candles in church, and the spiritual need to respect something beyond herself. In the telling, she creates a portrait of beauty, anger, and independence. "Spirituality which inspires activism and, similarly, politics which move the spirit—which draw from the deep-seated place of our greatest longings for freedom—give meaning to our lives." Some knowledge of Spanish may be helpful with these writings, but even without it Cherríe Moraga's words will touch your heart and your mind.

H.S.

Moses, Man of the Mountain, Zora Neale Hurston, *1939, United States,* NOVEL

According to the author's brief and pithy introduction, stories of Moses abound in Africa, Asia, and the Near East, "but not because of his beard nor because he brought the laws down from Sinai. . . . What other man has ever seen with his eyes even the back part of

God's glory? . . . That calls for power." Here is the story of Moses told from the ground up, the story of law told by the bearers—of children, of law, of labor—not the makers or the decreers. It starts with the women hiding to give birth, the sounds of their labor stifled in terror of the greater agony of having their infant sons taken away and drowned. How does life continue under such a law? What do people do to survive? To grow? Enter Moses, an illegal boy born in gagged silence and floated away on the river inside a reed basket with his parents' sobbing hope his only strength. Rescued and raised by the pharaoh's daughter, Moses grows up to become the savior of his people. As Moses learns, being a savior is not an easy or trouble-free life, and it's not just the Pharaoh causing the problems. In prose full of rhythmic strength and humor, Zora Neale Hurston tells the story of Moses—an ancient human heritage story deeply enmeshed in the psyches and souls of many races and cultures—from the inside out, with all the guts and raggedy edges visible.

J.L.

My Place, Sally Morgan, *1983, Australia,* AUTOBIOGRAPHY

This is a story of extended family, the treatment of aboriginals, and history lost and found. Nan, the author's grandmother, wants to "forget" about her heritage. She teaches her grandchildren about birds and bullfrogs to make sure they know nature's side of life and instills in them a certain distrust of white people, but she won't talk about her past. Late in his life, Great-Uncle Arthur is eager to tell of his past, the fair and the unfair, even though it makes his sister Nan angry, for his stories bring forth painful memories she buried long ago. Gladys, the author's optimistic mother, has allowed her past to fade from her consciousness: with a sick husband and four children she has plenty of other things on her mind. And finally there is the author, Sally Morgan, who was told her family was from India and didn't realize for years that they were Australian Aborigines. Although this autobiography centers upon the author's early life, it is the stories of her mother, great-uncle, and especially her grandmother that make this a moving book. When Sally Morgan's mother and grandmother allow themselves to remember their pasts, they affirm the power of the mind and the spirit. *My Place* demands that we respect what people want and are able to remember—and let some secrets stay buried.

H.S.

Nervous Conditions, Tsitsi Dangarembga, *1988, Zimbabwe,* NOVEL

"I was not sorry when my brother died." So begins Tambu, narrator of *Nervous Conditions*, as she looks back on her childhood. Tambu grew up on her family's impoverished farm within a traditional native society; her determination to get an education, however, brings her into contact with British colonialism in the form of mission schools. As an African woman, Tambu comes to understand that oppression has many forms; it is never simple, and solutions are hard to come by. The patriarchal traditions of her own culture oppress women, while British colonial education takes native children from their parents, literally and figuratively. Tambu grows maize to earn her school fees, because there is only enough family money for her brother—only to have her brother steal her produce and give it to friends. She tells of her cousin Nyasha, raised in England and brought back to Zimbabwe; unable to live in either culture, she self-destructively turns her struggle inward. Tambu talks of how she herself has changed. Despite the pain and oppression that she has witnessed, Tambu loves her country. Bitterly, with barely repressed irony, she points out wrongs, and then lovingly describes a pathway, a pool, the face of a woman. A strong, intelligent, loving girl/woman, Tambu is a character to stay with and care about, even—perhaps especially—as the conditions she describes enrage us.

E.B.

Obasan, Joy Kogawa, *1981, Canada,* NOVEL

When Naomi was a young child living in Vancouver, British Columbia, her mother left to visit relatives in Japan. Soon after, the Japanese bombed Pearl Harbor. Naomi's mother was not allowed to return, and Naomi's family was "relocated" by the Canadian government. When *Obasan* begins, Naomi is thirty-five, a woman determined to ignore her past. But the death of the man who helped raise her, and her aunt's refusal to forgive the Canadian government, force Naomi to remember. Naomi's initial memories are of a big house with a backyard and a father who loved music, of handcrafted boats and communal baths with her great-aunt. Then the memories shift and she remembers families divided, chicken coops assigned as "houses," parents dying away from their children, and a government that took away rights based on ethnic heritage, not on actions. *Obasan* uses a combination of personal narrative, lyrical outpourings, official letters, and dreams to protest the treatment of Japanese-Canadians during World War II. Varying in style and emotional intensity, the novel's voices clash and mesh, building upon each other until they reach a stunning ending that forces us to reconsider all that has gone before.

E.B.

Once Upon an Eskimo Time, Edna Wilder, *1987, United States,* BIOGRAPHY

Once Upon an Eskimo Time is the tale of the tenth year in the life of Nedercook, as told to her daughter, Edna Wilder. Nedercook's narrative begins in the spring at the end of "the cold, dark days of winter." While her descriptions of the Bering Sea and surrounding land on the Seward Peninsula are filled with beautifully crafted prose, the dialogue portrays a people whose lives are dictated by thought directly related to action: "Today we go on big hunt." "Son needs help." "Young be happy." "Big storm come." Nedercook's delicately rendered descriptions tell of events, ceremonies, and details in the daily life of people from the far north. This is a land where every day's weather determines what each person will do to find, cook, and store food; where the people will relieve themselves; where the moss used for personal hygiene, menstruating women, and baby diapers will be found; what will be wrapped around the newborns who, within hours of birth, are strapped to their mothers' backs. Interwoven with these particulars of daily life are the ancient legends, told to Nedercook by her parents with the delightful requirement that she herself tell them again and again until she gets them right. This story of one year in a young Eskimo girl's life is a powerful and tender tribute to some of America's first peoples.

J.L.

Praisesong for the Widow, Paule Marshall, *1983, Caribbean/ United States* (*United States*), NOVEL

Throwing into suitcases all she brought with her on this Caribbean cruise, Avey Johnson knows she has to go home. She wonders why she has been dreaming of her childhood, of the months of August spent on a small island with her great-aunt. Were these dreams of the Shout Ring and her great-aunt's stories of the slave ships from Africa causing the knots in Avey's stomach? Then, forced to wait overnight in Grenada for the plane home, Avey loses herself in memories of her marriage. It was a "successful" marriage, one that took her from Harlem to Brooklyn to White Plains, New York. But now she feels that her and her late husband's financial gains were made at the cost of their history and passion for life. The next morning, as she walks on the beach in a dreamlike trance, emotionally drained from her night of memories, she encounters a man about to leave on his annual trip to his native island of Carriacou. His dancing the Juba dance triggers Avey's memories, and she is talked into going with him. On Carriacou, sixty-five-year-old Avey comes to understand in new ways traditions she has long forgotten—and the importance of knowing, and remembering, her past.

H.S.

Proud Shoes: The Story of an American Family, Pauli Murray, *1956, United States,* NONFICTION

Spurred by the 1950s civil rights movement in the United States, Pauli Murray interrupted her law career for four years to investigate and document her family's history. Meticulously researched and eloquently written, *Proud Shoes* is at once an engrossing story of one family and a historical overview of race relations in the United States spanning almost one hundred years. Pauli Murray grew up in the South with her grandparents, Cornelia and Robert Fitzgerald, two strong-willed individuals of vastly different backgrounds. Cornelia—the child born of the rape of a beautiful house slave by the master's son—was brought up in a Southern household, both heir and slave. Robert grew up in the North, the sickly child of free black Thomas and his white wife Sarah Ann, who through her marriage "enlisted in a cause which called for raw courage and no retreats." Educated and brave, Robert refused to pass for white, and waited impatiently until the Union allowed blacks into the military; his determination and heroism on and off the battlefield served as a constant example and a psychological shield against the racism of young Pauli's world. As Pauli Murray traces her family's history, she shows the Civil War from two sides and describes a world of North and South, before and after emancipation, filled with family stories, laws, injustice, bravery, and heroes and villains of both races. She never shrinks from truth, and her loving pride is ever-present.

E.B.

The Roots of Ticasuk: An Eskimo Woman's Family Story, Ticasuk (Emily Ivanoff Brown), *1974, United States,* AUTOBIOGRAPHY

The Roots of Ticasuk contains the stories Ticasuk learned from her elders, stories that tell the history of six generations of her family. After a battle of her early Unalakleet ancestors with the Indians of interior Alaska, Masu, the childless sister of the Unalakleet chief, discovers a male child survivor. This story describes how she smuggles him into her camp and how, because he is a special gift, he is adopted and trained to become the tribal chief. "Malquay" tells about the baby Malquay, great-granddaughter of Masu, whose mother dies when she is an infant. The tale of "Chalavaluk" recounts the legend of how a brave new mother forces the Unalakleets to stop female infanticide in times of famine by placing her baby girl on her parents' doorstep and disappearing into the night. The history of Chalavaluk's daughter, Chikuk, follows: how her people save her life to honor her mother's courage; her introduction to white culture; her marriage to a Russian trader; the birth of their only child, Stephan; her untimely death. In the final set of stories, we learn how Stephan and Malquay meet, marry, and bear Ticasuk: "I am Ticasuk, the last child of Stephan and Malquay of the lineage of Alluyagnak of Unalakleet. I have three children . . ." With loving and beautiful descriptions of the great Alaskan landscape as a background, Ticasuk's depictions of the particulars of everyday Eskimo life fill this collection with the warmth, strength, and pride of a long and strong tradition.

J.L.

The Seventh Garment, Eugenia Fakinou, *translated from Greek by Ed Emery, 1983, Greece,* NOVEL

The first voice is from a tree: "In the old days, the maidens from the distant North would come and we would talk together. Then came the priestesses, clad in white, with their copper gongs, and garlands in their hair. In their white robes, they would lie down and wait and listen for the whispering of my leaves." The next voice is that of Roula, who lives in Athens: "My mother always used to say that you can tell a bad day from the way it starts. Well, she wasn't wrong." Out in the Greek countryside where Roula's relatives live, other voices speak—those of Eleni and her mother, who live near the tree. Through the course of the book, the voices come together to tell of the suffering of the women and men of Greece. Eleni's mother loved her husband, the man who stroked her belly and painted pictures all over her body, but the Turks killed him, and his severed head landed in the water near her boat. Eleni is one of eight children her mother later conceived with *him*, the man who raped her, knowing she had no place else to go. A death brings the family together and, following tradition, Eleni becomes the spiritual medium for seven generations of male family members. The stories of dead men blend with the voices of living women to relate a history of Greece dating back to the 1820s.

E.B.

Spring Moon, Bette Bao Lord, *1981, China* (*United States*), NOVEL

Spring Moon is a big and engrossing novel, the literary equivalent of a rich, indulgent dessert. Spanning five generations of a Chinese family, the book illuminates the social and political upheavals of late-nineteenth- and twentieth-century China through its focus on Spring Moon, the cherished, if headstrong, daughter of the wealthy and powerful house of Chang. Spring Moon's feet are bound when she is seven, and when she screams in pain she is told, "It is for your own good, child. . . . No matter how beautiful, how rich, how filial, no man will marry feet that flop like a yellow pike." Although she is part of a household that continues the old traditions, Spring Moon is determined to learn to read, and she soon becomes the favorite of her uncle, who once studied in America. The love that develops between them, and continues despite their marriages to others, threatens many of the traditions and codes of honor that are the foundation of the house of Chang. Their affair raises in microcosm many of the ethical controversies faced by a changing China. As the generations pass, as large and illustrious households disappear, as a mother's secret and personal transgressions are replaced by her daughter's open rebellion and revolutionary fervor, we witness the immense changes in China on both an intimate and a grand scale.

E.B.

Talking Indian: Reflections on Survival and Writing, Anna Lee Walters, *1992, United States,* ESSAYS/SHORT STORIES

Anna Lee Walters writes: "I am an American Indian, but this simply does not say enough to satisfy the past, the present, or future. I am a Pawnee. I am an Otoe. My husband is a Navajo. And my children are all three." *Talking Indian* is about words and memory: their cultural context, their power and meaning when spoken and written, their presence and absence. It is also a book about time, "Indian time." These are essays and stories—"Oral Tradition," "Talking Indian," and "World View"—that weave childhood memories through oral tribal history. "Buffalo Wallow Woman" is a beautiful and haunting story about a woman in a mental hospital who knows her name is not Mrs. Smith. "The Web" is an allegorical tale about listening to all life forms. In the middle of the book is "Family Photographs," a series of handsome black-and-white pictures. The last section is prefaced by an essay on time that teaches: "Eight o'clock promptly on the dot is an artificial time measurement, for time is not measured. Rather, its dimensions are noted. Life experience and the duration of a people are recorded in generations of offspring who carry on the perceptions." A blend of fable, fiction, and fact, *Talking Indian* is a powerful, spiritually enriching, and rewarding work.

J.L.

This Bridge Called My Back: Writings by Radical Women of Color, Cherríe Moraga and Gloria Anzaldúa, editors, *1979–1983, United States,* ESSAYS

From the forewords by Cherríe Moraga and Gloria Anzaldúa, through the poems, essays, and pieces Toni Cade Bambara calls "cables, esoesses, conjurations and fusile missles," this is a work of bringing-togetherness that gives the reader a clear-eyed view of life in the United States. From "I Paid Very Hard for My Immigrant Ignorance," by Mirtha Quintanales, to "who told you anybody wants to hear from you? you ain't nothing but a black woman!" by hattie gossett, to "I Don't Understand Those Who Have Turned Away from Me," by Chrystos, *This Bridge Called My Back* is a showing-and-telling, a volume of reflections of stunning color: raging, gentle, powerful. First published in 1983, and winner of the 1986 Before Columbus Foundation American Book Award, this collection was an important addition to the steadily growing voice of the world's silenced people, especially women of color. *This Bridge Called My Back* is a gift of wisdom, of strength, of womanhood. As Gloria Anzaldúa puts it in her foreword: "Haven't we always borne jugs of water, children, poverty? Why not learn to bear baskets of hope, love, self-nourishment and to step lightly?"

J.L.

Tracks, Louise Erdrich, *1988, United States,* NOVEL

The time is the early twentieth century. Epidemics, harsh winters, and the greed of white men are rapidly destroying the land and its Native American people. *Tracks* is the story of the Chippewa Indians and in particular of one woman, Fleur, told through the voices of two opposing Native American viewpoints. Nanapush, respected male elder, relays to Fleur's rebellious daughter the history of her people and the power of her mother. But to awkward and rejected Pauline, who latches on to Catholic doctrine and twists her life into one of mortification and revenge, Fleur is an evil woman who couples with the water spirit in the lake. Aware of each other but always speaking to others, the alternating voices of Nanapush and Pauline rise and clash like the two ways of life they represent. Whose representation is correct? Where does knowledge of the earth and its mysteries end and magic begin? And what is the fate of the Native American people in light of these different ways of knowing? This is a lyrical and passionate novel about belief, and about love for nature and individuals.

E.B.

The Woman Warrior: Memoirs of a Girlhood Among Ghosts, Maxine Hong Kingston, *1975, United States,* AUTOBIOGRAPHY

Maxine Hong Kingston grew up in two worlds. There was "solid America," the place her parents emigrated to, and the China of her mother's "talk-stories." In the talk-stories, women were warriors and her mother was still a doctor who could cure the sick and scare away ghosts, not a harried and frustrated woman running a stifling laundromat in California. But what is story and what is truth? In China, a ghost is a supernatural being; in America it is anyone who is not Chinese. In addition, underlying even the most exciting talk-stories of Chinese women warriors is the real oppression of Chinese women: "There is a Chinese word for the female 'I'—which is 'slave.' " In an attempt to figure out her world, Maxine Hong Kingston finds herself creating stories of her own, filling in the blanks her mother has not told her because her daughter is, after all, not true Chinese and thus cannot be completely trusted. Can these new stories explain why she had trouble speaking in the American schools? Can they help her understand the aunt who committed adultery and whose existence is denied? The new stories refuse to fall into traditional forms, and the realizations that come from them often bring out a beautiful, passionate anger that practically burns through the pages. This is powerful, experimental writing, a combination of love, hate, frustration, and sheer beauty.

E.B.

Identity

Identity is a socially and an individually constructed reality, a unique combination of factors. For some, understanding the origin and impact of the various parts of one's identity is a quest. How much of who we are is created by ancestors, education, work, poverty or prosperity, spirituality, loves, memories from childhood? Lydia Minatoya journeys through Asia looking for her roots; the title character of *Fiela's Child* may never know whose child he in fact is. For some, the quest is complicated by a growing knowledge that their identities do not conform to the prevailing social structures. In *The Jailing of Cecelia Capture*, Cecelia seeks strength and a sense of self as a Native American living in the United States. Lorene Cary writes of what it was like to be black and working class at an elite, predominantly white prep school; Rachel in *The Worry Girl* listens to and tells stories that provide her with pieces of herself. Radclyffe Hall, H. D., Terri de la Peña, and Becky Birtha write coming-out stories from completely different points of view. Entwined in tradition, women from Spain, Brazil, Chile, England, Canada, and the United States share a common struggle to find and live a life they believe in. Sometimes learning who you are is a battle; sometimes knowing who you are is a release. Always it is a journey of searching and discovery, for both author and reader.

Black Ice	Lorene Cary
Breakthrough	Mercedes Valdivieso
Corregidora	Gayl Jones
Disappearing Moon Cafe	Sky Lee
Dora, Doralina	Rachel de Queiroz
Emma	Jane Austen
The False Years	Josefina Vicens
Fiela's Child	Dalene Mathee
HERmione	H. D.
The Jailing of Cecelia Capture	Janet Campbell Hale
Jane Eyre	Charlotte Brontë
Jerusalem Plays Hide and Seek	Ariella Deem
Lover's Choice	Becky Birtha
Margins	Terri de la Peña
Nampally Road	Meena Alexander
The Odd Woman	Gail Godwin
The Pegnitz Junction	Mavis Gallant
Rebellion	Minnie Bruce Pratt
The Shawl	Cynthia Ozick
Solitude	Victor Català
The Street	Ann Petry
Talking to High Monks in the Snow	Lydia Minatoya
Weeds	Edith Summers Kelley
The Well of Loneliness	Radclyffe Hall
The Worry Girl	Andrea Freud Loewenstein

Black Ice, Lorene Cary, *1991, United States,* MEMOIR

In 1971, Lorene Cary was a fourteen-year-old black girl from Philadelphia who went to public school and worked part-time at the food counter at Woolworth's. "I smelled as if I had scrubbed the grill with my uniform. . . . I felt irritable and entitled to it, as adults seemed to be when they finished their work for the day." When she learned the prestigious Saint Paul's School in New Hampshire had recently gone co-ed and was looking for female students—particularly those of her skin color—she applied, was accepted, and decided to go. In *Black Ice,* Lorene Cary—who later went on to teach at Saint Paul's and to sit on the school's board of directors—looks back on those school years. She talks of fitting in and of feeling like an outsider, of defenses and offenses on all sides, of friendships that cross any boundary. Most of all, she remembers trying to figure out who she was in the midst of all her different environments: "I had a whiff, as subtle as the scent of the old books that lined the wall, of my utter aloneness in this new world." We watch her change from a defiant freshman to a returning student determined to make honors. What she has to say is enlightening, and her descriptions are often beautiful surprises that take this book beyond straightforward reminiscence: "Black ice is an act of nature as elusive as grace, and far more rare. I did not learn about either until much later."

E.B.

Breakthrough, Mercedes Valdivieso, *translated from Spanish by Graciela S. Daichman, 1961, Chile,* NOVEL

"I got married like everyone else does," begins the nameless narrator of *Breakthrough.* "I was nineteen, strong willed, passionate, beautiful." Subdued after the death of her father and compelled by her mother and grandmother to be silent and obedient, she stays constantly on the alert for a way to escape her female fate of enforced helplessness. Although married life does allow her some new freedoms, she finds herself living with a man who wants "to substitute control for his lack of real communication," a man who watches her "with growing fear. There was danger in a twenty-year-old wife who could drink with gusto, avoided mass, and had no plans for the future." After five years of marriage and the birth of her only child, she does the unthinkable and leaves her husband. Widely praised as one of Latin America's first revolutionary feminist novels, *Breakthrough* is a superb account of one woman's struggle for autonomy.

J.L.

Corregidora, Gayl Jones, *1975, United States,* NOVEL

When Ursa Corregidora is five years old and questions the truth of her great-grandmother's stories, her great-grandmother tells her, "I'm leaving evidence. And you got to leave evidence too. And your children got to leave evidence. And when it come time to hold up the evidence, we got to have evidence to hold up. That's why they burned all the papers, so there wouldn't be no evidence to hold up against them." Ursa's great-grandmother was raped and then used as a whore by her white slave owner, Corregidora, as was her daughter after her. Ursa had a black father, but her skin more closely resembles the color of Corregidora, the man who is both her grandfather and her great-grandfather. Ostracized by darker-skinned women who resent the added value her light skin gives her among black men, and unable to trust any man, black or white, because of the stories she was raised on, Ursa Corregidora sings the blues and fights both the past and the present to maintain mental and physical autonomy. Internal monologues, dreams, and remembered stories intermingle with present-day reality until it becomes difficult for the reader or Ursa to draw the lines between them—a task made doubly difficult when black men echo the proprietary attitudes (and sometimes words) of dead slave owners. Gritty, full of rage and pain, *Corregidora* presents a searing denunciation of racism and sexism in both white and black communities.

E.B.

Disappearing Moon Cafe, Sky Lee, *1990, Canada,* NOVEL

"I thought that by applying attention to all the important events such as the births and the deaths, the intricate complexities of a family with Chinese roots could be massaged into a suant, digestible unit. Like a herbal pill—I thought I could swallow it and my mind would become enlightened." Kae Ying Woo, whose ancestors immigrated to Vancouver, British Columbia from China in 1892, has been nurtured on family stories and traditional ceremony. Upon the birth of her first child in 1986, she begins to question her upbringing: "I get tricked because I want to be so damned perfect all the time. Now I've found that nobody has told me the whole messy truth about anything!" Weaving fiction with fact, moving between China and Canada, the past and the present, *Disappearing Moon Cafe* is an impressive and poignant story about a family's struggle for identity on a new continent, and an individual's struggle to come to terms with and bring an end to a tradition of female silence. With a voice that combines mythical lyricism and contemporary wit, Kae Ying Woo illuminates the legacy behind her indomitable strength of spirit: "So, having swallowed the pill, here I am, still waiting. For enlightenment. Disappointed, yet eternally optimistic!"

J.L.

Dora, Doralina, Rachel de Queiroz, *translated from Portuguese by Dorothy S. Loos, 1975, Brazil,* NOVEL

"What kills you today is forgotten tomorrow. I don't know if this is true or false because all that's real for me is remembrance." In her old age, Dora reflects on the major influences in her life: her mother, her career in the theater, and her one true love. Set in Brazil in the early part of the century, *Dora, Doralina* is a story about power. Through her fierce resistance to her mother, and in her later life as a working woman and widow, Dora attempts to define herself in a time and culture that places formidable obstacles before women. Married off by her mother to a man she does not love, told what to wear and eat, Dora's journey to reclaim herself is full of both discovery and rage. For her, independence is the right to protect herself and make her own choices. After a life confined by religion and "respectability," even her passionate attachment to a hard-drinking smuggler represents an act of free will previously unavailable to her. *Dora, Doralina* is an intimate, realistic, and vivid glimpse of one woman's struggle for independence, for a life in which she owns her actions, her pleasure, and her pain.

S.L.

Emma, Jane Austen, *1816, England,* NOVEL

First published in 1816, *Emma* is generally regarded as Jane Austen's most technically brilliant book. But that's not the reason to read it. Read it to see how a scheming heiress who is determined not to marry ends up embracing love and growing in maturity without dying or becoming impossibly insipid—the fate of so many nineteenth-century heroines. As her fourth novel was taking shape, Jane Austen noted, "I am going to take a heroine whom no one but myself will much like." She was wrong. It is easy to love Emma Woodhouse. A snob, a meddler, and a spoiled child, she is also smart, funny, generous, and compassionate. Determined to control the arrangements of other people's lives, Emma takes on the self-appointed role of matchmaker in a world that grants little public power to women. Small wonder that Emma, who has a "mind lively and at ease," wastes her considerable creative powers dreaming up romantic scenarios that consistently and comically fail all reality checks. As in all of Jane Austen's works, the simple theme of courtship here belies the complexity of her vision of human nature and of our need for power. Technical brilliance? Yes. Moral brilliance? Most definitely.

C.K.

The False Years, Josefina Vicens, *translated from Spanish by Peter G. Earle, 1982, Mexico,* NOVEL

"Do you know what it is to remain at the edge of yourself, just looking at yourself?" This is nineteen-year-old Luis Alfonso Fernandez's question to himself as he visits his father's grave on the fourth anniversary of his death. Luis, the pampered son and namesake of the fast-drinking, gambling man who killed himself while playing with a gun, knows he is—or is he?—his father. "We've all come to see us," he mumbles as he reads his own name on the headstone and watches his mother and twin sisters, "thirteen and exasperatingly alike," do the work of maintaining the grave. Now the "man-of-the-house," he simultaneously mourns and scorns his former place in the family as his mother's son. Through rambling memories, dialogue, and description, Luis Alfonso relives his life with his father and contemplates the slow transfer of his father's life to his own: the change in his relationship with his mother, the job with the dirty politicians, the mistress, Elena, and his "ineffable, delicious horror of sharing her." Written in spare and fluidly descriptive prose, this young man's private graveside monologue provides a unique and poetic critique of contemporary Mexican society.

J.L.

Fiela's Child, Dalene Mathee, *1986, South Africa,* NOVEL

One night a three-year-old boy wanders away from his home in a clearing, out into the surrounding Knysa forest; one night a little boy arrives at Fiela Komoetie's farm on the plains, miles and mountain ranges away. Fiela raises the child as her own, even though she and her family are black and he is white. When he is twelve, the census takers discover the boy and take him away to judge if he is, indeed, the little boy who was lost. The child, Benjamin (or Lukas), is "returned" to the van Rooyens, who greet him as a son and brother and promptly put him to work. But who is Benjamin/Lukas? Is he a white child with a black mother? Is he really the lost son of the lazy, scheming forester Elias van Rooyen? Benjamin/Lukas is determined to discover the real—as well as his own—truth. Through vivid details and characters, with a true storyteller's ability to create a world while spinning a tale, Dalene Mathee takes us into the dark Knysa woods, where elephants wreak revenge and foresters chop down the trees that are their future, and onto the plains, where ostriches represent financial freedom as Fiela struggles against racism. Through Benjamin/Lukas's search for his identity, *Fiela's Child* shows us a land composed of white and black, of opportunism and motherly love.

E.B.

HERmione, H. D. (Hilda Doolittle), *1928* (*1981*), *United States,* NOVEL

HERmione is the semiautobiographical tale of Hilda Doolittle's early twenties. A young, confused woman about to come of age, Hermione Gart is split between her old self and a new, true identity. She is ill at ease with her life after returning home from a failed career at Bryn Mawr and a brash relationship with George Lowndes (a thinly veiled portrait of Ezra Pound). "I am HER, HER, HER," H. D.

writes. "Names are in people; people are in names. God is in a word. God is in HER." The depth of Hermione's painful self-reflection is beautifully transcribed in this eerie interior monologue, which describes the twists and turns of the H. D. character, her torrid affair with George Lowndes, and the beginnings of her relationship with Fayne Rabb. Hermione's relationship with Fayne, the turning point in her life, forces her to gather her fragmented self together into a whole person. Primarily known for her poetry, H. D. has produced here a lush, vivid portrayal of the inner psyche, written in an experimental, disjointed style that creates a tapestry of Hermione's deepest feelings.

H.D.

The Jailing of Cecelia Capture, Janet Campbell Hale, *1985, United States,* NOVEL

On the day after her thirtieth birthday, Cecelia Capture, a mixed-blood Native American law student, wakes up in a holding tank in the Berkeley, California, jail. Booked on a drunk-driving charge, she begins to contemplate her life through a series of flashbacks. Her search for identity goes back to the Idaho reservation where she was raised by an alcoholic full-blood father and a crazy halfbreed mother. As she reflects on the various phases of her life, including a bittersweet romance with a soldier just leaving for Vietnam who became the father of her son, and her loveless marriage to a white liberal teacher, she begins to see patterns in the apparent meaninglessness of her life. Despite pain and setback, Cecelia is a survivor, and her Native American identity gives meaning and purpose to her life. She comes close to suicide, but her vision of what she can be for her people and herself carries her on. "She was not able to return to the beginning, of course, and remake her life more to her liking, but now she was free to go on with the life she did have." The author, a member of the Coeur d'Alene tribe, writes in a calm and dispassionate voice with real understanding of how it feels and what it means to be Native American today. To reach Cecelia's level of self-understanding, to really like oneself, requires an often painful self-examination, a process that Janet Campbell Hale depicts brilliantly in this book.

N.M.

Jane Eyre, Charlotte Brontë, *1847, England,* NOVEL

Early responses to *Jane Eyre,* first published in 1847, were mixed. Some held the book to be anti-Christian; others were disturbed by a heroine so proud, self-willed, and essentially unfeminine. The modern reader may well have trouble understanding what all the fuss was about. On the surface a fairly conventional Gothic romance (poor orphan governess is hired by rich, brooding Byronic hero type), *Jane Eyre* hardly seems the stuff from which revolutions are made. But the story is very much about the nature of human freedom and equality, and if Jane was seen as something of a renegade in nineteenth-century England, it is because her story is that of a woman who struggles for self-definition and self-determination in a society that too often denies her that right. But self-determination does not mean untrammeled freedom for men or women. Rochester, that thorny masculine beast whom Jane eventually falls for, is a man who sets his own laws and manipulates the lives of those around him; before he can enter into a marriage of equals with Jane, he must undergo a spiritual transformation. Should the lesson sound dry, it's not. *Jane Eyre* is full of drama: fires, storms, attempted murder, and a mad wife conveniently stashed away in the attic. This is very sexy stuff—another reason Victorian critics weren't quite sure what to make of it.

C.K.

Jerusalem Plays Hide and Seek, Ariella Deem, *translated from Hebrew by Nelly Segal, 1976, Israel,* NOVEL

Jerusalem—a sensuous city which evokes emotional, sometimes hysterical passion—is the mirror in which Ariella Deem reflects her tale. Like the city, she plays hide and seek with her readers, interspersing her novel with historical narrative, obscuring the places where fiction and fact part ways. One warm autumn day in Boston, Ariella Deem happens upon a metal box filled with antique glass slides. Through them we are introduced to Hiram Alistair, the photographer who left his American comfort to document the "Holy Land" in 1888. As the pages flash black-and-white pictures of stone walls and stark landscape, so dry you can taste the dust, the tale of Yosef Levi is revealed. In 1882, at the age of eight, Levi arrives in Jerusalem, impoverished and neglected, and is befriended by Um Ibrahim, who teaches him the arts of healing. *Jerusalem Plays Hide and Seek* is the story of the slides and their circuitous journey from the cave where they were left by Alistair and found by Levi, to Boston where they were eventually brought by Yosef Levi's friend. With fluid, lyrical prose, Ariella Deem interweaves first- and third-person narrative, biblical references, Hebrew poetry, and accounts of current events amid the strands of Yosef Levi's tragic life to reveal the fragile relationships among characters, time, and the author herself.

P.L.

Lover's Choice, Becky Birtha, *1987, United States,* SHORT STORIES

Lover's Choice takes the reader on short trips into the lives of eleven different women. Becky Birtha creates a sense of continuity throughout her stories by blending strength, passion, pain, and ingenuity in each character. Ms. Moses makes clear that the government doesn't really help the poor: "Ain't no reason for you to be gaping at me. I pay my taxes, just like everyone else." Sahara "never wanted a man. . . . Sometimes it seems she has spent her whole life finding ways to get close to other people's children." Camped out under the stars, she thinks back over those children and opens her heart to yet another one. Maurie questions her taste in women: "White Anglo-Saxon Protestants. The Bourgeoisie. What the hell was she doing in love with someone . . . like that?" And Johnnieruth, who can ride her bike as fast as the boys and resents her mother trying to rein her in because she's a girl, watches in a park as two women greet each other with a kiss on the lips. For the first time, she sees herself mirrored. *Lover's Choice* is unusual in its ability to show the interconnectedness of eleven separate lives. Becky Birtha makes the reader care for and relate to each character as an individual, and as part of the whole that we call woman.

S.C.

Margins, Terri de la Peña, *1992, United States,* NOVEL

In the eight months since her car accident, Veronica has been going to physical therapy to heal her leg, and writing short stories to heal her emotional wounds. Joanna, her only lover and best friend since kindergarten, was killed in the accident. Though they hadn't meant to live a secret life, the timing just never seemed right for them to come out. Now rumors are being spread about her and Joanna. A new woman in Veronica's life refuses to hide the fact that she is a lesbian and expects the same openness of Veronica. Although this novel is a bit slow with character development, it gains depth: once Veronica starts her journey out, there is no turning back. Her Chicano upbringing is at the forefront of her identity, and she fears the reaction of the Catholic church and especially of her family. In talks with her sister, who is a nun, Veronica ponders: "Rejecting the Church entirely is like rejecting Chicanismo, like denying a whole part of myself. How can I justify doing that?" Through conversations with family and friends, Veronica comes to understand herself; through learning what she will accept for herself, she becomes less afraid. With insights from many perspectives, *Margins* offers readers much to reflect on. If you don't read Spanish, a Spanish-English dictionary may be helpful.

H.S.

Nampally Road, Meena Alexander, *1991, India,* NOVEL

After four years of study in England, twenty-five-year-old Mira returns to India, grateful to have obtained a teaching position. She arrives in Hyderabad, a city that pulsates with a power struggle brought on by political corruption, and sees firsthand its effects on the lives of people who dare to defy politics as usual or happen to be in the wrong place at the wrong time. Though writing and poetry have always provided meaning in Mira's life, her awareness of her country's political corruption causes her to question the necessity of teaching English poetry in India. She feels she lacks the words to describe her society: "The lines sucked in chunks of the world, then collapsed in on themselves. Our streets were too crowded, there was too much poverty and misery. The British had subdued us for too long and now that they had left, the unrest in rock and root, in the souls of men and women, was too visible, too turbulent already to permit the kinds of writing I had once learned to value." Through Mira's talks with Little Mother, with a holy man, and with her boyfriend, Meena Alexander makes real the struggles for morality and survival in a society that is politically immoral.

H.S.

The Odd Woman, Gail Godwin, *1974, United States,* NOVEL

Jane is a thirty-two-year-old professor of English at a Midwestern university, aware of the "ever present problem of her unclear, undefined, unresolved self." She considers characters and authors of nineteenth-century novels as friends and converses with them, wondering how they might react, what they might choose, how they might define Jane in their novels. The death of her staunchly supportive grandmother, Edith, brings Jane home to bury this woman whose influence feels almost bigger than life. Edith, proper and always knowing, never seemed to consider the questions that constantly haunt Jane. Kitty, Jane's mother, who recently turned to God, has become "so serene, so distant." Even Gerta, Jane's "oldest" friend, now driven by feminist zeal, leaves Jane wondering if history is all they have in common. And Gabriel, Jane's married lover—what does he provide in her life? Where is the truth in that relationship? Jane has thoughts that are "flying wildly abroad, knocking one another down, flinging themselves against impenetrable windows, barriers of other times, other places"—thoughts that demand her time and attention as she remembers Edith, talks with Kitty, confronts Gerta, and allows herself to be honest about Gabriel. *The Odd Woman* is an introspective romp; it may make you want to reread nineteenth-century novels, review your own relationships, and reaffirm your own truths.

H.S.

The Pegnitz Junction, Mavis Gallant, *1984, Canada/France* (*Canada*), SHORT STORIES

Characterized by sparseness of detail and elegance of style, *The Pegnitz Junction* comprises a novella and five short stories that evoke a vivid picture of post–World War II Europe. Mavis Gallant's writing is precise and pointed, yet opens doors to larger questions of identity and freedom in a world devastated by war. In the multivoiced narrative of the title piece, a young woman on a train is conscious of the thoughts and feelings of her fellow passengers. Nearly all the "interference" she receives from those around her concerns moments in their lives they cannot move beyond: old grudges, wounds that won't heal. "Decide what the rest of your life is to be. Whatever you are now, you might be forever," she silently advises a man returning to the scene of a childhood memory. Mavis Gallant beautifully illustrates the idea that sometimes, in a passing glance, we can tell everything about a person's life, and at the same time she explores the paralysis that such a vision can leave us with. In her stories, she explores the ways in which people deal with pain and betrayal: the concentration camp victim in "Old Friends," the compromises of marriage in "Alien Flower." She suggests, with subtlety and gentle acceptance, that in order to live we must also endure a thousand small deaths. Mavis Gallant's portrait of these moments is both moving and full of respect.

S.L.

Rebellion: Essays 1980–1991, Minnie Bruce Pratt, *1991, United States,* ESSAYS

In the title essay of *Rebellion*, Minnie Bruce Pratt writes from her experience as a white woman in the South, where "to embroider the surface of doom with style and manners was the only way to keep your reason." Her personal rebellion involves extending herself beyond the boundaries of style and manners to some comprehension of the obstacles and possibilities between people. In her poetry, Minnie Bruce Pratt has explored the capacity of words to expand and communicate her experiences; through her essays she examines this process and tests its limits. She writes of when she first discovered her "outsider" status as a lesbian: "I did not yet understand that to come to a place of greater liberation, I had to risk old safeties. Instead, I felt I had no place; that, as I moved through my days, I was falling through space." She uses insights into her own "loss of place" to explore the dynamics of privilege and difference in other contexts, within other cultural, racial, political, religious, and sexual contexts. Each essay in this collection approaches the writer's identity from a different angle, and each offers a challenge to assumptions concerning that identity. Minnie Bruce Pratt honors her readers with a trust: she takes us to the edge of her own understanding and invites us to go further with her, as well as on our own.

K.B.

The Shawl, Cynthia Ozick, *1981, 1984, United States,* NOVELLA/SHORT STORY

This short story and novella, both O. Henry Prize winners, together create a picture of Rosa Lubin's life. The title story tells of Rosa's fifteen-month-old daughter's death in a concentration camp, and of the shawl that provided the daughter with a comfort Rosa's breasts could no longer give. "Rosa," the novella, takes place more than thirty years later in southern Florida—where it is "Summer without end, a mistake!" Rosa has been exiled to Florida after destroying her shop in Brooklyn; she had to leave the state or be put in a mental institution. With financial help from her niece, who Rosa thinks is evil, she is able to stay in Florida. She knows she can depend on her niece because Rosa saved her life in the concentration camp; Rosa knows, too, that her niece was the cause of her daughter's death. Rosa lives in two worlds: she functions in her daily life, but her real world is where her long-dead daughter lives. In letters to her daughter, she comments about her niece: "Because she fears the past she distrusts the future—it, too, will turn into the past. As a result she has nothing." Rosa is a woman who, through the loss of her country, her family, and her daughter, has lost herself. Cynthia Ozick's spare writing leaves a lasting image of Rosa and her life, showing us that people do get lost and are sometimes never found.

H.S.

Solitude, Victor Català (Caterina Albert i Paradís), *translated from Catalan by David H. Rosenthal, 1905, Spain,* NOVEL

Beautiful, industrious, and intelligent Camilla is taken to an isolated hermitage in the Pyrenees by her lazy and insensitive husband, Matias. There she contends not only with her rapidly failing marriage but with her attraction to her young neighbor Arnau; her growing admiration and respect for the older shepherd named Gaieta; and the violent intentions of the bestial Anima. Through Gaieta's guidance, Camilla finds strength and a sense of self in the mountains: "Forcing her to gaze over every steep precipice, teaching her how to twist her body and secure her footing in dangerous spots, making her look down when they were halfway up a cliff and laughing at her terror, he helped conquer her fears. . . . And now she loved the excitement she felt on those peaks and the way the yawning depths seemed to suck her soul out of her." Faced with debt, deprivation, and violence, she must make choices for and ultimately by herself. While Caterina Albert i Paradís had little choice but to use a male pseudonym, she wrote *Solitude* from an intensely feminine viewpoint, delving deeply into the thoughts and emotions of a young woman caught by circumstance. It has been called "the most important Catalan novel to appear before the Spanish Civil War," when Franco took power and repressed the Catalan language and culture for more than thirty-five years. To find it translated into English and in print is remarkable indeed.

E.B.

The Street, Ann Petry, *1946, United States,* NOVEL

Ann Petry puts forth a painfully honest treatise on black-white relations in *The Street*, and while it was written nearly fifty years ago, her unblinking insights and powerful commentary on the dynamics of race in the United States remain accurate today. Lutie Johnson, an intelligent, strong, and beautiful black woman, is the vehicle for Ann Petry's message. Separated from her husband, Lutie is doing her best to raise an eight-year-old son, achieve independence from her father, advance in her job, and work her way out of the Harlem streets, which she calls "The North's lynch mobs . . . the method the big cities use to keep Negroes in their place." Streetwise, she is able to avoid being conned and to exploit a con artist to get ahead. Though her self-knowledge is thorough, it can't stop her from becoming entangled in a tradition of oppression and an upbringing that blames whites for present afflictions. Her goals and values are her strength, enabling her to make decisions when there is no apparent choice and to face a justice system fraught with injustice. She ultimately escapes, but not without a sacrifice that rips apart any woman's heart.

S.L.S.

Talking to High Monks in the Snow, Lydia Minatoya, *1992, Asia/United States* (*United States*), MEMOIR

The lyrical title of this memoir is a prelude to the gentle writings of Lydia Minatoya. Born in the 1950s in the United States and raised as part of a generation used to having its way, she is fired from an unfulfilling teaching position and seeks a freedom she's never allowed herself. With a carefully planned itinerary, she leaves the United States to travel and teach in Asia and to visit her relatives in Japan. Though her Japanese ancestry opens doors in Asia, it also creates confusion. She comes to understand why her mother was reluctant to let her daughter travel to Japan and be subjected to the expectations of her heritage. Describing her life, she writes: "Taking detours, I pause here and there to sample the hospitality of strangers. Wondering, Is this where I belong? But I always return to my road, wanting to find home, before the darkness falls." In her travels she learns of a force called grace, the presence of ghosts, the importance of taking risks, and the power of trust. Eventually her road leads her back to the United States with a new confidence. Lydia Minatoya is not interested in competing or comparing herself with others. She takes to heart every lesson, every adventure, and together they provide the stepping stones for her self-discovery.

H.S.

Weeds, Edith Summers Kelley, *1923, United States,* NOVEL

"In the backwoods corners of America, where the people have been poor and benighted for several generations and where for as many generations no new blood has entered . . . the children are mostly dull of mind and scrawny of body. Not infrequently, however, there will be born a child of clear features and strong, straight body, as a reminder of earlier pioneer days when clear features and strong straight bodies were the rule rather than the exception." Judith Pippinger is one of these strong, straight children, brought up in poverty on the family farm, determined to escape the life she sees around her but inexorably pulled into it by pregnancy, marriage, and unending work. Despite the hardships, there is something triumphant in this story that comes both from Judith's indomitable, fighting personality and from Edith Summers Kelley's ability to show the raw beauty in a world laden with pain and frustration. There are moments of wonder and intimacy, often between unlikely combinations of people. Most of all, there is life, which Edith Summers Kelley describes unflinchingly, even down to a graphic description of childbirth which was edited out by the publishers when *Weeds* was first issued in 1928. Though bleak in general outlook, the novel is lush with details and emotions, and gathers power from its unconquerable heroine and from the author's resolution to look life straight in the eye.

E.B.

The Well of Loneliness, Radclyffe Hall, *1928, England,* NOVEL

The Well of Loneliness is a pathbreaking novel. Published by Radclyffe Hall herself in 1928, it was immediately banned in Britain due to its lesbian theme, and was allowed in the United States only after a long court battle. Once it was available, *The Well of Loneliness* sold more than 20,000 copies its first year, and paved the way for other works with lesbian themes. The novel concerns a girl, born into a wealthy English family at the turn of the century and named Stephen by her father, who desperately wanted a boy. Practically from birth, Stephen is described as "different." While Radclyffe Hall delivers the powerful message that lesbianism is natural, she also asks the reader to have pity on Stephen Gordon—for, along with the popular psychoanalysts of her day, Radclyffe Hall describes lesbianism as an "inversion." The "terrible mark of Cain" compels Stephen to forsake the woman she loves in order to protect her from a life of ostracism. This message, along with Radclyffe Hall's portrayal of lesbians in stereotypical "butch" and "femme" roles, caused the book to be written off by feminists in the late 1970s and early 1980s. In addition, many readers today may find the writing long-winded and the characters one-dimensional, with the exception of the thinly veiled portrait of the author as Stephen Gordon. Nonetheless, *The Well of Loneliness* is worth reading because it shattered the silence of oppression and conveys a message about homophobia and internalized shame relevant to lesbians even today.

H.D.

The Worry Girl, Andrea Freud Loewenstein, *1992, United States,* SHORT STORIES

With chunks called "From the Stories That Came Before" and pieces named "The Grandmothers' Stories," this pithy collection—"fictional composites of memory, imagination and invention"—is Rachel Freud's story of growing up. "Look how we make here a nice picnic, a little herring, a little cucumber zalade—come Puppi you're hungry?" asks Grandmother Oma as she guides Rachel through the photo album. Parents' stories, school stories, and friendship stories follow, each told in the voice of the teller, mostly the voice of Rachel. Her famous great-grandfather, Sigmund Freud, is a distant but important part of family history. So are Nazi Germany, World War II, fascist extermination camps, and American schools. Rachel's family isn't rich or poor; Rachel isn't gorgeous or quick-witted or small. Even worse, she's afraid of the dark, terrified to be without her mother, and cannot learn to tell time. She's also a storyteller and secret writer. Lucky us.

J.L.

Imagined Worlds

What if? It's a question that unleashes the imagination. With two words, it vaults us out of a reality where things "are" because they "always have been." By turning society slightly, or completely, upside down authors can make readers see their own world differently, and sometimes more clearly. Octavia Butler and Marge Piercy explore the complexities of slavery, racism, and sexism through time travel. *The Painted Alphabet, The House of the Spirits, The Amber Gods, The Ship of Fools,* and *The Löwensköld Ring* dance on the edge of the supernatural to teach us about class struggle, innocence, politics, ethics, and spirituality. Marion Zimmer Bradley recasts the Arthurian legend from a female perspective; Maryse Condé re-creates the life of the only black woman accused of witchcraft in Salem; Angela Carter reconstructs the life of Lizzie Borden. Marlen Haushofer examines the reactions of a woman who believes she is the last person alive. Mary Wollstonecraft Shelley questions the limits of science. *The Maid of the North* gives us alternatives to folktale myths of mean old women and beautiful, passive young ones. Through their books, these authors show us that reality can be whatever the mind can imagine.

The Amber Gods and Other Stories	Harriet Prescott Spofford
A Bag of Stories	Edla Steen
Eve's Tattoo	Emily Prager
Family Album	Claribel Alegría
Frankenstein	Mary Wollstonecraft Shelley
The House of the Spirits	Isabel Allende
I, Tituba, Black Witch of Salem	Maryse Condé
The Iguana	Anna Maria Ortese
Kindred	Octavia Butler
The Löwensköld Ring	Selma Lagerlöf
The Maid of the North	Ethel Johnston Phelps
The Mists of Avalon	Marion Zimmer Bradley
Mrs. Vargas and the Dead Naturalist	Kathleen Alcalá
New Islands and Other Stories	María Luisa Bombal
Out of Time	Paula Martinac
The Painted Alphabet	Diana Darling
Saints and Strangers	Angela Carter
The Ship of Fools	Cristina Peri Rossi
Through the Arc of the Rain Forest	Karen Tei Yamashita
The Wall	Marlen Haushofer
Woman on the Edge of Time	Marge Piercy

The Amber Gods and Other Stories, Harriet Prescott Spofford, *1863, United States,* SHORT STORIES

When Harriet Prescott Spofford first submitted her work in the mid-nineteenth century, the editor at the *Atlantic Monthly* refused to believe that an unworldly woman from New England had written such eerie and unsettling stories. Her style, though ornate by our twentieth-century standards, enhances the stories' atmosphere, like heavy, Baroque furniture in a large and creepy house. The title story presents a self-centered and captivating woman who ruthlessly steals her orphan cousin's lover. In "Circumstance," a pioneer woman returning home through the woods at night is caught by a panther; her husband, who has come to save her, can only watch from the ground as, pinned in a tree, she sings for her life. A train engineer hallucinates again and again that he is running over his wife. And Mrs. Craven, who's a bit "weak" in the head, mindlessly repeats, "Three men went down cellar and only two came up." These stories combine elements of the best ghost stories—timing, detail, and character—with just enough chill to make you think twice about turning out your lights at night.

E.B.

A Bag of Stories, Edla Steen, *translated from Portuguese by David George, 1991, Brazil,* SHORT STORIES

A Bag of Stories contains fourteen highly structured and multilayered short stories told in a variety of voices and narrative styles. "Period (Under the Influence of Soap Operas)" is dying Lavanía's last letter to Gabriel, a runaway lover she has not seen for years. "Good Enough to Sing in a Choir" is a poignantly sad and slightly bizarre story of a wig-wearing father who nurses his infant—and eventually ungrateful—son with an artificial breast. "A Day in Three Movements" tells about young Leonor's first job, her lecherous boss, and her oblivious mother, with regular interruptions suggesting rewrite ideas: "But Leonor (or Greta?) might prefer to be placed in a bright modern building . . . In that case, the custodian could be used in another text. Clip and save." In "The Pledge," Alba, a married woman about to turn fifty—"a half century of experience, a century of sorrow"—visits her mother for the first time in thirty years.

"CAROL head LINA heart" begins and ends as a two-column, two-narrator tale of Carolina's meeting with an old lover. "In Spite of Everything" tells about a death from the perspectives of several people, including the victim's. Because Edla Steen's characters all follow an inner path, each narrative is unpredictable and unconventional. *A Bag of Stories* provides an evocative view of how peculiar, complicated, and creative human beings can be.

J.L.

Eve's Tattoo, Emily Prager, *1991, United States/Germany* (*United States*), NOVEL

Eve has always felt fear about the Holocaust. Her readings have given her more questions than answers: How had Hitler come to, and remained in, power? What was the role of women under his reign? Eve worries that when the last Holocaust survivor dies, so will the memory. On her fortieth birthday, she has her arm tattooed with the number of an Auschwitz victim, a woman in a picture who reminds Eve of herself and whom she names Eva. The man Eve loves is appalled by the tattoo and wants her to have it removed, but she can't; it has taken on its own meaning. When people ask about the tattoo, Eve makes up stories about Eva, and in these stories she finds answers to her questions. In Eve's stories Eva becomes, at different times, a Red Cross nurse, a poor German woman, a nun with commitments to a power higher than the Third Reich. As a gynecologist performing an illegal abortion, Eva "was in the middle of the curettage when the Gestapo started pounding on the door. She gestured to Heidi [her assistant] to sit quietly and do nothing while she calmly and methodically finished up just as they smashed in the door glass." All these Evas suffered at the hands of Hitler; it didn't matter if they supported, were indifferent to, or opposed him—he took their lives.

H.S.

Family Album, Claribel Alegría, *translated from Spanish by Amanda Hopkinson, 1966, Nicaragua/Spain* (*El Salvador/Nicaragua*), NOVELLAS

This is a collection of three stunning, ethereal novellas. Karen, the adolescent protagonist in "The Talisman," is doing poorly in Catholic boarding school. Every time she attempts to memorize facts, people from her past burst into her imagination: her mother, Natalia, often appears and begs Karen to understand Mark, Natalia's boyfriend; sometimes Mark arrives smelling like alcohol and tells Karen stories that require him to feel her body; always her friends, Missouri and Nicolasa, come to comfort and advise. In the title story, anecdotes about Ximena's Nicaraguan family are told through memory, conversation, and descriptions of often faceless photographs. Ximena, a middle-class woman living in Paris, wants to understand the relationship of her own comfortable French life to the tortured existence of her relatives in Somoza's Nicaragua. "Village of God and the Devil" is the story of the magic village of Deya, where ghosts are as real as memory and imagination. Written in deceptively simple and imaginative prose, *Family Album* is a dynamic blend of the natural and supernatural.

J.L.

Frankenstein, Mary Wollstonecraft Shelley, *1817, England,* NOVEL

After being rescued from an iceberg, Dr. Frankenstein relates his autobiography to the ship's captain, complete with vivid descriptions of his idyllic childhood and passionate cries of regret that not even his love for Elizabeth could control his fanatic ambition. Dr. Frankenstein has been consumed by his desire to create a fully grown living creature. When he reaches his goal, he perceives his creation as a monster, immediately regrets his work, and promptly abandons it. We also hear the poignant voice of the monster as he describes the spurning and the physical attacks he has endured because of his ugliness; his desolate pain and loneliness; how he learns to love; how he finally finds and tries, unsuccessfully, to make peace with his maker; how he learns to hate. A story within a story, *Frankenstein* is a subtle and ironic prophecy that raises the question of who is the real monster in this story.

J.L.

The House of the Spirits, Isabel Allende, *translated from Spanish by Magda Bogin, 1982, Chile,* NOVEL

"Many children fly like birds, guess other people's dreams, and speak with ghosts, but . . . they all outgrow it when they lose their innocence." *The House of the Spirits* is a book about magic, politics, families, dreams, passion, obsession, and reconciliation. It is a book about almost everything, yet the relationship between innocence and natural and supernatural power is at the heart of all of these themes. Clara, the matriarch of the Trueba family, is blessed and cursed with a childhood clairvoyance that follows her into adulthood. Her capacity to foretell tragedy and truth casts an extraordinary light on the personal and political epic of her family, but hers is only one of the many stories within the larger story. Isabel Allende does not limit herself to any single perspective, so the fantastic events in *The House of the Spirits* are shown from different angles, in different lights. Though reality is relentless, it is not absolute: the miraculous pervades the most petty and commonplace circumstances, the most morbid and terrible events. At the same time, spectacular occasions and divine moments are marked by the vulgar demands of the body or the crude interference of fate. This is storytelling on a grand scale, yet each detail is touched with intimacy and authenticity.

K.B.

I, Tituba, Black Witch of Salem, Maryse Condé, *translated from French by Richard Philcox, 1986, Barbados/United States,* NOVEL

Tituba, a slave from Barbados, was the only black person accused during the Salem, Massachusetts, witch hunts of the late 1600s. Maryse Condé constructs a fictional life for Tituba from the little that is known about her, and quotes excerpts from the trial transcript to create an exalted and at times farcical life tale. In her early life, Tituba is initiated "into the upper spheres of knowledge" through the use of herbal remedies, and learns to call on her personal spirits for guidance. As the novel moves between Barbados and the United States, her medicinal skills make her legendary in both places. In a scene full of irony, Tituba meets Hester Prynne of *The Scarlet Letter* while in a Salem prison, and they discuss the fate of women and their visions of the future. Tituba is a woman who loves her men, and though she is warned by those in the afterworld that the cost of her love will be great and that her self-satisfaction through physical love is frowned upon, this love is a part of her being. Through Tituba's very candid first-person narrative, Maryse Condé expands on history to educate the reader about both the Puritans' widespread persecution of women and the lives of slaves in Barbados in the 1600s.

H.S.

The Iguana, Anna Maria Ortese, *translated from Italian by Henry Martin, 1965, Italy,* NOVEL

One of Anna Maria Ortese's best-known examples of Italian magical realism, *The Iguana* is a complex story of twists and turns, with roving aristocrats, uncharted islands, poetry, religion, class struggle, introspection, philosophical debate, and a servant who is an old woman—no, a large, ancient lizard—no, a young lizard—no, a beautiful girl in a lace dress—no, a servant in gray rags. Abrupt plot shifts intermingle with high-flying rhetoric: "If excitement strikes you as a target hardly congruent to the vast potentialities of money, then consider the strict correlation between financial abundance and the impoverishment of the senses." There are echoes of Kafka and Shakespeare's *The Tempest*; there are dark cellars, deep wells, and tall, gray towers. Read in a singleminded quest to unravel the mystery, the novel careens and jolts like a funhouse ride and ends with more questions and uncertainties than it began with. If, on the other hand, readers approach *The Iguana* like a two-thousand-piece puzzle—pick up the pieces and look at each shape as well as how they fit together, read sentences more than once just to feel the rhythm, marvel at word choice, and try to figure out the implications in what the characters are saying—they will be amply rewarded with more answers and more mysteries.

E.B.

Kindred, Octavia Butler, *1979, United States,* NOVEL

Kindred utilizes the devices of science fiction in order to answer the question "How could anybody be a slave?" A woman from the twentieth century, Dana is repeatedly brought back in time by her slave-owning ancestor Rufus when his life is endangered. She chooses to save him, knowing that because of her actions a free-born black woman will eventually become his slave and her own grandmother. When forced to live the life of a slave, Dana realizes she is not as strong as her ancestors. Unable to will herself back to her own time and unable to tolerate the institution of slavery, she attempts to run away and is caught within a few hours. Her illiterate ancestor Alice succeeds in eluding capture for four days, even though "She knew only the area she'd been born and raised in, and she couldn't read a map." Alice is captured, beaten, and sold as a slave to Rufus. As Dana is sent back and forth through time, she continues to save Rufus's life, attempting during each visit to care for Alice, even as she is encouraging Alice to allow Rufus to rape her and thus ensure Dana's own birth. As a twentieth-century African-American woman trying to endure the brutalities of nineteenth-century slavery, Dana answers the question, "See how easily slaves are made?" For Dana, to choose to preserve an institution, save a life, and nurture victimization is to choose to survive.

D.N.-W.

The Löwensköld Ring, Selma Lagerlöf, *translated from Swedish by Linda Schenck, 1925, Sweden,* NOVEL

In 1909, Selma Lagerlöf became the first woman and the first Swede to win the Nobel Prize for literature; today, she is almost completely unknown in the United States. Only recently have present-day readers had access to an English translation of *The Löwensköld Ring,* a gripping, moving novel that combines a ghost story with political, cultural, and psychological analysis. The story is told by one of a long line of women who have sat round the fire, spinning, weaving, and telling stories. It begins with a splendid ring, given to General Löwensköld for service to King Charles XII. The general wants the ring buried with him. Even though the ring, if it were sold, could feed many of the farmers left hungry by years of war, it is buried. But the ring is stolen from the tomb, and from that point on, the general's ghost walks abroad, exacting revenge. There is far more to this story than the supernatural effects, however. Like one of the women sitting around the fire, combining work and stories, Selma Lagerlöf maintains the tension of the ghost story while at the same time giving us insights into eighteenth-century Sweden, life among the elite and working classes, the role and lot of women, and the essential question of certainty itself. How do we judge innocence?

How do we know our own motives? And who, or what, makes us do what we do?

E.B.

The Maid of the North: Feminist Folk Tales from Around the World, Ethel Johnston Phelps, *1981, United States,* SHORT STORIES

In her two collections, *Tatterhood* and *The Maid of the North*, Ethel Johnston Phelps sets out to counterbalance traditional fairy tales such as Snow White, where women are either beautiful and passive or ugly and evil. *The Maid of the North* gathers folk and fairy tales from Scandinavia, Africa, Britain, Russia, and Pakistan, and from several North American Indian cultures. The women, girls, and female animals in these stories are bright, brave, crafty, determined, loving, and moral. They protect themselves and others; they can ride on the wind and choose whom (or if) they will marry. Ethel Phelps retells these stories in plain language, creating the lulling sensation of truth found in fairy tales while highlighting the differences between these tales and their grimmer counterparts. Read them to children, keep them for yourself, give a copy to a teenage girl who might need to be reminded that women are courageous and intelligent; these fairy tales transcend age barriers.

E.B.

The Mists of Avalon, Marion Zimmer Bradley, *1983, United States,* NOVEL

"There is no such thing as a true tale. Truth has many faces and the truth is like to the old road to Avalon; it depends on your own will and your own thoughts, whither the road will take you." *The Mists of Avalon* is a story of another time and place. It's the legendary saga of King Arthur and his companions at Camelot—their battles, love, and devotion—told this time from the perspective of the women involved. Viviane is the Lady of the Lake, the magical priestess of the Isle of Avalon, a special mist-shrouded place which becomes more difficult to reach as people turn away from its nature- and Goddess-oriented religion. Viviane's quest is to find a king who will be loyal to Avalon as well as to Christianity. This king will be Arthur.

Gwenhwyfar, Arthur's queen, is an overly pious, fearful woman who successfully sways her husband into betraying his allegiance to Avalon. Set against her is Morgaine of the Fairies, Arthur's sister, love, and enemy—and the most powerfully believable person in the book—who manipulates the characters like threads in a tapestry to achieve her tragic and heroic goals. *The Mists of Avalon* becomes a legend seen through new eyes, with details, majestic language, and haunting foreshadowing that hold the reader through its more than eight hundred pages.

G.B.

Mrs. Vargas and the Dead Naturalist, Kathleen Alcalá, *1992, United States,* SHORT STORIES

This collection of fourteen short stories is rich with visionary language that sets the imagination wandering. Kathleen Alcalá shows the everyday in a brilliant light; tales of family history, expectations, disappointments, and interactions with strangers and animals leave the reader full and reflective. Set mainly on the United States–Mexican border, these stories take the reader into the land of dreams, death, and hope. In "The Canary Singer," "Birdy always left her audience with the assurance that they could overcome all obstacles, that this beautiful sound, this feeling of floating euphoria induced by her voice, was her personal gift to them." In "Reading the Road," we meet Lucy, who "read tire tracks the way others read cards or tea leaves. . . . Lucy knew that the blood of California flowed through its roads and highways, and the highway leading west went past her front door." Through mothers, sisters, sons, and friends we feel the impact of disappearing children, lost loves, and the influence of God. Weaving the tangible, physical realities with the spiritual world, *Mrs. Vargas and the Dead Naturalist* visits many lands and times—places where, with Kathleen Alcalá's gentle writing, we gladly go.

H.S.

New Islands and Other Stories, María Luisa Bombal, *translated from Spanish by Jorge Luis Borges, 1940s, Chile,* SHORT STORIES

Each of the female protagonists in these five stories faces the grinding social expectation and reality of quiet compliance to the desires of men. And each, in her own way, creates entirely new, often magical worlds through her imagination. In "The Final Mist," a middle-aged spinster marries her first cousin a year after the death of his beloved first wife. At first she is only mildly distressed by this loveless union and by her boring husband, a man who wears decorum "as though it were a suit of armor," but she is changed forever after a silent and intensely passionate night with an unknown man. Who was he? Where is he? Was he only a dream? In "The Tree," Brigida, known for being "as silly as she is pretty," marries her father's old friend, Luis. There is no love, but she doesn't mind; she has the quiet, cool intimacy of her dressing room with a window shaded by a rubber tree that fixed the room "in shadow, quiet and ordered. Everything seemed to be held in an eternal and very noble equilibrium. That was life." In the title story, both Don Sylvester and Juan Manuel fall in love with Yolanda, but her magic cannot protect them from the pain of love and death. Written in fluid and acutely observant prose, *New Islands* is a collection of fablelike stories about the secret lives many women live.

J.L.

Out of Time, Paula Martinac, *1990, United States,* NOVEL

Seeking shelter from the rain, Susan steps inside a Manhattan antique store. She finds a scrapbook and looks "the pages over quickly, taking in the faces of four amazing women." For this amateur collector of old books about lesbians, the photo album seems too good to be true: "it was almost like holding the women, protecting them from the silence of time." The photos—of Harriet, an actress during the 1920s, her partner Lucy Warner Wier, a writer, and another couple, Elinor and Sarah—stop in 1927. Susan's search to find out what happened to them affects her own life; the more involved she becomes with the photos, the more strained becomes her relationship with her partner, Catherine. The scrapbook women become real to Susan; she seeks and visits places they visited, and before long is conversing with them, but she is afraid to share this with Catherine. Though some of the action wraps up a little too neatly, Paula Martinac's engaging writing makes *Out of Time* a fun romp through the twists and turns of the past and present—a mystery, a history, and a love story in one.

H.S.

The Painted Alphabet, Diana Darling, *1992, Indonesia* (*United States*), NOVEL/FOLK TALE

A traditional Balinese folk tale with a modern setting, *The Painted Alphabet* is told by American-born sculptor Diana Darling, a resident of Bali for more than ten years. This is an epic tale of moral questions and decisions encountered by its many players. Siladri wants to know the "whys" of life; finally his inner turmoil compels him to leave his village with his wife and niece, Sari, to study with Mpu Dibiaja, a wizened, gentle old man who knows that all ascetics are witches—it's a choice about how one uses personal power. After many years of study, Siladri and Sari take Mpu Dibiaja's place when he dies. During their years with Mpu Dibiaja, the powerful archwitch Dayu Datu also has a student—Ni Klinyar, a girl who was "conceived in sin and signified by a secret climate of curse." Ultimately their paths cross in battles involving earthquakes, monsters, monkeys, and fire. In *The Painted Alphabet,* we see that evil and good are not always clearly defined—there are philosophical paradoxes throughout. Diana Darling's writing illuminates the importance of the spirit world in the daily life of the Balinese, and immerses the reader in the smells, sounds, and beauty of Bali.

H.S.

Saints and Strangers, Angela Carter, *1985, England,* SHORT STORIES

In *Saints and Strangers,* Angela Carter takes real people and literary legends—most often women—who have been mythologized or marginalized and recasts them in a new light. In a style that is sensual, cerebral, almost hypnotic, "The Fall River Axe-Murders" portrays the last hours before Lizzie Borden's infamous act: the sweltering heat, the weight of flannel and corsets, the clanging of the factory bells, the food reheated and reserved despite the lack of adequate refrigeration, the house "full of locked doors that open only into other rooms with other locked doors." In "Our Lady of the Massacre," the no-nonsense voice of an eighteenth-century prostitute–runaway slave questions who is civilized: the Indians or the white men? "Black Venus" gives voice to Charles Baudelaire's Creole mistress, Jeanne Duval: "you could say, not so much that Jeanne did not understand the lapidary, troubled serenity of her lover's poetry but, that it was a perpetual affront to her. He recited it to her by the hour and she ached, raged and chafed under it because his eloquence denied her language." "The Kiss" takes the traditional story of Tamburlaine's wife and gives it a new and refreshing ending. Sometimes disquieting, sometimes funny, always thought-provoking, Angela Carter's stories offer a feminist revision of images that lie deep in our collective psyche.

E.B.

The Ship of Fools, Cristina Peri Rossi, *translated from Spanish by Psiche Hughes, 1984, Uruguay,* NOVEL

"A stranger. Ecks. Estranged. Expelled." For reasons we come to assume are political, thirty-odd-year-old Ecks can never go back to his unnamed country. Traveling, learning new streets, leaving again, he is an exile. In numerous short chapters prefaced by dreams, biblical quotes, and dreamlike descriptions of an ancient tapestry, Ecks' wanderings bring him to places with no names, and to eccentric characters who share his intense soul-searching interest about their place in a confused and polluted world. We first meet Ecks on a ship with Chinese lanterns that, when darkened, "hang like forgotten trophies, lonely witnesses, spent fireflies." A gentle man to whom women are drawn, Ecks knows that "the best way for a foreigner to get to know a city is to fall in love with one of its women, someone inclined to mother a man far from home and also appreciative of different pigmentation. She will trace him a path that does not figure on any map and instruct him in a language he will never forget." And Ecks, the perennial foreigner, finds delightfully unusual women to guide him in what is ultimately a series of loosely related stories about sex and power. Reading this unconventional novel is a bit like floating on an unknown sea filled with surprising possibilities.

J.L.

Through the Arc of the Rain Forest, Karen Tei Yamashita, *1990, Brazil (United States),* NOVEL

Through the Arc of the Rain Forest is a burlesque of comic-strip adventures and apocalyptic portents that stretches familiar truths to their logical extreme in a future world that is just recognizable enough to be frightening. In an author's note, Karen Tei Yamashita writes that her book is like the Brazilian soap operas called *novelas*: "the *novela's* story is completely changeable according to the whims of the public psyche and approval, although most likely, the unhappy find happiness; the bad are punished; true love reigns; a popular actor is saved from death . . . [it is] an idyll striking innocence, boundless nostalgia and terrible ruthlessness." The stage of the novel is a vast, mysterious field of impenetrable plastic in the Brazilian rain forest; the action is set against a backdrop of rampant environmental destruction, commercialization, poverty, and religious rapture. *Through the Arc of the Rain Forest* is narrated by a small satellite hovering permanently around the head of an innocent character named Kazumasa. Through no fault of his own, Kazumasa seems to draw strange and significant people into his orbit and to find himself at the center of cataclysmic events that involve carrier pigeons, religious pilgrims, industrial espionage, magic feathers, big money, miracles, epidemics, true love, and the virtual end of the world. This book is simultaneously entertaining and depressing, with all the rollicking pessimism you'd expect of a good soap opera or a good political satire.

K.B.

The Wall, Marlen Haushofer, *translated from German by Shaun Whiteside, 1962, Austria,* NOVEL

Thirty years after its acclaimed publication in Europe and twenty-two years after the author's death, *The Wall* has finally been published in the United States. This novel is narrated by a woman with no need for a name, who, while in the countryside, awakens to find an invisible, impenetrable wall surrounding the fields. She believes the wall is the result of a government experiment and that she is the last person alive. In time the wall becomes "a thing that is neither dead nor alive, it really doesn't concern me." With her are a dog, a cow, and a pregnant cat, who become her family. Her interactions with this family and her philosophical musings make this an extraordinary work. As the number of matches for lighting fires dwindles, she wonders how we got so removed from the basics of life, and realizes she "had forgotten how to see things with my own eyes, . . . but loneliness led me, in moments free of memory and consciousness, to see the great brilliance of life again." Though she is content with her family in her unique Garden of Eden, the reader knows changes will occur. In *The Wall*, Marlen Haushofer explores the strength of the individual and questions human drive and ambition, giving us a picture both broader and more focused than most of us ever see.

H.S.

Woman on the Edge of Time, Marge Piercy, *1976, United States,* NOVEL

With honest and compelling prose, Marge Piercy delves into the mind of thirty-seven-year-old Consuelo (Connie) Ramos, a woman who exists on the fringes of life in contemporary New York City. Early in the novel Connie beats up her niece's pimp and is committed—again—to the psychiatric ward in Bellevue Hospital. The novel shifts between the horrible conditions of the psychiatric wards, and events in the year 2137, as Connie at first talks to, then time travels with Luciente, a person from that future time. Luciente lives in a nonsexist, communal country where people's survival is ensured based on need, not money. A sense of freedom, choice, and safety are part of Luciente's world; Connie's world is the complete opposite. Though Connie struggles to stand up for herself and others in the treatment centers, she knows that the drugs she is forced to take weaken her in every way. She knows she shouldn't be there, knows how to play the game, and tells herself, "You want to stop acting out. Speak up in Tuesday group therapy (but not too much and never about staff or how lousy this place was) and volunteer to clean up after the others." But she knows she is stuck. She spends more time "away" with Luciente, trying to develop a way out of her hell. Ultimately Connie makes her plan of action, and the book leaves us with our own questions about Connie's decisions—and her sanity.

H.S.

Mothers and Mothering

No one else inspires such conflicting feelings of love, frustration, hate, and adoration as our mothers and our children. Mothers are our first loves, our most powerful teachers, to be replaced only by our children. Many of the novels and memoirs included here examine this bond on an intimate level. Vivian Gornick and Kim Chernin look at their own mothers' lives. In Susan Straight's novel, Marietta struggles to raise her big, powerful, "blue-black" twin boys in the South. Beverly Donofrio relates her life as a single mother; Carol Schaefer tells of finding the son she gave up for adoption eighteen years earlier. Gladys Milton fights for her job as a midwife; the title character of *Virginia* must choose between the needs of husband and children. Shay Youngblood, Simone Schwarz-Bart, and Anne Cameron remind us that the connection need not be biological nor confined to one person, and show us the beauty and richness that can come from a circle of mothers. Other writers invite us to consider motherhood as a social institution with a history. Adrienne Rich works on personal and theoretical levels to explore the history and culture of motherhood, while in *The Fifth Child*, Doris Lessing scares us into reconsidering myths that are the bedrock of western European thinking. Here are books that can reinforce our own experiences, and authors that bring out the complexity and power—positive and negative—of this most fundamental relationship. They give us mothers and children at their best and worst: strong, loving, confused, overwhelmed, overjoyed.

Anywhere But Here	Mona Simpson
The Bean Trees	Barbara Kingsolver
The Big Mama Stories	Shay Youngblood
The Bridge of Beyond	Simone Schwarz-Bart
Child of Fortune	Yúko Tsushima
Child of Her People	Anne Cameron
Fierce Attachments	Vivian Gornick
The Fifth Child	Doris Lessing
I Been in Sorrow's Kitchen and Licked Out All the Pots	Susan Straight
In My Mother's House	Kim Chernin
The Kitchen God's Wife	Amy Tan
Mary O'Grady	Mary Lavin
A Mom's Life	Kathryn Grody
Of Woman Born	Adrienne Rich
The Other Mother	Carol Schaefer
Praxis	Fay Weldon
Pride of Family	Carole Ione
Riding in Cars with Boys	Beverly Donofrio
Virginia	Ellen Glasgow
Why Not Me?	Wendy Bovard and Gladys Milton
Wild Swans	Jung Chang
The Woman Who Was Not All There	Paula Sharp

Anywhere But Here, Mona Simpson, *1986, United States,* NOVEL

Anywhere But Here touches on many of the great American myths: the sanctity of the family, upward mobility, the promise of the West. When Ann and her mother Adele head to California, away from the boredom (and safety) of their family home in the Midwest, they are dreaming of a new future in which Adele can marry rich and Ann can become a child star. It is a world in which Adele believes that the right "look," the right "smile" can change their lives. But it is also a world dominated by chance, a life of constant moves away from the past toward some undefined happiness. Comprised of several compelling narratives and an all-female cast of characters, *Anywhere But Here* evokes many of the ways in which women have struggled to find meaning and dignity in their lives. Ann, a clear-headed and thoughtful twelve-year-old, as well as Ann's gentle grandmother, her shy aunt, and her mother, Adele, all have their say, speaking eloquently about the past, the future, and the gap between their expectations and the realities of their lives. Bound together in this funny, very real novel, they give us a vivid picture of the resilient power of family ties, and the struggle both to escape and to honor them.

S.L.

The Bean Trees, Barbara Kingsolver, *1988, United States,* NOVEL

Marietta Greer's mama called her Missy, because, according to family legend, when she was three, she stamped her foot "and told my own mother not to call me Marietta but MISS Marietta, as I had to call all the people including children in the houses where she worked Miss this or Mister that." Her growing-up years in Pittnam County, Kentucky, taught her two things: don't get pregnant, and get out as quick as you can. With Mama's expert training in old-car troubleshooting, Marietta hits the road in her windowless, jump-start 1955 Volkswagen, determined to rename herself after the first place she has to buy gas. Relieved at missing Homer, Illinois, and keeping her "fingers crossed through Sidney, Sadorus, Cerro Gordo, Decatur, and Blue Mound," she "coasted into Taylorville on the fumes." Now Taylor Greer, she discovers that car trouble can change more than just her name: when her rocker arm breaks in Oklahoma, she is "given" a baby; when she has two flat tires in Tucson, she limps into Jesus Is Lord Used Tires, where she begins to learn that her troubles are minor compared to those of people hiding from Guatemalan death squads. *The Bean Trees* is written in the spirited language of a Kentucky-raised working woman with a generous heart and an audacious imagination.

J.L.

The Big Mama Stories, Shay Youngblood, *1989, United States,* SHORT STORIES

The narrator of *The Big Mama Stories* grew up in "the projects," an area with "lines that marked us" and where the best blackberries flourished in the black cemetery. When her biological mother deserted her at five, the narrator was left with Big Mama, who was neither big nor her mother: "Just regular. A old Black woman who had a gift for seeing with her heart." Big Mama, however, is only one of this young girl's mothers—and they're not all female. Through their interconnected stories we learn their histories and hear their advice. Big Mama's explanation about why she uses snuff becomes a lesson on black pride. From Miss Corrine, the hairdresser, the narrator learns the truth about her mother along with some advice: "If you got to dance or dream or anything at all, take it a step at a time and don't let nothing and nobody get in your way when you doing right." There's Miss Tom, "who was not a pretty woman, she was handsome like a man," and Uncle Buck, who tells her, "Sometimes I love Jesus and sometimes I think he hard of hearing." On occasion all the mothers come together, to heal an illness or to celebrate a rite of passage, and during these events the narrative soars. Whether quiet or jubilant, sad or defiant or thoughtful, each story has power and pride, given freely to the narrator, and through her, to us.

E.B.

The Bridge of Beyond, Simone Schwarz-Bart, *1972, Guadeloupe,* NOVEL

This aptly titled novel takes the reader to many "beyonds." Through the life of Telumee Lougandor we meet a proud line of women who live in small villages in Guadeloupe: women whose lives are beyond Africa, beyond the slavery that in theory has been abolished, and beyond the physical restrictions of their difficult existence, which is eased only by their faith in the spirit world. In the day-to-day life Telumee leads with her grandmother Toussine—washing clothes at the river, tending a garden, working as a house servant, and interacting with others in the villages—Simone Schwarz-Bart shows lives linked by common suffering. Ma Cia, a witch "closer to the dead than the living," soundly advises young Telumee: "Be a fine little Negress, a real drum with two sides. Let life bang and thump, but keep the underside always intact." While doing their "women's work"—work they must do to survive—the Lougandor women not only endure, they grow. They love, lose at love, and allow themselves to love again. They know the meaning of oppression—sometimes at the hands of other villagers or the men in their lives, and always at the hands of the whites. *The Bridge of Beyond* is a view of unending hardships made bearable by the love and wisdom of elders—especially grandmother Toussine—and the healing power of the spirit world.

H.S.

Child of Fortune, Yúko Tsushima, *translated from Japanese by Geraldine Harcourt, 1978, Japan,* NOVEL

Thirty-six-year-old Koko is a single mother in contemporary Japan; her adolescent daughter, Kayako, wants a traditional home like those of her schoolmates, so she lives with Koko's sister and visits her mother once a week. When a casual relationship with an old friend ends, Koko takes the time to look at her life. She realizes she has often only moved through the motions and been passive about her choices: she got married because she was pregnant, divorced because her husband wanted to, and got jobs through friends because it was convenient. She questions how she got so removed from her daughter and from herself. When her body begins feeling different, she suspects she is pregnant. "But now, just for the moment, she wanted to find an answer to this problem and be done with it—to let sheer momentum carry her there. She was on the way to a featureless but comfortable place known as 'common sense.' " The decision Koko makes about her pregnancy is one that doesn't please many. But with it, Koko's self-respect grows and Kayako gains a new appreciation for her mother. Together they work at bridging some of the gaps in their lives, even when everything does not turn out as planned.

H.S.

Child of Her People, Anne Cameron, *1987, Canada,* NOVEL

"For a story to be told, it must be told properly, and to tell a story properly, it must be told with respect." Child of Her People, an orphaned white infant, is found and adopted by Woman Walks Softly, the daughter of Strong Heart Woman. In her new family, Child of Her People is taught the ways of Cree warrior women through story and example. "She learned to talk the language of children, and all the games she played were preparation for the training she would need to become one of the adults." Then Newcomer Crazies—incomprehensible beings who kill for no reason—flood onto the Good People's lands. Through changes of season, age, time in life, and circumstance—those inevitable changes and the unexpected changes forced by the Newcomers—Child of Her People is challenged, wounded, renewed, and challenged again. *Child of Her People* is a story rich in captivating detail, ancient stories, and the magic that imbues strength and trust in the relationships between Cree mothers and daughters.

J.L.

Fierce Attachments, Vivian Gornick, *1987, United States,* AUTOBIOGRAPHY

Fierce Attachments captures a kind of love particular to mothers and daughters—messy, obsessive, and at times blissfully simple. Vivian Gornick grew up in the Bronx, the child of Jewish "urban peasants." Now middle-aged and divorced, she writes for a living and takes long walks through the city with her mother while they carry on conversations that quite often turn into heated debates. Through their present-day discussions and Vivian Gornick's memories, her mother emerges as strong-willed and opinionated, a woman with a level of sensitivity and curiosity that enables her to discern the emotional climate of the neighborhood by listening to the rise and fall of voices through windows. Her attachment to her husband is deeply sentimental; his early death threw her into a prolonged depression which had profound ramifications for her daughter. Standing in contrast to the author's mother is the widowed Nettie—beautiful, sensual, and the only non-Jewish resident in their apartment building. In *Fierce Attachments*, Vivian Gornick describes her neighborhood and her life as she tries to understand the effect that these two women had on her and her relationships with men. The result is a memoir lush with detail and deeply introspective.

E.B.

The Fifth Child, Doris Lessing, *1988, England,* NOVEL

The Fifth Child is not a book for pregnant women or even young mothers. It is the chilling, obsessive story of Harriet and David, a young middle-class English couple determined to achieve their dream of a big house full of children. They find their dream house before they can afford it; for them to buy it requires money from wealthy parents and extra hours at work for David. The children come—four of them—faster than expected. But for all the stress, the house *is* big and warm, full of huge, happily anticipated family gatherings—all of which require more money. Then comes the fifth child, who is different and terrifying from the moment of conception. This novel magnificently brings alive fears many of us have about ourselves and society, fears we would rather not think about. Where *do* our children come from, anyway? What is the real cost of the big house and all the myths that come with it? How does society deal with what is "abnormal"? Doris Lessing tackles social issues with sentences and rhythms that could be read simply for their own beauty. In *The Fifth Child* she has used her art to create a book that frightens deep and leaves its questions to linger in your mind well after the creepiness has waned.

E.B.

I Been in Sorrow's Kitchen and Licked Out All the Pots, Susan Straight, *1992, United States,* NOVEL

At fifteen, Marietta is over six feet tall, "blueblack" like her blueblood father from Africa. Her father is dead—killed, somehow, no one really talks about it—and her mother is dying. In 1959, there aren't many places for a big, hard-looking black woman. During Marietta's life, "sorrow's kitchen" has many locations: Pine Gardens, where she was born, where the people speak Gullah and Mr. Ray wants to re-create plantation life for the tourists; Charleston, where Marietta conceives her twin boys and works day and night jobs to support them; southern California, where Marietta's now-grown boys are "living large" playing professional football and Marietta's daughter-in-law has long fingernails covered with polish. Following Marietta through it all, Susan Straight tells a thick, rich story, full of small details and large insights. Marietta takes in the little things about motherhood—the feel of small hands on her back, the stickiness of peach juice dripping down a small body, the fear for fragile knees on a football field. She also knows she is the mother of two huge boys, as blueblack as herself, living in a country where white motorists still run down black people for target practice, so she stays hard—"Big Ma," who wears man's pants and a headwrap. In her, Susan Straight has created a tough and beautiful woman.

E.B.

In My Mother's House, Kim Chernin, *1983, United States,* BIOGRAPHY

In My Mother's House is more than a story about four generations of women; more than a documentation of communism, socialist idealism, and its subsequent disillusionment; more than proof of the existence of women who have struggled to fight for what they believed in with bravery and persistence. More than any of this, *In My Mother's House* is about healing. The book begins with conflict: Rose Chernin asks her daughter, Kim, to write down the story of Rose's life as a Communist organizer. Through years of struggling with her own identity and her mother's ideal vision of her, Kim Chernin has separated herself from her mother, and she is wary of the project, not wanting to "face their secrets and silences" or "wake the family's ghosts." Her powerful and persistent mother persuades her, however, and with relaxed sentences that drift into stories of the past, Kim Chernin skillfully, colorfully, and with great affection brings us into the culture of Russian Jews. In the end, she finds writing down the pain in daring honesty allows growth, empathy, and finally understanding, and takes down the walls separating mother and daughter. And as Kim Chernin says "Tell me a story Mama," she keeps alive a flame handed down to her, one that she will pass on to her own daughter.

G.B.

The Kitchen God's Wife, Amy Tan, *1991, China/United States* (*United States*), NOVEL

Winnie is a powerhouse who has fought, laughed at, and struggled with life; Pearl is the daughter who grew up in Winnie's shadow. Pearl has a secret she doesn't want her mother to know because Winnie will blame herself, worry, be mad she wasn't told right away. Winnie has secrets she doesn't want to tell Pearl: she's afraid she won't understand, that she'll be hurt. Auntie Helen knows their secrets and thinks it is time for each of them to tell. Winnie was born in China seventy years ago and experienced her mother's desertion, a cultural revolution, and a very bad marriage. How can she explain these things to her American-born daughter, the one who keeps to herself and wouldn't even allow herself to cry when her father died? But as Winnie lets Pearl in, Pearl learns more than just her mother's story. She learns about herself, about the costs she and her mother pay to keep their secrets—and she learns to share her own secrets. Mothers can both support our roots so we can stand on our own and remove the topsoil that nurtures us; this is a story of mothers doing both.

H.S.

Mary O'Grady, Mary Lavin, *1950, Ireland,* NOVEL

As a newly married young bride in Dublin, Mary O'Grady takes a daily stroll to deliver a hot lunch to her husband, Tom, at work in the tram barn. Her walk takes her past the Grand Canal, a place which reminds her of the rural area where she grew up. As the babies come—Patrick, Ellie, Angie, Larry, and Rosie—she ignores her neighbor's offer to help with the children. She finds a pram good company, and besides, the children give her good cause to linger on the canal edge that glows with "the full splendour of a country meadow." The O'Gradys are Catholics whose faith runs through their veins like their blood, unquestioned and rarely celebrated. Mary's inner life is full and rich with the cares of her home and children; she allows no shadows or even a dangerous word like "delicate" to fall on them: "Let there be no talk about delicacy. That word was like a curse. . . . If a boy or a girl had any little weakness the best thing to do was to fight against it." But life brings painful changes that even Mary's heroic efforts cannot avert. Written in deliberate and sensitive prose, *Mary O'Grady* is a moving and hard-to-put-down novel about one woman's love for her family.

J.L.

A Mom's Life, Kathryn Grody, *1991, United States,* MEMOIR

A Mom's Life captures mothering in the nineties in a way you'll never find in Dr. Spock or any other how-to-parent book. Provoked by naïve friends who ask "Are you working now or just staying home having fun with the kid?" Kathryn Grody sets out to describe one day in the life of a mother of two young boys. The result is hilarious and insightful, full of the joy, fear, anger, frustration, and exhilaration that make up a full-time mom's days. She writes of husbands: "I think how sometimes the dad knows the difference between the kids' needs and his own too well, and how for the mom, there is no difference." She writes of sense of self: "Actually, I don't remember who I used to be before this totally dependent-upon-me creature arrived. . . . I listen to friends tell stories about the old me like great fiction." She writes of early mornings, getting-dressed games, negotiations over sugar and swearing, nap times during which she accomplishes nothing because there is so much to do, fear of nuclear war and pesticides, moments of bliss. At once fast-paced and full of reflection, *A Mom's Life* covers much more than one day's events. For those who are mothers, it is both welcome reinforcement and a source of delight; for those without children, it should provide insight into "the planet called Momdom," a place where "you become invisible to anyone unless they live there with you."

E.B.

Of Woman Born: Motherhood as Experience and Institution, Adrienne Rich, *1976, United States,* NONFICTION

Asking "But what was it like for women?" with "painful consciousness of my own Western cultural perspective and that of most of the sources available," Adrienne Rich examines pregnancy, childbirth, and motherhood from historical, physical, religious, institutional, political, and personal angles. In her introduction to the 1986 edition, she explains "I did not choose this subject; it had long ago chosen me. . . . I only knew that I had lived through something which was considered central to the lives of women . . . a key to the meaning of life; and that I could remember little except anxiety, physical weariness, anger, self-blame, boredom, and divisions within myself." A stimulating combination of poetic rhythms, scholarly precision, feminist perspective, and personal reflection, *Of Woman Born* is both an engrossing read and an affirmative, potentially life-changing examination of what it means to be of woman born.

J.L.

The Other Mother, Carol Schaefer, *1991, United States,* AUTOBIOGRAPHY

In 1965, at age nineteen, Carol Schaefer gave her son up for adoption. Sent to a Catholic home for unwed mothers, where she wasn't allowed to use her last name or share personal information, she was told repeatedly that she had made the right decision for the baby, that she would soon forget. But she never forgot, and remembers the home as a place of great loss. She recalls signing the adoption papers: "The consequences of those signatures would permeate every aspect of my life, my son's life, Chris's [the father's] life, and many, many other lives, forever. I had no legal counsel, no psychological counseling. I was nineteen and alone. I sat for a while, stunned, overcome by my desolation." When her baby was two days old he was taken away, and she vowed to find him when he was eighteen. She married and had two more sons, all the time remembering that she had another child, one she might walk past and not recognize. Carol Schaefer's honesty about how the social pressures of her times affected her touches deeply: her feeling that adoption was a middle-class disease, the shame and secrecy surrounding her pregnancy, and the effects giving up her child had on her self-esteem and on her future. Strength, sadness, joy, and the power of undeniable love abound in this book.

H.S.

Praxis, Fay Weldon, *1978, England,* NOVEL

An astonishingly vivid and wickedly funny portrait of a woman and her times, *Praxis* is a story told from two viewpoints—those of Praxis as a young girl and Praxis as an old woman. At age five, Praxis Duveen is "the pretty one," while her sister, Hypatia, is "the artistic one, and very sensitive"; their mother, Lucy, "clearly valued sensitivity above prettiness." While Lucy fights to protect her place in the heart of her children's father—not her husband—and in the eyes of a society not of her choosing, Hypatia collects awards in school and Praxis propels herself into life and love. Looking back as an old woman, Praxis cannot forgive her mother or cherish her memories: "I, Praxis Duveen, being old and scarcely in my right mind, now bequeath you my memories. They may help you: they certainly do nothing to sustain me, let alone assist my bones to clamber out of the bath." Neither the young nor the old Praxis are especially likable, and both are given to wild errors in judgment. Fay Weldon pulls no punches in her pointed and witty observations of British middle-class values and behavior as she creates a discomfitingly believable picture of an ordinary woman in a society that does not value women.

J.L.

Pride of Family, Carole Ione, *1991, United States,* AUTOBIOGRAPHY

Carole Ione was in her thirties when she decided to write an article about the women in her family. One of a third generation of only daughters, she grew up in the homes of her mother, grandmother, and great-aunt, all of whom were very quiet on the subject of family history. What little she learned was from the men of her family, people she rarely saw and barely knew. When she remembers that her other grandmother kept a diary, she asks to see it, and new doors open. For the next eighteen years she researches her family and uncovers much about herself in the process. She finds out that her ancestors were not only African, but European and Caribbean, suffragettes and slave owners. She learns about the family prejudices—preferences for fair skin over dark and for those with "good hair" over those without—and of the repetition of secrets hidden for generations. Finally, she reaches an understanding of the women who raised her and comes to terms with her life. *Pride of Family* may leave you with questions about your own background and cultural assumptions: all may not be what it seems.

H.S.

Riding in Cars with Boys, Beverly Donofrio, *1990, United States,* AUTOBIOGRAPHY

Beverly Donofrio portrays a world of babies having babies and children raising children. She acknowledges right away that she's not a conventional mother, that she and her son, Jason, don't have a traditional home life. She was seventeen when Jason was born, and they spent eight of the next ten years on welfare. A spunky, spirited woman with a defiant streak, she wages a constant struggle with herself: Is Jason an anchor pulling her down, or does he provide ballast? At times he seems to grow in spite of her. Her love for him isn't in question, but will she ever be able to comprehend his needs? Motherhood is never easy, but hers was made more difficult by a society ready to cast judgment on young, single mothers, by a family who finds it easier to criticize than support her, and by her own struggle to reach a long-held dream of a college education. As Beverly Donofrio's sense of who she is increases and she realizes her goals, Jason challenges her understanding of life and contributes to their growth together.

H.S.

Virginia, Ellen Glasgow, *1913, United States,* NOVEL

Ellen Glasgow set out to write an ironic novel about Southern ladies; in the end, however, sympathy for her character took over, turning "a comedy of manners into a tragedy of human fate." The resulting novel follows Virginia through her early life as the daughter of a pastor and his submissive wife, into Virginia's romantic marriage to a handsome, dynamic man, and on to her increasingly difficult life as a wife with children. In contrast to Virginia is her friend Susan, caught in expectations of filial duty, who tries to find another way to live. The situations and decisions here are never easy. Is passionate love preferable to life with a steady, less exciting man? Who comes first—husband, children, or self? Is submission a necessary aspect of life as wife and mother? This novel provides no simple answers. Through the lives of Virginia and Susan, Ellen Glasgow considers and attacks the traditions and expectations of turn-of-the-century Southern society, the Church, and the feminists of her day.

E.B.

Why Not Me? The Story of Gladys Milton, Midwife, Wendy Bovard and Gladys Milton, *1993, United States,* ORAL HISTORY

The opening chapter of *Why Not Me?* is a courtroom scene: *State of Florida Health and Rehabilitative Services* v. *Gladys Milton*, age sixty-four, for providing illegal medical care. From this point, Gladys Milton looks back, telling her story to Wendy Bovard, a midwife and one of Gladys's many patients. Gladys is raised by her midwife aunt in rural Florida during the years when white doctors and hospitals refused to care for brown- and black-skinned people. By the time she is a teenager, Gladys has helped her aunt deliver dozens of babies. In 1958, after her marriage and the birth of her seven children, Gladys is asked by a school nurse to study to become a lay midwife as part of the state's plan to improve rural health care. Although initially reluctant, Gladys finally agrees, swayed in large part by the encouragement of her husband and children. In 1988, after thirty years of delivering thousands of healthy babies—many remembered in exquisite detail—and after several personal tragedies, Gladys Milton is asked to "retire" from midwifery by the state agency that trained her. When she refuses, she is threatened with "serious charges." Although adamant that "anyone who knows me knows that I'll run a hundred miles out of my way to avoid a fight," she unearths the courage to face her challengers in court. Buoyed by her faith and by far-reaching support, Gladys Milton proves her family's adage: "Success comes in cans, failure comes in can'ts."

J.L.

Wild Swans, Jung Chang, *1991, China,* AUTOBIOGRAPHY

Jung Chang's autobiography tells recent Chinese history from a personal perspective. Jung's grandmother was a concubine with bound feet who saw the father of her only child three times in ten years. Her child, Jung's mother, grew up to be a passionate, committed Communist, who married one of Mao's most ardent supporters. Jung's father always put the party before the family: he once sent his mother-in-law away after she had walked hundreds of miles to be with them because he felt feeding her would be taking advantage of his position. Jung grew up with the belief that Mao was the savior of China; because of him she had adequate living quarters, enough food, and a good education. But as the momentum of the Cultural Revolution grew, things changed: in school, students were required to memorize every word Mao said; in the community, personal vendettas were settled by betrayals. "The whole of China was like a prison. Every house, every street was watched by the people themselves. In this vast land, there was nowhere anyone could hide." Jung's parents and countless others suffered a myriad of attacks that included denunciations, beatings, and imprisonment in labor camps. Many people were killed or died spiritually at the hands of Mao, a man who "created a moral wasteland and a land of hatred." Jung Chang survived, and with her life story shares her confusion, tears, and triumphs in a world seemingly gone mad.

H.S.

The Woman Who Was Not All There, Paula Sharp, *1988, United States,* NOVEL

Marjorie LeBlanc's husband "had misled her for so long that she learned to lean away from life to keep from falling over, like a woman walking a large dog." When they finally split up, she removes his name from their mailbox and wearily begins trying to understand what happened, and to figure out how she will raise four rambunctious children—Sam, Karen, Carla, and Ruth—alone. After work, Marjorie watches TV, reads, and plays cards on the porch with her women friends and neighbors, all of whom have their own sad man-stories to tell. Marjorie's loneliness makes her son Sam brood and stare at the ground, "as if he were building up his resistance against inevitable attacks of loneliness in his adult future." Karen abandons the family to stay with her grandmother and live "normal," where hard-drinking housewives don't play cards, swear, and have lesbian friends. Ruth and Carla, hard-assed tomboys determined to stay tough at any cost, make sure to get home before dark if their mother is alone in the house. In wonderfully inventive prose and sharp-tongued, witty dialogue, Paula Sharp shows us how, with the help of her friends, Marjorie's spirit prevails almost in spite of herself.

J.L.

Observations

Sue Hubbell waits in silence as her new swarm of bees enters its hive. Agatha Christie's detective takes note of the passengers on a train, knowing one of them is a killer. A former slave, now a seamstress, Elizabeth Keckley observes her employer, the wife of Abraham Lincoln. Whatever we study, we see through the lens of our own histories and passions. The authors in this section play with the concepts of observation and subjectivity in a variety of ways. Elisabeth Bumiller, Margaret Wettlin, Elizabeth Warnock Fernea, and Annie Dillard consciously make themselves and their reactions to, respectively, India, Iraq, Russia, and Tinker Creek, a part of the environments they describe: what could have been "objective" studies bloom into complexity as these authors acknowledge and celebrate their own involvement. Some authors attempt to make readers first-hand observers: Mercè Rodoreda uses stream of consciousness to place the reader directly in Natalia's mind as she looks back over her life, while Flannery O'Connor's detached style gives the reader the feeling of looking through a camera lens. Cora Sandel, Carol Shields, and Christina Stead hold ordinary characters up to the light as if they were precious stones. As the authors here describe rural Missouri, fourteenth-century Europe, a small village in England or Italy, the guests at a hotel in Switzerland, Mexican revolutionaries, and Arab society, they not only teach us about their subjects, but about what happens when human beings observe.

After Henry	Joan Didion
And the Bridge Is Love	Faye Moskowitz
Behind the Scenes	Elizabeth Keckley
Cora Sandel: Selected Short Stories	Cora Sandel
A Country Year	Sue Hubbell
A Distant Mirror	Barbara W. Tuchman
Distant View of a Minaret	Alifa Rifaat
Excellent Women	Barbara Pym
Fifty Russian Winters	Margaret Wettlin
Flowering Judas	Katherine Anne Porter
A Good Man Is Hard to Find	Flannery O'Connor
Guests of the Sheik	Elizabeth Warnock Fernea
The Little Hotel	Christina Stead
The Little Virtues	Natalia Ginzburg
May You Be the Mother of a Hundred Sons	Elisabeth Bumiller
Murder on the Orient Express	Agatha Christie
The Nocturnal Naturalist	Cathy Johnson
Pilgrim at Tinker Creek	Annie Dillard
The Portable Dorothy Parker	Dorothy Parker
The Time of the Doves	Mercè Rodoreda
Various Miracles	Carol Shields
Women of Sand and Myrrh	Hanan al-Shaykh
The World and the Bo Tree	Helen Bevington

After Henry, Joan Didion, *1992, United States,* ESSAYS

Joan Didion has the ability to evoke a time and place with a crystalline intelligence that sees and makes far-reaching connections. *After Henry* is a collection of essays which captures the essence and opens provocative discussions of, among other things, the fire season in California, the "jogger" rape case in New York, the history and impact of the *Los Angeles Times,* the 1988 presidential campaign, the Reagan administration, the real estate and entertainment industries in southern California, and Patty Hearst. Each topic is the center of a rapidly expanding series of thoughts, a chance to reveal and contrast one of the "narratives" the media presents and people prefer to believe with what may be actually occurring. Joan Didion's essays are impressively researched; her sentences have the power and grace of a thoroughbred at full speed. A piece that explores "the use of other nations as changeable scrims in the theater of domestic politics" begins: "In August of 1986, George Bush, traveling in his role as vice president of the United States and accompanied by his staff, the Secret Service, the traveling press, and a personal camera crew wearing baseball caps reading 'Shooters, Inc.' and working on a $10,000 retainer paid by a Bush PAC called the Fund for America's Future, spent several days in Israel and Jordan." Fascinating and eye-opening, *After Henry* challenges us to recognize the sometimes messy, sometimes discomfiting reality that lies under the "stories" that have splashed across our newspapers and television screens.

E.B.

And the Bridge Is Love: Life Stories, Faye Moskowitz, *1991, United States,* ESSAYS

Faye Moskowitz offers her impressions of life in this collection of essays. *And the Bridge Is Love* is about illness, family, birth, death, and the power and pleasure of reading and food. She takes a hilarious look at the problem of attending a wedding while trying to stay on a diet—for her, the two just don't mix. As her son says, "In this family, food is the recreational drug of choice." She confronts anti-Semitic attitudes at a yard sale, then wonders if she helped or hurt her cause. She lovingly and movingly tells of a friendship with a neighbor, with whom she thought she'd have nothing in common, but from whom she learns much about life as her friend confronts and succumbs to breast cancer. When her husband complains that there have been no washcloths in the house for ten years, she writes: "When you've been married for forty years, it's convenient to argue in decades." The twist of a phrase or the choice of a word works its way into your mind, and Faye Moskowitz's writing lingers long past the closing of the book. "Life Stories" is a fitting subtitle; these are stories to read aloud and read again.

H.S.

Behind the Scenes, or, Thirty Years a Slave and Four Years in the White House, Elizabeth Keckley, *1868, United States,* AUTOBIOGRAPHY

Elizabeth Keckley's post–Civil War life story is part slave narrative, part gossip column, part Horatio Alger story. It blends autobiography with—is there a word to describe a biography that *disparages* its subject? Although Elizabeth Keckley lived longer as a slave than as modiste to first lady Mary Todd Lincoln, most of her engrossing autobiography is devoted to her White House years. The opening three chapters establish her as a woman to be reckoned with: the "school of slavery," as she calls her bondage, taught her to be fiercely self-reliant, persevering, and defiant, though more than one slavemaster tried to beat her into submission. Having worked as a reputable seamstress for three years while also performing her full-time duties as a slave woman, she finally manages to buy freedom for both herself and her son. After a brief, unhappy marriage, she begins her rapid social ascent from seamstress for the solid South's "best ladies" to Mary Todd Lincoln's best friend and confidante. Elizabeth Keckley's narrative is riveting as she describes life in the White House during the Lincoln administration in meticulous detail. *Behind the Scenes* will engage equally the history buff, the gossip monger, and the lover of literature.

J.M.

Cora Sandel: Selected Short Stories, Cora Sandel, *translated from Norwegian by Barbara Wilson, 1960, Norway,* SHORT STORIES

These stories are a series of detailed, sympathetic portraits of people often ignored or judged without being understood: Lola, the conniving artist's model; Shit-Katrine, the prostitute; Adele, the aging prima donna, and her nondescript sister Tora; Mrs. Larsen, the shopkeeper, who thought she caught a romantic dream only to realize she had merely been caught. The son of a couple who has everything but happiness "doesn't suspect that he constitutes the living chain of flesh and blood and nerves binding two incompatible people together, and that he will have to pay for it." The young girl who resists taking on the trappings of womanhood comments, "To dress up in all that, strut around in it, stumble in the long skirts, mimic the grown-ups and make them laugh where they sat on the garden steps, was fun enough for a while. But it was nothing to base a life on." Through the intensity of her own gaze, Cora Sandel makes us look closely at these people, and understand the intricacies of individual moral dilemmas, the courage of small rebellions, and the tragedy of any one person's everyday life. Dismissing the operating morality of society, she sees through clear eyes and describes the beauty, sadness, and strength of lives that are often overlooked.

E.B.

A Country Year: Living the Questions, Sue Hubbell, *1986, United States,* JOURNAL/ESSAYS

"My chicken operation, I like to believe, is one of the few straightforward bits of farming that goes on at my place. But during the past weeks I have been trying to get the chickens organized to sleep inside the coop, and in doing so I've been forced to think like a chicken, which is not very straightforward at all." Sue Hubbell is wise enough to know there are many things she may never understand, such as the bees she keeps on her Ozark place, or why her marriage failed, or why it takes a good rain to settle the mud. This fifty-year-old librarian turned commercial beekeeper/honey-seller/farmer/amateur naturalist/journal writer wonders "where we older women fit into the social scheme of things once nest building has lost its charm." With gentle, rustic elegance, Sue Hubbell shares her understanding of how daily details shape how we see the world.

J.L.

A Distant Mirror: The Calamitous 14th Century, Barbara W. Tuchman, *1978, Europe* (*United States*), NONFICTION

In *A Distant Mirror*, historian Barbara Tuchman reveals in harrowing detail a "tortured century" with parallels to our own. People in the fourteenth century were subjected to natural and man-made disasters, including the Hundred Years War, the Crusades, insurrection, lawlessness, the schism of the Catholic church, massacres of Jewish people, and the Black Death, which claimed the lives of nearly half the population living between India and Iceland. Barbara Tuchman introduces a nobleman, Enguerrand de Coucy (1340–1397), a "whole man in a fractured time," who takes the reader through the century and gives a personalized context through which to understand the events and attitudes of the day. *A Distant Mirror* goes beyond the recording of facts to analyze the psychology of the age. It follows Enguerrand from one battle to the next, observing how bankruptcies, crop failures, revolts, and plagues effectively forced people apart, so that "emotional response, dulled by horrors, underwent a kind of atrophy." Suggesting that the "relative emotional blankness of a medieval infancy may account for the casual attitude toward life and suffering," she illustrates the discrepancy between the ideal and the real apparent in upper-class traditions of chivalry, in the practice of Christianity, and in the impossible regulations imposed on nobles, priests, and commoners alike. Pessimism inevitably resulted, for "man had lost confidence in his capacity to construct a good society." This fascinating portrayal of a tumultuous time provides insights into the present and hope for the future.

L.A.

Distant View of a Minaret, Alifa Rifaat, *translated from Arabic by Denys Johnson-Davies, 1983, Egypt,* SHORT STORIES

Through fifteen short and short-short stories, Alifa Rifaat unveils the world of contemporary Cairo and explores the importance of Islam in the lives of her characters. There are marketplaces and gardens, traffic, and in the distance always the call for prayers, reminding everyone of the time of day, of Allah, of their position in life. A daughter longs to ask her mother about men's infidelities, but realizes it is one of many subjects they won't talk about. An elderly woman is sure that her eyesight is failing because of the tears she's shed throughout her life, and knows no doctor can help her, since the "cure lies in the hands of Allah alone." A woman falls in love with a djinn—an Islamic spirit that appears to her in the form of a snake —and is riveted by her passions as she describes their encounters: ". . . sipping the poisons of my desire and exhaling the nectar of my ecstasy." Upon the death of his father, a man learns that a grandfather can love a grandchild he has never met. The life lessons in these stories are rarely about great changes; they are about everyday incidents, the strength and faith needed to live, and always, always about Allah. *Distant View of a Minaret* takes the reader down narrow alleyways and into people's homes and hearts to show how people find what is important.

H.S.

Excellent Women, Barbara Pym, *1952, England,* NOVEL

Mildred Lathbury, the narrator of *Excellent Women,* is washing up after providing her neighbors with tea and yet another opportunity to impress their problems upon her. Mildred maintains a tolerant and wonderfully wry perspective on her supporting role in the melodramatic lives of others, but she has no desire to be "always making cups of tea at moments of crisis." In fact, she has complicated and often inappropriate ideas about her relationships to people around her. She examines the social psychology of each situation afterward as if she were inspecting a soapy cup for lingering stains: "My thoughts went round and round and it occurred to me that if I ever wrote a novel it would be of the 'stream of consciousness' type and deal with an hour in the life of a woman at the sink." *Excellent Women,* however, goes beyond Mildred's introspection to include a bevy of curates, anthropologists, gossips, and ingrates in parochial, academic, and domestic contexts. In Barbara Pym's fiction, the preoccupations are petty, the daydreams disappointing, the romance unromantic, and the intelligent woman who does all the work is bound to be unappreciated. Oddly enough, these elements add up to delightful reading. Honesty, insight, feminism, and some terribly funny remarks are hidden among the teacups and conversations. If you are patient with *Excellent Women* you may discover an entirely unexpected story sandwiched between the lines.

K.B.

Fifty Russian Winters, Margaret Wettlin, *1992, Soviet Union* (*United States*), AUTOBIOGRAPHY

In 1932, Margaret Wettlin purchased tickets for a month's tour of Soviet Russia, took a leave of absence from her job as a high school teacher in Pennsylvania, and sailed off to see "The Great Social Experiment" for herself. Forty-two years later she returned to the United States. In that time she had taught English at a Russian-American automobile plant in Gorki, married a Russian theater director, lived in a log cabin in Outer Mongolia, made a home in Moscow, raised her children, and believed in the new society she was helping to build. Her book is an intensely personal account of an American woman who adopted the Soviet Union as her home and lived the life of an average Russian citizen through a half-century of tumultuous Soviet history. She searched for sufficient housing for her family, stood in food lines, was solicited as an informer by the KGB, huddled against the onslaught of the purges, was evacuated from Moscow, and spent the first two years of World War II as a refugee searching for safety for her family. Margaret Wettlin provides a bridge to understanding the strength of the belief that propelled a nation to sacrifice for a future greater than their past, and the gradual demise of that hope as a result of privations, government excesses, and corruption.

K.B.-B.

Flowering Judas, Katherine Anne Porter, *1930, Mexico/United States* (*United States*), SHORT STORIES

Flowering Judas is a collection of ten masterfully written stories about people struggling to survive in a world filled with conflict. Braggioni, a Mexican revolutionary in the title story, is a man with a "vast cureless wound of self-esteem" who has "taken pains to be a good revolutionist and a professional lover of humanity." To his chagrin, Laura, the "gringita" he pursues, loves the revolution without being in love with any man in it. In "Maria Concepción" Maria slaves long and hard to save enough to be married in the church, a symbol of status she comes to value more than life itself. In "The Jilting of Granny Weatherall," the excruciating memory of George —the groom who deserted her more than fifty years earlier—returns to Granny Weatherall to erase all other sorrow, even her fear of death. In "Magic," Madam Blanchard's cook gives her a charm so powerful that "even your enemy will come back to you believing you are his friend." These compassionate portrayals of ordinary lives filled with joy, anguish, and anger resonate with gentle courage and strong truth.

J.L.

A Good Man Is Hard to Find, Flannery O'Connor, *1948–1955 (1976), United States,* SHORT STORIES

With a keen eye for the dark side of human nature, an amazing ear for dialogue, and a necessary sense of irony, Flannery O'Connor exposes the underside of life in the rural South. One of the powers in her writing lies in her ability to make the vulnerability of one into that of many; another is her mastery of shifting "control" from character to character, making outcomes uncertain. Sexual and racial attitudes, conditions of poverty and wealth, and the passages of adolescence, old age, and being thirty-four (which "wasn't any age at all") are only some of the issues touched on in this collection. When Ruby has to walk up the "steeple steps . . . [that] reared up" as she climbed to her fourth-floor apartment, we feel her pain as she "gripped the banister rail fiercely and heaved herself up another step." Flannery O'Connor, a 1972 National Book Award winner, reminds us that none of the roles in our lives is stagnant, and that wearing blinders takes away more than just a view. Through her stories we see that what we blind ourselves to is bound to appear again and again.

H.S.

Guests of the Sheik: An Ethnography of an Iraqi Village, Elizabeth Warnock Fernea, *1965, Iraq (United States),* MEMOIR

There are 800 million Muslims in the world today, yet Islam is one of the world's least understood and appreciated religions. The culture of Islamic women and the mystery of a veiled society have endured any number of uninformed or hostile interpretations. Elizabeth Warnock Fernea spent the first two years of her marriage in the 1950s living in El Nahra, a small village in Southern Iraq, and her book is a personal narrative about life behind a veil in a community unaccustomed to Western women. She arrived speaking only a few words of Arabic and feeling dubious about her husband's expectation that she adapt completely to the segregated society in order to accommodate his anthropological study. When she left two years later she was an accepted and loved member of the village, inspired for a lifetime of work in Middle Eastern studies. The story of her life among the Iraqis is eye-opening, written with intellectual honesty as well as love and respect for a seemingly impenetrable society. Although the book was originally published in 1965, it surfaced again during the Gulf War in 1991, when many small villages were destroyed in Southern Iraq. This book gives readers a fuller sense of those communities, and brings home the cost of war waged against civilians.

R.S.

The Little Hotel, Christina Stead, *1973, Switzerland (Australia),* NOVEL

The Little Hotel is an in-depth examination of the longings and dreams of the owners, workers, and guests of a "fourth-rate" Swiss hotel shortly after World War II. Through Selda, one of the owners, a woman "always astonished at how people can muddle their lives," we learn about the guests and the staff as well as how she keeps order and calm amid clashing personalities. There is an Englishwoman of fifty, slowly dying of boredom; the "Mayor of B" from Belgium, constantly issuing unnecessary documents he keeps in the hotel safe; the wife of a doctor who is sure her husband is trying to kill her with prescription drugs. The hotel staff includes fifty-year-old Clara, who has worked there many years and vies for power over the other staff and guests; Luisa and Lina, sisters from Italy; and Rosa, a young German waitress who wants to be an actress. The staff tries to decipher the whims of the guests and deal with their own situations, and while many of the guests see the staff as friends, it is not an equal relationship—a difference that is not lost on the workers. Irony, humor, and sadness emerge as this unlikely mixture of people goes about the art of living.

H.S.

The Little Virtues, Natalia Ginzburg, *translated from Italian by Dick Davis, 1962, Italy,* ESSAYS

Natalia Ginzburg's essays are like pen-and-ink drawings. Her vocabulary is elemental, her style is not lush; through the simplicity come thoughts that are deep and generous. Included here are essays about living under fascism, descriptions of her old city and her little village, stories of friends who have died. She talks of raising children: "I think they should be taught not the little virtues but the great ones. Not thrift but generosity and an indifference to money; not caution but courage and a contempt for danger; nor shrewdness but frankness and a love of truth; not tact but love for one's neighbor and self-denial; not a desire for success but a desire to be and to know." Natalia Ginzburg writes with love about writing, with disdain about England, and with insight and honesty about how people grow up. This is a book to be read in small bits during the slow and quiet moments when the children are asleep or the work day is over. It takes you out of the everyday and reminds you of the difference between the little and great virtues in life.

E.B.

May You Be the Mother of a Hundred Sons: A Journey Among the Women of India, Elisabeth Bumiller, *1990, India (United States),* NONFICTION

It is difficult to articulate fully the rich, diverse, and poignant lives of the women of India, whose silent presence has carried that vast culture through famine, floods, and political upheavals. *May You Be the Mother of a Hundred Sons* attempts this, even if it stops somewhat short of showing the full strength of Indian women. Elisabeth Bumiller spent four years in India, and her observations offer insights into the conditions of rural Indian women, Bombay actresses, and powerful political figures. Though the writing is at times journalistic, Elisabeth Bumiller skillfully portrays individual women's lives often beset by arranged marriages, harassment over dowry, female infanticide, and oppressive family situations. Yet she also sees hope in the drive illiterate women have to get an education, and in the way creative women—painters, poets, filmmakers—emerge from the misery that surrounds them. No less exciting are the changes that the author herself undergoes: "Although I am still learning exactly what my journey to India meant to me, I do know that it transformed much of my thinking. It was in India that I had some of the most moving experiences of my life. . . . Ultimately, I realized my journey to India was a privilege. Rather than going to the periphery, I have come to the center."

B.K.

Murder on the Orient Express, Agatha Christie, *1934, England,* NOVEL

Murder on the Orient Express, a tour-de-force variation on the theme of the English house party, gathers a remarkable set of characters, each a secretive soul, for a journey on the fabled Orient Express as it travels from Istanbul to Paris. On hand to resolve the murder of an American passenger is Hercule Poirot, the dapper Belgian detective, dependent only on his wit, who tucks away obscure, seemingly unrelated minutiae in his facile mind. When he determines that the corpse was a renowned child kidnapper and killer, he begins to wonder about connections between the passengers and the victim. A misplaced button, overheard conversations, a monogrammed handkerchief, and an elusive figure clad in a scarlet kimono all become clues as Hercule Poirot interrogates the snow-trapped travelers and comes to his own conclusions. *Murder on the Orient Express*, with its skillful plot construction, adroit writing, and thought-provoking revelations, reminds us that what is "just" is not always what is legal.

V.S.

The Nocturnal Naturalist, Cathy Johnson, *1989, United States,* JOURNAL

"If one is willing to adapt, the darkness offers a place to step beyond the known edge and explore, a place of silence and sound, a place both unpopulated and populous, filled with things we may not see by day." Most of us live by day, and our realities are defined by light; *The Nocturnal Naturalist* allows us to see some of what we have missed. Cathy Johnson lives twenty miles outside of Kansas City, Missouri, in a once-rural area where opossums still hibernate in basements and you can hear peeper frogs in the spring, but land is divided into lots and yards. Sometimes she wanders at dusk or predawn, sometimes at midnight; sometimes she goes by car, sometimes she simply rambles around her own backyard. Always she tells us what she sees, hears, touches, smells, until the night becomes alive. Her words are lyrical, dense; her sense of detail is exquisite; her knowledge as a naturalist makes the book fascinating and educational. Her journal follows a year in which some seasons are longer than others, redefining our notions of calendars and days and reminding us how closely tied we are to the seasons and to nature—whether we are awake or asleep.

E.B.

Pilgrim at Tinker Creek, Annie Dillard, *1974, United States,* ESSAYS

Pilgrim at Tinker Creek is a series of essays that bring together scientific observation, philosophy, daily thoughts, and deep introspection with glorious prose. On the surface, Annie Dillard is exploring a place called Tinker Creek and its inhabitants: "It's a good place to live; there's lots to think about." But as her observations range well beyond the landscape into worlds of esoteric fact and metaphysical insight, each paragraph becomes suffused with images and ideas. Whether she is quoting the Koran or Albert Einstein, describing the universe of an Eskimo shaman or the mating of luna moths, Annie Dillard offers up her own knowledge with reverence for her material and respect for her reader. She observes her surroundings faithfully, intimately, sharing what can be shared with anyone willing to wait and watch with her. In the end, however, "No matter how quiet we are, the muskrats stay hidden. Maybe they sense the tense hum of consciousness, the buzz from two human beings who in silence cannot help but be aware of each other, and so of themselves." The precision of individual words, the vitality of metaphor, the sheer profusion of sources, the vivid sensory and cerebral impressions—all combine to make *Pilgrim at Tinker Creek* something extravagant and extraordinary.

K.B.

The Portable Dorothy Parker, Dorothy Parker, *1944, United States,* SHORT STORIES/POEMS/REVIEWS

Dorothy Parker doesn't just reveal the hypocrisies, vanities, myths, and foibles of her characters, she skewers them—in a style that is merciless, wickedly funny, and often sad. There is the rich and selfish Mrs. Whittaker: "Mrs. Whittaker's dress was always studiously suited to its occasion; thus, her bearing had always that calm that only the correctly attired may enjoy." And Mr. Durant, whose affair with his stenographer, Rose, has taken an unfortunate, one might say pregnant, turn: "Mr. Durant wished to God that he had never seen Rose. He explained this desire to her." "The woman with the pink velvet poppies" repeatedly and at great length assures her host that she can't wait to meet the guest of honor because "I don't see why on earth it isn't perfectly all right to meet colored people. I haven't any feeling at all about it—not one single bit." Then there is Hobart Ogden, "a very good-looking young man indeed, shaped to be annoyed," who works his way through an unlimited number of women. Sometimes related in the first person, sometimes by a third-person narrator, Dorothy Parker's stories show us what people cannot, or will not, see for themselves. These stories, along with the play and book reviews included in this collection, are quick, sharp, and dazzling.

E.B.

The Time of the Doves, Mercè Rodoreda, *translated from Catalan by David Rosenthal, 1962, Spain,* NOVEL

"To me a cork was like a stopper . . . I was like a cork myself. Not because I was born that way but because I had to be. And to make my heart like stone. I had to be like a cork to keep going because if instead of being a cork with a heart of stone I'd been like before, made of flesh that hurts when you pinch it, I'd never have gotten across such a high, narrow, long bridge." Natalia is a young woman living in a small village in Spain without a mother to give her advice. At a dance in the plaza she meets Quimet, with his "gleaming monkey eyes," who convinces her to reject her fiancé and marry him. Her decision marks the beginning a life of toil for Natalia which continues through the births of two children, the Spanish Civil War, Quimet's death, a second marriage, and finally into a feeling of rest. Told through Natalia's stream of consciousness, the novel is filled with precise observations, magical ramblings, exquisite metaphors, and a feeling as rushed, rippling, and languorous as a river running a long course. Mercè Rodoreda was twenty-six and just gaining recognition as an important author when Franco took power and repressed the Catalan language; she went into exile and did not write again for twenty years. *The Time of the Doves*, written when she was fifty-three, is a stunning re-creation of both a period in Spanish history and the life of one hardworking woman.

E.B.

Various Miracles, Carol Shields, *1985, Canada,* SHORT STORIES

Love, "capricious, idiotic, sentimental, imperfect and inconstant" —that longed-for state that "most often seems to be the exclusive preserve of others"—is what fills and informs these gentle and elegantly witty stories. The title character of "Mrs. Turner Cutting the Grass" is happily oblivious to the local girls' ridicule of her Bermuda shorts, the criticism of one neighbor for her use of pesticides on her lawn, and the scorn of another for her not having a catcher on her mower. In fact, "the things Mrs. Turner doesn't know would fill the Saschers' new compost pit, would sink a ship, would set off a tidal wave, would make her want to kill herself." In "The Journal," Sally records her trip to France, where she and her husband try to revive the sex life of their younger days. In "Others," Robert and Lila go to France for their honeymoon and briefly help a stranger named Nigel, who then initiates a correspondence that spans a period of thirty years. Although they never see each other again, Lila and Robert both fall secretly in love with letter-perfect Nigel and his wife, Jane. Each of the twenty-one stories in this volume offers warm, welcoming, and never simple understandings of life and love.

J.L.

Women of Sand and Myrrh, Hanan al-Shaykh, *translated from Arabic by Catherine Cobham, 1988, Lebanon,* NOVEL

Women of Sand and Myrrh focuses on four contemporary women living in an unnamed Middle Eastern country. Suha lives away from her home, war-torn Beirut, yet longs for the freedoms she had there: Why should she be confronted in the markets because she isn't covered? Why is she forbidden to drive? What part does her anger at this place and her overwhelming unhappiness with her husband play in her involvement in a lesbian relationship? Tamr, a native, sees the freedoms men have and wonders why those doors are closed to her. Even when she does succeed in opening a business, she is ever watchful for the self-appointed guards who will try to shut her down. Suzanne, from the United States, is excused for many of her actions because she is not an Arab. The unhappiness of her marriage is played out through a multitude of affairs. When her husband's job ends, will she be able to go back to the United States and be just another middle-aged woman? Wealthy, unhappy Nur wants only to be allowed to travel, but her husband has her passport. With all her money, she sits in a glass house and feels her dissatisfaction deepen. In Hanan al-Shaykh's intricate writing, sometimes whispered, sometimes shouted, is a desperate plea for liberation.

H.S.

The World and the Bo Tree, Helen Bevington, *1991, United States,* ESSAYS

Helen Bevington, a retired English professor, traveled extensively in the 1980s "in search of something—call it a bo tree, or Shangri-La, or earthly paradise—which is only another name for peace itself and these days is decidedly a fool's errand." Her essays and travels take us on a worldwide quest through Africa, Asia, Europe, North and South America. With each journey we get a history lesson, ancient or recent, enhanced by her extraordinary insight and global view of human life. In a remote area of Kenya, surrounded by thousands of wild animals, she encounters one of life's wonders: "I shut my eyes and listened to take the stillness in, to carry it away for future need—the measureless calm, the timeless serenity." Her observations and intimate writing style make reading *The World and the*

Bo Tree a personal adventure; you are with her for a sunrise in Tibet, watching the river rocks change "every shade from brown to magenta to shining gold," and feel anxious with her when she goes back to her hometown "to dispel the more persistent phantoms by looking with my eyes instead of my memory." Helen Bevington has strong political convictions and is not shy about criticizing President Reagan's policies and their global effects. But life itself is her primary interest: its bigness, its vastness, and the small but important role each of us plays.

H.S.

Pioneers and Seekers

A single mother of five, M. Wylie Blanchet takes her children in a twenty-five-foot boat to explore the treacherous Georgia Straits off Vancouver Island. Ida B. Wells launches an anti-lynching campaign in the United States. The women of the Resistance movement in France risk imprisonment and death in their fight against Hitler. Timid Lotty Wilkins and Rose Arbuthnot determine they *will* go to Italy in April, no matter what their husbands say. Here are stories of brave, intelligent women who broaden our vision of what is possible. The quest can be physical, spiritual, political, motivated by economic necessity or the sheer excitement of challenge. After her husband is killed, E. J. Guerin dresses as a man for thirteen years because she cannot support her children as a woman. Nadezhda Durova pretends to be a man in order to join the Russian cavalry; Isabella Bird, a Victorian gentlewoman, rides through ice storms and climbs 14,000-foot peaks; Mary Seacole leaves the Caribbean and travels around the world in a quest for adventure and economic freedom. The women who crossed the Overland Trail, and Mary Paik Lee, who came with her family from Korea to the United States in 1905, did not set out to be heroes, but became so in their determination to survive. These women and their stories are empowering, invigorating, and awe-inspiring.

All But the Waltz	Mary Clearman Blew
Annapurna	Arlene Blum
The Cavalry Maiden	Nadezhda Durova
Crusade for Justice	Ida B. Wells
The Curve of Time	M. Wylie Blanchet
Daughter of the Hills	Myra Page
The Devil Is Loose	Antonine Maillet
Enchanted April	Elizabeth von Arnim
Exile in the Promised Land	Marcia Freedman
Floreana	Margaret Wittmer
Heat and Dust	Ruth Prawer Jhabvala
The Hidden Hand	E.D.E.N. Southworth
A Lady's Life in the Rocky Mountains	Isabella Bird
Libby	Libby Beaman and Betty John
Living My Life	Emma Goldman
Mountain Charley	E. J. Guerin
My Ántonia	Willa Cather
A New Home—Who'll Follow?	Caroline Kirkland
Purple Springs	Nellie L. McClung
Quiet Odyssey	Mary Paik Lee
Spiritual Narratives	Sue E. Houchins, ed.
Tracks	Robyn Davidson
Two in the Far North	Margaret Murie
West with the Night	Beryl Markham
Women's Diaries of the Westward Journey	Lillian Schlissel
Women in the Resistance	Margaret L. Rossiter
Wonderful Adventures of Mrs. Seacole in Many Lands	Mary Seacole

All But the Waltz: A Memoir of Five Generations in the Life of a Montana Family, Mary Clearman Blew, *1991, United States,* MEMOIR

Mary Clearman Blew's *All But the Waltz* is both a compelling book about people and a saga of a powerful place that has dominated the lives of her family for more than a century. By telling the stories of her ancestors, people who began settling in central Montana in 1882, then weaving their tales with her own, she creates a revealing family portrait and a fascinating lesson in the social and economic history of Montana. Although she speaks of the beauty and the feeling of glorious space that comes to inhabit the souls of the homesteaders and their descendants, she also reveals the cruelties imposed by geography, distance, and climate. Debunking the modern-day myth that life in a place like Montana, beautiful and wild, could or should be close to ideal, Mary Blew courageously examines her own reality, and her options as a young woman longing to flee the confines of ranch life and faced with an unexpected pregnancy. Whether you are a Montana native or not, the significance of Mary Blew's "escape," and the profound and beautiful depiction of the people around her, will speak to you.

R.S.

Annapurna: A Woman's Place, Arlene Blum, *1980, Nepal (United States),* MEMOIR

Arlene Blum led the first American and first women's expedition to climb Annapurna I in the Himalayas. *Annapurna* is her story of the climb: from fund-raising (remember the T-shirts that said "A Woman's Place Is on Top"?); to organizing thirteen women, more than 150 boxes of gear, thousands of pounds of food, and numerous Nepalese guides and porters; to the summit ascent itself and the deaths of two climbers. Perhaps because it is told from the perspective of the leader of a team, this is as much a book about management and decisions as it is about climbing a mountain. There are poetic passages about the beauty of the ice, the fantasy of cloudwalking, the terrors of avalanches and crevasses, but more time is spent on the delicate balance that must be kept between native male guides and foreign women climbers, as well as among the women themselves. This is a book about working together under extraordinary conditions where the temperature in your tent can drop to ten degrees below zero and a tiny hole in a glove can mean the possible loss of a finger. It is about making decisions while an avalanche rushes by you with a wind that knocks you over. It is about risking death knowing that you have people you love at home; for a few it means working for years and years, and then choosing at the last minute not to go to the top. At times confusing (keeping track of all the base camps, sherpas, and climbers is a job in itself), at times preachy, this is, in the end, the compelling story of thirteen very different women—ranging in age from nineteen to fifty—each determined to get women to the top of a mountain whose name means "the goddess rich in sustenance."

E.B.

The Cavalry Maiden: Journals of a Russian Officer in the Napoleonic Wars, Nadezhda Durova, *translated from Russian by Mary Fleming Zirin, 1836, Russia,* DIARY

In the early nineteenth century, Nadezhda Durova ran away from home dressed as a man and joined the Russian calvary, where she maintained the secret of her gender and served with distinction as an officer for more than nine years. Her diary, published as *The Cavalry Maiden*, was one of Russia's first autobiographical works, making this book noteworthy both for its content and its place in literary history. Not every reader will enjoy the disjointed and occasionally impersonal style; nor will everyone be interested in Nadezhda Durova's recounting of Russian geography and military history, which takes up much of the middle portion of the book. Yet you don't have to be from the nineteenth century to sympathize when she writes: "I jump for joy as I realize that I will never again in my entire life hear the words: *You, girl, sit still! It's not proper for you to go wandering out alone.*" Nor need you be a scholar of Russian history to appreciate her descriptions of officers, horses, local citizens, and dress balls. Mary Fleming Zirin's introduction illuminates those areas where Nadezhda Durova was not exactly truthful (she was not sixteen and single when she ran away, but twenty-three, married, and a mother), and brings further understanding to this headstrong woman who, as a child, refused to knit shoelaces but "ran and galloped around the room in all directions, shouting at the top of my voice: 'Squadron! To the Right, face! From your places, charge—CHARGE!' "

E.B.

Crusade for Justice: The Autobiography of Ida B. Wells, Ida B. Wells, *Edited by Alfreda M. Duster, 1928 (1970), United States,* AUTOBIOGRAPHY

Toward the end of her life, realizing that her work was already becoming forgotten history, Ida B. Wells wrote the massive, unfinished memoirs that form *Crusade for Justice.* An outspoken and determined woman with seemingly limitless energy, Ida B. Wells began her crusade against the oppression of black people in 1884, when, at the age of sixteen, she sued the Chesapeake and Ohio Railroad for evicting her from a first-class car. She became a teacher and a journalist but when a close friend was murdered, she began a one-woman antilynching campaign. She traveled throughout England and later in the United States gaining support; got married; began the first clubs for black women in the United States; started a reading room, shelter, and employment service for black men in Chicago; investigated race riots; and had six children. Her children and husband remain almost invisible in this book, but what *Crusade for Justice* lacks in domestic detail, it makes up for in personal opinion. Ida B. Wells was a forthright woman who worked with many famous leaders of the early twentieth century, and she does not hesitate to blast her opponents, and to praise those who earned her respect—including President Woodrow Wilson, Booker T. Washington, Susan B. Anthony, and Frederick Douglass. Her history is packed with facts not often taught in schools, and filled with the fervor of a woman who spent her life proving that one person can and must make a difference.

E.B.

The Curve of Time, M. Wylie Blanchet, *1968, Canada,* MEMOIR

M. Wylie Blanchet was only thirty-six when her husband died in 1927, leaving her with an isolated home on Vancouver Island and five children, the smallest one two and a half years old. When relatives advised her that she couldn't manage alone, she sent back a telegram: "Can't I?" She proceeded to educate her children at home during the winter, and in the summer to take them on expeditions aboard their twenty-five-foot boat through the often treacherous straits off Vancouver Island. *The Curve of Time* recounts her memories of these expeditions—of encounters with cougars, deserted Indian villages, engine failures, and eccentric hermits; of long evenings and free trout. Those looking for a family saga or an explanation of how a single mother manages all the daily details of such expeditions will be frustrated. What we do get, beautifully and abundantly, is M. Wylie Blanchet's curiosity, the feeling of the water, and a strong sense of a family—fighting tides and rapids, swimming naked in the sun, and then looking up all their questions in the *Encyclopaedia Britannica* when they get home.

E.B.

Daughter of the Hills: A Woman's Part in the Coal Miner's Struggle, Myra Page, *1950, United States,* NOVEL

Daughter of the Hills (originally titled *With the Sun in Our Blood*) is a novel based on the true story of Dolly Hawkins Cooper's life—of her home in the Cumberland Mountains of Tennessee, of her coal-mining family and their heritage of labor and political struggle, of her love for the miner John Cooper and their enviable marriage, of his death, and of battles with the coal company to provide medical and environmental protection for its workers. As Dolly grows from girlhood into womanhood, so her sense of responsibility evolves from love and concern for her immediate family to a commitment to her community and eventually to mining communities throughout the country. The novel takes us through Dolly's husband's death; the preface and afterword describe Dolly's development into a speaker and community organizer, and her studies at Commonwealth College in Arkansas, an experimental college founded in the 1930s upon the themes of labor history, organizing strategy, and Marxist theory. It was there that she and her teacher, Myra Page, working together in the classroom and in the field, became close friends. Written in the tradition of social activism and the political literature of the 1930s, with ardent attention to the dialect, customs, music, folklore, and scenery of the Tennessee coal-mining world, *Daughter of the Hills* is both a powerful love story and a novel of social protest for the people and communities who live as victims of corporate power and greed.

K.B.-B.

The Devil Is Loose, Antonine Maillet, *translated from French by Philip Stratford, 1986, Canada,* NOVEL

"Around about the start of the Thirties, the weathercock of the world suddenly began spinning like crazy." So begins Antonine Maillet's rollicking, irreverent look at the effects of the Depression years and prohibition in Canada's French-speaking Maritimes. It's a tale of rumrunners and hunger, love and rivalry, storytellers and the supernatural. The heroine is Crache-A-Pic (Spit-In-Your-Eye), a true woman of the sea, whose stories are told in a wonderful, friendly style. As a young bootlegger (or "Galosh," as she prefers to call herself) she dazzles the villagers and infuriates her adversaries with her daring and clever feats. From raising a holy ruckus disguised as a nun, to deviously foiling her arch rivals' plans, she outsails and outwits her fellow bootleggers and the law. Sly, compassionate, and above all fearless, Crache-A-Pic spits in the eye of convention. This vibrant, well-woven, and entertainingly authentic book begs to be read out loud.

S.L.

Enchanted April, Elizabeth von Arnim, *1922, Italy/England (England),* NOVEL

Enchanted April is a book for anyone who feels stiff, unloved, or used up—a restful, funny, sumptuous, and invigorating vacation for the mind and soul. It begins one cold, rainy February afternoon soon after the end of World War I, when Mrs. Arbuthnot and Mrs. Wilkins come across an advertisement for a villa in Italy to rent for the month of April. Mrs. Arbuthnot, with the "face of a patient and disappointed Madonna," and Mrs. Wilkins, "her clothes infested by thrift," barely know each other, yet the fantasy of a wisteria-covered Italian villa sparks something in each and brings them together. They raid their meager nest eggs, find two more women—the formidable Mrs. Fisher and the unspeakably lovely but bored Lady Caroline Dester—to help defray costs, and set off for their dream of sunshine and beauty. At San Salvatore, remarkable changes occur. Mrs. Wilkins becomes Lotty—intuitive, sensual, self-confident; Mrs. Arbuthnot loses her religious self-righteousness. Lady Caroline finds herself with "that really rather disgusting suspicion that her life till now had not only been loud but empty," while Mrs. Fisher starts to feel a "very odd and exciting sensation of going to come out all over buds." Elizabeth von Arnim portrays these transformations in wickedly dry British humor interwoven with descriptions of the lush, soul-stirring terrain of San Salvatore. The effect is refreshing, charming, and romantic.

E.B.

Exile in the Promised Land, Marcia Freedman, *1990, Israel* (*United States*), MEMOIR

In 1967, realizing a long-held dream, Marcia Freedman moved with her husband and young daughter from the United States to Israel. Within four years she became a founding member of Israel's women's movement, fulfilling a need based on personal discoveries that "housework and childcare are exploitive when unshared; that anatomy need not be destiny; that anger is a rational response to oppression . . . I learned that like Blacks, like Jews, women needed a liberation movement." In 1973 she was elected, unexpectedly, to the Knesset, Israel's governing body. Issues she raised about wife abuse or abortion choices were met with ridicule and personal attacks; these escalated as she became an outspoken proponent of Palestinian autonomy. Political life took its toll, and her marriage of thirteen years ended as she came to acknowledge and accept herself as a lesbian. In addition to shedding historical light on a critical area of the world, Marcia Freedman shows us a woman who struggled with questions bigger than herself, a woman who found some answers and even more questions.

H.S.

Floreana: A Woman's Pilgrimage to the Galapagos, Margaret Wittmer, *1959, Ecuador* (*Germany*), MEMOIR

In 1932, Margaret Wittmer leaves Germany with her husband and stepson and travels to Floreana, a small, almost unpopulated island in the Galapagos chain, where they settle, clear land, and, after five months of living in old pirates' caves, move into the house they finish just in time for Margaret to have a baby. Over time, the Wittmers acquire a number of remarkable neighbors, including convicts, military personnel, and a mysterious baroness who aspires to build a hotel for millionaires. They receive visits from people as diverse as Franklin D. Roosevelt and Thor Heyerdahl, who comes to investigate a reported "head" much like the ones on Easter Island, only to find it was carved by Margaret's husband. There are wild bulls and boars, a dog named Lump that serves as a baby-sitter, a distant war, a daughter who would rather have a machete or a hoe than a doll, years of settled life, and finally grandchildren. At times the entire situation borders on the unbelievable, but Margaret Wittmer provides equal measures of intrigue, fantasy, and common sense as she writes in her down-to-earth and often very humorous fashion about her years on Floreana.

E.B.

Heat and Dust, Ruth Prawer Jhabvala, *1975, India,* NOVEL

Heat and Dust views India through the lives of two Englishwomen living fifty years apart. Olivia is the first wife of an English government official assigned to India in the 1920s. The unnamed narrator of the story—the young granddaughter of the same official by a later wife—is intrigued by family rumors about Olivia and travels to India seeking answers to Olivia's mysterious existence. How, in a segregated society, did Olivia meet an Indian prince of questionable character, and why did she leave her husband for him? What happened to her afterward? As the narrator stays in the town where Olivia lived, and visits places that influenced Olivia's life, we witness India's past through Olivia's letters and journals and the narrator's imagination. For Olivia, removed from the day-to-day existence of the Indian people, India "was like being not in a different part of this world but in another world altogether, in another reality." In contrast, the narrator sublets a room that shares a courtyard with an Indian family and learns much about their life. Ruth Prawer Jhabvala shows us India before and after independence, and exposes the similarities and differences of India's impact on each of these women.

H.S.

The Hidden Hand, E.D.E.N. Southworth, *1859, United States,* NOVEL

E.D.E.N. Southworth was one of the most popular and prolific writers of the nineteenth century, and her Capitola Black, or Black Cap—a cross-dressing, adventure-seeking girl-woman—was so well loved that the book was serialized three times between 1859 and 1888, and dramatized in forty different versions. When we first meet sharp and witty Capitola she is living among beggars and street urchins, dressed as a boy because a boy can get work and be safe, whereas a girl is left to starve for want of "proper" employment. Unknown to her, Capitola has a very rich elderly guardian who finds her at a providential moment and takes her back to his palatial mansion. Soon, she finds herself "decomposing above ground for want of having my blood stirred." But not to fear. There are bandits, true loves, evil men, long-lost mothers, and sweet women friends in Capitola's future—not to mention thunderstorms, kidnap attempts, and duels. The pace is fast, the action wonderfully unbelievable. This is escape literature at its nineteenth-century best, with a woman at its center who makes you feel strong, daring, and reckless.

E.B.

A Lady's Life in the Rocky Mountains, Isabella Bird, *1879, United States (England),* LETTERS

In 1854, at the age of twenty-two, Isabella Bird left England and began traveling as a cure for her ill health. Over the years she explored Asia, the Sandwich Islands, Hawaii, and both the eastern and western United States. *A Lady's Life in the Rocky Mountains* contains letters written to her sister during her six-month journey through the Colorado Rockies in 1873. Traveling alone, usually on horseback, often with no clear idea of where she will spend the night in what is mostly uninhabited wilderness, she covers more than a thousand miles, mostly during the winter months. A well-educated woman who had known a comfortable life, she thinks nothing of herding cattle at a hard gallop, falling through ice, getting lost in snowstorms, and living in a cabin where the temperatures are well below zero and her ink freezes even as she writes. She befriends desperadoes and climbs 14,000-foot mountains, ready for any adventure that allows her to see the unparalleled beauty of nature. Her rare complaints have more to do with having to ride side-saddle while in town than with the life-endangering conditions she faces in the mountains. An awe-inspiring woman, she is also a talented writer who brings to life Colorado of more than one hundred years ago, when today's big cities were only small collections of frame houses, and wild and beautiful areas were still largely untouched.

E.B.

Libby: The Alaskan Diaries and Letters of Libby Beaman, 1879–1880, as Presented by her Granddaughter Betty John, Libby Beaman and Betty John, *1879–1880* (*1987*), *United States,* DIARY/LETTERS

In 1879, Elizabeth Beaman accompanied her husband to the Alaskan Pribilof Islands on his government assignment to oversee the slaughter of fur seals. Her diary and letters, put in a narrative form by her granddaughter, recount her life during this period. Libby Beaman was an amazing woman—she had a job as a mapmaker when "respectable" women were not allowed careers; she sustained a four-year secret courtship and convinced her fiancé to change his career in order to facilitate an introduction to her family. It was Libby's personal petition to President Rutherford B. Hayes that was responsible for her husband's assignment in the Pribilofs (a fact she never told her husband). As the first white woman on the Pribilof Islands, Libby was a curiosity to the natives and a source of resentment and passion for her husband's superior. Libby and her husband survived violent sea storms, raging jealousy, and an Arctic winter that nearly killed them. Through it all, Libby appears indomitable, and above all, curious—about the people, the seals, the wildlife around her. Her husband resents the experience; she relishes it. The easy continuity and the novelistic rise and fall of action make this more an adventure story than a diary (and might cause problems for a purist who would prefer that gaps were not "filled in" by Libby's granddaughter). What makes this book important, however, is this strong-willed, spirited woman and the life *she* chose to lead.

E.B.

Living My Life, Emma Goldman, *1931, United States,* AUTOBIOGRAPHY

In *Living My Life*, Emma Goldman, called "Red Emma" or "The Anarchist Queen" by the United States government and other detractors, describes her philosophical and political journey through life. We witness the politicization of this young Russian immigrant as she arrives in the United States in 1886, begins her first job in a sweatshop, and becomes inflamed by the Haymarket labor riots of 1887. Over the next forty years of her life as an anarchist, she wends her way through the labyrinth of American, Russian, and European radical politics. *Living My Life* is a graphic description of the labor movement in the United States; of bitterly fought battles and ensuing jail terms over free speech, free love, and the right to birth control; and of day-by-day political and personal life in Russia immediately following the 1917 revolution. Emma Goldman applies the same unrelenting scrutiny to her political actions and the actions and philosophies of governments that she does to her personal relationships. The power of this book lies in the intimate nature of her narrative—in the daily accounts of the friendships, love affairs, doubts, and joys of Emma Goldman and her revolutionary colleagues—overlaid on the canvas of major world events.

K.B.-B.

Mountain Charley or the Adventures of Mrs. E. J. Guerin, Who Was Thirteen Years in Male Attire, Mrs. E. J. Guerin, *1861 (1968), United States,* AUTOBIOGRAPHY

Mountain Charley is a woman you won't soon forget. Widowed at fifteen with two small children and no means of support, she decides to dress as a man, not only out of economic necessity but also to gain greater access to her husband's murderer. Placing her children with the "Sisters of Charity," she works on Mississippi River steamboats for four years under her assumed identity. She is able to pay her children's fees and visits them whenever possible, dressed in women's clothing. Soon she discovers: "I began to rather like the freedom of my new character . . . the more convenient, healthful habiliments of a man, was in itself almost sufficient to compensate for its unwomanly character." In 1855, Mountain Charley takes the first of several trips out West. Over the years she works as a gold miner, owns a saloon, and herds cattle, and continues to dress as a man even after being "discovered." This book contains her autobiography, unchanged from the original 1861 self-published text, as well as newspaper articles of other "Mountain Charleys," including a lengthy report of one woman who fought in the Civil War. All these Mountain Charleys are fascinating, and their exploits and accomplishments provide entertaining and enlightening reading well over a century later.

H.S.

My Ántonia, Willa Cather, *1918, United States,* NOVEL

My Ántonia is set in Nebraska at a time when "there was nothing but land: not a country at all, but the material out of which countries are made." Through the eyes of young Jim Burden, the reader sees the land that rolls "as if the shaggy grass were a sort of loose hide, and underneath it herds of wild buffalo were galloping, galloping." The people who live here are immigrants—the tragic Russian brothers, Norwegian Lena Lingard with her violet eyes and her determination never to marry, and most importantly, Bohemian Ántonia Shimerda. Their stories stand out like framed portraits against the backdrop of the prairie, and remind us how many different countries make up the United States. Warm as the perfect summer, Jim's memories tell of the land and of Ántonia, a girl who works the fields like a man and who hears the songs of old Bohemian women in the cries of a cricket. In Ántonia, Willa Cather portrays one of the great women of literature—strong, capable, and honest. *My Ántonia* is a book to read to children to show them what women can be; or to read—and remind—yourself.

E.B.

A New Home—Who'll Follow?, or Glimpses of Western Life, Caroline Kirkland, *1839, United States,* NOVEL

A New Home—Who'll Follow?, or Glimpses of Western Life broke ground in early-nineteenth-century American writing for its forthright realism and keenly satiric narrative style. Using her own experience of moving to an unsettled village in Michigan in the 1830s, Caroline Kirkland not only describes the life and times of individuals immersed in the growth and establishment of a community, but also subtly imbues her text with a sophisticated cultural criticism. As a displaced Easterner and a newly identified Westerner, writing under the name Mary Clavers, she describes mud holes, drunken husbands, local politics, and Victorian American values in her witty and often sharply ironic voice: "I should be disposed to recommend a course of Michigan to the Sybarites, the puny exquisites, the world-worn and sated Epicureans of our cities. If I mistake not, they would make surprising advances in philosophy in the course of a few months' training." The idea for her regional description of village life was sparked when her friends responded enthusiastically to the letters she was posting from Pickney, Michigan—renamed Montacute in the book. When the book was published, however, she found that her satirizations of her neighbors' clothing, habits, romantic illusions, and gender conventions got her in so much trouble with her small community that she vowed never to be so honest in her writing again.

L.T.-S.

Purple Springs, Nellie L. McClung, *1921, Canada,* NOVEL

With courage and hard work, Pearl Watson's Irish immigrant parents carve out a living on a prairie farm in Manitoba in the early 1900s. In *Purple Springs*, the third of Nellie McClung's semi-autobiographical novels, Pearl is eighteen years old and glad to be home from Normal School, where she has created a sensation with her sweet disposition, excellent academic work, and outspoken opinions. Her hopes are high as she waits for wonderful young Dr. Clay to fulfill the promise he made three years earlier. When the promise does not come as expected, Pearl hides her disappointment and remembers her mother's warning: "There's lots of trouble for them that don't marry, and there's lots more for them that do." Faced with the need to earn her living in an era when single women are cruelly maligned and isolated, and married women have no legal rights, Pearl accepts a job as the teacher at Purple Springs. Here, new facts about people and politics force her to articulate unpopular truths. Filled with moral outrage at the devastating domestic situations faced by two of her students' mothers, Pearl plunges into the work of winning a public commitment to justice for women. Through lovely prose that celebrates "labor-honed" faces, domestic detail, changing weather, and the value of humor, we accompany Pearl through her struggle to maintain her belief in love and marriage while she fights to win disenfranchised Canadian women a legal voice.

J.L.

Quiet Odyssey: A Pioneer Korean Woman in America, Mary Paik Lee, *edited by Su Cheng Chan, 1990, United States,* AUTOBIOGRAPHY

Forced by Japanese soldiers to leave their home in Korea, Paik Kuang Sun (later Mary Paik Lee), her parents, and her brother emigrate to the United States in 1905, leaving behind their extended family and comfortable way of life. They spend one year in Hawaii, then move on to California, where they change locations every year or so in hopes of finding work that will allow them to feed and clothe their rapidly growing family. Mary Lee writes of "whites only" signs, of laws that prohibit Asians from renting or buying property, of the year they ate only biscuits and water. Through it all her father works at backbreaking and sometimes life-endangering jobs, always ready to give to others who are in need. Mary grows up to be a hardworking, honest, and caring woman, prepared to stand up for what she believes is right, particularly when it comes to racism. Written with the intimacy of an oral history, her memoir allows the reader into the life of one of the few (perhaps less than three dozen) Korean-born children growing up on the West Coast before 1910. Su Cheng Chan, the book's editor, has added an extensive introduction and appendix which place Mary Lee's autobiography within a detailed historical and cultural context without invading its boundaries. The result is a book that can be read both as a piece of a history and as the personal testament of one courageous woman.

E.B.

Spiritual Narratives, Sue E. Houchins, editor, *1835/1849/ 1886/1907, United States,* NONFICTION

Sue Houchins's *Spiritual Narratives* brings together the religious writings of four nineteenth-century African-American women: Maria Stewart, Jarena Lee, Julia Foote, and Virginia Broughton. Because each of these extraordinary black women accomplished significant feats despite fierce racial and gender oppression, this collection is a rare treat. The first American-born woman to address both blacks and whites, men and women, Maria Stewart was an electrifying orator; her writings are full of passion and are political as well as pious. Like Maria Stewart, Jarena Lee was a Northern, free-born black woman who spoke out against such injustices as sexual discrimination and slavery; while her text is sometimes cumbersome because of its precise and laborious detail, it tells a triumphant story. Julia A. Foote's narrative is characterized by a bold, sassy style; it challenges stereotypes of nineteenth-century black women as docile, illiterate, or envious of white privilege. Virginia W. Broughton's autobiography is unusual for its third-person perspective. Unlike the other three writers here, all Northerners, Virginia Broughton, born in Virginia, was college-educated; her memoir describes her work in "colored schools" throughout the post-emancipation South. Skeptical and devout readers alike will be moved to contemplation and admiration by the broadly divergent rhetorical power and piety of these four women.

J.M.

Tracks, Robyn Davidson, *1982, Australia,* MEMOIR

Why does Robyn Davidson walk 1,700 miles across the Australian desert accompanied by four camels? *Tracks* is a quintessential adventure, yet the adventurer's relationship to her own quest is ambivalent and nuanced. She never directly explains her motivations, but it's clear that she's been driven to the starkness and isolation of the desert by something so personally powerful that she may not understand it herself. Ironically, when she accepts the financial backing of the *National Geographic,* her private "trial by fire" is doused by the popular concept of romantic independence she represents to others: "I was beginning to see it as a story for other people, with a beginning and an ending." She feels pursued and invaded by the photographer assigned to follow her, by the people who intercept her with questions and interpretations. Yet her ultimate confrontations are with her own rage and desperation, with the personal and cultural repercussions of racism and misogyny in her own experience, and with the paradoxical ugliness and beauty of the rural Australia she encounters. The integrity of this articulate and impassioned account is evident in the fact that Robyn Davidson does not find glib solutions to inner or outer conflicts. Like her camel companions, she seems temperamental, insatiable, and slightly crazy, but also determined, direct, vulnerable, and splendid.

K.B.

Two in the Far North, Margaret Murie, *1962, United States,* AUTOBIOGRAPHY

Two in the Far North is the life story of Margaret Murie, who grew up in Alaska before it was a state, tramped its wild lands before they were mapped, and has worked hard to preserve its wild places. She went north at age nine to a new life in a log cabin in Fairbanks. Her childhood was filled with the dangers and thrills of life on the frontier: the night the town caught fire and her father and the other men burned the town's bacon supply to keep the water pump going; an exciting cross-country trip on the last dog sled mail run of the year over rivers that were breaking up; the dazzling weekly arrival of the mail sleigh with its flamboyant driver. When she graduated from college, she married—at three a.m., just before the arctic sun rose—a young biologist named Olaus Murie. Together they spent the next fifty years exploring and mapping the wilderness of Alaska, researching, studying, and counting its wildlife by dogsled, snowshoe, ski, boat, and floatplane—sometimes with a baby in tow. She shares all of these adventures in buoyant, lively prose. For Margaret Murie, it is the people as much as the place that make Alaska home, and her book is a loving tribute to both.

M.L.

West with the Night, Beryl Markham, *1942, Kenya,* AUTOBIOGRAPHY

West with the Night is an exceptional autobiography filled with a strong spirit, fascinating events, and beautiful words. Beryl Markham was raised by her father on a large farm in British East Africa in the early twentieth century; as a child she preferred spear hunting with the native Muranis to learning her school lessons. At seventeen, when her father lost their farm and went to Peru, she chose to stay in Africa and began a highly successful career as a race horse trainer. In her twenties she gave up horses and started flying airplanes, becoming the first woman in East Africa to be granted a commercial pilot's license, then the first woman to fly the Atlantic from east to west. Lyrically and philosophically, *West with the Night* covers each of these parts of her life. Beryl Markham writes hunting stories filled with danger and tension, then turns and discusses the different qualities of silence, or what it is like to fly alone over water for forty hours: "Being alone in an aeroplane for even so short a time as a night and a day, irrevocably alone, with nothing to observe but your instruments and your own hands in the semi-darkness, nothing to contemplate but your own small courage. . . . Such an experience can be as startling as the first awareness of a stranger walking by your side at night. You are the stranger." This is the story of an extraordinary woman—and that alone might be enough to recommend it. The fact that it is also extraordinarily well written makes it a gift.

E.B.

Women's Diaries of the Westward Journey, Lillian Schlissel, *1982, United States,* HISTORY/DIARIES

After the depression of 1837, the prospect of "free land" and gold prompted more than 250,000 people to emigrate to Oregon and California between 1840 and 1870. History, relying predominantly on men's writings, often presents this journey in terms of mythic adventure. But what was it like for women? After studying the writings of 103 women, Lillian Schlissel determined, "If ever there was a time when men and women turned their psychic energies toward opposite visions, the overland journey was that time." In *Women's Diaries of the Westward Journey*, she explores her findings, quoting at length from her sources and including a selection of diaries and reminiscences at the end. Although unmarried adolescents were often exuberant about their experience, for the married women, particularly those with young children, the trip was fraught with danger and fear. Children could fall under wagon wheels, or be left behind in the confusion of traveling with as many as one hundred other wagons. There were buffalo stampedes, Indian attacks, snakebites, dysentery, starvation, and cholera; many women note individual graves, sometimes one per mile. In addition, one of every five women was pregnant when the journey began or became so in the course of a trip that guidebooks said would take three to four months, but often took six to eight. Through Lillian Schlissel's fascinating and extremely readable account, we gain a fuller understanding of the journey few of these women wanted to take.

E.B.

Women in the Resistance, Margaret L. Rossiter, *1986, France (United States),* NONFICTION

Margaret L. Rossiter is a professor of history, and her book on the role of women in the French Resistance during World War II reads like a well-researched textbook: the tone is unemotional, the thesis is clearly stated in the preface, the facts are chronologically presented and accompanied by twenty-eight pages of footnotes and twelve pages of bibliography. The subject matter, however, transforms the work from a scholarly documentation of historical facts into a collection of heroic stories. A virtual manual on the workings of the French Resistance from 1940 to 1945, *Women in the Resistance* is filled with the details of organizing and leading escape lines, clandestinely gathering and transmitting military information, publishing and circulating underground newspapers, sabotaging targets, and fighting in partisan combat. The women who perform these feats—smart, courageous, strong, and dedicated—range in age from teenagers to older women with grandchildren. Their stories make us wonder: Could I have been this strong of spirit and body and mind? How would I have stood up to such a threat to my home and life? This book takes us from the global stage of world history to the inner world of personal courage, carefully documenting both as it shows us how women were propelled into extraordinary action by their determination to defy and defeat Hitler.

K.B.-B.

Wonderful Adventures of Mrs. Seacole in Many Lands, Mary Seacole, *1861, Jamaica/Panama/Crimea (Jamaica),* MEMOIR

Mary Seacole, a free-born Jamaican Creole, claims that from her Scottish father she received her energy and vitality, and from her Jamaican "doctress" mother she learned the healing skills that she used throughout her life. As a child living near an English military base, Mary Seacole watches and helps her mother treat the military personnel seeking medical attention, and develops a lifelong feeling of affection for the British. When her husband dies, Mary earns her living by doctoring. In Panama, Yankees who admire her skill offer to bleach her "yeller" skin. Her response is typically blunt: "As to the society which the process might gain me admission into, all I can say is, that, judging from the specimens I have met here and elsewhere, I don't think that I shall lose much by being excluded from it." The Crimean War breaks out in 1854, and Mary learns that many British officers she knew in Jamaica are fighting there. With characteristic perseverance, in spite of obstacles placed in her path, she finally arrives there. Though she describes her battlefield experiences with much humor, she feels deeply the horrors of war and loss of life. A woman independent beyond her times, Mary Seacole still has much to teach.

H.S.

Places and Homes

A piece of land, a mountain, a river—all can exist without a human presence. People have rarely had this capacity for separation, however. Wherever they are, they send out their tendrils of associations, memories, needs, and questions, intertwining themselves into the landscape, making it a home. When Gretel Ehrlich goes to Wyoming to make a film, she finds a land of "no alibis, no self-promoting schemes." She stays. Sandra Cisneros, Lynda Barry, Cherry Muhanji, and Rosellen Brown re-create the energy, conflict, and vibrancy of four urban neighborhoods. Rosario and Aurora Morales create homes through family traditions in New York, Puerto Rico, and Chicago. Barbara Grizzuti Harrison and Ann Cornelisen both come as outsiders to Italy: one writes a lush, philosophical travel guide that revels in the country's beauty and culture; the other organizes child care centers and describes the almost overwhelming poverty that exists in rural southern towns. Writing from Australia and Utah respectively, Oodgeroo Nunukul and Terry Tempest Williams recall the wonder of childhood haunts and mourn the destruction caused by those who see nature as an opportunity for exploitation. In their conscious and sometimes unconscious interactions with the land around them, these authors remind us how integral and influential are the relationships that exist between humans and our environments.

Bake-Face and Other Guava Stories	Opal Palmer Adisa
Beka Lamb	Zee Edgell
A Belfast Woman	Mary Beckett
Getting Home Alive	Aurora Levins Morales and Rosario Morales
The Good Times Are Killing Me	Lynda Barry
Hannah Senesh: Her Life & Diary	Hannah Senesh
Her	Cherry Muhanji
The House on Mango Street	Sandra Cisneros
The Irish R.M.	E. Somerville and Martin Ross
Italian Days	Barbara Grizzuti Harrison
The Land of Little Rain	Mary Austin
Lemon Swamp and Other Places	Mamie Garvin Fields with Karen Fields
Mute Phone Calls and Other Stories	Ruth Zernova
My Mother's House	Colette
Now in November	Josephine Johnson
Out of Africa	Isak Dinesen
Refuge	Terry Tempest Williams
River Time	Janet Lembke
The Solace of Open Spaces	Gretel Ehrlich
Stradbroke Dreamtime	Oodgeroo Nunukul
Street Games	Rosellen Brown
Talking to the Dead	Sylvia Watanabe
Winter Wheat	Mildred Walker
Women of the Shadows	Ann Cornelisen
Womenfolks	Shirley Abbott

Bake-Face and Other Guava Stories, Opal Palmer Adisa, *1986, Jamaica (United States),* SHORT STORIES

These warm, descriptive stories bring to life the existence of four rural Jamaican women. "Bake-Face" has escaped an abusive family through her marriage to a kind man, but it's a marriage without love. Bake-Face and Mr. Johnson have had an affair for five years, an affair in which she "discovered that laughter found her and she could cry. . . . She cried without fearing that the ground would open up and take her in." In "Duppy Get Her," a very pregnant Lilly is told by her cousin, "Dis a definite boy picknie yuh a guh ave. See how yuh belly pointed and de sonofabitch won gi yuh nuh peace." During her pregnancy and after her son's birth, Lilly has encounters with duppies—ghosts—which makes her an object of both respect and fear from others. "Me Man Angel" tells of a young child's impact on the village and how, even after his death, "whenever two or more women gather in the community of Monstrance, their talk always comes around to Perry." In "Widow's Walk," June-Plum is tempted again and again to give herself to Yemoja, mistress of the sea. The spirit world is a powerful presence in these stories, which invite the reader to feel and appreciate its force.

H.S.

Beka Lamb, Zee Edgell, *1982, Belize,* NOVEL

Twelve-year-old Beka Lamb lives in Belize City, "a relatively tolerant town" where people with their roots in Africa, the West Indies, Central America, Europe, North America, Asia, and other places, "lived in a kind of harmony. In three centuries, miscegenation, like logwood, had produced all shades of black and brown, not grey or purple or violet." Beka knows her family's history from Gran, who tells of "befo' time," when they were slaves, and now, when Beka can win an essay contest at the Convent school: "Befo' time . . . Beka would never have won that contest. . . . But things can change fi true." And change they do. Before she won the essay contest, Beka's days were filled with family, domestic work, food, school, neighbors, politics, hurricanes, and dreaming with her best friend, fourteen-year-old Toycie. Before the contest, Sundays were the days she and Toycie walked Beka's baby brother through the rich neighborhoods to the seashore and planned the redecorating they would do when they owned the houses they passed, the days Beka waited patiently while Toycie talked to her boyfriend. Before the contest, Beka lied, got caught, got punished, and lied again. Before the contest, Toycie was still alive. *Beka Lamb* is a beautiful and lovingly told story of a few months in the life of a young woman growing up in a time and place of constant change.

J.L.

A Belfast Woman, Mary Beckett, *1980, Ireland,* SHORT STORIES

This collection of eleven trenchant short stories centers on what it means to be a woman in Catholic Ireland, where marriage is expected, a wife's criticism of her husband is unacceptable, and divorce is impossible. "The Excursion" recounts nervous Eleanor's plan to ask her silent husband James for the money to go on a trip to Dublin. In "Theresa," the presence—and gifts—of American soldiers during the war years liven up the life of young Theresa. Even her unexpected pregnancy does not seriously threaten her confidence as she reassures her mother: "Oh, don't go on like that . . . I'll have the baby in the hospital and I'll leave it in the home and I'll be back to work the same as I always was." The title story describes a few days in the life of a Catholic widow, residing in a Protestant neighborhood, who receives a threatening letter: "Get out or we'll burn you out." Each skillfully rendered portrait of an ordinary Irish woman celebrates the extraordinary inner strength necessary to survive the emotional and physical poverty often engendered by this frequently embittered tradition.

J.L.

Getting Home Alive, Aurora Levins Morales and Rosario Morales, *1986, United States/Puerto Rico,* ESSAYS/SHORT STORIES

Rosario and Aurora Morales are mother and daughter; Rosario was born in Puerto Rico, the daughter of Russian Jewish immigrants who moved to New York when Rosario was young; Aurora was born in New York and as a child moved with her parents to Puerto

Rico. *Getting Home Alive* is their book. Written in alternating voices, these sketches, short stories, and poems, spanning continents, generations, languages, religions, and cultures, celebrate the lives of mothers, daughters, grandmothers, sisters, friends, and family. Home is where the children are born, the food smells of garlic and oregano, the language is loose and round and rolls fluidly from the mouth, and green hillsides are outside kitchen windows. Home is in any kitchen, wherever it is, when the tablecloth woven by one grandmother, "dyed by another, embroidered by another still . . . [is] put there in the center every year in memory of our mothers." Home is all the places both have lived; "even Chicago, grim old gritty dust heap of a city had its blues its trains, had its Northern Black Irish Polish Russian Hillbilly Puerto Rican Ojibwe meatpacking railroad citylake city spirit, worthy of love." Home is sadness for the English language when it is "robbed of the beat your home talk could give it, the words you could lend, the accent, the music, the word-order reordering, the grammatical twist." Home is in the hearts from which Rosario and Aurora speak.

J.L.

The Good Times Are Killing Me, Lynda Barry, *1988, United States,* NOVEL

In the first of forty-one short chapters, young Edna Arkins invites us to "Come over here and look out this window. You see that street? That's my same old street. I know everything that has ever happened on it." The neighborhood is changing: "In the beginning of this street it was a mainly white street. That was a long time ago, but I can remember the houses went White, White, White, Japanese, White, White." When Bonna Willis moves close to Edna, their on-again off-again friendship begins; now that they've finished seventh grade, it's off: "I already know she won't be caught dead talking to no honky bitch this year, and the same goes for her from me only backwards using the word I won't say." Edna's memories are triggered by music, which makes her wonder how "hearing a certain song can make a whole entire time of your life suddenly just rise up and stick in your brain." Tales about family breakups, nervous breakdowns, betrayals, fights, and teenagers having babies mingle with tales of sisters, brothers, Girl Scouts, aunts, best friends, and mean music teachers. The stories, superbly written in plain "white" English that sings and rocks with pain and pride, are accompanied by a "Music Notebook" at the end: seventeen color reproductions of Lynda Barry's gorgeous mixed-media musician paintings. *The Good Times Are Killing Me* is an absolute treat.

J.L.

Hannah Senesh: Her Life & Diary, Hannah Senesh, *translated from Hebrew by Marta Cohn, 1933–1944 (1966), Hungary/Israel,* DIARY/LETTERS

During her brief life, 1921–1944, Hannah Senesh became a national hero in Israel. Her diary begins in 1933 in her native Budapest. In the midst of entries about school, boys, and travel, her growing awareness of herself as a Zionist emerges; while she is learning Hebrew and making plans to move to Palestine, thoughts on the impending war pepper her writing. In 1939, she moves to Palestine to attend the Girl's Agricultural School and work on a kibbutz. That same year, World War II is formally declared. Hannah feels powerless in the face of its horrors: "We can do nothing else; we're forbidden to take action, though there is certainly a difference between passivity and inactivity." But she volunteers, the only female, for a parachute troop with a secret mission to land behind enemy lines in Yugoslavia, sneak into occupied Hungary, and warn the Jewish population, including her mother, of their imminent fate. Tension is strong in her last letter, penned the day she parachutes into Yugoslavia. The next section of the book is written by two fellow parachuters who provide more details about their mission and portray Hannah Senesh as a brave, wise, and compassionate woman. The last section is written by her mother, who was imprisoned in Budapest when Hannah was captured and brought to the same jail. There Hannah was tortured and died at age twenty-three.

H.S.

Her, Cherry Muhanji, *1990, United States,* NOVEL

"Houses collect things: old newspapers, junk mail—Her. She had come under cover of night, a stowaway with Brother's child tucked in the bottom of her belly. He had stuck his Alabama dirt farmer finger in her Dee-troit urban-ghetto Ford Motor Company hi-yellah hole and she had went from somewhere to nowhere, somehow." From the opening sentence, *Her* is a novel whose words refuse to be constrained by the boundaries of its pages. Like jazz that reaches out to both heart and gut, it is deep, throaty, and rich; its language and characters wail, leap, glide, and moan as Cherry Muhanji describes Detroit in the late 1950s and in particular a place called John R. Street. During the day John R. is filled with black women on their way to clean white women's houses and black men going to the factory where "the metal would roll out as they 'picked' their way through the field of Henry Ford's new invention—the assembly line." At night, the neon lights come on and John R. is "the strip" —full of nightclubs, pimps, hookers, female impersonators, and cruising johns. Whether day or night, John R. Street and its inhabitants are painfully, angrily, vibrantly alive, fighting a world that prefers light skin over dark, heterosexuality over homosexuality, money over spirit. From a central core of strong women characters, Cherry Muhanji experiments and elaborates, playing variations, solos, and combinations up and down the register. Her creation is both eye-opening and sensual.

E.B.

The House on Mango Street, Sandra Cisneros, *1991, United States,* SHORT STORIES

Esperanza and her family didn't always live on Mango Street. Right off she says she can't remember all the houses they've lived in, but "the house on Mango Street is ours and we don't have to pay rent to anybody, or share the yard with the people downstairs, or be careful not to make too much noise, and there isn't a landlord banging on the ceiling with a broom. But even so, it's not the house we thought we'd get." Esperanza's childhood life in a Spanish-speaking area of Chicago is described in a series of spare, poignant, and powerful vignettes. Each story centers on a detail of her childhood: a greasy cold rice sandwich, a pregnant friend, a mean boy, how the clouds looked one time, something she heard a drunk say, her fear of nuns: "I always cry when nuns yell at me, even if they're not yelling." Esperanza's friends, family, and neighbors wander in and out of her stories; through them all Esperanza sees, learns, loves, and dreams of the house she will someday have, her own house, not on Mango Street.

J.L.

The Irish R.M., E. (Edith) Somerville and Martin (Violet Florence) Ross, *1899–1915, Ireland/England,* SHORT STORIES

Written in concert by E. Somerville and Martin Ross in the late nineteenth and early twentieth centuries, these stories have as their narrator Major Sinclair Yeates, a young man returning to Ireland after being educated in England. As resident magistrate (R.M.), he is provided with a title, an office, a low salary accompanied by high social expectations, and every problem—small and large—of the local inhabitants. Yet the major finds his appointment to the rather unattractive job of R.M. in the village of Shreelane "glittering with possibilities" because it provides him with the means to make a successful proposal to the lovely Philippa. The cast of characters includes Mrs. Cadogan, the irrepressibly grumpy housekeeper; Dr. Hickey, the lovelorn, ambitious, and utterly humorless Englishman; Flurry, the local horse trader and unquenchable huntsman; and, of course, beautiful Philippa, a young woman whose capacity to laugh "unsuitably" shows her lack of even "the most rudimentary capacity for keeping her countenance." While horses and fox hunts provide most of Major Yeates's discomforts, domestic problems also assail him, like the chairs in his new house, with their "aggressive knobs in unexpected places." As the straight-man narrator, observer, and regular butt of hundreds of hilarious trials and mishaps, Major Yeates never ceases to be surprised, is usually not amused, and can't stop himself from loving his neighbors.

J.L.

Italian Days, Barbara Grizzuti Harrison, *1989, Italy (United States),* NONFICTION

Barbara Grizzuti Harrison's travel journal is one of the most comprehensive, revealing, and interpretive books of its genre. And yet *Italian Days* does not fit neatly into a category; lyrical, philosophical, anecdotal, it never pretends merely to give guidance or instruction to the traveler. The book is divided into eight chapters, each covering a city or specific region from Milan to Sicily. Barbara Harrison meanders through Italy, sharing her ideas about the people she encounters, and all the while thinking—about architecture, religion, politics, food, society, nature, family, and history. Her prose is joyful and informed, her descriptions of the people and places quite exhilarating: "The bus went slowly, like a swimmer who loves the water too much to race and challenge it, and the world unfolded like a child's picture book: gardeners turning over the soil with gnarled, patient hands; bronzed youths of Etruscan beauty casually strolling by the roadside as if here were just anywhere and everywhere was beautiful . . . laughing nuns pushing children on orange swings, their heavy habits floating on magnolia-scented air." This is a book to be read in small bits, so each detail and sentence might be savored, a book to relish whether or not you ever intend to visit Italy.

R.S.

The Land of Little Rain, Mary Austin, *1903, United States,* NONFICTION

"To understand the fashion of any life, one must know the land it is lived in and the procession of the year." Mary Austin was one of this country's early writers of natural history and natural philosophy; in her classic *The Land of Little Rain* she explores the deserts of Arizona and Southern California, recording details of landscape and wildlife in prose that is as expansive and exacting as the desert itself. To survive and even flourish in such a harsh environment, the inhabitants (human and nonhuman) must adapt themselves to the demands of the climate and terrain—and to each other. The experiences that shape personal truth must be grounded in the hard, dry soil of concession and nourished by relentless attention to the rapport between self and surroundings. Going beyond the role of the observer to become a participant in the ecology of the desert, Mary Austin describes a world that does not support or encourage human purposes, but follows a more compelling imperative. She recognizes this imperative, combining a deferential relationship to resources like water—"one expects to find springs, but not to depend upon them"—with an ultimate respect for the personal resources that enable individuals to live with the limitations, the risks, and the magnificence of such a place.

K.B.

Lemon Swamp and Other Places: A Carolina Memoir, Mamie Garvin Fields with Karen Fields, *1983, United States,* AUTOBIOGRAPHY

Karen Fields, professor of sociology at Brandeis University, spent a year taping her grandmother's stories—sipping okra soup, laughing over her kitchen table, and listening. The result is *Lemon Swamp*, Mamie Garvin Fields's memories of her childhood and her life as an educated black woman in early-twentieth-century Charleston, South Carolina. Born in 1888, Mamie Fields was part of an extended family and a large neighborhood. Keeping track of all the names and places makes the early chapters hard work, but there's a reason for the details, and almost every one has a story. Mamie Fields tells of Charleston parks where blacks were not allowed to sit on the benches, and describes jubilant picnics in the country, filled with food, families, dancing, and games of hide-and-go-seek. There is her grandfather's plantation, with its Lemon Swamp, where her grandmother was "lost" during Sherman's march. And there are the schools on the Sea Islands—"a place behind God's back"—where Mamie Fields taught. In *Lemon Swamp*, Mamie Fields remembers what blacks were not allowed to do in the South, and won't let anybody forget what they accomplished. When other teachers told her, " 'Don't bother with the white people to get necessities for your school' . . . [her] attitude was 'He's a man and he speaks English. I will ask him.' " She did ask and she did accomplish—often without asking. She's a remarkable woman, and she and her granddaughter bring a remarkable history to life.

E.B.

Mute Phone Calls and Other Stories, Ruth Zernova, *translated from Russian by Ann Harleman, Martha Kitchen, and Helen Reeve, 1961–1991, Russia,* SHORT STORIES

With a few exceptions, the stories in this collection are firmly rooted in particular places and times, taking readers back twenty or fifty years, to other countries and ways of thinking. One story evokes the tragedy of the Spanish revolution; another recalls the climate of anti-Semitism in Russia during the 1940s; a third describes the tensions and dynamics among women in a Soviet labor camp. A background in twentieth-century Spanish and Russian history will help, but it is not crucial; the American translators have included footnotes that aid the reader in seeing the universal qualities in each of these stories. In "Elizabeth Arden," Ruth Zernova reminds the reader of the connections that take her stories beyond their immediate context: "Jews in America were exposed as Communists; Jews in the Soviet Union as anti-Communists. And once again we didn't suspect that those winds were one and the same; and we wouldn't have believed it if we'd been told. . . . For one and the same idiot wind blows around our little globe, our green spaceship with the light-blue sails." While not strictly autobiographical, each of these stories draws on Ruth Zernova's experiences, re-creating the atmosphere of revolution, oppression, and exile, and celebrating the human spirit.

E.B.

My Mother's House, Colette, *translated from French by Una Vicenzo Troubridge and Enid McLeod, 1953, France,* ESSAYS

"The house was large, topped by a lofty garret." This house and the rural early-twentieth-century French town in which it is located are the center of Colette's childhood world. It is a world filled with characters—a loving, opinionated mother; an absentminded father infatuated with his wife; an older sister who lives next door without communicating; the people of the town. There are memories of playing until dirty and exhausted; of Henriette Boisson, seven months pregnant, who "will not get married, and I may as well give up expecting it"; of Colette's early fascination with words and the day she encountered the word *presbytery*; and of a trip to Paris which reminds Colette how much she loves the animals and people at home. One especially beautiful piece describes the last years of Colette's mother's life, when she slowly had to give up her independence and all the tasks that went with it, yet fought to retain her self-reliance. One morning Colette caught her: "Dressed in her nightgown, but wearing heavy gardening shoes . . . her back bent in the attitude of the expert jobber, my mother, rejuvenated by the indescribable expression of guilty enjoyment, in defiance of all her promises and of the freezing morning dew, was sawing logs in her own yard." This gentle, poetic book creates moods and visions as much as it tells stories. It is worth reading slowly.

E.B.

Now in November, Josephine Johnson, *1934, United States,* NOVEL

In 1934, Josephine Johnson won the Pulitzer Prize for her first novel, *Now in November.* A bleak and beautiful work, it tells the story of a Midwestern farming family and their desperate efforts to make a living. Like John Steinbeck's *The Grapes of Wrath* (published several years later), it portrays the unrelenting harshness of hard work and drought set against the life-giving beauty of the land and the fierce determination of its people. Margret, the narrator, and her family come to the farm when she is a young girl; ten years later she tells of her family's fight to pay off their mortgage and keep their land: "There was a bitterness in sowing and reaping, no matter how good the crop might be . . . when all that it meant was the privilege of doing this over again and nothing to show but a little mark on paper." Always struggling, always tired, never secure, they still hear the constant refrain from outsiders: "You farmers have got stuff to eat anyway. That's something, ent it?"

E.B.

Out of Africa, Isak Dinesen, *1937, Kenya (Denmark),* MEMOIR

From 1914 to 1931, Danish aristocrat Baroness Karen Blixen owned and operated a coffee plantation in Kenya. After the plantation failed, she returned to Europe and began to write under the pen name Isak Dinesen. *Out of Africa* reads like a collection of stories in which she adheres to no strict chronology, gives no explanation of the facts of her life, and apologizes for nothing. First published in 1937, *Out of Africa* is not free of the colonial or racist attitudes of its time; yet, within that context, Isak Dinesen is an enlightened observer and participant as she describes the experience of living in British East Africa before World War II. She portrays in rich detail the vast land around her, alive with strange and wonderful human populations; the thrilling terror of a nocturnal lion hunt; a shooting accident among the Africans on her farm, and its repercussions; raising and freeing an orphaned antelope fawn; getting to know the Africans and the colonial adventurers who found their way into her life. "If I know a song of Africa," she writes, "of the Giraffe, and the African new moon lying on her back, of the ploughs in the fields, and the sweaty faces of the coffee-pickers, does Africa know a song of me?" *Out of Africa* is that song.

L.A.

Refuge: An Unnatural History of Family and Place, Terry Tempest Williams, *1991, United States,* NONFICTION

Refuge chronicles Terry Tempest Williams's intimate relationships with the terrain of Utah and with the women of her family. In 1983, the waters of the Great Salt Lake rose to record heights, flooding fragile wetlands and destroying the Bear River Migratory Bird Refuge, the beloved environment of Terry Tempest Williams's childhood. During the same period, both her mother and grandmother were diagnosed with cancer. With a naturalist's concern for detail, a poet's sense of language, and the tenderness of a daughter and granddaughter, Terry Tempest Williams invites the reader into her thoughts as she struggles to understand her loss and grief. Ultimately, "a poetics of landscape becomes a politics of landscape" as she discovers that when she was a child, she and her family witnessed nuclear bomb tests conducted in Utah by the government; although she has no proof, she becomes convinced that it was the nuclear fallout that caused the devastating illnesses in her family. In *Refuge,* we learn that our relationship to the place we live in echoes our relationships with our loved ones, and it is our connections to our communities, to the natural environment, and to our families and friends that provide us our refuge.

A.C.

River Time: The Frontier on the Lower Neuse, Janet Lembke, *1989, United States,* NONFICTION

There are a lot of places in the world people want to learn about; if it wasn't for Janet Lembke, however, the Great Neck Point on the Lower Neuse River of North Carolina probably wouldn't be on the list. To begin with, it's hard to find; it's "cut off by water on one side, by a sea of green pines on the other," and the nearest town is twenty-two miles away. The people here are different, too, their sense of time and material possessions deeply affected by the river running near their doors. "On the riverfront *house* is a word that can be appropriately applied to only a few dwellings." People keep dogs, which Jake the Dogkiller occasionally knocks off, as well as goats, mallards, and their own business. Knock at these doors in the middle of the night and, if you are a stranger or even a "weekender," you could wait all night long; if you are a neighbor, there's nothing they won't do. Janet Lembke is a recent but permanent resident who sees herself as in "a halcyon season, the calm that comes after years of child-rearing, the calm before infirmity overtakes the one parent left to us, before we ourselves lose our vigor." Her descriptions of this place and its people are loving, acerbic, enlightening, and entertaining, and while she and her neighbors wouldn't want you to visit, you might just end up wanting to.

E.B.

The Solace of Open Spaces, Gretel Ehrlich, *1985, United States,* ESSAYS

Gretel Ehrlich is the kind of writer who teaches you that prose can be poetry. In *The Solace of Open Spaces* she writes about coming to terms with the death of the man she loves, about her life in Wyoming, and about what it means to live in wide spaces and interact primarily with animals. Each of these essays is a piece unto itself; sentence after sentence can be savored like hard candy until every bit of flavor comes out. There is much to learn about Wyoming here; Gretel Ehrlich has a mind for details, and the reader comes away fully educated about sheepherding, rodeos, cabin fever, and the value of water. But it is how Gretel Ehrlich writes as much as what she writes that makes her work exceptional. Her words soar and swoop and remind us that writing can always be more than just telling what happened: "The truest art I would strive for in any work would be to give the page the same qualities as earth: weather would land on it harshly; light would elucidate the most difficult truths; wind would sweep away obtuse padding."

E.B.

Stradbroke Dreamtime, Oodgeroo Nunukul, *1972, Australia,* MEMOIR/FOLK TALES

Oodgeroo Nunukul, one of seven children, was born in 1920 on the island of Stradbroke, off the Australian coast. *Stradbroke Dreamtime* combines her growing-up memories with creation folklore from Aborigine myths, which play off her memories and offer insights to their origins. Although Oodgeroo's father is employed by the government, his pay is so low the family hunts and fishes to have enough to eat; every child has a slingshot and a fishing line and knows how to make bandicoot traps. Her father's tribal totem is the carpet snake, and much to their mother's dismay, Carpie, a ten-foot pet snake, slithers around their home. Oodgeroo fondly remembers Carpie; she "used to sit in the lavatory for hours and tell him my innermost secrets, and it was very satisfying the way old Carpie would never interrupt the conversation or crawl away." The author recalls being ridiculed at the government school because she was left-handed, and embarrassing her mother by showing up in town with dirty clothes and feet. While her stories tell of a home full of love and an upbringing close to nature, Oodgeroo Nunukul weaves in a thread of bitterness at the loss of the island's natural beauty to mineral exploration, tourism, and white settlement.

H.S.

Street Games, Rosellen Brown, *1991, United States,* SHORT STORIES

Each story in *Street Games* takes place at one of fourteen specific addresses on George Street in Brooklyn, New York. In "268, Corner Leon. I Am Not Luis Beech-Nut," Luis talks, in a fretful and day-dreaming monologue, about himself—"Little shit, this Luis"—and his life as the owner of a corner store, where all day long people are "going by the store so fast you think I'm selling the plague in here two for a dollar." From "245, Migdalia Colon's third floor rear," an unnamed wife thanks her recently dead, drug-addicted husband for dying before he "had to hock your children's eyes and little toes," and celebrates the right to call herself "I" instead of "we": "I. I. I. I . . . I want to put it on the mailbox. Use it for my signature. Frame it and hang it on the wall all gold. . . . Show it around like a fat new baby. It's the best baby we never had, the one I made myself, after the children had gone to bed, just before you died." In "259, Upper Duplex," a young, liberal white bureaucrat laments: "I am too bored to move." Through an impressive variety of voices and accents, Rosellen Brown reveals moments in the lives of a few people on George Street, a neighborhood teeming with connections, a hard street in hard times that is alive with anger and love.

J.L.

Talking to the Dead, Sylvia Watanabe, *1992, United States,* SHORT STORIES

Talking to the Dead is a series of interconnected stories describing the inhabitants of a small Hawaiian town, a collection with the intricate beauty of a spider's web. Sylvia Watanabe, who "wanted to record a way of life which I loved and which seemed in danger of dying away," explores fragile lives and tenuous connections in stories that glimmer with moments of pain, wonder, realization, and rebellion. Haru Hanabusa chants and feeds the hungry ghosts in order to stay safe: "She kept it all down in a little notebook which she referred to from time to time, but no matter how many things she could think of to be kept safe from, there was always something more." Missy decides not to leave the island to go to college: "You can want a place with your whole skin, the way you want a person. It can fill your thoughts, without your even knowing; you can only know that, if it wasn't there anymore, maybe you wouldn't have any thoughts at all." Doc McAllister runs every morning, "but whether McAllister was in retreat or pursuit" his wife is not sure. Each story has its own catharsis or revelation; the themes set up in the initial story evolve and build, becoming more complex and subtle, allowing the reader brief, gentle, intimate insights into human frailties and strengths.

E.B.

Winter Wheat, Mildred Walker, *1943, United States,* NOVEL

With an arid "dry-land" wheat farm as both its geographic and metaphorical center, *Winter Wheat* tells the story of eighteen-year-old Ellen Webb. Her Vermont-born father and Russian-born mother, married during the First World War, have come as homesteaders to Barton, Montana—a grain elevator and a general store. It is 1940, the year Ellen will start college if the wheat harvest is good; it is September, "like a quiet day after a whole week of wind. I mean that wind that blows dirt into your eyes and hair and between your teeth and roars in your ears after you've gone inside." The harvest pays and Ellen goes off to college, where she immediately falls in love: "I hadn't meant to fall in love so soon, but there's nothing you can do about it. It's like planning to seed in April and then having it come off so warm in March that the earth is ready." Ellen and Gil plan their marriage for after the summer harvest. But Gil arrives and doesn't find Montana or the life of dry-land wheat farmers beautiful. Ellen begins to see everything, including her parents, with new and critical eyes in this unsparing and poignant examination of love and life.

J.L.

Women of the Shadows: The Wives and Mothers of Southern Italy, Ann Cornelisen, *1977, Italy (United States),* NONFICTION

The Italy of most foreigners' imaginations centers on pastoral vineyards or the glamour of Rome, but there is another part of Italy—the South—a "bleak land and dour people who see no joy in this life, but only an eternal struggle they cannot quite win." Ann Cornelisen arrived in 1954 to study archaeology; she ended up spending ten years establishing nurseries in poverty-stricken villages in Southern Italy. "Regret[ting] my own intrusion as a filter," she wanted to record the lives of the women she met because "before they disappear to become the ghostly shadows behind a myth, I think they should have their say." *Women of the Shadows* focuses on five women, describing their lives of endless work, frustration, anger, and pain. Husbands who can find no work locally leave for Germany and return once or twice a year. Their wives stay home and "do whatever else no one has done. That's what we're taught; that's what we're supposed to do. Men work and talk about politics. We do the rest." Out of horrendous conditions emerge women of amazing strength and resourcefulness, individuals who are capable of supporting nine children, living in a one-room house without light or water, or finessing their ways through government regulations to gain a job or a hospital operation. Ann Cornelisen's portrayal of these women and their impoverished land is written with clear-sighted sympathy.

E.B.

Womenfolks: Growing Up Down South, Shirley Abbott, *1983, United States,* NONFICTION

Womenfolks is an illuminating blend of scholarly history, personal reflection, and political essay, spiced with a smattering of "what-if" historical fiction. Shirley Abbott's research encompasses diaries and journals of early Southern immigrants and visitors, family stories, academic histories of the South, and Southern historical fiction, all of which she uses methodically to disentangle Southern myth from history: "Most Southerners, even those who descend from some distinguished old family or another, can also look back, at quite close range, on at least one line of half-literate farmers who scratched their living out of the dirt one way or another and moved along every generation or so, searching for cheap land and sweet water and the chance to start over again." At the center of her study is the juxtaposition between the generations of the women of her family and the legendary Southern belle. Who were the majority of Southern foremothers? What is a Southern belle, or, more importantly, what is a Southern belle supposed to be and why? In this book, a new version of Southern history emerges, one that debunks the enslaving myth of Southern bellehood and reveals women as a pivotal force. In witty and lucid prose, Shirley Abbott, a native daughter of Hot Springs, Arkansas, offers new ways—and reasons—for looking at the places we come from.

J.L.

Power

There is power in a dream achieved or destroyed, in the lust for control of a corrupt and dictatorial government, in the passion of two people for each other, in the unshakable faith of a spiritual foundation. In *The Yellow Wallpaper*, a young woman fights against the medical authorities, including her husband, whose "cures" for depression are driving her to insanity. Sofia Petrovna, Lady Hong, and Mary, Queen of Scots, try to navigate their ways through the complicated and often violent politics of, respectively, Stalin's purges, eighteenth-century Korea, and sixteenth-century England. Susan Faludi exposes the backlash against feminism in the United States; Rigoberta Menchú speaks out against the Guatemalan government that is destroying her people; Elaine Brown describes her own rise to power within the Black Panther Party. Stephanie Golden examines the myths about and the real lives of homeless women. The black citizens of one sleepy North Carolina town decide to fight for their rights in *Praying for Sheetrock*; across the ocean in South Africa, Lauretta Ngcobo exposes the oppressive restrictions of the apartheid government. Linda Hogan provides a fictional re-creation of the clash that occurred in the early twentieth century between the Osage and the white men who wanted their oil-rich land in Oklahoma. *Grandmothers of the Light* portrays the strength of Native American traditions; Charlotte Watson Sherman shows us a need-driven faith that allows escaping slaves to walk across the surface of a river. Here are battles and revelations, moments and centuries of defeat and triumph. Here is the power of beauty, of greed, of hate, and of love.

And They Didn't Die	Lauretta Ngcobo
Awaiting Trespass	Linda Ty-Casper
Backlash	Susan Faludi
The Beggars' Strike	Aminata Sow Fall
City of Kings	Rosario Castellanos
The Daughter of Time	Josephine Tey
God Bless the Child	Kristin Hunter
Grandmothers of the Light	Paula Gunn Allen
The House of Ulloa	Emilia Pardo Bazán
How to Suppress Women's Writing	Joanna Russ
I, Rigoberta Menchú	Rigoberta Menchú
John Dollar	Marianne Wiggins
Kelroy	Rebecca Rush
Killing Color	Charlotte Watson Sherman
The Living Is Easy	Dorothy West
Mary, Queen of Scots	Antonia Fraser
Mean Spirit	Linda Hogan
Memoirs of a Korean Queen	Lady Hong
Oroonoko, The Rover and Other Works	Aphra Behn
A Persian Requiem	Simin Daneshvar
Praying for Sheetrock	Melissa Fay Greene
Sister Outsider	Audre Lorde
Sofia Petrovna	Lydia Chukovskaya
Sultana's Dream and Selections from The Secluded Ones	Rokeya Sakhawat Hossain
A Taste of Power: A Black Woman's Story	Elaine Brown
The Threshing Floor	Barbara Burford
A Vindication of the Rights of Women	Mary Wollstonecraft
Women, Culture, & Politics	Angela Y. Davis
The Women Outside	Stephanie Golden
The Yellow Wallpaper	Charlotte Perkins Gilman

And They Didn't Die, Lauretta Ngcobo, *1990, South Africa (South Africa/England)*, NOVEL

And They Didn't Die is a magnificent novel that weaves together compelling characters and a powerful narrative with an in-depth examination of the effects of apartheid rule on various black communities in South Africa. Lauretta Ngcobo's main character, Jezile, lives in the impoverished rural community of Sigageni; Siyalo, her husband, works in the faraway city of Durban. As the novel opens, Jezile is despondent because she does not manage to conceive during the two weeks per year that Siyalo is allowed to return home; while she does eventually have children, her hardships only seem to multiply in number. Siyalo is sent away from Durban for suspected "political" activities, then is arrested in Sigageni for stealing milk from a nearby white farmer. It does not matter that he took only a pint a day, to feed his starving child—he is sentenced to ten years in prison. And this is only the beginning. Jezile, Siyalo, and their families are trapped, both by the relentless oppressions of the white government and by the restrictive conventions of their own society. Lauretta Ngcobo's portrayal of their suffering, of the strength of the community of women in Sigageni, and of the enduring bond between Jezile and Siyalo, create a novel that is powerful, angry, and uplifting.

E.B.

Awaiting Trespass, Linda Ty-Casper, *1985, Philippines,* NOVEL

Linda Ty-Casper examines life in the contemporary Philippines through the behavior and memories of relatives and friends during the three-day wake of Don Severino Gil. Severino's sudden death and his closed casket are cause for much speculation. His three sisters, all past eighty, mourn with the expected display of grief, and with one eye open to see who comes to the vigil. Severino's "favorite niece," Telly, arrives. The family has forgiven her for being forty-nine and divorced because she is a "poet," though she knows "she writes poetry only in her mind . . . to silence the furious screech that suddenly—with much cunning, always catching her by surprise—twists through her until her head begins to feel like an expanding circle." Father Sevi, Severino's only legitimate heir, estranged from his father for many years, brings with him reservations about involving himself with his family again, and wonders: "Was it pride all along that made him want to be a priest, that kept him a priest: weakness hiding in weakness?" Through Telly, Father Sevi, and others, a picture emerges of a country ruled by corruption and greed, of people who benefit from inequities and people who want to expose them. A powerful book, *Awaiting Trespass* is currently banned in the Philippines.

H.S.

Backlash: The Undeclared War Against American Women,
Susan Faludi, *1991, United States,* NONFICTION

In this monumental investigative work, Pulitzer Prize–winning journalist Susan Faludi offers exhaustive and disquieting evidence of a "powerful counter-assault on women's rights"—a backlash—intent on reversing the hard-won gains of the feminist movement. *Backlash* sounds the alarm on the cultural forces that would coax women into believing that the independence, equality, and power they have struggled to achieve are actually the *source* of their problems—from cellulite and infertility to sexual harassment and career burnout. Susan Faludi exposes the methods employed in the backlash—manipulated statistics, beguiling turns of language, and condescending fashion dictates. She gracefully ushers us into the offices and homes of various captains of the backlash, turns on her microphone, and lets these opponents of feminism indict themselves. She exposes the New Right, with its strong-minded women who drop their kids at day care, "report to their offices in suits and issue press releases demanding that women return to the home"—to protect family values, of course. The cruel irony of these New Right women being at once victims and purveyors of the backlash typifies the insidiousness of the trend. The unyielding 450-plus pages of research and documentation that make up *Backlash* bear the mark of an indefatigable journalist who dares to challenge her adversaries and stir her readers. The end of the book contains more than 80 pages of citations, as well as an extensive index. This provocative book will stand for a long time.

C.M.

The Beggars' Strike, or The Dregs of Society, Aminata Sow Fall, *translated from French by Dorothy S. Blair, 1979, Senegal,* NOVEL

The beggars are becoming a problem in the capital; their physical deformities and constant presence are scaring away the tourists. It is up to Mour Diyae, director of public health and hygiene, to clear the streets, a job he quickly passes on to his competent assistant Keba Dabo. While Mour sees the problem as a way to self-promotion, Keba approaches the task with a zeal born out of his own childhood of poverty and pride. Soon, after beatings and repeated imprisonment, the beggars leave the streets, but a new problem arises. People must give alms to the poor to insure spiritual favor and earthly rewards. A marabout, or holy man, tells Mour Diyae that he will become vice president if he gives certain gifts to real beggars on the streets. But the beggars now congregate and receive alms at a house far out of town, and they see no need to return to the streets to help the man who persecuted them. Mour Diyae's dilemma is made all the worse by his polygamous marriage to a new young second wife and the frustrations it causes both wives. Quick and sharp, Aminata Sow Fall moves like a bantamweight fighter through this fast-paced, satirical novel, jabbing deftly at her targets of patriarchy, polygamy, privilege, and hypocrisy.

E.B.

City of Kings, Rosario Castellanos, *translated from Spanish by Gloria Chacon de Arjona and Robert S. Rudder, 1960s, Mexico,* SHORT STORIES

Set in Ciudad Real—the *City of Kings*—these stories center on the centuries-old traditions of deceit, debasement, and disaster heaped on the Chiapa people by the "ladinos," the "caxlanes," the white men. "Death of a Tiger" mythically recounts the history of the decimation of the Bolometic community, who, driven from their land, become wanderers, until they are finally desperate enough to look for work in Ciudad Real. There they fare no better: "The years came in grimly, and hunger wandered freely from house to house, knocking on all doors with its bony hand." In "The Wheel of Hunger," Alicia Mendoza travels on a donkey for days and nights through rain and wind over treacherous mountain passes to reach her post as nurse in the Indian Aid Mission. There she finds an embittered doctor who lets babies die and believes in nothing more than the sound of the watches he collects. Anthropologist José Antonio Romero's attempt to help a starving Chiapa child leaves him searching for answers in "The Gift, Refused." American Arthur Smith finds "salvation" with the knowledge that he is on the "side of good. His religion was the true one, his race was superior, his country was powerful." This collection exquisitely and relentlessly exposes the indiscriminating pain and deformation that result when civilizations are built on race and class degradation.

J.L.

The Daughter of Time, Josephine Tey, *1951, England,* NOVEL

Since its publication in 1951, Josephine Tey's insightful mystery *The Daughter of Time* has become a major resource for historians researching the death of the nephews of Richard III. It opens with a bored Detective Alan Grant, stuck in his hospital bed with a wounded hip and broken leg. His actress friend, Marta Hallard, notices he is not reading and brings him some portraits to occupy his mind. Alan Grant becomes transfixed with the face of Richard III, which "had that incommunicable, that indescribable look that childhood suffering leaves behind." Thus begins Grant's travel through time to solve a five-hundred-year-old mystery: Did Richard III kill his two nephews and have them buried in the Tower of London in order to eliminate all possible contenders for the throne? Initially Grant drafts all his friends to help in his search; finally he hires Mr. Carradine as a real research assistant. Historical fact is related to the audience through the readings of the characters, especially of the frustrated, curmudgeonly Detective Grant. Due to the detective's confinement, there is far less fast-paced action than one often expects from mysteries, but the dialogue and interplay between Grant and Carradine is crisp and wonderful, and the conclusion is fascinating.

V.S.

God Bless the Child, Kristin Hunter, *1964, United States,* NOVEL

This is a novel filled with a rage reminiscent of Ralph Ellison's *Invisible Man* and Ann Petry's *The Street. God Bless the Child*'s Rosie Fleming grows up in an apartment where killing roaches is a childhood game. Her grandmother has always cared for and idolized rich white folks, and admires anything that has the faintest whiff of "culture." Rosie's mother is a woman whose experiences as a hairdresser and single mother have given her insights into people, but she is also an alcoholic who brings home "uncles" to spend the night, and Rosie doesn't listen to her mother's advice. Rosie grows up fast. Who needs school when you could be earning money? Why earn just straight money when crooked money might come faster? For Rosie, money must bring happiness—and she needs money the way her mother needs five or seven drinks a night. Rosie doesn't understand yet what Kristin Hunter makes clear: as a black person in the United States, and particularly as a black woman, she will never get power through her money. Rosie's destruction is painful to watch, especially because Rosie is so vibrantly alive: "It's as natural for people to touch her as it is for them to warm their hands at a fire." The title comes from one of Billie Holliday's most famous songs: "Mama may have and Papa may have, but God bless the child that's got his own." After reading about Rosie, you might well ask, What "own" can a black child hope to have?

E.B.

Grandmothers of the Light: A Medicine Woman's Sourcebook, Paula Gunn Allen, *1991, United States,* NONFICTION

Through her introductory essays to sections entitled "The Living Reality of the Medicine World," "Ritual Magic and Aspects of the Goddesses," and "Myth, Magic, and Medicine in the Modern World," Paula Gunn Allen dissects modern "monotheistic" English understandings of ancient New World goddess cultures. Each of these scholarly essays is followed by stories she learned from family and friends that show "how the disciplines of the medicine woman—including the way of the daughter, the way of the mother, and the way of the wise woman—are open to all women, and how the commitment to 'walk in a sacred manner' can yield increasing spiritual power throughout one's life." These stories hold the kind of magic in their telling that makes flying, transforming, and disappearing humans completely believable, and the kind of power that makes us feel our kinship to "grandmothers of the light."

J.L.

The House of Ulloa, Emilia Pardo Bazán, *translated from Spanish by Paul O'Prey and Lucia Graves, 1886, Spain,* NOVEL

The House of Ulloa is a classic of Spanish literature, its author one of the innovators of the modern Spanish novel. It focuses on three characters: Julian, the spiritual, effeminate, and ultimately ineffectual chaplain at the manor at Ulloa; the marquis of Ulloa, the rough aristocrat who prefers hunting to intellectual pursuits; and Primitivo, his majordomo, who cleverly impoverishes his employer while increasing his own power and wealth. Through them, Emilia Pardo Bazán portrays the struggle between the aristocracy and the peasant class as well as the spiritual turmoil of the Glorious Revolution of 1868. Readers with a knowledge of Spanish history will find more subtle meanings, but such a background is not essential. In fact, the latter portion of the novel, which focuses on a local election, may surprise readers with its contemporary relevance. A proponent of Spanish realism, Emilia Pardo Bazán delves into the details of rural life with verve, although in her attempts to combine realism with her theme of the decline of the aristocracy she tends to stereotype peasants as earthy and animalistic. Her feminism, however, is unusual for her time—she condemns both wife-beating and the prevailing sexual double standard—and her descriptions of babies and of the nurturing love of the chaplain for the marquis's baby daughter provide a beautiful contrast to the account of the corrupt and often violent society that surrounds them.

E.B.

How to Suppress Women's Writing, Joanna Russ, *1983, United States,* NONFICTION

"She didn't write it. She wrote it but she shouldn't have. She wrote it but look what she wrote about. She wrote it but she isn't really an artist, and it isn't really art. She wrote it but she had help. She wrote it but she's an anomaly. She wrote it BUT . . ." *How to Suppress Women's Writing* is a meticulously researched and humorously written "guidebook" to the many ways women and other "minorities" have been barred from producing written art. In chapters entitled "Prohibitions," "Bad Faith," "Denial of Agency," "Pollution of Agency," "The Double Standard of Content," "False Categorization," "Isolation," "Anomalousness," "Lack of Models," "Responses," and "Aesthetics," Joanna Russ names, defines, and illustrates the barriers to art-making which we may have felt, but which tend to remain unnamed and thus unremovable. With the apparent proliferation of women writers in the last decade, is this book still relevant? Ask yourself: how many women do you know who are trying to make art? And how many find the time, resources, and support to succeed? So long as poverty, lack of leisure, and sexism—those "powerful, informal prohibitions against committing art"—exist, *How to Suppress Women's Writing* remains timely.

J.L.

I, Rigoberta Menchú: An Indian Woman in Guatemala, Rigoberta Menchú as told to Elisabeth Burgos-Debray, *translated from Spanish by Ann Wright, 1983, Guatemala,* AUTOBIOGRAPHY

"This is my testimony. I didn't learn it from a book and I didn't learn it alone. . . . My personal experience is the reality of a whole people." Born in the mountains of Guatemala into the Quiché, one of twenty-three mestizo groups, Rigoberta Menchú tells her story. The Quiché people's spirituality, much of which must not be told to outsiders, affirms community responsibility for village children and intensely personal relationships with the land and the natural world. The celebration of her ancient culture is all that strengthens Rigoberta

Menchú in the face of a brutally repressed and poverty-stricken existence. Two of her brothers die as infants from malnutrition. When the Quiché begin their fight to keep the government and big-business people from stealing any more of their land, her family is forced to watch her youngest brother be tortured and burned alive; later her mother is tortured to death, and her father murdered. Obligated by circumstance and unquestionable responsibility to her people, Rigoberta Menchú assumes the role of organizer/leader. These interviews—conducted in Spanish, a language she had spoken for only three years—center on her role as a Quiché woman. Her politics are deeply personal: "They've killed the people dearest to me. . . . Therefore, my commitment to our struggle knows no boundaries nor limits." Despite the layered nature of her written story—from oral history to transcriber to translator—Rigoberta Menchú's unadorned and selfless words ring like a clear and beautiful bell sounding both wonder and warning.

J.L.

John Dollar, Marianne Wiggins, *1989, Burma* (*United States*), NOVEL

John Dollar is a devastating, strangely beautiful novel that renders appalling events in exquisite prose. The book begins by tracing the fortunes of Charlotte Lewes, a grieving World War I widow whose life in England is passionless and empty. She comes to Rangoon, Burma, to teach, and there recovers her sensual nature and experiences a reawakening of love with the sailor John Dollar. In Rangoon, she is barely tolerated by the "mannered, pre-emptive, supercilious" English, who build their lives around the re-creation of an England which to them is "myth and memory, a place more real in microcosm, in its recreation, than in any actuality." The focus then shifts to a patriotic sailing expedition to the Andaman Islands, which ends in disaster: Charlotte's eight female pupils are cast ashore with John Dollar, who is paralyzed in the accident. The girls attempt to survive and keep hope alive by establishing familiar hierarchies and rituals from their own colonialist and Christian culture; yet it is these structures and beliefs that catalyze an increasingly horrifying chain of events. A riveting novel, *John Dollar* illuminates the racism, viciousness, and arrogance inherent in colonialism, and the potential for the misuse of power that exists within both imperialism and organized religion.

P.H.

Kelroy, Rebecca Rush, *1812, United States,* NOVEL

Kelroy is easily compared to many early-nineteenth-century British novels of manners and sensibility. America has never been Britain, however, and the differences are obvious in *Kelroy*, in which British irony becomes straightforward American criticism, villains are both more obvious and more deliciously alive, and class and money take on new meaning in a newly democratic nation. The plot centers on Mrs. Hammond, "a woman of fascinating manners, strong prejudices, and boundless ambition," who, with the death of her rich but improvident husband, is left with two daughters and "the prospect of comparative indigence, which suited neither her habits nor her temper." Determined to regain a fashionable standard of living, and fully aware of the power of beauty, she focuses her attention on making her daughters suitable for marriage to wealthy men who will support her as well. In Lucy she succeeds in creating an elegant, cold, marketable product. Emily, "who felt she had a heart," is another matter. And so the complications begin. Through the love affairs, financial reversal, hypocrisy, and deceit that follow, Rebecca Rush provides both a condemnation of avarice, and, perhaps unintentionally, a fascinating look into early America's efforts to find its own place between its British class-based heritage, a democratic ideal, and a rapidly developing hierarchy based upon economic success.

E.B.

Killing Color, Charlotte Watson Sherman, *1992, United States,* SHORT STORIES

These are stories of power—the power of belief, rage, ritual, passion, healing. Deep, rough, muddy, and pure, at times they speak of forces so elemental or complex that story turns into song. A woman who talks with her eyes stands in front of the courthouse and stares; every night she gets into a different car and another Ku Klux Klan member disappears, just as her husband disappeared years ago. A man and a woman make love to the sound of the earth's humming. A young girl walks on water—just like Jesus, just like the slaves who walked away from the plantation and couldn't swim across the river that blocked their way: "*mlongo mlongo hmmhmmhmmhmm o-o-*. They knew they couldn't turn back so they kept on hummin that song and then they feet sank in the red mud at the edge of the river and come up covered with green sprouts climin on they ankles and circlin round and tiny wings grew from each ankle and started flappin back and forth, back and forth, gentle at first and then faster and faster. And they could feel the cold of them chains deep in the wet earth and the wings beatin harder and then they took a step into the yellow water but they first foot didn't go down." Not every story reaches as deep or achieves the same level of aesthetic liberation; those that do explode the conventions of literature.

E.B.

The Living Is Easy, Dorothy West, *1948, United States,* NOVEL

The Living Is Easy takes a close, critical look at upper-class black society in Boston around the time of World War I. At its center is Cleo Jericho Judson, born in the South, the oldest of several sisters, a woman who exploits or creates weakness in others to gain her place in society and to maintain her role as the focus of her sisters' dependent admiration. Cleo is conniving, self-serving, domineering, as well as beautiful, dramatic, and breathtaking in her audacity. She hears of a house in a higher-class part of Boston where "there wasn't another colored family she knew who had beaten her to it." The rent is thirty-five dollars; she tells her husband it is fifty, convinces the landlord to accept twenty-five, and pockets the difference. Once she has the house, she convinces her sisters and their children to "visit" her; five months later, only Cleo still has a marriage and the sisters have nowhere else to go. Yet if Cleo is unethical, there is a clarity to her motives that is lacking in the Boston-born society she is determined to join, an elite society consisting of light-skinned, college-educated daughters and sons of self-made businessmen who—when the money runs out—find themselves caught between their own pride and the racism of the rest of the world. Dorothy West knew the society she wrote about—in fact, many of the characters are based on real people—and her observations are both sharp-edged and empathetic.

E.B.

Mary, Queen of Scots, Antonia Fraser, *1969, Scotland (England)*, BIOGRAPHY

The tragic life of Mary, Queen of Scots, has long fascinated students of history and dreamy young girls alike. In this scholarly, comprehensive, and moving biography, Antonia Fraser skillfully guides the reader through the genealogical labyrinths and convoluted intrigues of the Scottish, English, and French courts. Born in 1542, six days before the death of her father, Mary Stuart was crowned Queen of Scotland in her infancy, and began her life as the pawn of the powerful who surrounded her. Raised in Catholic France and married at fifteen to the young dauphin in alliance against the Protestant English, Mary became Queen of France at sixteen and a widow at eighteen. Returning to Scotland, Mary—culturally a Frenchwoman—faced the challenges of ruling an unpredictable, fractious, still militantly Protestant society. Her determination to remain a Catholic distanced her from her subjects and antagonized her cousin and nemesis, Queen Elizabeth of England, who was intensely aware of Mary's legitimate place in the English succession. Eventually, Elizabeth imprisoned Mary and later ordered her execution. In lucid prose, Antonia Fraser examines and interprets the complex drama of one of history's most compelling figures—her transformation, significance, and paradoxical victory.

L.A.

Mean Spirit, Linda Hogan, *1990, United States,* NOVEL

Mean Spirit is more than just the story of the Osage people in the oil-rich Oklahoma of 1922: it is a poet's picture of her people, drawn with careful and tender detail. Linda Hogan allows us the privilege of getting to know much about the Osage people's wisdom, warmth, and world view. This novel, woven from history, is neither romanticized nor idealized. Oil wells, oil fires, oil towns, and oil money are attended by a certain amount of dirt and danger. Violent death is common; so is murder. No one, Osage, Sioux, or "American" (as Caucasians are called in *Mean Spirit*), is all good or bad. Sometimes the villains—each one someone's trusted friend—know what they are doing, sometimes they don't. The drama of the struggle for land between indigenous inhabitants and industrial profiteers may tempt you to read quickly to see what happens next; but give yourself time to dream-read and feel this beautifully written, tragic story. Through it, Linda Hogan gives each of us some of the great strength and hope of her heritage.

J.L.

Memoirs of a Korean Queen, Lady Hong, *translated from Korean by Choe-Wall Yang-hi, circa 1796, Korea,* MEMOIR

In her sixtieth year, Lady Hong began this memoir for her grandson, King Sunjo, in order to explain the "Imo Incident" and to clear her family name of any wrongdoing associated with the tragedy. At age ten, Lady Hong became the wife of Crown Prince Sado, next in line to be the king of Korea. Unfortunately, the prince suffered from paranoia and delusions that intensified over time. In response to the prince's physical and sexual mistreatment of servants, family members, and people off the street, his father—the king—killed him in a bizarre and horrifying manner. This murder became known as the Imo Incident. Its effect on Lady Hong was all-encompassing: "In the face of this disaster it seemed as if heaven and earth touched each other and the sun and moon turned pitch black, and I had no desire to remain any longer in this world." For years prior to her husband's death, she had longed to talk with the king, to ask for help; because of royal protocol, all she was allowed to do was watch her husband's violent abuses. *Memoirs of a Korean Queen* provides a rare example of writing by a Korean woman during this period, and an equally rare view of her life and the lives of those around her. Two hundred years later, Lady Hong shines through as a thoughtful, intelligent woman whose life was circumscribed by the custom, culture, and Confucianism of her time—the same custom, culture, and religion that provided her with the strength to endure.

H.S.

Oroonoko, The Rover and Other Works, Aphra Behn, *1677–1689, England,* NOVELS/PLAYS/POEMS/LETTERS

Aphra Behn, considered the first professional female writer in English, produced literature in a variety of genres during the middle of the seventeenth century. Her work combines themes of passion, intrigue, and honor, in classically romantic prose. The pieces in this volume, a mixture of reportage and high adventure, are as enlightening as they are entertaining. In "The Fair Jilt," the beautiful and treacherous Miranda is chaperoned in a convent while deciding which of her many suitors she will have. When denied her first choice, she is quick to exact her revenge. "Oroonoko" is the tale of a young African prince who is tricked into slavery and brought to Suriname. When he meets up again with the lover he believed was dead, he is doubly determined to live free or die. What is remarkable about these stories is the tremendous willpower of the characters. Aphra Behn's protagonists clearly reflect her own passion for life, a spirit which led her to write in a letter to a male colleague: "All I ask is the privilege . . . to tread in those successful paths my predecessors have so long thrived in. . . . If I must not because of my sex, have this freedom, but that you will usurp all to yourselves; I lay down my quill and you shall have no more of me." Fortunately, Aphra Behn persevered, and her work, like her life—unhampered by either modesty or apology—exudes a rare vitality.

S.L.

A Persian Requiem, Simin Daneshvar, *translated from Persian by Roxane Zand, 1969, Iran,* NOVEL

A Persian Requiem is the first published novel written by an Iranian woman, and one of the most widely read novels in Iran. It begins on the eve of World War II, as two landholder brothers, Yusef and Abol-Ghassem, react in opposite ways to the British request for their grain harvests. Through Zari, Yusef's wife, we hear, see, and feel the power struggle created by each brother's choice. Yusef refuses to sell his grain out from under the people of his homeland to feed a foreign army. Abol-Ghassem seeks personal gain by accepting British policies and supporting their determination to keep Iran's oil out of Hitler's control, and he tries to persuade his brother to sell. Zari believes she must be the family peacemaker, a difficult role in these troubled times: "She kept thinking about her past, and wondering whether she had always been a coward or whether she had become one." *A Persian Requiem* emanates the heat of the Iranian summer and the longing for the coolness of water. Here are the lives of individuals in a country caught in an international power struggle: landowners and their families, servants who know much but hold their tongues, nomadic tribes whose lands are being controlled by outside forces, and Zari, a woman who must come to understand her role within her family, her country, and the world.

H.S.

Praying for Sheetrock, Melissa Fay Greene, *1991, United States,* NONFICTION

Praying for Sheetrock is a book about social change and the way it can really happen—in small measures, in individual homes, among participants who are simultaneously victims and heroes. The setting for this warmly written history is McIntosh County, Georgia, at the beginning of the 1970s. The civil rights movement has been in full force elsewhere in the South for years, but the black citizens of sleepy, tidewater McIntosh County continue on in unquestioned powerlessness in the personal fiefdom of Sheriff Tom Poppell. Though African-Americans make up fifty percent of the county's population, they are grossly excluded from participation in county politics. With great affection and intimacy, Melissa Fay Greene tells this story of the black citizens' fight for representation in local government. She introduces us to members of the community and lets us watch their day-to-day lives and listen to their conversations. We learn from what depths these people draw up the courage to participate in lawsuits to challenge their white neighbors. She also gives us an outsider's view of how the acquisition of legal and personal power changes the lives of the members of the community. In the end, after all the legal battles have been fought and won, the story is one of human nature and the noble and ignoble uses of power. This is a great book—an excellent history and a wonderful story.

K.B.-B.

Sister Outsider, Audre Lorde, *1984, United States,* ESSAYS/ SPEECHES

"Perhaps . . . I am the face of one of your fears. Because I am a woman, because I am Black, because I am a lesbian, because I am myself—a Black woman warrior poet doing my work—come to ask you, are you doing yours?" This is how Audre Lorde introduces herself in a paper entitled "The Transformation of Silence into Language and Action." Audre Lorde takes personal responsibility for this essential, perpetual transformation. In *Sister Outsider* she enters into dialogue with listeners and readers, lending us her voice and challenging us to speak and act for ourselves. She insists that we pay attention, that we confront the limitations we set upon ourselves and each other; her words have weight and resonance because she listens as rigorously as she speaks. She asks and risks more of herself than might seem possible; the political is personal on many levels of her life. She writes about facing the threat of cancer, about being part of an interracial lesbian couple raising a son; about sex, poetry, rage, and restraint. She is a fiercely intelligent writer, addressing racism, sexism, and heterosexism from the heart of her individual experience. Audre Lorde demonstrates how each of us must speak for and from our most intimate knowledge, yet simultaneously extend the boundaries around ourselves to include the "outsider," to include more than we have been, more than we thought we could imagine.

K.B.

Sofia Petrovna, Lydia Chukovskaya, *translated from Russian by Aline Werth, 1965, Russia,* NOVEL

Sofia Petrovna is an unusual book—one of the few novels about Stalin's purges written shortly after they occurred. It was almost published in the Soviet Union in 1963, but, after receiving sixty percent of her royalty advance, Lydia Chukovskaya was told that the work contained "ideological distortion" and would not go to press. In response, she sued for the rest of her advance—and won. Two years later, the work was published in Paris. The novel opens with Sofia Petrovna, a mother who has recently discovered the joys of having a paying job as a typist. Sharing her apartment with several other families, attending mandatory meetings at work—these are simply parts of her daily life as a Soviet citizen, as unquestioned and necessary as brushing one's teeth or washing dishes. When the purges begin and the director of her office is taken away, even after her own son is arrested, she tries to believe in both the government and in the innocence of people she loves. But as Sofia Petrovna stands in line after line—attempting to gain information, pass along money, plead for her son—she slowly loses her innocence and her sanity. Sofia Petrovna is not Lydia Chukovskaya, but the emotional background for her story came from the experience of the author, whose husband was arrested and murdered during one of Stalin's purges. In this slim novel, Lydia Chukovskaya was determined to describe, through the life of an ordinary woman, "an educated society driven to loss of consciousness by lies."

E.B.

Sultana's Dream and Selections from The Secluded Ones, Rokeya Sakhawat Hossain, *nonfiction selections translated from Bangla by Roushan Jahan, 1905, Bangladesh,* SHORT STORY/ NONFICTION

The story "Sultana's Dream" first appeared in print in 1905. Written by a Muslim woman, it reverses the role of purdah, the practice of seclusion and segregation of women. Through a dream, the narrator visits a country run by women where the men are hidden; on her tour she sees gardens everywhere, a transportation system that is efficient, and kitchens that are clean and pleasant to work in. When the narrator questions her guide about how this happened, the guide challenges her: "Why do you allow yourselves to be shut up? . . . You have neglected the duty you owe to yourself and you have lost your natural rights by shutting your eyes to your own interests." This amazing story reads very quickly, but it is not light reading. Following "Sultana's Dream" are selections of Rokeya Sakhawat Hossain's observations of women who live under purdah, including accounts of her own experiences: "Ever since I turned five, I have had to hide myself from women even . . . I had to disappear as soon as strangers approached." Rokeya Sakhawat Hossain, who lived between 1880 and 1932, devoted her life to the education of women and the recognition of sexual equality. She was a thought-provoking, far-sighted woman with visions of a world beyond the realities of her life.

H.S.

A Taste of Power: A Black Woman's Story, Elaine Brown, *1992, United States,* AUTOBIOGRAPHY

In her autobiography *A Taste of Power: A Black Woman's Story,* Elaine Brown chronicles her life from her childhood through her rise to the head of the Black Panther Party. She describes her feelings of powerlessness and fear as a black girl growing up in a poor section of North Philadelphia, and her desire to assimilate in order to become like her elementary school classmates—white and affluent. It is not until after college and several eye-opening relationships with white men that she becomes politicized and turns to the Black Panther Party. She feels that their struggle is her struggle, their problems are her problems—but she rapidly finds herself in conflict. In the midst of a Black Panther Party that has become obsessed with armed revolution, she fights for social programs such as food banks, schools, and medical assistance. During her rise to leadership she repeatedly has to confront the machismo of the Panther Party: "A woman in the Black Power movement was considered, at best, irrelevant. . . . If a black woman assumed a role of leadership, she was said to be eroding black manhood, to be hindering the progress of the black race. She was an enemy of black people." Elaine Brown journeys from belief to disagreement to violent opposition, and eventually flees in fear for her safety. *A Taste of Power* is an insightful, detailed, and fast-moving look into her struggles against oppression and opposition before and during the era of the Black Panther movement.

D.N.-W.

The Threshing Floor, Barbara Burford, *1987, England,* SHORT STORIES

Brown-skinned, brown-eyed, black-haired women are at the center of each of the seven short stories in this collection. "Dreaming the Sky Down" features Donna, a teenager who practices flying only in her dreams until she learns to face the abusive school nuns. In "The Pinstripe Summer," a loyal and bored bookkeeper falls in love "with such tensile insidiousness, that although she had not been consciously aware of its spangled ambush, she was able, once knowing, to plot the ways and steps of its arrival." The title story, an intense novella about love and art, is told through Hannah, a young working-class glass artist recovering from the breast-cancer death of her partner, Jennifer Harrison. Despite the fact that Jennifer is a white, middle-class poet, she and Hannah had done the hard work necessary to make a good life together. Grieving alone in the home Jennifer's family abandoned, the home she and Jennifer remodeled to make their own, Hannah must make her way past memories of Jennifer and through her own nearly forgotten shame to find new life and love. The deeply evocative prose in these stories vibrates with the wisdom of experienced passion.

J.L.

A Vindication of the Rights of Women, Mary Wollstonecraft, *1792, England,* NONFICTION

A Vindication of the Rights of Women was written during a time of revolutionary fervor, when the principle of inalienable rights for all men had caused and was causing political turmoil in the United States, France, and Britain. What Mary Wollstonecraft did was relatively simple in premise but complicated in reality: she applied the concept of inalienable rights to women as well as men. Her attack on those who perpetuate a sexual double standard is direct and pointed: "I must declare what I firmly believe, that all writers who have written on the subject of female education and manners, from Rousseau to Dr. Gregory, have contributed to render women more artificial, weak characters than they would otherwise have been; and consequently, more useless members of society." Mary Wollstonecraft blasts the imbalance of power between the sexes, pointing out that, as with governments, an imbalance of power corrupts both the oppressed and the oppressor. She seeks instead an education for women and men that will produce individuals with reason, knowledge, and virtue. An eloquent, self-educated, and self-supporting woman, she was rewarded for her efforts in *A Vindication of the Rights of Women* with the label "a hyena in petticoats." Her writing, like most prose of her time, tends to be verbose by today's standards, yet her arguments have passion and insight that speak across more than two centuries.

E.B.

Women, Culture, & Politics, Angela Y. Davis, *1990, United States,* ESSAYS

"Politics do not stand in polar opposition to our lives. Whether we desire it or not, they permeate our existence, insinuating themselves into the most private spaces of our lives." In this collection of speeches, essays, lectures, and conference reports written between 1983 and 1987, Angela Davis—world-renowned teacher and political activist for the past thirty years—continues her unrelenting effort to bring the light of intelligence, internationalism, and inclusion to United States politics. A classically trained scholar who took her learning to heart and put it into action despite the personal risks and political persecution that resulted, she makes her message clear: "The roots of sexism and homophobia are found in the same economic and political institutions that serve as the foundation of racism in this country." In sections called "On Women and the Pursuit of Equality and Peace," "On International Issues," and "On Education and Culture," she explores the unbroken history of African-American women's organizational efforts to confront the causes and change the conditions that create the dismal living and working conditions of the majority of working-class women, regardless of race. Drawing from a vast store of knowledge, using sources gathered from statistics, history, classic literature, contemporary poetry, political speeches, international events, and official government policies, Angela Davis offers wisdom and hope in her ruthless analysis of how things are and her elegant vision of how things could be.

J.L.

The Women Outside: Meanings and Myths of Homelessness, Stephanie Golden, *1992, United States,* NONFICTION

"How is it," asks Stephanie Golden, "that I could be going home while the women I had just left had no home?" This question leads her to research and write this impressively well documented and eloquent text on the social psychology of female powerlessness in America and England. In "Real Life Outside"—the first of five sections—she describes the images and realities of homeless women in New York City, and tries to answer questions about who they were before and what drove them outside. The second section, "Mythmaking," explores the power of English-language witch-based myths and fairy tales that enforce social fears of female individuality and of women—especially old women—alone, without family. "Homeless Women Have Always Existed" details and compares the history of male and female homelessness from the ancient world through contemporary times in England and America. "In Praise of Folly" dissects the connections between "mental illness" and homelessness and demonstrates how the bags "full of junk" and the layers of clothing are often all that's left of the lost—given away, denied—"self" of the woman without a home. The conclusion—"At the Margins"—summarizes the social modes and dangers of scapegoating, or relegating people to the periphery of humanity. With unrelenting thoroughness, dispassionate rhetoric, and warm compassion for the "women outside," Stephanie Golden sheds significant light on the history and psychology of women in English-speaking societies.

J.L.

The Yellow Wallpaper, Charlotte Perkins Gilman, *1892, United States,* SHORT STORY

The unnamed narrator and her doctor husband, John, live in "a colonial mansion, a hereditary estate." She believes the house is haunted. "John laughs at me, of course, but one expects that." She believes she is ill but her husband and her brother, also a physician, say it is only "temporary nervous depression—a slight hysterical tendency." They insist on "phosphates or phosphites—whichever it is—and tonics," and absolutely forbid work until she is well again. She believes "personally . . . that congenial work, with excitement and change, would do me good. Personally, I disagree with their ideas. But what is one to do? I did write for a while in spite of them; but it does exhaust me a good deal—having to be so sly about it, or else meet with heavy opposition." She is confined to rest in a room she hates, with wallpaper she finds hideously ugly: "The color is repellent, almost revolting: a smoldering unclean yellow . . . dull yet lurid orange in some places, a sickly sulphur tint in others." It is in this room that she writes her secret journal that is this story. She struggles to believe in her husband's and brother's "kindness" and "care" while, with terrifying starkness, she narrates her journey into madness.

J.L.

Trials and Adversity

Adversity is the mountain we never planned to climb, the illness we have to overcome, the poverty that shrinks our stomachs and chafes our minds; a society, an army, a person that threatens our lives. These are the battles women fight; the books here sometimes constitute the only public recognition of their struggle. Eugenia Ginzburg survives an eighteen-year imprisonment in Russia. Fadwa Tuqan fights sexism within her own family and works to promote the Palestinian cause. Sarah E. Wright describes a life of grinding poverty. Edith Wharton examines the suffocating restrictions of upper-class turn-of-the-century New York society. Harriet Jacobs lives for seven years in a three-foot-tall garret rather than return to slavery. Nancy Mairs describes her life as a woman with multiple sclerosis. Buchi Emechta's autobiographical novel tells of one woman's determination to gain a better life for herself and her children despite the sexism of her Nigerian husband and the racism of England. A young woman must battle the memory of her husband's dead first wife. Sylvia Fraser faces the fact of incest. Wanda Coleman writes about living in Watts. Zhang Jie's characters are affected by the tragedies of the Chinese cultural revolution. Trapped by circumstances not of their making, these women do what they can—yell, cry, hit out with both fists, find an escape, make peace within themselves. They do not always succeed, yet these books carry a feeling of triumph, for they look adversity in the face and capture it in prose.

Anne Frank: The Diary of a Young Girl	Anne Frank
The Bell Jar	Sylvia Plath
Berji Kristin	Latife Tekin
The Censors	Luisa Valenzuela
Christabel	Christabel Bielenberg
Daughter of Earth	Agnes Smedley
A Daughter of Han	Ida Pruitt
The Girls of Slender Means	Muriel Spark
The Hour of the Star	Clarice Lispector
The House of Mirth	Edith Wharton
The House with the Blind Glass Windows	Herbjørg Wassmo
Incidents in the Life of a Slave Girl	Harriet Jacobs
Journey into the Whirlwind	Eugenia Semyonovna Ginzburg
Love Must Not Be Forgotten	Zhang Jie
Magic Eyes	Wendy Ewald
A Mountainous Journey	Fadwa Tuqan
My Father's House	Sylvia Fraser
Nectar in a Sieve	Kamala Markandaya
Or Else, The Lightning God & Other Stories	Catherine Lim
Our Nig	Harriet E. Wilson
Plaintext	Nancy Mairs
Rebecca	Daphne DuMaurier
Second Class Citizen	Buchi Emechta
This Child's Gonna Live	Sarah E. Wright
A War of Eyes and Other Stories	Wanda Coleman

Anne Frank: The Diary of a Young Girl, Anne Frank, *translated from Dutch by B. M. Mooyaart-Doubleday, 1947, Holland,* DIARY

In 1942, on her thirteenth birthday, Anne Frank is given a diary, which she promptly puts to use. In many ways, Anne Frank is like any other thirteen-year-old—concerned about boyfriends and passing on to the next grade ("though I'm not too certain about my math"), relieved to have a diary because, while she has "darling parents" and many friends, she has no one she can really talk to. History sets her diary apart, however: less than a month after her birthday, her family is forced to go into hiding to escape from the Gestapo. Her diary records her two years secluded in an attic with seven other people: the fights, the scares, the frustration of having to sit for days without talking or moving, her growing affection for the son of the other family that shares their "Secret Annex." Her journal mixes the personal reflections of a young girl turning into a woman with horror stories of the world outside. She is emotional, introspective, mischievous, and determined to be hopeful: "I've found that there is always some beauty left—in nature, sunshine, freedom, in yourself: these can all help you." Her words are haunting; after two years the Gestapo invaded the attic and took all its inhabitants to concentration camps, where Anne Frank died two months before Holland was liberated. Her diary was miraculously overlooked in the raid; it is a poignant and important memoir of World War II.

E.B.

The Bell Jar, Sylvia Plath, *1963, United States,* NOVEL

Sylvia Plath's autobiographical novel is a somber, circling journey through a severe depression. Nineteen-year-old Esther Greenwood, on a one-month internship with a fashion magazine in New York City in the early 1950s, wonders what life is all about and feels increasingly confused by her thoughts. When she returns to her mother's home, Esther's feelings of despair become apparent. The reader is awake with Esther when she hasn't slept for seven days, fourteen days, twenty-one days, and feels her suffering when she refuses to wash her clothes or hair because "it seem[s] so silly." At her mother's insistence, Esther sees a doctor, who asks her what she thinks is wrong. Contemplating her response, she realizes that the question "made it sound as if nothing was really wrong, I only thought it was wrong." She is given shock treatment—"a great jolt [that] drubbed me till I thought my bones would break and the sap fly out of me like a split plant"—which causes her to wonder what she has done to deserve this. Later, she spends extended time in private sanitariums. Her awareness throughout her ordeal that many of the accepted realities of life are not her realities makes her struggle even more heart-wrenching. Her pain is real and tangible; it is with sadness that the reader learns that Sylvia Plath committed suicide only one month after *The Bell Jar*'s publication.

H.S.

Berji Kristin: Tales from the Garbage Hills, Latife Tekin, *translated from Turkish by Saliha Paker and Ruth Christie, 1983, Turkey,* NOVEL

Based on actual events in the city of Istanbul, *Berji Kristin* gives life to people who own nothing. These people come to the city for work and make their homes upon the garbage hills from whatever material is available—tin, cardboard, cast-off wood. The wind blows down these fragile structures during the night, taking away babies "asleep in the roof-cradles." The people rebuild. The city sends trucks that knock down the shelters and huts. Again they rebuild. In time, industries that provide jobs rise up near the stench of the garbage hills. But the factories bring a river of blue hot water that can peel away layers of skin; they send clouds of the most beautiful colors into the sky and rain snow upon the hills even in the summer. Each exploitation becomes part of history; the people from the garbage hills compose songs about the blue water, write poems about the wind. The workers form unions and chants become battle cries against the many injustices they suffer. Gullu Baba, an old blind man, is their spiritual leader; Honking Alhas, so named because of a nasal obstruction, is their historian; and Fidan of Many Skills leads the fight for clean water. These tales of spirit and survival show how both personal and corporate greed can be exposed through the influence of rumor and the healing of laughter.

H.S.

The Censors, Luisa Valenzuela, *translated from Spanish by Hortence Carpentier, J. Jorge Castello, Helen Lane, Christopher Leland, Margaret Sayers Peden, and David Unger, 1976, Argentina,* SHORT STORIES

The Censors stretches and enlivens the conventional literary definition of "story" to include brief, poetic, and poignant creations that portray moments of life in Argentina. In "The Snow White Watchman," a desperately bored bank security guard changes more than his daily routine when he requests permission to look after the bank's plants. "The Best Shod" describes the life of a person who sells dead people's shoes to beggars, mismatched shoes recovered from severed legs "found in the underbrush," although "this doesn't happen very often, usually corpses are found with both shoes intact." In "One Siren or Another," an old lighthouse keeper holds a ship's captain hostage after the ship rams and sinks his imaginary continent. The last story, "The Place of Its Quietude," is an autobiographical account of a writer living in a city controlled by fear. When writing in cafés is outlawed, she hides: "Though I'm quiet these days, I go on jotting it all down in bold strokes (and at great risk) because it's the only form of freedom left." Luisa Valenzuela's superhuman characters, fantastic plots, and symbolic settings are unified through an eloquent and urgent understanding that these stories can and will "bear witness to the truth."

J.L.

Christabel, Christabel Bielenberg, *1968, Germany/England,* MEMOIR

Christabel Bielenberg was born in England, the daughter of middle-class English-Irish parents. She became a German citizen in 1934 when she married Peter Bielenberg, a young law student from a prominent Hamburg family. *Christabel* is memoir as history, covering the war years 1932 through 1945, and written with "one advantage perhaps over those whose knowledge must needs depend on documents: I am English, I was German, and above all I was there." At the time of their marriage, she and Peter brush off her family's warnings about problems in Germany and concentrate on finding an appropriate house. Peter finishes law school, and Christabel gives birth to two sons. By 1939, however, it becomes obvious that "something had gone terribly wrong with the works. [Germany] had become like some prison turned inside out, with the criminals in command." When harassment of communists, labor leaders, and Jewish people is legalized, no one, not even their neighbors, can be trusted anymore. When Peter joins a military organization intent on ousting Hitler from power in late 1939, Christabel supports his decision and they begin a dangerously secret life. Written from the perspective of a stay-at-home wife and mother and filled with political, cultural, and domestic detail, *Christabel* presents a lucid, important, and often-neglected view of the anti-Hitler movement in the German military during World War II.

J.L.

Daughter of Earth, Agnes Smedley, *1929, United States,* NOVEL

Branded as a "radical," a "premature fascist," and a "red sympathizer" who saw her books burned during the height of the McCarthy period of the 1950s, Agnes Smedley was largely excised from American literature until the 1973 reissue of *Daughter of Earth.* With fierce and painful honesty, this autobiographical novel describes her recurrent attempts to survive the scars of the poverty, child abuse, ignorance, and pain she experienced growing up in Midwestern and Western mining towns during the early part of this century, and portrays her involvement as an adult with revolutionary movements in India and China. This rare example of the self-transformation of an ordinary working-class woman into a feminist, teacher, writer, tireless activist for social change, and revolutionary is powerful and compelling. Writing in 1929, Agnes Smedley describes marriage as "a relic of human slavery" and refuses to be owned by any man; instead she insists that her allegiances to humankind are first as a daughter of earth, an individual, and second as a servant to the cause of human justice: "Subjection of any kind and in any place is beneath the dignity of man . . . the highest joy is to fight by the side of those who for any reason of their own making or ours, are unable to develop to full human stature."

S.S.

A Daughter of Han: The Autobiography of a Chinese Working Woman, Ida Pruitt, from the story told her by Ning Lao T'ai-t'ai, *1945, China (United States),* ORAL HISTORY

Ning Lao T'ai-t'ai, born in the seventh year of T'ung Chih, 1867, lived a full and difficult life; she bore and buried children, worked as a maidservant, begged for food, and felt pride in her old age at sharing a home with her son and his family. A lively, driven woman who wants only to provide for her family, often without the support of her opium-addicted husband, Ning Lao wonders how life would have been different had she received a formal education: "I might have been somebody in the world." When her husband sells their kitchenware, she gets it back; when he sells their daughters, she gets them back, then must give one up because she's unable to feed her. As a maidservant, she often works for Christian missionaries but refuses to accept their religion. When told she should thank God for her strong arms and legs, she responds that she had them before she'd ever heard of God. She describes the importance of neighbors and self-reliance in the life of a peasant, stating bluntly: "I am not afraid of hard work but I am afraid of hunger." Her life is recorded in conversations with Ida Pruitt over a two-year period. Unfortunately, the book ends in 1938 with the Japanese occupation of Peking, and the rest of Ning Lao's life is unknown.

H.S.

The Girls of Slender Means, Muriel Spark, *1963, England,* NOVEL

"Long ago in 1945 all of the nice people in England were poor . . ." So begins Muriel Spark's *The Girls of Slender Means.* Set in a "home for young ladies" in wartime London, it is a funny and sharply drawn portrait of a group of young women struggling to survive in a world in which men and money are vital but scarce commodities. The "girls" are polite and well bred, with eyes that gleam with "an eager spirited light that resembled near genius, but was youth merely." Jane craves time to do her "brainwork" and supports herself through various schemes; beautiful Selina is not above accepting clothing rations from any one of her "weak" men; and Joanna, the rector's daughter, is much taken with poetry. In this atmosphere of genteel poverty and youthful chaos, these women, practical yet romantic, ruthless yet tender-hearted, negotiate their passage to the end of the war and the end of an era. Muriel Spark's gift for characters and dialogue make this little book both satirical and compassionate in its vision. The war years were a time when women, socialized to be dependent, were forced by circumstances to be autonomous. The ways in which these young women coped with the daily compromise in their lives without ultimately feeling "compromised" makes for both entertaining and illuminating reading.

S.L.

The Hour of the Star, Clarice Lispector, *translated from Portuguese by Giovanni Pontiero, 1977, Brazil,* NOVEL

The Hour of the Star, or "The Blame Is Mine," or "She Doesn't Know How to Protest," (or one of eleven more choices of subtitle) is a compact, compelling, and disturbing book. The narrator, Rodrigo S. M., writes the story of Macabea, his young female clerk, almost against his will: "Before this typist entered my life, I was a reasonably content chap despite my limited success as a writer. Things were somehow so good that they were in danger of becoming very bad because what is fully mature is very close to rotting." Stream-of-consciousness writing filled with Rodrigo's personal anguish is interspersed with the telling of Macabea's story. "Born with a legacy of misfortune, a creature from nowhere with the expression of someone who apologizes for occupying too much space," Macabea is an ugly, undernourished native of rural northeast Brazil who loves Coca-Cola and Marilyn Monroe, lives on a steady diet of hot dogs, and believes that "to be well educated was the same as knowing how to tell lies." Her daily life is constricted by the bleakest poverty, her spirit is squeezed into voiceless want, her intelligence is choked with unknown need. In less than one hundred pages, Clarice Lispector tells a brilliantly multifaceted and searing story.

J.L.

The House of Mirth, Edith Wharton, *1905, United States,* NOVEL

The most compelling aspect of *The House of Mirth* is Lily Bart's descent of the social ladder, as she changes from an alluring, fashionable decoration at lavish country estates to a wild-eyed, disheveled woman living in a shabby hotel, addicted to tea and sleeping drops. The most frightening aspect of the book is that the progress seems somehow both inevitable and avoidable at nearly every turn. Here is a physically beautiful and psychologically complex woman who has become or been made into an object for consumption by a society that values the material world exclusively. As Lily approaches thirty, still unmarried, and without financial resources, her value—in this society—declines. In part, her misfortune can be ascribed to her lack of a maternal influence, her own irresolution, the weakness of her primary suitor, and the viciousness of the other rich women in the novel; but ultimate blame has to fall on a society that made her "so evidently the victim of the civilization that produced her, that the links of her bracelet seemed like manacles chaining her to her fate." Nearly ninety years after its publication, this novel is still chillingly accurate in its remorseless critique of a society willing to sacrifice any and all who do not conform to its expectations.

C.T.

The House with the Blind Glass Windows, Herbjørg Wassmo, *translated from Norwegian by Roseann Lloyd and Allen Simpson, 1981, Norway,* NOVEL

The House with the Blind Glass Windows is a searing look into a small Norwegian village ten years after World War II, viewed through the life of pre-adolescent Tora. Tora's stepfather, Henrik—injured in the war, often drunk, and always angry—rapes her repeatedly. Although she longs to tell, she feels an undeserved guilt and knows that telling would only add another burden to her mother's difficult life. With regret we watch a chasm develop between Tora and her mother, even as Tora continually searches for hope. Her imagination becomes her powerful, if temporary, ally, a place where life holds promise. Her spirit is fed by three people: her aunt, who, unaware of the abuse, consciously guides Tora; a teacher who provides inspiration in an otherwise stifling environment; and a young deaf-mute friend, another child who can't talk. *The House with the Blind Glass Windows* exposes the struggles of the whole village: the harsh realities of the fishing wharf, the humiliation of buying food on credit, the winter coldness of the tenement apartments, the lingering effects of German occupation. Herbjørg Wassmo brings the reader in touch with the villagers' daily battles and Tora's constant search for safety and comfort.

H.S.

Incidents in the Life of a Slave Girl, Harriet Jacobs, *1861, United States,* AUTOBIOGRAPHY

"Slavery is terrible for men, but it is far more terrible for women," Harriet Jacobs wrote in 1861. At that time she was an escaped slave living in the North, but the Fugitive Slave Law of 1850 meant that she could not consider being in the Northern states a guarantee of freedom or safety. Her book is an eloquent recital of the suffering that is slavery. Families broken apart; promises of freedom made but never kept; whippings, beatings, and burnings; masters selling their own children—all are recounted with precise detail and a blazing indignation. Harriet Jacobs's master started pursuing her when she was fifteen; in disgust she continually refused and avoided him. Her first attempt at revenge and escape failed: she became the lover of a local unmarried white man and with him had several children, but even then her master refused to sell her. Finally, in desperation, she ran away and hid in an uninsulated garret, three feet high at its tallest point, with almost no air or light. She stayed there for seven years, enduring cold, heat, and a crippling lack of movement, always hoping to catch a glimpse of her children through a crack in the walls as they walked by on the road below her. At last she had a chance to escape to the North. Her story is a remarkable testimony to her strength and courage, and an unrelenting attack upon the institution of slavery.

E.B.

Journey into the Whirlwind, Eugenia Semyonovna Ginzburg, *translated from Russian by Paul Stevenson and Max Hayward, 1967, Russia,* MEMOIR

In 1989, the Sovremennik Theatre in Moscow brought Eugenia Ginzburg's memoir to the stage for the first time. When the curtain came down an emotional audience rose up and applauded for twenty-four minutes. The tragedy of an entire nation had finally been dramatized in one woman's poignant account. Nineteen thirty-seven, the year that Eugenia Ginzburg was arrested and falsely charged as a Trotskyist terrorist counterrevolutionary, was only the beginning of Stalin's purges. Nearly six million people were arrested on trumped-up charges, and millions were executed or perished in prisons and camps. Eugenia Ginzburg, a historian and loyal Communist Party member, chronicles her own terrifying arrest, interrogation, and eighteen-year imprisonment. She speaks with brutal honesty; her ability to recount the minutes and hours of her internment is surpassed only by her extraordinary will to survive. This memoir is important for those who wish to understand Russian history and for anyone who has ever wondered how they might survive in a maelstrom, facing constant betrayals, overwhelming physical hardship, agonizing loneliness, and a longing for the past. Eugenia Ginzburg shows us "how thin the line is between high principles and blinkered intolerance," and yet she emerges from these pages as a compassionate woman with the "conviction that dignity and honor are not just empty words."

R.S.

Love Must Not Be Forgotten, Zhang Jie, *translated from Chinese by Gladys Yang, W. J. F. Jenner, Janet Wang, Stephen Hallett, and Yu Fanquin, 1986, China,* SHORT STORIES/ NOVELLA

The horrors of the Chinese Cultural Revolution linger in the memories and lives of Zhang Jie's characters in this engrossing collection of six short stories and a novella. In the title piece, a daughter, by not following her mother's deathbed wishes, learns of the great love of her mother's life. An elderly man in "An Unfinished Record" wonders: "Do we really have to wait until it's too late to do anything, before we remember all those countless old debts great and small that we've no way of settling now?" A young student learns an important life lesson about his own frailty from a woman who sells tickets for the bus in "Who Knows How To Live?" The novella, "The Ark," describes three single women who "were quite used to hardship, so much so that they often failed to notice if there was an easier way." Though these are stories of often painful lives, they also remind us of the powers of love, commitment, and endurance.

H.S.

Magic Eyes: Scenes from an Andean Girlhood, Wendy Ewald from stories told by Alicia and María Vásquez, *1992, Colombia* (*United States*), ORAL HISTORY

" '(Your papa) passed the power of evil from his eyes to yours. Now you must live with the burden of evil for the rest of your life.' I wanted to ask her what evil was, but she clamped her hand over my mouth. Her hands were dirty, they smelled like the earth. That smell—that must be what evil is." *Magic Eyes* tells in words and photographs the story of Alicia Vásquez's peasant childhood in Colombia. Transcribed by Wendy Ewald from conversations with Alicia and her mother, María, *Magic Eyes* recounts Alicia's struggle to overcome poverty and the stigma of the evil eye. Despite the difficulty of daily life and her troubled relationships with her mother, with the villagers, and with men, Alicia achieves self-reliance and respect. Her move to the squatters' camps on the outskirts of Bogotá, followed by skirmishes with police and involvement with unions and cooperatives seen by the government as subversive, illuminates the government's inability to deal with the increasing urbanization of peasant societies in Colombia. A selection of photographs, taken by Wendy Ewald and her fifth-grade students in Bogotá and in the small Andean village where Wendy Ewald lived and taught, is interspersed with sections of text, and resonates with meaning. Through her belief in herself, Alicia transcends the onus of the evil eye and seeks another destiny for herself. *Magic Eyes* is a powerful, magical testament to the complexities of female existence and the ever-hopefulness of the human spirit.

L.A.

A Mountainous Journey, Fadwa Tuqan, *translated from Arabic by Olive Kenny, 1985, Palestine,* AUTOBIOGRAPHY

To read this melodious autobiography, you may need three bookmarks: one to keep your place in the text, one for the notes listed in the back, and one to help you find the author's poetry as she refers to it. From these pages a compassionate, opinionated Palestinian woman emerges. Fadwa Tuqan was born in 1917; her mother couldn't remember the date this daughter was born, only what she cooked that day. When Fadwa is an adolescent, a young man passes her a sprig of jasmine, and she recalls her first feelings of love as "borne on a jasmine flower redolent with scent that fastened itself to the walls of my heart." When she is restricted to her home because of her interaction with the young man, her small world collapses. Her brother, however, teaches her poetry; with his encouragement and guidance she becomes one of the Arab world's most distinguished poets. When Palestine falls in 1948, "Arab society [is] shaken, politically, socially and culturally," and Fadwa Tuqan's world grows: now she is able to meet in coffeehouses with friends, both female and male, to travel, and to write poetry that reflects her budding political awareness. But by 1967 she recognizes: "The reality we were living every moment of our lives was one of sheer pain and misery." Since then she has written little poetry and has devoted her time to Palestinian causes. Fadwa Tuqan emerged from her life of dictated attire and seclusion to become a politically active feminist. With her autobiography she allows the reader to accompany her on her fascinating and difficult journey.

H.S.

My Father's House, Sylvia Fraser, *1987, Canada,* AUTOBIOGRAPHY

Sylvia Fraser grew up in a home where her father worked at a respectable job, was active in church, and provided for his wife and two daughters. Sylvia was a rebellious child who became an outstanding high school student; she was also a victim of incest for years and years, but no one acknowledged it. In her forties, after a divorce she didn't understand, an affair with the father of a high school friend, and continual dreams of a past she didn't recognize, Sylvia Fraser finally learned of her "shadow-self." This person inside her held terrible secrets: "She knew passion where I knew only inhibition, then grief where I knew guilt, then terror where I knew anger. She monitored my every thought, manipulated my actions, aided my survival and sabotaged my dreams, for she was I and I was she." She begins to understand some of the choices she has made, her actions and reactions to life. To admit the violation of trust and love was part of her road to healing; to write this deeply painful book was another part. Going beyond her own suffering, Sylvia Fraser reaches out to help readers understand the pain of victims who don't heal. *My Father's House* can give you renewed respect for the power of the human spirit and new insight into those who have experienced such violation.

H.S.

Nectar in a Sieve, Kamala Markandaya, *1954, India,* NOVEL

Rukmani, a peasant from a village in India, lives a life of constant struggle, yet she is a source of strength for many. At age twelve she marries a man she has never met and moves with him to his rented farmland. Over the years their marriage fills with love, mutual respect, and children: one daughter and many sons. A tannery built near their village forever alters Rukmani's life, for the tannery takes away farmland and silence, and while it provides jobs, they come at great costs. The changes as the village is transformed from an agricultural to an industrial community frighten Rukmani; her life becomes one of "Hope and fear. Twin forces that tugged at us first in one direction and then in another. . . . Fear, constant companion of the peasant. Hunger, ever present to jog his elbow should he relax. Despair, ready to engulf him should he falter." Kenny, a white doctor in Rukmani's village, watches with a palpable foreboding his patients' daily struggle to survive. He leaves the village suddenly and often, and just as suddenly reappears, as if life there is too much for him yet he can't stay away. Rukmani and Kenny's conversations make apparent their individual and shared suffering, and while their experiences of the world are completely different, their friendship is based on respect and mutual reliance. *Nectar in a Sieve* is a powerful, depressing, but ultimately hopeful novel of a life lived with love, faith, and inner strength.

H.S.

Or Else, The Lightning God & Other Stories, Catherine Lim, *1980, Singapore,* SHORT STORIES

Singapore is a mixture of nationalities, religions, and classes, and Catherine Lim seems to represent them all. Stories of joss sticks and temples, alcohol and money, spouses, parents, and children—all are included in this collection. Her stories tell of people struggling with abject poverty and enduring everyday situations. Often the catalyst in the story is a peripheral character, one who may never even speak but who provides the impact, and many times the irony, that make these haunting stories. One man reacts to a conversation with someone he just met: "What had lain dead in him all these years stirred uneasily to life: his heart filled, his mind crowded with dim visitations and images. He was awash in a tide of feeling too great to resist, so he wept." Many of these stories are sad: a character climbs a hill, only to find a mountain. Catherine Lim peeks and pokes into lives, uncovering unconscious weaknesses and unexpected strengths.

H.S.

Our Nig; or, Sketches from the Life of a Free Black, in a Two-Story House, North, Showing that Slavery's Shadows Fall Even There, Harriet E. Wilson, *1859, United States,* NOVEL

Ignored by critics upon its publication, and "lost" for more than one hundred years, *Our Nig* was rediscovered and reprinted in 1983 and is currently considered to be the first novel by an African-American published in the United States. This fascinating book combines elements of nineteenth-century slave narratives and domestic novels; it defied the social conventions of its time by portraying interracial marriage, child abandonment, cruel Northerners, and an African-American heroine who is full of energy, intelligence, and imagination, bowed only by prolonged and arduous toil. The story begins with six-year-old Frado, deserted by her white mother after the death of her black father, and left to live as a servant with the

Bellmonts. While some Bellmont family members are sympathetic, Frado is treated like a slave by the mistress of the house and her daughter. By the time Frado is an adult she fulfills duties in "all departments—man, boy, housekeeper, domestic, etc." One by one, Frado's allies are taken from her, replaced finally by a man with whom "she opened her heart to the presence of love"—and who then deserts her. With an ironic play off the beginning of the story, *Our Nig* is Frado's—and the author's—attempt to provide financial support so she can keep her child.

E.B.

Plaintext: Deciphering a Woman's Life, Nancy Mairs, *1986, United States,* ESSAYS

In lucid, forthright essays, Nancy Mairs examines acute anxiety, suicidal depression, and the physical realities of coping with multiple sclerosis. She also writes about what she loves and what she has learned: "I am wounded easily, but I am just as easily delighted." Since the rigors of MS and agoraphobia make many of life's usual "adventures" impossible for her, Nancy Mairs redefines adventure within her own parameters, not by what one does but by the passion or thoroughness with which one does it. Her feminism, like her sense of adventure, begins in personal experience and extends to something larger than the plain details. Describing her stay in a psychiatric hospital as a young mother, she recounts each agonizing step of her survival (not "recovery") and relates this experience to the "madwoman" paradigm that haunts women who have confronted raw frustration and existential panic. And while she hates her physical limitations and refuses to be defined by them, she is determined to expand her outlook even through the experience of being "crippled" (the word she chooses to use). Empathy complicates and enriches her struggles: "in searching for and shaping a stable core in a life wrenched by change and loss . . . I must recognize the same process . . . in the lives around me." This writer teaches, by her living and working example, the ways we may incorporate and transform the obstacles in our lives.

K.B.

Rebecca, Daphne DuMaurier, *1938, England,* NOVEL

Rebecca is a novel of mystery and passion, a dark psychological tale of secrets and betrayal, dead loves and an estate called Manderley that is as much a presence as the humans who inhabit it: "When the leaves rustle, they sound very much like the stealthy movement of a woman in evening dress, and when they shiver suddenly and fall, and scatter away along the ground, they might be the pitter, patter of a woman's hurrying footsteps, and the mark in the gravel the imprint of a high-heeled satin shoe." Manderley is filled with memories of the elegant and flamboyant Rebecca, the first Mrs. DeWinter; with the obsessive loyalty of her housekeeper, Mrs. Danvers, who observes the young, timid second Mrs. DeWinter with sullen hostility; and with the oppressive silences of a secretive husband, Maxim. Rebecca may be physically dead, but she is a force to contend with, and the housekeeper's evil matches that of her former mistress as a purveyor of the emotional horror thrust on the innocent Mrs. DeWinter. The tension builds as the new Mrs. DeWinter slowly grows and asserts herself, surviving the wicked deceptions of Mrs. Danvers and the silent deceits of her husband, to emerge triumphant in the midst of a surprise ending that leaves the reader with a sense of haunting justice.

V.S.

Second Class Citizen, Buchi Emechta, *1974, Nigeria/England,* NOVEL

An autobiographical novel, *Second Class Citizen* follows its main character, Adah, through her years in Nigeria and England. As a young girl, Adah dreams of going to school and then to the United Kingdom, whose name, "when pronounced by Adah's father sounded so heavy, like the type of noise one associated with bombs." Unfortunately, Adah's father dies, and she is sent to be a servant among relatives. Despite all obstacles she manages to make her way through school, but when she graduates, she is faced with a problem: society says she must marry to have a home. The man she chooses turns out to be self-centered, lazy, and chauvinistic, proud of his educated wife who can stay in Nigeria and financially support his own academic program in England. Adah follows him to England with their two children, only to discover that England presents both old and new trials. This is a book of intense anger and tremendous strength. Adah is inspiring, not only in her unwavering desire for education and her love for her children, but in her growing determination to change her life.

E.B.

This Child's Gonna Live, Sarah E. Wright, *1969, United States,* NOVEL

Mariah and Jacob battle against grim and desperate poverty. One baby dies after her navel is bound with an unsterile bandage; another dies from pneumonia, worms, and poison. Neighbors attack and gossip, hurling words in their own hopeless frustration at trying to make a living out of the used-up land and oyster beds of Tangierneck, Maryland: "Wonder was that it hadn't all been washed away, the way that big, wide, bossy, ocean-going Nighaskin River keeps pouring water down into the mouth of the Neck until Deep Gut swallows all it can hold and backs the rest of it out for the ocean." It is a bleak and awful world, and Sarah Wright's language swirls up out of it, making the water, trees, and buzzards seem sentient and symbolic. There is little hope and much determination, little forgiveness and far too many things to forgive in this place. The Paddy Rollers come around and lynch black men, the nearest school is still far away, and nothing seems to cure Mariah's children of their constant illnesses. Yet Mariah keeps on, intent on getting her children out of the Neck, on finding a way out of a place without hope. Sarah E. Wright describes a horrible reality in stunning, beautiful, almost surreal language; her novel burns in your mind like the hallucinations of a fever.

E.B.

A War of Eyes and Other Stories, Wanda Coleman, *1988, United States,* SHORT STORIES

A "struggling welfare mother," Wanda Coleman says she was "a brash, abrasively frank young woman, her few sponsorships were frequently aborted by her naivete, her stubbornness or socio-economic contingencies." Here are twenty-five Watts, Los Angeles, stories that whisper, scream, moan, and sing about people who "smile and act nice to you but they ain't your friends," pretty newborn babies, dressed-up pimps, women who sell their bodies—but not their anger—to feed their kids, and sweet, loving friends. In "A War of Eyes," a black dancer handpicked by "Blue-Eyed Soul-Mama" to perform in an "artistic statement on racial harmony," learns "that the real war will be fought on other ground." In "Hamburgers," James David Poke, in a desperate attempt to save enough money to "do right" by his girlfriend, disciplines himself to eat one hamburger a day and sleep in his car, where he dreams his last dream of love and dignity. In "Dream 5281," "Mother's Day" is the twice-monthly day that checks are sent to county aid recipients, some of whom are mothers who can't stop looking for a place to live that "looks like 'somethin'—and no pets. By pets she meant roaches and mice." Through deft use of dialogue, dream, description, and shimmering language, Wanda Coleman writes stories that feel and sound rough, gorgeous, strong, half-dead, brave, and terrified.

J.L.

Violence

Is violence only that which is committed with a knife, a gun, a fist? What happens to our perceptions if we expand our concept of violence to include a mental or physical invasion of privacy, a poverty that endangers the mind long before it kills the body, a systematic denigration of one's identity? The books in this section open our definition of violence and help us to see it as something both more amorphous and more prevalent. When Migael Scherer is attacked, violence is not only the act of rape, but all that comes after; in *Beloved* and *The Butcher's Wife* it is not just the crime upon which the book centers, but all that comes before it. The Mozambiquan peasants described in *Dumba Nengue* endure not only individual acts of brutality, but the fear that surrounds these attacks and the way that fear rules and directs their lives. *Regeneration, Beirut Fragments, Cartucho/My Mother's Hands, A Chorus of Stones*, and *A Woman's Civil War* describe the mental as well as physical effects of war on civilians and soldiers. Keri Hulme's *The Bone People* considers the larger sociological origins and impact of child abuse. Carolina Maria de Jesus's spare, heartrending diary depicts a life of unending deprivation in the slums of Brazil. Susan Brownmiller defines rape as a crime of domination that affects all women. Cries of pain, howls of protest, quiet reflections of much-needed healing, these books show us the many faces of violence and help us to understand what surrounds, shapes, and encourages it.

Against Our Will	Susan Brownmiller
Beirut Fragments	Jean Said Makdisi
Beloved	Toni Morrison
The Bone People	Keri Hulme
Burmese Looking Glass	Edith T. Mirante
The Butcher's Wife	Li Ang
Cartucho/My Mother's Hands	Nellie Campobello
Child of the Dark	Carolina Maria de Jesus
A Chorus of Stones	Susan Griffin
Cracking India	Bapsi Sidhwa
Dogeaters	Jessica Hagedorn
Dumba Nengue	Lina Magaia
"G" Is for Gumshoe	Sue Grafton
The History of Mary Prince	Mary Prince
The House Tibet	Georgia Savage
The Loony-Bin Trip	Kate Millett
The Montreal Massacre	Louise Malette and Marie Chalouh, eds.
Regeneration	Pat Barker
Scraps of Life	Marjorie Agosin
Still Loved by the Sun	Migael Scherer
A Woman's Civil War	Cornelia Peake McDonald
Yes Is Better Than No	Byrd Baylor

Against Our Will: Men, Women and Rape, Susan Brownmiller, *1975, United States,* NONFICTION

Whether you come away feeling furious, stronger, and/or terrified, you will not be unaffected by this book. Susan Brownmiller's thoroughly researched, ground-breaking history is one woman's determined effort to make the world see rape as a crime of violence and power that achieves a political purpose: "That *some* men rape provides a sufficient threat to keep all women in a constant state of intimidation . . . men who commit rape have served in effect as front-line masculine shock troops, terrorist guerrillas in the longest sustained battle the world has ever known." *Against Our Will* begins with early legal definitions that treat rape as an act of damaging (a man's) property, then gives graphic descriptions of rape during war that remove any doubt that this is a crime of domination, not sexual gratification. Susan Brownmiller then examines other instances of rape—by gangs, fathers, murderers, and casual acquaintances—and provides an illuminating contrast between the reluctance of public officials and psychoanalysts to investigate rape and the widespread attention it receives in the popular media, particularly when the victim is young, beautiful, and white. She includes testimonies from women victims, whose voices resound with startling honesty and clarity against the background of bureaucracy, psychological jargon, and popular myths, and calls for women to empower themselves and for men to take "psychologic responsibility for the nature of [the rapist's] act." Gut-wrenching, eye-opening, *Against Our Will* is a book to make you reconsider the world and how you live.

E.B.

Beirut Fragments: A War Memoir, Jean Said Makdisi, *1990, Lebanon,* MEMOIR

How does one understand a war that has been waged in one's hometown for fifteen years? In this moving and troubling memoir about life in war-torn Beirut, Jean Said Makdisi tries to answer this question for both herself and her readers. Her background gives her a unique perspective: a Christian born in Jerusalem, she went to English schools in Cairo, then attended college in the United States, where she lived for fifteen years before moving to Beirut in 1972 with her Lebanese husband and three young sons. The descriptions of her life before Beirut are insightful and set the framework for the rest of the book. While she defines herself as a member of the "privileged class," she makes it clear that war affects each person, that when a city has no electricity or running water or food, it means none for everyone. Through the long years of war, Lebanese citizens, including Jean Makdisi, "have looked evil in the face . . . we have asked ourselves the questions that most people are spared." Her answers, at times, surprise her as she comes to realize that "one either suffered from [the continued violence], or allowed it, there was no middle ground." Amidst daily atrocities and continual false hopes of cease-fires, Jean Makdisi finds strength and true hope with her fellow humans in a community of diverse religions and ideologies.

H.S.

Beloved, Toni Morrison, *1988, United States,* NOVEL

When slavery has torn apart one's heritage, when the past is more real than the present, when a dead baby's rage can literally rock a house, then the traditional novel is no longer an adequate instrument. And so Pulitzer Prize–winner *Beloved* is written in bits and images, like a mirror smashed on the floor and left for the reader to put together. In a novel that is hypnotic, beautiful, and elusive, Toni Morrison portrays the lives of Sethe, an escaped slave and mother, and those around her. There is Sixo, who "stopped speaking English because there was no future in it," and Mister, the overseer who defines slaves in terms of "human" and "animal" characteristics. There is Baby Suggs, who makes her living with her heart because slavery "had busted her legs, back, head, eyes, hands, kidneys, womb and tongue"; and Paul D, a man with a rusted metal box for a heart and a presence that allows women to cry. At the center is Sethe, whose story makes us think and think again about what we mean when we say we love our children or our freedom. The stories circle, swim dreamily to the surface, and are suddenly clear and horrifying. Because of the extraordinary experimental style as well as the intensity of the subject matter, what we learn from them touches at a level deeper than understanding.

E.B.

The Bone People, Keri Hulme, *1985, New Zealand,* NOVEL

The Bone People weaves its story together with dreams, myths and legends, the world of the dead, and the ways of ancient cultures. The result is an unconventional and powerful novel which, after being rejected by major New Zealand publishers, was published by a women's collective and won the prestigious Booker Prize in 1985. *The Bone People* explores the potential within families for both destruction and healing, as well as the great personal costs of the disintegration of individual connections to traditional communities and cultures—in this case, the indigenous Maori culture of New Zealand. The novel centers on a strange trinity of characters, each isolated, each spiritually adrift. Simon, a mute child surrounded by mysteries, is found on a beach and is adopted by Joe, a Maori man embittered by the loss of his wife and son and thwarted in his desire for familial, religious, and cultural ties. The two are bound together by "a bloody kind of love that has violence as its silent partner." Simon and Joe come into the life of Kerewin, a part-Maori woman estranged from her family. She is a strong and compassionate woman, a sensualist who delights in color and landscape, food and archaic language, but who is also wary and conflicted. The three come together, break apart, and experience great pain and loss and eventual healing. Ultimately, the family they create stands as Keri Hulme's assertion of the potential for vitality and regeneration in individuals, families, and traditional cultures.

P.H.

Burmese Looking Glass: A Human Rights Adventure and a Jungle Revolution, Edith T. Mirante, *1993, Burma (United States),* NONFICTION

While studying art in Thailand in 1983, Edith Mirante, a twenty-nine-year-old artist from the United States, makes her first of many illegal border crossings between Thailand and Burma. Curious about Burmese history, she learns that four ethnic groups have fought over land control for years and that many independent hill tribes have lived a nomadic existence on Burmese soil. Ne Win, the dictatorial, xenophobic ruler of Burma, and Khun Sa, the drug kingpin of northern Burma, have an unspoken pact to stay out of each other's way, while both benefit from conflicts among the ethnic groups and hill tribes.

Outraged by the atrocities committed by the Burmese army against so many, Edith Mirante joins the hill tribes' battle for survival. With detailed descriptions of people and places, she takes the reader through monsoons and into hamlets and jungles on her quest for knowledge and the liberation of the generous, capable people caught up in a civil and economic war. She charges the Burmese government with numerous human rights violations; she indicts the Thai government, which allows the drug trade to thrive in return for money and access to Burma's rain forests; she exposes the United States government's donation of chemicals that eradicate opium poppies but also destroy the vegetation, pollute the rivers, and kill and injure the people. A powerful, rapidly moving book, *Burmese Looking Glass* is one of Edith Mirante's responses to her understanding that "knowledge breeds responsibility."

H.S.

The Butcher's Wife, Li Ang, *translated from Chinese by Howard Goldblatt and Ellen Yeung, 1983, China,* NOVELLA

In 1930s China, one woman defied the cultural assumption that a woman would only murder her husband in order to be with a lover; in this instance the woman insisted she had killed her husband to stop his abuses. Five decades later, Li Ang's novella *The Butcher's Wife*, which uses the real-life murder as its basis, created both a literary sensation and widespread outrage about its subject matter. Li Ang's style is graphic and brutal, mirroring the life of its lead character, Lin Shin, and the sexism and cultural superstitions that surround her. After a childhood of starvation and hard work, Lin Shin marries a pig butcher named Chen Jiangshui. He is a violent, abusive husband, but Lin Shin's relief at finally having enough food to eat and less work to do helps her to endure the frequent rapes and beatings. Conditions worsen, however, and she is isolated by the vicious gossip of neighbors who condemn her for screaming aloud: "As women, we're supposed to be tolerant and put our husbands above everything else. Who ever heard of anyone raising such a stink over a little pain once in a while!" Trapped without guidance or support, Lin Shin follows her husband's example. While *The Butcher's Wife* is not an easy read, it is an important book on a neglected issue, which, by its very outspokenness, has profoundly affected Chinese literature.

E.B.

Cartucho/My Mother's Hands, Nellie Campobello, *translated from Spanish by Doris Meyer and Irene Matthews, 1931, Mexico,* SHORT STORIES

The first part of this volume, *Cartucho: Tales of the Struggle in Northern Mexico,* contains fifty-six rapid-fire sketches of the Mexican Revolution as witnessed by Nellie Campobello in her childhood. These direct and deceptively simple stories from "a country where legends are invented and where people lull their pain listening to them" simultaneously denounce war and pay tribute to the common soldier. More accustomed to the boom of cannons than the songs of birds, young Nellie finds the sight of "more than three hundred men shot all at once . . . quite natural." When she and her sister discover that the pretty red things in a basin carried by the soldiers are guts, they move "up closer to see them. . . . 'Guts. How nice! Whose are they?' we said, our curiosity showing in our eyes." The second collection, *My Mother's Hands,* is a selection of sketches and vignettes which pay loving tribute to the author's mother: "Everything was natural in our world. . . . Laughter, flour tortillas, milkless coffee, dead bodies, rifle volleys, the wounded, men rushing past on horseback . . . everything was ours—everything—for that was our life. Mama's singing, her scoldings and her lovely face were ours too." Together, the two literary masterpieces in this volume offer a compelling depiction of the Mexican Revolution.

J.L.

Child of the Dark: The Diary of Carolina Maria de Jesus, Carolina Maria de Jesus, *translated from Portuguese by David St. Clair, 1960, Brazil,* JOURNAL

Written between 1955 and 1960, *Child of the Dark* is the daily journal of an artist—a writer who, as the single mother of three young children, supports her family by picking through garbage for paper and scraps to sell. They live in a cardboard and wood-scrap shack in a Brazilian slum, a *favela,* where there is no plumbing, and one public cold-water spigot is the only clean water source for several hundred people. Carolina de Jesus wants her journal to document the lives *favelados* are forced to live. "July 24 I got up at 5 o'clock to carry water." She often understates: "June 18 Today it dawned raining. Yesterday Vera spit two worms out of her mouth. She has a fever. There is no school today in honor of the Prince of Japan." Carolina de Jesus is a poet of intense dignity, without physical or spiritual nourishment. "July 15 Today is the birthday of my daughter Vera Eunice. I can't give her a party for this would be just like trying to grab ahold of the sun with my hands. Today there's not going to be any lunch." Her novels are rejected, but her journal is accepted for publication in 1959 and eventually becomes very popular in Brazil. This makes her happy but does not immediately change her life: "January 1, 1960 I got up at 5 and went to get water."

J.L.

A Chorus of Stones: The Private Life of War, Susan Griffin, *1992, United States,* NONFICTION

"Perhaps every moment of time lived in human consciousness remains in the air around us." With these words Susan Griffin begins to draw the connections between personal histories and the violent and often unspoken events of this century. Believing that "each solitary story belongs to a larger story," she tells us the sad and violent tale of her childhood. Her calm and mesmerizing style builds to a crescendo as she ties her memories to the life stories of more powerful individuals—the architects of modern war who have shaped our history. Susan Griffin presents some disturbingly provocative accounts of war's atrocities, the stories of bomb makers and bomb victims, and the contents of once-classified government documents. Not only does she bring us face to face with the horrific underbelly of war and fascism, she makes us look fresh at our journey from innocent child to ruthless warmonger or war enabler. Adamant that society's gender biases continue to coerce men into the shadow of war, she challenges us to understand that not a shred of our violent past is ever forgotten, that in our conscious lives we have entered into a collective silence which erodes our ability to see truth and act responsibly. *A Chorus of Stones* is a profound and accessible book which infuses insight into the overwhelming moral dilemmas of our time.

R.S.

Cracking India, Bapsi Sidhwa, *1991, Pakistan,* NOVEL

"One man's religion is another man's poison." The child narrator of *Cracking India* learns this lesson as she experiences the partition of India in 1947. Comic, violent, turbulent, and full of life, this novel functions vividly on both domestic and historical levels, illuminating the uprooting of seven million Muslims and five million Hindus and Sikhs in "the largest and most terrible exchange of population known to history." In particular, *Cracking India* explores the effect of partition on the subcontinent's greatest underclass: women. Events are refracted through the eyes of five-year-old Lenny, the indulged daughter of a Parsee family whose tumultuous extended household includes an array of neighbors, servants, and relatives, and Lenny's beloved Ayah. For Lenny, the domestic manifestation of partition is sudden and menacing: "One day everybody is themselves—and the next day they are Hindu, Muslim, Sikh, Christian. People shrink, dwindling into symbols." Witnessing the inexorable cracking apart of her world, with its affection, humor, and balance superseded by bigotry and violence, Lenny comes to a painful understanding of "human needs, frailties, cruelties and joys." In focusing on the domestic drama engendered by a national cataclysm, and by rendering it in the voice of an uninformed but perceptive young girl, Bapsi Sidhwa fully evokes the personal costs of a historical event.

P.H.

Dogeaters, Jessica Hagedorn, *1990, Philippines (United States),* NOVEL

Dogeaters presents a montage of Filipino people during the Marcos era, and the circumstances that define their motivations. It is a metaphorical album of raw snapshots: of Joey Sands, the classic victim, son of a prostitute and an African-American soldier; of the adolescent Rio Gonzaga, who reassesses the dynamics of her well-to-do family and concludes that she will be different; of military henchmen, movie stars, and the obscenely wealthy; and of the sacrificial leaders of the anti-Marcos opposition. The pictures are graphic and conflicting, sometimes brutal, sometimes shimmering with the intoxicating, seductive mood of the American movies that seem to be the characters' only means of momentary escape. Joey describes the river where his mother committed suicide: "a watery grave black with human shit, every dead thing and piece of garbage imaginable." Rio writes of her mother's "mysterious, mauve rooms": "Wherever she looks in any of her mirrors it is always night and she is always beautiful." Out of the fragmentary confusion and the preoccupation with appearances that characterized the Marcos era, Jessica Hagedorn sets out to resurrect a country's cultural identity.

M.J.R.K.

Dumba Nengue: Run for Your Life: Peasant Tales of Tragedy in Mozambique, Lina Magaia, *translated from Portuguese by Michael Wolfers, 1988, Mozambique,* NONFICTION

"And I heard it being said that there was civil war in Mozambique. Civil war!? What is civil war? Wars, whether civil or not, are waged between armed contingents. That's not what's happening in Mozambique. There's no civil war in Mozambique. In Mozambique there is genocide perpetrated by armed men against defenseless populations. Against peasants." These true accounts are Lina Magaia's attempt to bring to an international public the reality of rural life in her country, where people are terrorized by the Mozambique National Resistance (MNR), a group with clear ties to the South African apartheid regime and to ex-colonialists now in Portugal. While members of the MNR are often represented as "freedom fighters" in the American and British press, Lina Magaia's refutation is deadly clear. The events she relates are horrific and gut-wrenching. The stories vary in style; sometimes they are short and as shocking as an axe to the neck, sometimes they are drawn out like a keening wail. Others start out slowly—telling the reader about the beauty of what one woman has been able to produce from the land, or the love of a young couple—only to end up with a brutal description of total, barbaric destruction. This is not a book for the weak of heart; it is easier to pretend such things do not exist. But they do, and Lina Magaia's book makes closing one's eyes impossible.

E.B.

"G" Is for Gumshoe, Sue Grafton, *1990, United States,* NOVEL

Kinsey Milhone is a thirty-three-year-old twice-divorced, self-employed private investigator—a witty, philosophical woman who wears jeans and tennis shoes and cuts her own hair every six weeks with a nail scissors: "If I were asked to rate my looks on a scale of one to ten, I wouldn't. I have to say, however, that I seldom wear makeup, so whatever I look like first thing in the morning at least remains consistent as the day wears on." As *"G" Is for Gumshoe* opens, Kinsey is hired for what appears to be a simple case: to find Agnes Gray, Irene Gersh's missing mother. Shortly thereafter, a friendly district attorney warns Kinsey there is a contract out on her life because of her involvement in another case, and suggests she hire Robert Dietz, a burned-out private investigator, for protection. Within a few pages, Sue Grafton presents multiple plot lines that she masterfully weaves together with tantalizing clues, fast action, and upbeat dialogue. Mrs. Gray is pursued, found, lost, found, and dies while dropping clues as secretive as her nature about a crime committed in 1940. The situation with the hit man turns out to be more complicated than anticipated; so, too, is Kinsey's relationship with Robert Dietz. The pace quickens as Kinsey finds her answers and the hit man finds her. Kinsey is sharp and womanly, and her cases are thought-provoking and full of excitement. For the reader, when Kinsey signs off the novel with her characteristic "Respectfully submitted," it is like leaving a much-loved friend at the end of a delicious afternoon.

V.S.

The History of Mary Prince, a West Indian Slave, Related by Herself, Mary Prince, *edited by Moira Ferguson, 1831, West Indies/England,* AUTOBIOGRAPHY

"I was born in Brackish-Pond, in Bermuda, on a farm belonging to Mr. Charles Myners. My mother was a household slave; and my father, whose name was Prince, was a sawyer belonging to Mr. Trimmingham, a ship-builder at Crow-Lane." In this brief, straightforward, and often poetic narrative, Mary Prince describes her life of labor as a household and field slave, and the illness and pain brought on by the abject cruelty of her masters. The text of this autobiography, the first by a female slave to be published, is prefaced and followed by letters written by British people attesting to the honor of her character and the truth of her testimony. Mary's heartfelt and unself-pitying life story, often so wrenching that she cannot bring herself to remember or describe the details, contrasts sharply with the polite words of her white protectors' proclamations about the truth of her words. Moira Ferguson's excellent introduction and a critical afterword by Ziggi Alexander give a historical perspective to this lucid and powerful story.

J.L.

The House Tibet, Georgia Savage, *1988, Australia,* NOVEL

The tough, naïve voice of thirteen-year-old Morgan, the narrator of *The House Tibet*, calls for the reader to feel personally responsible for this character's survival from the very first sentence. The story begins with incest: "While it was happening I watched the moon. It was a piece of sky behind his shoulder." Afterward, Morgan seeks support from her family and is repeatedly rebuffed with a bluntness that is almost as horrifying as the rape itself. When she and her mute younger brother run away and join a band of vagabond kids, her story becomes increasingly surreal as Morgan learns that survival depends upon a combination of ruthless detachment and fierce loyalty. Though Georgia Savage ties up all the loose ends a bit too neatly in the end and occasionally resorts to convenient explanatory dialogue along the way, even her clichés have twists to them. The sharp, ironic turns of thought and plot make this novel and its narrator unforgettable. Morgan herself comments upon the process of telling this story: "I was going to write it as if I had everyone I knew sitting in a circle listening while I told them. *I'll put in everything* I thought. *So they start to understand what it's like being a girl at war . . . practically every MINUTE of your life.*"

K.B.

The Loony-Bin Trip, Kate Millett, *1990, United States,* MEMOIR

Dedicated to "those who've been there," *The Loony-Bin Trip* is the brilliantly written memoir of a period in Kate Millett's life when she was diagnosed as "constitutionally psychotic" and the thirteen years she spent using prescribed drugs that deadened her mind and obscured her consciousness. With scrupulous detail, she think-talks us through the disbelief; the terrors of betrayal, restraint, incarceration, isolation, drugs, and shock treatment; the despair when her fears of betrayal prove real; and her urgent need not to forget: "It is the integrity of the mind I wish to affirm, its sanctity and inviolability." This insider's look at what happens to people diagnosed with schizophrenia, manic depression, paranoia, and personality disorders, "all illnesses which are established upon behavioral and not physical grounds," reveals a body of law that allows people to be deprived of "any and all rights, civil, constitutional or human." But stripping institutionalized patients of their legal rights and depriving them of elementary human needs such as privacy, cleanliness and meaningful activity is not "treatment" enough, these patients are also routinely forced to take such drugs as Thorazine, Stelazine, and Haldol, which cause permanent, irreversible side-effects—involuntary spasms, physical disfigurements—or lithium, which threatens the kidneys and the heart. Readers are lucky that Kate Millett is one of the fortunate ones: a Caucasian scholar and writer with enough money, influential friends, and guts to survive, get out, and write about it.

J.L.

The Montreal Massacre, Louise Malette and Marie Chalouh, editors, *1991, Canada,* ESSAYS/LETTERS

The Montreal Massacre is a translation of essays, letters to editors, and poetry about the impact of the December 1989 deaths of fourteen women, all engineering students, murdered by a gun-wielding man out to kill "feminists." In words both tender and scathing, its writers struggle to place the killings in their social context. Working to make the connections between personal grief and political action, the writings include a critique of the media, who for the most part reduced the tragedy to the isolated work of a "madman": "If this is madness, never has it been so lucid. . . . Never has madness left such a clear message." Another author addresses the way in which all misogyny has become "medicalized," and crimes such as rape, wife abuse, and incest viewed as "diseases" of individuals versus a reflection of society in general: "The real nature . . . is camouflaged, and the attackers appear to be the victims." Still others speak of the general reluctance to recognize the shootings as part of a larger framework: "Crimes against women have no history. This history, swept aside, wiped out, has only begun to be written." *The Montreal Massacre* articulates the shock, rage, and sadness that many women have felt since the day the killings occurred. It addresses the silences that exist for both women and men, and that allow such acts to be treated as nonpolitical ("Have we ever questioned that Hitler was a politician because he was mad?" one writer asks), and gives voice to those calling urgently for change.

S.L.

Regeneration, Pat Barker, *1992, England,* NOVEL

In the summer of 1917, as more than 100,000 English soldiers are dying in World War I, Captain William Rivers continues to build a reputation for curing mentally "broken-down" officers in a London war hospital. Captain Sassoon, well-bred English gentleman, poet, and decorated war hero, is committed to the same hospital as an alternative to court-martial for his public letter denouncing the government and the war. Pat Barker seamlessly interweaves fiction with facts gleaned from the journals and writings of these real-life military men to probe the depths of the conflicts and contradictions they face. Captain Rivers is moved by Captain Sassoon's antiwar position, and torn by his own duty to cure broken men so they can return to the front, to a "resumption of activities . . . that were positively suicidal." Captain Sassoon can't believe they are powerless to stop the carnage. Both men struggle with the war's many paradoxes, especially the fact that "this most brutal of conflicts should set up a relationship between officers and men that was . . . domestic. Caring . . . maternal." This feeling tortures Sassoon with questions about what it means to be a man. Both men struggle, with each other and internally, as a terrible, unaskable question haunts them: What kind of "automatic or unquestioning allegiance" does one owe to "a society that devours its own young?"

J.L.

Scraps of Life: Chilean Arpilleras, Chilean Women, and the Pinochet Dictatorship, Marjorie Agosin, *translated from Spanish by Cola Franzen, 1987, Chile* (*Chile/United States*), NONFICTION

During the years 1980 to 1985, Marjorie Agosin returned often to her native Chile to visit the Arpillera workshops of the Association of Families of the Detained-Disappeared. Although she acknowledges, "the more I learned about what the military could do, *with absolute impunity*, the more terrified I became," she decided "not to be afraid of fear" and reaffirmed her commitment to tell the stories of the women who make Arpilleras, embroidered and appliquéd pictures that tell the true story of what is going on in Chile. These Arpilleristas search for any trace of relatives who have been picked up by the authorities and never seen or heard about again. Although most live with small children in crowded hovels with no food, electricity, or running water, these women have banded together to fight back in every way they can. With the help of the Catholic Church's Vicarate of Solidarity—which, despite the fact that these Arpilleras are illegal to sell in Chile, provides the materials, and buys and markets the finished work to the outside world—the Arpilleristas create art from "scraps of life": hair clippings, clothing scraps, and pictures and messages about their detained or disappeared loved ones. *Scraps of Life* brings together a brief history of the rise of the Pinochet dictatorship and moving descriptions of Marjorie Agosin's experiences with these revolutionary artists.

J.L.

Still Loved by the Sun: A Rape Survivor's Journal, Migael Scherer, *1992, United States,* MEMOIR

In twenty minutes, Migael Scherer's life changed forever. On a Tuesday morning at a local laundromat, a man stabbed her, raped her, and said, when he unclenched his hands from her throat, "You're a very lucky woman." *Still Loved by the Sun* is Migael Scherer's journey down a road traveled by an estimated one in three women in the United States. In her honest and unsparing journal, she captures the emotional hell and the lasting repercussions of her assault and the trial of her rapist, and the importance of the support of her husband and close friends. We feel her inability to concentrate, to be alone, to keep from crying. One month after the rape, when asked if she feels connected with her body, she realizes "Of course! The sense of my body as separate, almost dangerous, accounts for so much: my feeling translucent, my intense need for physical intimacy, my skewed time sense." When she feels strong enough, she attends group sessions with other rape survivors, and through their stories, Migael Scherer sees her experience in a larger context, as part of rape's effects on society. *Still Loved by the Sun* brings home rape's full impact—the fear, the lack of control, the deep invasive sadness, and the daily struggles to keep emotionally afloat.

H.S.

A Woman's Civil War, Cornelia Peake McDonald, *edited by Minrose C. Gwin, 1861–1865 (1935), United States,* MEMOIR

Forty-year-old Cornelia McDonald, mother of nine children ranging in age from infancy to adolescence, begins her diary in March 1862, when her husband leaves to fight for the Confederacy in the United States Civil War. In 1875, wanting to record the war years for her children, she reconstructs pages that were lost during the war and adds recollections of the year 1861. Her home is Winchester, Virginia, a Confederate town that is occupied off and on by the Union army. She recalls Confederate soldiers on one side of town, Union soldiers on the other, and remembers being on the porch with four of her children, two servants, and several wounded and dying Union soldiers, all of them surrounded by the "booming of the cannon, the screaming of shells and the balls of light [that] go shooting over our heads . . ." In August, 1863, she is forced from her home, and in Lexington, Virginia, the kindness of strangers and money from the sale of her valuables keep her family from starvation. In December, 1864, her husband dies, and she begins another struggle in her life, to keep her children with her. Cornelia McDonald's journal shows us the personal costs of war through the eyes of a courageous woman.

H.S.

Yes Is Better Than No, Byrd Baylor, *1991, United States,* NOVEL

Maria Vasquez passes Saint Jude's statue, nods him a promise to notice him tomorrow, and heads for the B-29 bar where she knows there will be no white people and where she hopes there will be dancing: "It would be good to dance all night. When you're dancing it doesn't really matter whether there is a board nailed across the front door or not." Maria is worried: she already has to lie and say she only has four kids, because the welfare worker warned her not to have any more before her fifth was born. Mrs. Domingo, Maria's friend and neighbor, is a basket weaver who knows how to forget her English when tourists talk "movie-Indian" at her. A woman whose house was started twenty-three years ago and still doesn't have a roof, she enters every contest she hears about, even when the prize is a swimming pool. Gabriel Soto is a proud young man who has his traditional dress and history all mixed up, has to keep a low profile with authorities, and paints wonderful pictures. One thing all the Papago people in these stories know about surviving in an Arizona city run by white people: "They have each learned long ago to try to give answers which will most please the questioner. At times this is hard to figure out, but they try. . . . Another thing. If a yes or no answer is required, they try to say yes."

J.L.

Ways of Knowing

Reading the books in this section is like looking at the world through a kaleidoscope. As these authors show us the world through their different lenses, reality shifts, bends, brightens, and becomes confused. Patricia Tichenor Westfall writes about how various cultures experience time; Diane Ackerman reacquaints us with the power and influence of our five senses. Lillian Faderman writes of the changing definitions of lesbianism over the past century. Other authors use their experiences to challenge too-commonly accepted visions of the world: working-class women depict life inside the academy; Brenda Peterson touches the earth and feels a current flow through her; Ruth Sidranksy describes growing up as a hearing child of deaf parents. Patricia Hill Collins examines daily life and feminism from the viewpoint of African-American women, while Sue Bender seeks a new perspective from the Amish. Placing their focus on language and images that affect our ways of knowing at an unconscious level, Dale Spender, Carolyn Kay Steedman, Susan Sontag, and Carolyn G. Heilbrun examine how our realities are shaped by the words, metaphors, and stories we use—or don't have. We come away from these books knowing that the ground under our feet is deeper and less stable than we thought, and that the possibilities for new questions and understandings are endless.

AIDS and Its Metaphors	Susan Sontag
Black Feminist Thought	Patricia Hill Collins
Ceremony	Leslie Marmon Silko
Dinner at the Homesick Restaurant	Anne Tyler
Dreams of an Insomniac	Irena Klepfisz
How We Survived Communism and Even Laughed	Slavenka Drakulić
I Heard the Owl Call My Name	Margaret Craven
In Silence	Ruth Sidransky
Landscape for a Good Woman	Carolyn Kay Steedman
Living by Water	Brenda Peterson
Mama Day	Gloria Naylor
Man Made Language	Dale Spender
Mohawk Trail	Beth Brant
My Story	Kamala Das
A Natural History of the Senses	Diane Ackerman
Odd Girls and Twilight Lovers	Lillian Faderman
Plain and Simple	Sue Bender
Real-Farm	Patricia Tichenor Westfall
Sassafrass, Cypress & Indigo	Ntozake Shange
The Second Sex	Simone de Beauvoir
The Straight Mind (and Other Essays)	Monique Wittig
Talking Back	bell hooks
Typical American	Gish Jen
Waterlily	Ella Cara Deloria
Women's Ways of Knowing	Mary Field Belenky et al., eds.
Working-Class Women in the Academy	Michele M. Tokarczyk and Elizabeth A. Fay, eds.
Writing a Woman's Life	Carolyn G. Heilbrun
Yours in Struggle	Elly Bulkin, Minnie Bruce Pratt, Barbara Smith

AIDS and Its Metaphors, Susan Sontag, *1989, United States,* ESSAY

Susan Sontag begins: "One cannot think without metaphors. But that does not mean there aren't some metaphors we might well abstain from or try to retire." She continues with a precise and cogent examination of the ancient body-as-society, illness-as-war, and, more recent, AIDS-as-plague metaphors common to contemporary Western European culture. The body-as-society metaphor introduced by Plato and Aristotle creates perceptions of society that are related to the body's orientation in space, as in the economically punishing concepts of upper and lower, and forward and backward, where "upper" and "forward" have worth and "lower" and "backward" do not. According to Susan Sontag, it is precisely this kind of metaphoric thinking that makes "an authoritarian ordering of society seem inevitable, immutable." She argues convincingly that the body-as-society metaphor gives birth to the metaphor of illness/disease-as-war with disastrous results for the ill: armies and diseases invade populations, military and medical personnel are armed for attack, an enemy agent can be a spy or bacteria. Citing philosophical, literary, and medical history, and Christian doctrines of plague-as-God's-war-against-sin, *AIDS and Its Metaphors* is a brilliant essay on how the metaphor of the body-as-society can lead even well-meaning people to consider the body as a battlefield, AIDS as a war, and people with AIDS as the enemy.

J.L.

Black Feminist Thought: Knowledge, Consciousness, and the Politics of Empowerment, Patricia Hill Collins, *1990, United States,* NONFICTION

In her introduction, Patricia Hill Collins states that her work is informed by the totality of her experience as the daughter of working-class parents, her education as a sociologist and educator, and her daily "non-scholarly activities" as wife, mother, community activist, sister, and friend. *Black Feminist Thought* is the first history and analysis of "Black women's ideas" told in a voice that is "both individual and collective, personal and political, one reflecting the intersection of my unique biography with the larger meaning of my historical times."

In it we discover new meanings for selected and neglected traditional female themes like gossip, hair, TV, movies, food, and clothing. We get a fresh look at where and how knowledge is produced; learn about self-definition and about kitchens, factories, and neighborhoods as "alternative locations for intellectual work." The implications for readers of her chapters "The Ethic of Caring," "The Ethic of Personal Accountability," and "Reconceptualizing Race, Class, and Gender as Interlocking Systems of Oppression" are enormous and compelling. For readers interested in the sources and definitions of knowledge—especially those readers whose history and intellectual tradition have been lost, denied, or denigrated—*Black Feminist Thought* is one of the most inspiring, exciting, and valuable books you'll ever read.

J.L.

Ceremony, Leslie Marmon Silko, *1977, United States,* NOVEL

Tayo is a half-white Laguna Indian emotionally stricken by white warfare and almost destroyed by his experiences as a World War II prisoner of the Japanese. Unable to find a place among Native American veterans who are losing themselves in rage and drunkenness, Tayo discovers his connection to the land and to ancient rituals with the help of a medicine man, and comes to understand the need to create ceremonies, to grow and change, in order to survive. He finds peace by "finally seeing the pattern, the way all the stories fit together—the old stories, the war stories, their stories—to become the story that was still being told." *Ceremony* is somber in tone, its narrative interspersed with fragments of myth, imbued with the grace and resonance of a ceremonial chant. It powerfully evokes both a natural world alive with story and significance, and the brutal human world of Highway 66 and the streets of Gallup, where Navajos, Zunis, and Hopis in torn jackets stand outside bars "like cold flies stuck to the wall." *Ceremony* is deeply felt, but avoids glib mysticism; it is informed not by bitterness and racial animosity, but by a larger sense of sorrow and an awareness of "how much can be lost, how much can be forgotten." Tayo's spiritual healing becomes an offering of hope and redemption for tribal cultures.

P.H.

Dinner at the Homesick Restaurant, Anne Tyler, *1982, United States,* NOVEL

Anne Tyler is known for her ability to explore and make real the ways in which "unexceptional" people create families out of what might be seen as a hopeless muddle of failed or failing relationships. The Tull family—frazzled and sometimes abusive mother Pearl, missing father Beck, jealous and manipulative son Cody, troubled but finally contented daughter Jenny, and loving, placid baby Ezra—resembles families most of us know. First we witness Pearl's memories as she wanders back through her life while lying on her deathbed; next, Cody's point-of-view takes over, and by the end of the book we have experienced each family member's perspective. Out of their often differing stories a picture emerges of Pearl: how her traveling salesman husband left her with three children to care for, how she tried to provide them both emotional and financial support, and how she failed (more or less, depending upon the perspective) to give them a loving and secure home. Her children create families for themselves with varying degrees of success—Cody with his brother's girlfriend, Jenny with a second husband and his built-in family, Ezra with his restaurant—but never seem able to make it through a single dinner together without conflict. Lovable in the complicated way only family members can be, they speak to us in the raucous manner of guests at a dinner party.

C.T

Dreams of an Insomniac: Jewish Feminist Essays, Speeches and Diatribes, Irena Klepfisz, *1990, United States/Poland,* ESSAYS

Irena Klepfisz was fourteen when she and her mother escaped from Poland to America during World War II, the only members of their family to survive the Holocaust. Among the twelve essays in this collection is "Resisting and Surviving America," in which she recalls that her "first conscious feeling about being Jewish was that it was dangerous, something to be hidden." Now, decades later, she questions how to comprehend what is meant when she hears academics and intellectuals speak of being "turned off by the Holocaust." In "Women Without Children/Women Without Families/Women

Alone," she examines the social and cultural meanings, messages, interpretations, and results of her decision to forgo motherhood. "The Distance Between Us: Feminism, Consciousness and the Girls at the Office" analyzes both the work and the relationships at work in an office. She notes how she has learned to stop admitting she has a Ph.D. in job interviews after prospective employers worried she will get bored: "What deliberate ignorance and callousness to people—high school drop-out and Ph.D. . . . —would allow for the conclusion that anyone would find this work anything but boring?" In "Jewish Lesbians, the Jewish Community, Jewish Survival," she writes about the high costs of "passing" for what you think or worry others want you to be. Irena Klepfisz draws on the history of artistic and political commitment that has long informed her precise and well-loved poetry, and her words have the power to penetrate and awaken.

J.L.

How We Survived Communism and Even Laughed, Slavenka Drakulić, *1991, Europe (Croatia),* ESSAYS

Despite its title, *How We Survived Communism and Even Laughed* is not a funny book. This informative, passionate, articulate series of essays looks at how communism in Eastern Europe affected—and still affects—the lives of women. Written for a Western audience, these essays explore the lives of individual Eastern European women through the details of their days, because, as Salvenka Drakulić states, "Life, for the most part, is trivial. It was this relationship between political authority and the trivia of daily living, this view from below, that interested me most. And who should I find down there, most removed from the seats of political power, but women." She takes mundane topics such as laundry, tampons, makeup, toilet paper, shared apartments, and soup and allows the larger implications to ripple out until the reader can see an entire system, a way of knowing and believing. Describing the widespread attitude that created the stockpiles of plastic bags, medicine, fabric, and food in her grandmother's cupboards, she comments: "If the politicians had only had a chance to peek into our closets, cellars, cupboards and drawers—looking not for forbidden books or anti-state material—they would have seen the future that was in store for their wonderful plans for communism itself. But they didn't look." Accessible, fascinating, and extremely timely, these essays offer an understanding of communism as it was lived on a daily basis.

E.B.

I Heard the Owl Call My Name, Margaret Craven, *1973, Canada (United States),* NOVEL

A quiet, graceful testimonial to a vanishing way of life, *I Heard the Owl Call My Name* is Margaret Craven's first book, written when she was sixty-nine. It tells of a young vicar named Mark, sent to a remote Kwakiutl village not knowing he has less than three years to live. In the village, Mark comes to understand the Kwakiutl Indians around him and sees how their traditions are being destroyed through the influence of white men. He watches the "English woman anthropologist" who comes to study the natives and insists upon calling the villagers "Quackadoodles"; he witnesses the impact when the government declares it legal for Indians to buy liquor and when traders cheat the villagers out of their cultural treasures; he sees the children lose their ties with their families and heritage while living in residential schools among whites. In striking contrast to the avarice and arrogance of most whites is the selflessness of the Kwakiutls and the beauty of running salmon, tall trees, and tribal festivals. Mark becomes a part of the Kwakiutl world, learning its language and ways, until finally "Time had lost its contours. He seemed to see it as the raven or the bald eagle, flying high over the village, must see the part of the river that had passed the village, that had not yet reached the village, one and the same." Gentle, full of profound philosophy, this is a book that both calms and disquiets, saddens and exhilarates.

E.B.

In Silence, Ruth Sidransky, *1990, United States,* AUTOBIOGRAPHY

"If there were a way, if I could, I would write this book in sign language." Ruth Sidransky was born in 1929, a hearing child of deaf parents; her first language was sign language. *In Silence* looks back at a childhood full of lush conversations told with hands that become gentle, funny, forceful, lucid. Her mother asks if colors have sound, and Ruth, persuasively, gives them sound. Then her mother admits, "To say truth, I never believe colors have noise, but nice to think so." Her father, Daddy Ben, instills a love of life in his daughter; his questions make her laugh, think, and learn. Lying on the grass in Central Park, he doesn't believe Ruth when she signs that the earth doesn't talk. "I deaf like old shoes, hear nothing. Not you. You listen. Learn earth's speech." She listens and understands: "He knew the earth's song and lifted me into its music." This is a story of living in two worlds—the hearing and the silent—and having a voice in both; of a home rich with love though financially poor; and of a religion that provided spiritual meaning, yet did not allow Ruth's father to have his bar mitzvah in the temple. Throughout her story, Ruth Sidransky gives us new perspectives of both sign and vocal language.

H.S.

Landscape for a Good Woman: A Story of Two Lives,
Carolyn Kay Steedman, *1987, England,* NONFICTION

Carolyn Steedman's 1950s South London childhood was shaped by her mother's longing: "What she actually wanted were real things, real entities, things she materially lacked, things that a culture and a social system withheld from her. . . . When the world didn't deliver the goods, she held the world to blame." When Carolyn Steedman grows up and begins to look for reflections of her and her mother's lives in history, theory, and literature, she finds that "the tradition of cultural criticism that has employed working-class lives, and their rare expression in literature, has made solid and concrete the absence of psychological individuality—of subjectivity." Through an in-depth comparison of personal experiences with prevailing political and social science theories on the psychology and attitudes of working-class people, *Landscape for a Good Woman* challenges an intellectual tradition that denies "its subjects a particular story, a personal history, except when that story illustrates a general thesis." In this poignantly written and thoroughly researched work, the common theoretical conclusion that the survival struggles of working-class people precludes the time necessary for more genteel "elaboration of relationships" is shot full of delightfully life-affirming holes.

J.L.

Living by Water: Essays on Life, Land and Spirit, Brenda Peterson, *1990, United States,* ESSAYS

Every geographic region influences how its inhabitants view the rest of the world. In *Living by Water,* Brenda Peterson considers the Pacific Northwest, with its mountains, its ever-present water, and its Native American beliefs. "Success in, say, Los Angeles, where the sun always shines, or New York, where city dwellers equate the sun with Con Edison, is a much more external affair. . . . But in the misty San Juan Islands, in the gray, rain-swept cityscapes of Seattle, in the high, snowed-in hollows of the Olympics and the cloud-shadowed deserts of Eastern Washington there is so much hidden about the land, the lives. Here, what you see is not what you get." Brenda Peterson writes of how the energy of the earth has surged through her like lightning, of her work as an environmental writer, and of growing up eating wild game. She draws parallels between the women who have been murdered by the Green River killer and the environment we seem to care so little for. She describes the joy of swimming with dolphins. In each essay she jumps from one idea to the next like a child leaping across rocks—but after a while you realize that form is meaning here. As you swoop from idea to idea, your path connects everything.

E.B.

Mama Day, Gloria Naylor, *1988, United States,* NOVEL

Gloria Naylor's fictional island, Willow Springs, is home to a few black families who have lived there since the time of Sapphira Wade, a "true conjure woman" who could "walk through a lightning storm without being touched" and who, as legend has it, may or may not have murdered the white landowner who was first her owner and then her husband and/or lover. Located between Georgia and South Carolina but a part of neither, Willow Springs is a place that resembles and yet makes strange the rest of the world. Like women anywhere, women from Willow Springs worry about not having children and are jealous of their spouses—but here they use secret rituals to become pregnant and cast spells over rivals. Here Ophelia Day (nicknamed Cocoa) returns every August from New York City, eventually bringing her new, native northeastern husband George; here, a hurricane, evil spells, jealousy, and tragedy teach her about the power of love and family. Here also is Mama Day, Sapphira's great-granddaughter and Cocoa's great-aunt, who has powers that the sophisticated Cocoa only senses and the practical George recognizes much too late. His sacrifice and Mama Day's love for her family and respect for her world teach us, "It ain't about right or wrong, truth or lies; it's about a slave woman who brought a whole new meaning to both them words, soon as you cross over here from beyond the bridge."

C.T.

Man Made Language, Dale Spender, *1980, Australia,* NONFICTION

In chapters such as "The Lesser Value of Women's Words," "Experience Without a Name," and "The Problem is Power, Not Women," Dale Spender presents a compelling and practical analysis of the androcentric construction of the English language: its social context, vocabulary, syntax, history, and usage. Starting from the understanding that "Language helps form the limits of our reality," she examines the male-oriented assumptions of the science of linguistics, specifically the premise of "female deficiency" predominant in earlier research: "When the starting premise is that women lack the forcefulness and effectiveness of men's language, then hypotheses and explanations are formulated to account for female hesitancy." In "Plus and Minus Male" she adds weight to Julia Stanley's earlier groundbreaking linguistic research—now widely accepted—showing that "masculinity is the unmarked form: the assumption is that the world is male unless proven otherwise. Femininity is the marked form: it is the proof of otherwise." Examples abound: doctor, woman doctor; writer, woman writer. There are literally fewer nouns in English to refer to females; when the female noun does exists, it often denigrates through the use of suffixes denoting "lesser," as in waitress, stewardess, majorette. If you are interested in the English language, make time to read this feminist classic so that you might think, laugh, get mad, get sad, and maybe change the ways you talk and listen.

J.L.

Mohawk Trail, Beth Brant, *1985, United States/Canada,* SHORT STORIES

Beth Brant is Degonwadonti, whose father is Joseph of the Mohawk Turtle Clan from the Bay of Quinte Theyindenaga reserve in Ontario. Degonwadonti is Beth Brant, whose mother is Hazel of Irish-Scots ancestry from Michigan. *Mohawk Trail* is a collection of singing stories that remember and honor this heritage. In the first section, called "Native Origins," we hear the legends of the grandmothers' birth traditions in the longhouse with the fire that must not go out, "the smell of wood smoke, sweat and the sharp-sweet odor of blood," and the whisper "Don't forget who you are." "Detroit Songs" sings stories of people in their own sweet, sad voices: "Daddy" talks about work: "It was every minute you thought about a job, about feedin' your family." In "Garnet Lee," Beth Brant's maternal grandmother tells about a Kentucky mining town, housekeeping jobs, black lung, and mine explosions. In stories named for them, Terri, Beth Brant's "Chippewa-Polack" friend, relates why she dresses up sexy to dance for tips in a lesbian bar on the weekends; Danny tells how he loved wearing dresses and why he had to kill himself; and Mama talks about taking care of "all those kids." The last selections, "Long Stories," describe two mothers living one hundred years apart whose children were stolen, and show us the life of a halfbreed girl growing up in Detroit. Each story a song, each song a poem, each poem a story, *Mohawk Trail* reverberates with the rhythmic strength of courageous and enduring love.

J.L.

My Story, Kamala Das, *translated from Malabar (translator unknown), 1976, India,* AUTOBIOGRAPHY

In her preface, Kamala Das tells us that she began writing her autobiography while seriously ill, that the serialized version in an

Indian journal brought much embarrassment to her family, and that she derived great pleasure from emptying her soul. Born in Calcutta in 1934, Kamala Das attended British schools, where she was always a minority: a brown-skinned girl among Caucasians, a Hindu among Christians. She affectionately remembers time spent with her grandmother at the ancestral home, knows her marriage to a distant relative at age fifteen is anything but a union of love, and struggles to understand this silent man whose bed she shares. In her constant search for love, Kamala Das often falls in love, as a child with students and teachers, as an adult with men who take the time to know her. It is her sons and her poetry that give meaning to her life. Enveloped by loneliness and sadness that last through years of nervous breakdowns and heart problems, she expresses her feelings through poetry that she sends to journals: "My grief fell like drops of honey on the white sheets on my desk. My sorrow floated over the pages of magazines darkly as heavy monsoon clouds do in the sky." Eventually Kamala Das gains recognition as a poet, despite her unorthodox approach to the role of women and her frank commentary on sexuality. Her autobiography is filled with honest, painful, and thought-provoking insight.

H.S.

A Natural History of the Senses, Diane Ackerman, *United States, 1990,* NONFICTION

To read Diane Ackerman's *A Natural History of the Senses* is to dive headlong into a sensuous feast. These delightful, inspired essays on the five senses—smell, touch, vision, hearing, taste—mix biology, psychology, history, anthropology, and poetry into voluptuous prose. Who could fail to pause over Diane Ackerman's description of Cleopatra welcoming Marc Antony to her bed in a room awash in a foot and a half of rose petals? Learn why orange juice tastes bitter when you drink it after brushing your teeth. Crawl in total darkness, feeling your way through the blaring confusion of textures in the San Francisco Touch Dome. Visit a laboratory in suburban Chicago where they levitate objects with ultrasound, or meet a "professional nose" who has "composed" scents for everything from perfume to laundry detergent. A rich book, where even the rhythm and movement of the sentences can be awe-inspiring, *A Natural History of the Senses* is not meant to be gobbled in huge helpings, but to be savored and browsed through like a box of exquisite chocolates. You'll come away from each reading with keener senses—seeing colors more deeply, hearing your favorite music anew, savoring complex flavors on your tongue.

M.L.

Odd Girls and Twilight Lovers: A History of Lesbian Life in Twentieth-Century America, Lillian Faderman, *1991, United States,* NONFICTION

For those readers unfamiliar with Stonewall, Lesbian Nation, Daughters of Bilitis, lipsticks, or "romantic friendships"—or for those readers who want to learn more—*Odd Girls and Twilight Lovers* provides an accessible, wide-ranging, meticulously researched history. Drawing from varied sources including literature, sociological and psychological studies, newspaper articles, military pamphlets, and movies, Lillian Faderman sets out to show the metamorphosis of a movement. Although the generalizations that occur as a result of a panoramic approach work against Lillian Faderman's stated wish to acknowledge the diversity among lesbians, these generalizations also serve to show the broad sweeps and clashes in what has been a rapidly changing and often tumultuous history. Beginning with nineteenth-century "romantic friendships" and the first all-women's colleges, progressing through the sexology of the 1920s and the openness of the war years, the McCarthy era, the radical 1960s and 1970s, and the more diversified 1980s and 1990s, Lillian Faderman documents "the extent to which sexuality, and especially sexual categories, can be dependent upon a broad range of factors that are extraneous to 'sexual drive.' " Perhaps the most revolutionary and exciting thing about this book is its ability to present lesbianism not only as a sexual orientation, but as a movement that has been both affected and defined by a constantly shifting economic, political, and cultural climate.

E.B.

Plain and Simple, Sue Bender, *1989, United States,* MEMOIR

In 1967, Sue Bender found herself mesmerized by the dark muted colors of the quilts and the haunting beauty of the faceless stuffed dolls of the Amish. The quiet simplicity of these crafts eventually led her on a journey of self-discovery to two Amish communities in 1982. Sue Bender, an overachiever with two master's degrees and two careers, found herself strongly attracted to the predictable rhythm of Amish life. This simple book describes both the ways of the Amish and their effect upon the author; like the author's extended retreat, the book is an escape for the reader. There are glimpses into Amish life: the wagon built to transport benches to the weekly home prayer groups, teenage girls who wear electric blue Nikes under their long black dresses, the democratic selection of a minister by drawing lots, and a no-holds waterfight among the nine Beiler children. Set against this background is Sue Bender's quest to discover inner wealth, to quiet the ramblings of ego, and to explore the part of her existence that values simplicity. With the Amish women as her mentors, she questions the obvious limits of their lives as well as her own frenzied pace. Walking to town one hot sunny day, Sue calls out to the horse-drawn buggies, "Am I on the right road?" It's a question we should all ask ourselves.

M.M.

Real-Farm, Patricia Tichenor Westfall, *1989, United States,* ESSAYS

On the surface, *Real-Farm* looks like one of many similar books: a city-bred, academic couple, full of illusions, buys a farm in Iowa, only to find that the reality of farming is far from what they imagined. In the end, however, *Real-Farm* goes beyond a description of the trials and tribulations of farm life to become a philosophical exploration of ways of perception, grounded in immediate daily details. What can we learn about marriage by watching geese? What *is* a bull snake, and does one's perception change if the bull snake is in the woods or in one's basement? How many ways can one measure a tornado? Patricia Westfall is an inquisitive person who has a talent for relaying the information she (sometimes literally) digs up. In *Real-Farm* she writes about the history of windmills, the mythology of snakes, and the development of corn; she explains how to drill a well and ponders what time means to different cultures around the world. While the abstract nature of much of this information could distance her from us and her surroundings, her writing is personal and concrete. In her hands metaphysics, weed control technology, and little red refrigerators are all equally understandable, interesting, and real.

E.B.

Sassafrass, Cypress & Indigo, Ntozake Shange, *1977, United States,* NOVEL

Sassafrass weaves tapestries, Cypress dances, Indigo makes magnificent dolls and plays a wild violin. Their originality is present in every part of their lives; even the time-honored transition into womanhood provides Indigo with an opportunity for expression: "Indigo, I don't want to hear another word about it," her mama says, "I'm not setting the table with my Sunday china for fifteen dolls who got their period today." The novel gives a brief but expressive glimpse of Indigo's future and then moves across the country with Sassafrass and Cypress as they, like Indigo, reinterpret, re-create, and challenge the predictable events of their evolving adult lives. Although some of the language might seem clichéd these days, it should be remembered that this book was among the first modern creative experiments that combined tradition with innovation, spirituality with passion, and celebration with grief and fury to express African-American women's experiences in distinctive and explicit terms. Ntozake Shange plunges headlong into the passions of her characters and blends the powerful, rhythmic patterns of poetry, music, and speech into her prose, pressing between the pages recipes, herbal remedies, choreography, letters, and dreams, like bright leaves to be preserved. Her novel can be read silently or aloud, but it can also be felt in Cypress's dancing, seen in Sassafrass's weaving, and heard in the unrestrained voice of Indigo's violin.

K.B.

The Second Sex, Simone de Beauvoir, *translated from French by H. M. Parshley, 1949, France,* NONFICTION

This massive, classic tome is still a delight to read. Simone de Beauvoir is intelligent, scholarly, lucid, and witty; her thesis is simple: Early Western philosophers established the female sex as "the other" to rationalize and promote the development and growth of the fledgling patriarchy. " 'The female is a female by virtue of a certain lack of qualities,' said Aristotle; 'we should regard the female nature as afflicted with a natural defectiveness.' " Referring to the earlier research of noted anthropologist Claude Lévi-Strauss on the development of the category of "other"—"as primordial as consciousness itself" in all known human cultures—Simone de Beauvoir analyzes the depth, breadth, purpose, and result of the Western notion of woman as not-man. The book is subdivided into two sections, "Facts and Myths" and "Woman's Life Today," in which she examines and documents such subjects as "The Data of Biology," "History," "Myths," "The Formative Years," "Situation," and "Justification," and ends with a chapter entitled "Towards Liberation." Simone de Beauvoir—literary artist, philosopher, and founding mother of twentieth-century feminism—wrote *The Second Sex* "less by a wish to demand our rights than by an effort towards clarity and understanding." Forty-five years after the book's publication, it remains true to its intent.

J.L.

The Straight Mind (and Other Essays), Monique Wittig, *1980–1989, France,* ESSAYS

The Straight Mind is French literary theorist Monique Wittig's first collection of essays centering on women's struggle for liberation from sexism and classism. These nine essays comprise a thoughtful and unique approach to the study of historical materialism and dialectics, and traverse philosophical, political, and literary theory. Monique Wittig describes this collection as a focus on "lesbian materialism," in which she examines men and women as *distinct classes* rather than as "essentialist" categories. "Lesbians are not women," writes Monique Wittig, and she presents powerful ideas about how the idea of "woman" is socially constructed and used to convey certain images. It is not enough, she argues, to transform economic oppression, because not all oppression is, at the source, economic. Sexism will continue to exist even in a society where all people have equal economic opportunities. Only by transforming our thought processes, and in turn our language, can we transform our society into one in which there is no longer the dominant and the dominated: "In other words, this means there cannot any longer be women and men, and that as classes and categories of thought or language they have to disappear, politically, economically, ideologically." Controversial and abstract, these essays challenge and provoke on both intellectual and emotional levels.

H.D.

Talking Back: Thinking Feminist, Thinking Black, bell hooks, *1989, United States,* ESSAYS

In her introduction, bell hooks writes about how difficult it is for her to write about her real, personal, Gloria Watkins self: "It has to do with punishment—with all those years in childhood and on, where I was hurt for speaking truths, speaking the outrageous, speaking in my wild and witty way, or as friends sometimes say, 'do we have to go that deep?' " In this collection of twenty-five essays with such enticing (uncapitalized) titles as "feminist scholarship: ethical issues," "on being black at yale: education as the practice of freedom" and " 'whose pussy is this': a feminist comment," she examines deeply and speaks unsparingly. Of particular concern in *Talking Back*, bell hooks's second major theoretical work, is "how deeply connected" the split between our private and public selves is in ongoing practices of domination, especially in our "intimate relationships, [the] ways racism, sexism, and class exploitation work in our daily lives, in those private spaces—that it is there that we are often most wounded, hurt, dehumanized; there that ourselves are most taken away, terrorized, and broken." *Talking Back* is a book that can be used by any interested reader to shape new ways of knowing through its thoroughly examined and well-articulated understanding that "domination is not just a subject for radical discourse, for books. It is about pain. . . . Even before the words, we remember the pain."

J.L.

Typical American, Gish Jen, *1991, United States,* NOVEL

Ralph, Theresa, and Helen move from China to America to escape political turbulence. Once in America, they find their lives, their morals, their beliefs and dreams changing. Ralph achieves his goal of a Ph.D. in mechanical engineering and university tenure, but is dissatisfied and fantasizes about making money in this America where "you have money, you can do anything. You have no money, you are nobody. You are Chinaman!" Theresa, his sister, becomes a doctor and finds herself in an affair with a married man. Helen, a friend of Theresa's, for whom "family . . . wasn't so much an idea for her, as an aesthetic," marries Ralph and realizes her dream of a split-level house in the suburbs of Connecticut, while her vocabulary expands to include the terms *love seat, nook*, and *finished basement.* This is a story about their daily lives in this new country—how they adapt, learn, and change to fit this land where freedom is both a dream and a curse. Gish Jen, a delightful, powerful writer, creates unexpected images that tickle the imagination. Her commentary on Chinese and American society is constantly thought-provoking, while her technique of italicizing translated Chinese dialogue (with increasing amounts of English thrown in) helps to put us in Helen's, Ralph's, and Theresa's minds as they journey between languages, cultures, and ways of thinking.

E.B.

Waterlily, Ella Cara Deloria, *1944 (1988), United States,* NOVEL

The story of the people of the Plains Indian Dakota culture and the Sioux Nation is told through the life of Waterlily from her birth through motherhood. Waterlily is born in the late 1800s during her village's migration to a new site. With permission from her mother-in-law, Waterlily's mother, Blue Bird, steps out of the walking line to go into the woods where, "against a spinning world she struggled to think coherently. Just what was it her grandmother once told a woman—something about the best position to induce an easy birth? . . . An eternity passed—and then, the child was a girl." Within minutes, Blue Bird rejoins the line with Waterlily pressed against her heart. The fabric of life in Waterlily's Dakota camp circle is woven of kinship obligations, ties "that held the people together, impelling them to sacrifice for one another" through joyously observed gift-giving rituals. Waterlily is instructed by the quiet modeling and supervision of all her family, the village elders, and *kola*—voluntarily bonded friends. Her story is a beautifully written and loving tribute to the strengths and wisdom of Sioux women, and to a culture whose primary desire is to make "duties toward others a privilege and a delight."

J.L.

Women's Ways of Knowing: The Development of Self, Voice and Mind, Mary Field Belenky, Blythe McVicker Clinchy, Nancy Rule Goldberger, Jill Mattuck Tarule, editors, *1986, United States,* NONFICTION

Women's Ways of Knowing offers new and useful understandings of the epistemology of the development of women's knowledge. While this already classic scholarly work is neither easily nor quickly read, there are many excellent reasons to read, use, and appreciate it. Earlier research in epistemology concentrated on predominantly undergraduate middle- and upper-class Caucasian males. Based on interviews with 135 women of various ages from a variety of cultural and economic backgrounds, *Women's Ways of Knowing* creates five "not necessarily fixed, exhaustive, or universal categories" of how women know what we know. The results of this study are insightful and applicable to everyday life. The authors, instead of speaking from the distant land of "objectivity" in the voice of the omnipotent "one," say "we" and talk about their process: how and why they did this study, the details of their planning, what surprised them, how the results affected their thinking, plans, and progress. A good example of what's possible when love informs science, *Women's Ways of Knowing* illuminates—with warm and welcome light—scholarly theories about how people learn and know.

J.L.

Working-Class Women in the Academy: Laborers in the Knowledge Factory, Michele M. Tokarczyk and Elizabeth A. Fay, editors, *1993, United States,* ESSAYS

Written by teachers, students, and retired academics in styles ranging from the formal and academic to the informal and personal, each of these twenty diverse and enlightened essays makes an intense and powerful examination of the realities working-class women encounter in academic life. Several authors write of the difficulties inherent in taking part "in projects to which they are not completely committed," and the contradiction they experience when vying for jobs with "male-identified women" whose "career goals outweigh their sense of responsibility to their community of colleagues and of students." The majority discuss the often confusing and always painful privileged-class assumptions predominant in academic discourse. A few, especially those previously trained to perform manual tasks, speak of their difficulty in valuing the activities of reading and writing as real work. And, without exception, all address the academy's failure—often expressed as blatant and hostile refusal—to address the reality of class issues. This collection provides the first forum for many of these scholars to analyze and discuss the recurring affronts they experience as their language, concerns, traditions, and culture are rendered "invisible." Through these singular voices and histories comes a remarkably unified and penetrating analysis.

J.L.

Writing a Woman's Life, Carolyn G. Heilbrun, *1988, United States,* NONFICTION

In this concise and eloquent feminist classic, Carolyn Heilbrun examines English-language fiction, biography, and autobiography written by and about women, and confirms her suspicion that the truths of female experience have been altered to assure that literature conforms with a predetermined and narrow definition of woman. Prior to 1970, "biographies of women made certain facts unthinkable," such as the existence in women of anger, rage, an open desire for power, or deeply felt sexual passion of any kind. According to Carolyn Heilbrun, when people with drive and ambition have no models, no exemplars, no stories to guide them, they must struggle to make their own choices outside of "safety and closure, which have always been held out to women as the ideals of female destiny, [but] are not places of adventure, or experience, or life." Some women have dressed like men, others—such as George Sand/Aurore Dudevant and George Eliot/Marian Evans—have taken men's pen names. Countless others have made choices that denied both personal and social truths about what it means to be a woman and condemned themselves to the "ultimate anonymity, to be storyless." This book is about more than just literature, however; it's about the pain caused when human desire and drive are denied, and about the choices all women have to make to find the courage to be fully alive people with stories.

J.L.

Yours in Struggle: Three Feminist Perspectives on Anti-Semitism and Racism, Elly Bulkin, Minnie Bruce Pratt, and Barbara Smith, *1984, United States,* ESSAYS

These thought-provoking personal essays examine the political reality of racism and anti-Semitism from the perspectives of three lesbian activists of widely differing backgrounds and identities who share mutual respect for each other's work. White, Christian-raised Southerner Minnie Bruce Pratt asks: "Where does the need come from, the inner push to walk into change, if by skin color, ethnicity, birth culture, we are women who are in a position of material advantage, where we gain at the expense of others, other women?" Barbara Smith, an African-American, examines the difficulty of talking about anti-Semitism to black women and about racism to Jewish women because, in a white-supremacist patriarchy, "white skin, and if you have it, class privilege, definitely count for something, even if you belong at the very same time to a group or to groups that the society despises." Elly Bulkin, an Ashkenazi Jew, traces the roots and growth of racism and anti-Semitism and ends with an appendix of questions "intended to challenge, to reveal changes in attitudes . . . to underscore how much each of us still has to learn" about our own culturally ingrained racist and anti-Semitic thinking and feeling. As these authors offer righteous rage without anger, and detailed analysis without tedium, their experienced concern with everyday justice charges this work with life-affirming energy.

J.L.

Wives, Lovers, and Partners

A husband gently washes his wife's hair as she lies stricken with polio. A young, unmarried woman flees to France to hide the impending arrival of a child. Joana McIntyre Varawa, in search of adventure, flies to Fiji, marries a man there, and creates a life in his culture. Idgie and Ruth run the Whistle Stop Cafe and make each other happy. Love may be an almost universal goal among human beings, but the routes we take to find it are as infinitely varied and complicated as people themselves. In literature, there are mythical, incandescent romances—Catherine and Heathcliff of *Wuthering Heights*, the Princess of Cleves and the Duc de Nemors, Ramona and Alessandro, Laura Esquivel's Tita and Pedro—all-consuming passions often taken to greater heights because of the obstacles placed in the lovers' way. Equally important are the everyday realities—the enduring relationships of the couples in *Stones for Ibarra* and *A Farm Under a Lake*, the stormy but equally constant commitment of Nora and James Joyce, the blissfully happy Lazy La Rue and her lover Pubah S. Queen, and the "homemade love" of J. California Cooper's characters. Some books offer critical commentary: George Sand, Amalie Skram, Anne Brontë, Brigitte Schwaiger, Siân James, and Zaynab Alkali take aim at marriage and show us that becoming a wife does not insure love, happiness, or self-fulfillment. *The Impenetrable Madam X* is a rollicking satire of erotic novels; *Possession* mixes a critique of romance and literary scholarship with a riveting mystery. Within these books, there are heights of passion and valleys of calm, reflective joy. There is loyalty, anger, trust, pain, bliss, and discovery.

Changes	Ama Ata Aidoo
Changes in Latitude	Joana McIntyre Varawa
Constance Ring	Amalie Skram
The Coquette	Hannah Webster Foster
The Day I Began My Studies in Philosophy and Other Stories	Margareta Ekström
Disappearing Acts	Terry McMillan
A Farm Under a Lake	Martha Bergland
Fried Green Tomatoes at the Whistle Stop Cafe	Fannie Flagg
The Heptameron	Marguerite de Navarre
Homemade Love	J. California Cooper
The Impenetrable Madam X	Griselda Gambaro
Incantations and Other Stories	Anjana Appachana
Indiana	George Sand
Lantern Slides	Edna O'Brien
Like Water for Chocolate	Laura Esquivel
The Lone Pilgrim and Other Stories	Laurie Colwin
Nightwood	Djuna Barnes
Nora	Brenda Maddox
Pembroke	Mary E. Wilkins Freeman
Possession	A. S. Byatt
The Princess of Cleves	Madame de Lafayette
Ramona	Helen Hunt Jackson
The Riverhouse Stories	Andrea Carlisle
The Samaritan Treasure	Marianne Luban
A Small Country	Siân James
The Stillborn	Zaynab Alkali
Stones for Ibarra	Harriet Doerr
The Tenant of Wildfell Hall	Anne Brontë
Why Is There Salt in the Sea?	Brigitte Schwaiger
The Works of Alice Dunbar-Nelson, Volume I	Alice Dunbar-Nelson
Wuthering Heights	Emily Brontë

Changes, Ama Ata Aidoo, *1991, Ghana,* NOVEL

After six years of marriage, a young woman, frustrated and unsatisfied by the demands of her husband and marriage, obtains a divorce. Within a year, she is involved in an affair with a married man. The scenario is not unfamiliar to Western readers, but it has its own twist in the hands of one of Africa's staunchest feminists and best-known novelists. In a style that is brisk and straightforward, Ama Ata Aidoo relates a story that is anything but. Esi is a college-educated woman who loves her work in the Department of Urban Statistics. When her affair with Ali deepens, he asks her to marry him—as his second wife. On the surface, polygamy gives Esi many advantages—she can throw herself into her work without worrying about home commitments and still have an ongoing relationship that satisfies her emotional and sexual needs. But things are rarely as they seem. Through Esi's conflicts, Ama Ata Aidoo takes us into a society bound by old traditions and deeply mired in colonialist attitudes. Esi and the women around her endure oppressions from all the cultures that have touched western Africa, and in showing their lives, *Changes* moves beyond the romantic entanglement of two individuals to become a social and political critique.

E.B.

Changes in Latitude, Joana McIntyre Varawa, *1990, Fiji (United States),* MEMOIR

Joana McIntyre has a strong sense of self-reliance and a deep sense of loneliness. She moved from California to Hawaii many years ago; her son is now grown, and she is searching for meaning beyond her secure but boring job. Looking for adventure, she flies to Fiji, and in a short time "had met a man who wanted to marry me. The reasons were all wrong in terms of my own culture, but the offer was real." A story of insight, warmth, and acceptance, *Changes in Latitude* tells in fascinating detail of Joana McIntyre's marriage into a foreign culture and her greater understanding of her middle-class background. Though her sense of loneliness abates amid her new extended family in Fiji, living in a foreign land raises new issues. The people in her village are proud Methodists, who pray to the God above the earth and the God below the earth, with rituals and hierarchy well established and unquestioned. But she does question—and she and her husband laugh and fight over—the "perfected complications of my own culture" versus the realities of her chosen one. She thinks the two of them watching a sunset is romantic; he finds it lonely without the people of the village. Yet as she immerses herself in her new life, she comes to appreciate that "Life in this village is a continuous ceremony. A soft spirituality pervades. . . . It is a dance of manners, assured, customary; it grants order and peace to life."

H.S.

Constance Ring, Amalie Skram, *translated from Norwegian by Judith Messick with Katherine Hanson, 1885, Norway,* NOVEL

France had *Madame Bovary*, the United States had *The Awakening*, and Norway had *Constance Ring*—each was written at the end of the nineteenth century, and each condemns the prevailing institutions of marriage and patriarchy. In *Constance Ring* the attack focuses on the sexual double standard set for men and women. Although the men in this novel argue for widely varying positions of political and religious liberality, in their private lives they maintain identical philosophies: it is excusable, even expected, for a man to carry on an affair with a working-class woman without it affecting his relationship with the upper-class woman he "loves." Constance Ring is a protected, naïve woman who goes through a series of disillusioning marriages and affairs with men before she realizes how all-pervasive the double standard is. Although the lack of positive options for women in *Constance Ring* is depressing, Amalie Skram does an exceptional job of showing us how society—through religious, legal, economic, and social institutions—works to keep the system of oppression operating. When Constance wishes to leave her first husband, there is no one, male or female, to support her decision; when her first husband dies and she is left bankrupt, she finds herself a woman with no way of supporting herself, fit only to marry again or commit suicide. Piece by piece, Amalie Skram reveals the structures that encircle a vibrant, beautiful woman, and leave her no room to move and no air to breathe.

E.B.

The Coquette, or, The History of Eliza Wharton, Hannah Webster Foster, *1797, United States,* NOVEL

Of the many cautionary novels written at the end of the eighteenth century that describe the seduction and betrayal of a beautiful young woman, *The Coquette* is one of the most interesting for twentieth-century readers. The character Eliza Wharton is based on an actual person, and her story is told through a series of letters which gives the book stylistic complexity. But it is the character of Eliza Wharton herself that distinguishes this book. Eliza is no ingenuous sixteen-year-old; she is past adolescence, has opinions, and wants more from her life than the narrow path that has been allotted to her. She agrees to an engagement she does not want because "both nature and education had instilled into my mind an implicit obedience to the will and desires of my parents," but also because "I saw, from our first acquaintance, his declining health; and expected, that the event should prove as it has." After her fiancé's death, she rejects a second potential husband because he bores her, and becomes caught up in the flattery of the dashing Major Sanford as much for the sense of adventure as in hopes of matrimony. Her death was the required literary ending for a "fallen woman" in her time, but Eliza Wharton's dynamic, frustrated personality and the questions she raises about women's place in society make this both a cautionary tale and a critique of the world that made such tales necessary.

E.B.

The Day I Began My Studies in Philosophy and Other Stories, Margareta Ekström, *translated from Swedish by Eva Claeson, 1989, Sweden,* SHORT STORIES

Margareta Ekström's stories cherish life and the tenuous, common, beautiful connections between people that are a part of it. Even when life is painful—when her stories are about divorce, attempted suicide, or betrayal—it is still precious and solid. A man remembers caring for his wife stricken with polio: "How good [her head] felt in his hands when her black hair was slippery and full of soap and lay there like a sort of fine-mesh fabric beneath his hands. He knew every seam of her skull and the hollow in the back that got filled with a sea of sweat whenever she made a great effort." Half-asleep, a seventy-year-old woman sees hands—her own, her mother's, her grandmother's?—birthing a baby, milking a cow, touching a man—"as though it was something holy, then, jovial and impetuous, having fun now, they caressed and kneaded, and they rested with a handful of happiness that no one could see." After witnessing a fight between his parents, a boy climbs in bed with his sister and her fiancé: "They put their arms around him. With their bodies they reassure him that they exist and the world exists as well, even if it has cracked." This collection is less than a hundred pages, the stories themselves are delicate and narrow in focus, yet each one unfurls like a silken parachute until it seems to touch the whole world.

E.B.

Disappearing Acts, Terry McMillan, *1989, United States,* NOVEL

Why do women choose the men they do? There are no answers in this book. Instead we find Zora Banks, a music teacher with dreams of becoming a singing sensation and the raw talent to build a future. She falls for the beautiful, chocolate-colored, sometimes working Franklin, who fills her empty spaces with affection and soul-touching sex. For a time nothing matters but their passion, a passion that wanes in the midst of misunderstanding, lies, betrayal, and fear. Zora's friend warns her: "You even starting to fool yourself. You better be careful, or you gon' start disappearing a little bit at a time. . . . Won't even remember who Zora Banks was." Terry McMillan's writing is characterized by lively, sometimes explosive conversations between friends and lovers. The honesty grabs readers to remind them that truth is found in the most unusual places: "That's what's wrong with women anyway. Get fucked real good, think we're in love, then we spill our fuckin' guts, give 'em our love resumes in chronological order and what information do they give up?" *Disappearing Acts* creates an atmosphere in which we experience the dance with Franklin and Zora, a dance that is at times full of energy, life, and ecstasy, at other times painful, draining, and nightmarish.

S.C.

A Farm Under a Lake, Martha Bergland, *1989, United States,* NOVEL

Janet Hawn is driving back to rural Illinois, to the town and farms where she and her husband Jack grew up, to the place where they've always wanted to return. But life has taken paths neither Jack nor Janet envisioned, and now twenty years have passed. Janet has a job driving eighty-year-old May, a woman who no longer speaks, to May's daughter's house. While on this drive, Janet talks about her connections to Jack and to the land, putting yearnings into words for the first time, maybe because it's easier and safer with a listener who doesn't respond. Janet realizes "that I was making this trip to Illinois to learn what to say or what to do about who I was . . . I was trying to sort—with my skin and my eyes and my breathing and my remembering—what to keep, how far to draw a line of . . . what? Sisterhood? Eminent domain? Marriage? Duty? I don't yet know the terms for inside and outside." At the same time, watching and helping May, she can't help but wonder what her life will be like when she herself is eighty. Janet's journey is inward and poetic: she consciously senses and tries to understand how life can overtake you while you are living it, how you can suddenly find yourself somewhere you never thought you would be, and how this realization can put you on a new path.

H.S.

Fried Green Tomatoes at the Whistle Stop Cafe, Fannie Flagg, *1988, United States,* NOVEL

Set in a small Alabama train stop town in the 1930s, this gem of a book almost could have been shelved as just another light romantic comedy. The chapters jump back and forth through time as various women's voices tell anecdotes of Whistle Stop. We hear from Mrs. Threadgoode, reminiscing fondly from her nursing home in the 1980s, and the chatty Dot Weems, editor of the gossipy town newsletter (1929–1969), and then listen in on spirited dialogue set in the town of Whistle Stop itself. The storytellers never find use for the label "lesbian," nor do they see fit to take us behind closed doors, but this is nevertheless the irresistible story of a fierce and true love between two women, Idgie and Ruth. After Idgie saves Ruth from an abusive marriage, these two friends become partners in running the Whistle Stop Cafe, where no one, "not even hobos and colored," is turned away for inability to pay. Readers are set down in the corner booth to eavesdrop on the comings and goings of an array of eccentric, ragtag characters who drop in for buttermilk biscuits, Big George's barbecue, and, eventually, news about their own hometown murder mystery. Among revelations big and small, Fannie Flagg mixes descriptions of small-town life and direct confrontations with racism, sexism, and ageism—told in the colorful and endearing language of the depression-era South—with the cafe's recipes for grits, collard greens, and, of course, fried green tomatoes.

C.M.

The Heptameron, Marguerite de Navarre, *translated from French by P. A. Chilton, 1558, France,* SHORT STORIES

Although its authorship has never been conclusively proven, *The Heptameron* is generally accepted as the work of Marguerite de Navarre, queen of Navarre and the sister of François I. *The Heptameron,* which has parallels to both Chaucer's *Canterbury Tales* and Boccaccio's *Decameron,* presents some seventy very short stories told by five gentleman and five lady travelers who find themselves stranded in an abbey. Proposed as an edifying method of passing time, the storytelling—as well as the conversations that follow each one—rapidly (d)evolves into an all-out verbal battle between the sexes. Most often the tales concern lovers, romantic conquests, and women's virtue—an object of intense pride and considerable power, or a prize of questionable or infinite value, depending upon the point of view. The stories include intimate details of adultery, flattery, betrayal, rape, and war; their very boldness and honesty may surprise many twentieth-century readers. The author declares that these stories actually were told by a group at the court of François I; the tellers testify to the veracity of their individual tales, and scholars have substantiated the claims for as many as twenty of the stories. Fictional or true, *The Heptameron* provides a rare and fascinating glimpse into the sixteenth century. Alternately bawdy, violent, chaste, funny, scatological, and sad, *The Heptameron* is a book to delight, offend, and educate twentieth-century readers.

E.B.

Homemade Love, J. California Cooper, *1986, United States,* SHORT STORIES

Homemade Love is "love that is not bought, not wrapped in fancy packages with glib lines that often lie." The stories in this collection are narrated by friends, relatives, and nosy neighbors, in voices so direct and familiar they sound as if they were talking over the back fence: "Ain't life funny? This life thing will drive you crazy if you let it! Me? I'm a hundred-degree woman and I ain't goin let it! But life is funny, and some people don't know how to live it. They fools!" The obstacles the characters face seem insurmountable, but through real loving and hard work, they are overcome. As in life, true love is attained in different ways and according to different needs. Dearie B, the "simple" cousin, cuts a valentine into the exact number of people she loves. A lonely, unattractive man eventually finds humor in his disfigurement. These and other stories enlighten, enrich, and satisfy our yearnings for the characters' fulfillment. J. California Cooper espouses the belief that there is someone for everyone, and that someone is probably right here at home. As she says, "All I know is there ain't nothing like love."

D.N.-W.

The Impenetrable Madam X, Griselda Gambaro, *translated from Spanish by Evelyn Picon Garfield, 1984, Spain (Argentina),* NOVEL

The Impenetrable Madam X is a brilliant and hilarious spoof of an erotic novel. Undaunted by her prologue—"the erotic novel's greatest obstacle is the difficulty it has coming to a literary climax"—Griselda Gambaro plunges forth. Madam X, an aristocrat who lives in early twentieth-century Barcelona, Spain, has, by the "advanced age of twenty-seven," taunted lovers by refusing to reveal her name for so long that she has forgotten it herself. Ah, but not to worry. What's important is beauty. Passion. And mystery. Enter a mysterious suitor who, in the first of many letters, reveals himself as a man who knows how to get her attention: "I swell like the sails of a ship beset by a storm and then suffer the waning wind that renders everything limp, the deck slippery, the sails moist." Not surprisingly, his letters, soon accompanied by monumental exertions outside her second story bedroom window, obsess her. Meanwhile, Madam X, an agreeable woman in matters of passion, is often swayed—and otherwise detained and entertained—by her servants. Especially her maid Marie, who is as determined to have Madam X as Madam X is to have the gentleman destined to grow famous for "the size of his mast and the ferocity of his jet stream." Writing with extraordinarily wild, witty, and irreverent imagination, Griselda Gambaro manages to slip in many pointed and penetrating observations about the attempts of civil and religious authority to regulate human sexuality.

J.L.

Incantations and Other Stories, Anjana Appachana, *1991, India,* SHORT STORIES

In India—with its humid climate, spicy foods, bright flowers, and myriad religions—a country in the midst of change, we meet many personalities in these eight short stories. A curious schoolgirl finds out her classmate is no longer a virgin and watches for changes: "I could see no hidden fire in Rakesh's eyes, no answering flame in Amrita's." A wife wonders: "When did she get to retire? Was there ever any retirement from cooking and cleaning?" A woman, many years after her sister's rape and death, still feels the grief and thinks about rebirth and religion: "There is much to say about Hindu philosophy, for belief brings with it acceptance and hope. It denies the eternal damnation of Hell, makes explicable the inexplicable, is the only logical answer to the tormented why." Anjana Appachana delves into many subjects, especially the humanness of seeking and finding answers, sometimes in unexpected places.

H.S.

Indiana, George Sand, *translated from French by George Burnham Ives, 1832, France,* NOVEL

Indiana is the first of many novels written by George Sand, a woman whose behavior was often considered more shocking than her writing. Seen as a denunciation of marriage when it was published, the novel is the story of a naïve, love-starved woman abused by her much older husband and deceived by a selfish seducer. Indiana and her husband are terribly ill-suited to each other. He believes that "women are made to obey, not to advise"; Indiana is submissive, but "it was the silence and submissiveness of the slave who has made of hatred a virtue and of unhappiness a merit." Her seducer is an eloquent rake; as George Sand comments, "the most honorable of men is he who thinks best and acts best, but the most powerful is he who is best able to talk and write." What takes this novel beyond a simple romance of good women and bad men, however, is George Sand's ability to draw direct analogies between personal behavior and the trends and expectations of politics and society. When one character advises, "Do not break the chains that bind you to society, respect its laws if they protect you, accept its judgments if they are fair to you: but if some day it calumniates you and spurns you, have pride enough to do without it," the reader is reminded that George Sand knew what she was talking about.

E.B.

Lantern Slides, Edna O'Brien, *1990, Ireland,* SHORT STORIES

Lantern Slides is an aptly titled book: each story here has a translucent yet vividly colored quality. Whether they tell of people on holiday, people in love, or children struggling to understand their surroundings, the stories are subtle in their motive, but rich in understanding, creating a world of memory and desire as physical as our own in color, texture, and taste. The characters in *Lantern Slides* all seek love, that "bulwark between life and death." In "Oft in the Stilly Night," the reader is a traveler who is told numerous stories about the inhabitants of a small town—the madwoman, the cheating husband, the ambitious young beauty: "Perhaps your own village is much the same, perhaps everywhere is, perhaps pity is a luxury and deliverance a thing of the past." Set primarily in Ireland, these stories relate a kind of beautiful despair, the sadness of those able to mourn without self-pity and to hope without self-delusion. Edna O'Brien's language is poetic yet not abstract; the dilemmas of her characters are universal yet deeply personal. She portrays loss without descending into bleakness or cynicism, and she never dismisses the possibility of hope, of life—"tender, spectacular, all-embracing life"—which each of the characters struggles to capture.

S.L.

Like Water for Chocolate: A Novel in Monthly Installments, with Recipes, Romances and Home Remedies, Laura Esquivel, *translated from Spanish by Carol Christensen and Thomas Christensen, 1992, Mexico,* NOVEL

Like Water for Chocolate is a deceptively simple book—a love story set in Mexico, interspersed with recipes, told in unadorned, uncomplicated language. Yet when the ingredients are combined and simmer, subtle and unusual flavors emerge. On one level, this is the story of Tita, youngest daughter of the formidable matriarch Mama Elena, who forbids Tita to marry her true love Pedro because tradition says that the youngest daughter must care for her mother until her death. When Pedro marries Tita's oldest sister in order to be near Tita, it begins a life-long conflict filled with passion, deception, anger, and pure love. Interwoven throughout the narrative are the recipes, which, like an ancient Greek chorus, provide an ongoing metaphorical commentary on the characters and their culture. Finally, there is the food itself that Tita creates as head cook on the family ranch—food so vibrant and sensual, so imbued with her feelings of longing, frustration, rebellion, or love, that it affects everyone who eats it. The combination of all these elements, with a good measure of the supernatural thrown in, makes for an earthy, quirky book, sad and funny, passionate and direct, related by Tita's grandniece—who follows in her footsteps, using her cookbook and continuing a tradition quite different from the one her great-grandmother tried to impose.

E.B.

The Lone Pilgrim and Other Stories, Laurie Colwin, *1981, United States,* SHORT STORIES

Laurie Colwin writes about relationships with the kind of clarity we might wish we possessed in the midst of them; but instead of being a cold observer, she takes us straight into the hearts of the characters she portrays with simplicity and sympathy. The women are serious, funny, sensitive, and smart. The men are charming and utterly irresistible cads or rangy men with large, tender hearts. All are complicated, interesting, and vivid people who work as illustrators, professors, architects, ranchers; all are steady, happy, untroubled—until their lives are completely undone by their hearts. Laurie Colwin's gift is her ability to capture pivotal moments: a young woman crosses to adulthood when she's kissed unexpectedly by her friend's father; a woman realizes her lover now hates her for all the things he fell in love with her for; a girl discovers to her horror that she's fallen in love with exactly the boy her parents wanted her to fall in love with; the "lone pilgrim" of the title story yearns for the settled life of her married friends, only to find herself hesitating on the brink of her desired happiness. In Laurie Colwin's deft but gentle hands, we see the subtle twists of relationships and know what awaits these lovers long before they do. In spite of the falls and bruises of love, the reader comes away happy, feeling that love and life are messy, but ultimately satisfying.

M.L.

Nightwood, Djuna Barnes, *1937, United States,* NOVEL

Written in convoluted and poetic language, *Nightwood* is an obsessive romance illuminating the demonic and destructive aspects of love. It tells the story of a beautiful young woman, Robin Vote, and Nora and Jenny, the two women who desire her and are eventually overwhelmed and destroyed by their own passions. Robin Vote, elusive and paradoxical, angelic yet amoral, intriguing because of what is kept from the reader rather than what is revealed, is the pivotal point upon which the story turns. A gothic undercurrent charges the book with tension: human is transformed into beast, beast into human. This theme appears over and over, and Djuna Barnes's obsessive telling of the tale melds style with subject matter. Throughout the book, Djuna Barnes interjects monologues from Dr. Matthew O'Connor, a gender-bending character whose words illuminate the storyline and provide a cohesive understanding of the plot. Formal, dense, even verbose, yet fluid and vivid, *Nightwood* circles and spirals, swirling around the shadowy plot to create a timeless tale of love and tragedy.

H.D.

Nora: A Biography of Nora Joyce, Brenda Maddox, *1988, Ireland/France* (*United States*), BIOGRAPHY

In 1904, having known each other for only three months, a young woman named Nora Barnacle and a not-yet-famous writer named James Joyce left Ireland. He had refused to marry her, proclaiming his adamant opposition both to the institution of marriage and to the institution that would solemnize their vows. Yet this unholy exit from a struggling land was the beginning of an amazing partnership, which eventually led to marriage, and endured for thirty-seven years. Brenda Maddox's biography of Nora Joyce is a remarkable social history, revealing much about Irish life and character and providing a vivid reconstruction of the elegantly vagabond existence of the perversely charming and brilliant writer and his little Irish entourage. The book is about Nora Joyce, who emerges as a unique and fascinating character, but ultimately it is a portrait of her relationship with James Joyce and of the impact she had on his work. Nora Joyce was her husband's "portable Ireland," and he uses her words, her experiences, and her soul to create his female characters. Hers is an evolution from an unsophisticated but not simple Irish maid to the worldly woman whom James Joyce introduces as Molly Bloom in *Ulysses* and Gretta Conroy in *The Dead*. The Joyces' union was complicated, committed, and sometimes shocking, yet Nora emerges as a warm, intelligent woman who was a powerful force behind one of the great literary figures of the twentieth century.

R.S.

Pembroke, Mary E. Wilkins Freeman, *1893, United States,* NOVEL

Much of the strength of Mary Wilkins Freeman's work comes from its deep grounding in nineteenth-century New England culture. With a cool eye, she saw the eccentricities, pride, and religious self-righteousness of those who lived around her, and depicted these qualities in her work, sometimes lovingly, sometimes with scorn. *Pembroke* combines both this love and this scorn in its portrait of several couples. Barnabas and Charlotte are engaged to be married; one night Barney enters into a heated political discussion with Charlotte's father and is ordered from the house. He swears he will never return, even if that means giving up Charlotte. Barney's sister, Rebecca, falls in love with William Berry, but when her mother forbids the relationship, Rebecca sneaks out to see him, with disastrous results. Sylvia Crane has kept company with Richard Alger every Sunday night for twenty years, but he has just never managed to ask her to marry him. Time and again these couples come close to happiness; time and again one or both of them shove it away. It might be easy to dismiss these people, but Mary Wilkins Freeman makes sure we understand that they are just that—people, who deserve love, even as they hold the world at arm's length. Through their lives she lets us see what it is like to be cold, inside and out, when there is warmth to be had.

E.B.

Possession, A. S. Byatt, *1990, England,* NOVEL

Roland Mitchell, underpaid English research assistant, is on a search for nineteenth-century poet Randolph Henry Ash's copy of *Vico*, in the hopes that Ash will have written something enlightening in the margins. The book is brought up from the vaults of the British Museum, and in it Mitchell finds far more than Randolph Ash's thoughts on *Vico*. Hidden between the pages, unknown to anyone, are two rough drafts of a love letter to an unknown woman, written by Randolph Ash—a man scholars believed was faithfully married. From here on, the plot thickens, to include romance, poetry, parodies of feminist and Freudian criticism, trips to old houses and foreign countries, thefts, deceptions, and true love. *Possession* is a novel about literary scholarship—a hymn of praise and an attack—a book about modern romance and the lack of it. It is a novel of many voices and about the difficulty of knowing anyone's voice, even one's own. It is a magnificent read—thick and engrossing. A favorite with book clubs, *Possession* elicits great discussions; readers either love it or hate it, but everybody has an opinion.

E.B.

The Princess of Cleves, Madame de Layfayette, *translated from French by Robin Buss, 1678, France,* NOVEL

Written more than three hundred years ago, *The Princess of Cleves* transports the reader to seventeenth-century French court society, where "love was always allied to politics and politics to love. No one was untroubled or unmoved: each considered how to advance, to flatter, to serve or to harm; boredom and idleness were unknown, since everyone was engaged in intrigue or the pursuit of pleasure." The story concerns a strikingly beautiful young woman, raised in seclusion and brought to the court at marriageable age. She is married to the Prince de Cleves, a powerful, sensitive man who adores her and hopes she will eventually reciprocate his feelings. Unfortunately, Madame de Cleves falls passionately in love with the Duc de Nemors, a man "born with every predisposition for courtship and every quality tending toward its success." Lost letters, whispered messages, extensive introspection—all are described in minute detail as Madame de Cleves attempts to overcome her feelings and remain a virtuous woman. The obsession of these characters can seem excessive, yet Madame de Lafayette is careful to place this story within a larger historical context that shows the extraordinary influence that such intimate affairs had upon foreign and domestic policy. Her book gives an insider's view into the personal lives of Henry VIII, Mary Stuart, Queen Elizabeth, and others, as she initiates Madame de Cleves and the reader into the morals and political maneuverings of her time and class.

E.B.

Ramona, Helen Hunt Jackson, *1884, United States,* NOVEL

Along with *Uncle Tom's Cabin, Ramona* is considered one of the great propaganda novels of the nineteenth century. Helen Hunt Jackson was already part of the literary elite when she learned of the efforts of the Ponca Indians to keep their land in Nebraska. She spent six months researching and writing *A Century of Dishonor,* which describes the treatment of Native Americans by the United States government, then mailed a copy to every United States Senator. When her book had little effect, she wrote *Ramona,* the fictional love story of a beautiful, illegitimate Scots-Indian orphan and the handsome and courageous Indian Alessandro. Ramona has grown up a privileged, adopted child, unaware of her ancestry. When she chooses Alessandro, she becomes Indian. Persecuted and betrayed by individuals and the government, Ramona and Alessandro struggle and flee. Their deep and powerful love is portrayed in dramatic and classical terms, while the tragedy of their lives is the tragedy of their people, who endure brutal poverty and the loss of their land. *Ramona* succeeded where *A Century of Dishonor* did not; it achieved best-seller status and focused attention on an issue many had been unaware of. Unfortunately, the results were not always beneficial. The book has the flaws of being created by an author who, although deeply engaged and sympathetic, had not experienced the life she was describing. Still, it is a moving love story and a fascinating example of the use of fiction to attempt political change.

E.B.

The Riverhouse Stories: How Pubah S. Queen and Lazy LaRue Save the World, Andrea Carlisle, *1986, United States,* SHORT STORIES

As the introduction attests, *The Riverhouse Stories* was one of those books that had a hard time finding a publisher. And it *is* a difficult book to categorize. The stories are short (a few pages at most), and at first glance, incredibly simple. There is Lazy LaRue, contemplating a difficult cat, and Pubah S. Queen, determined to organize her life. There are stories on feeding ducks, seeing rainbows, and visiting friends. While the subject matter changes, the feeling does not: all are fanciful, glowing, thoughtful—childlike in the best meaning of the term. If you are one of those people who thinks the world needs to be saved by something more practical than love, you might be inclined to dismiss this book. But give yourself a chance. Enter Lazy and Pubah's houseboat, where all dreams are listened to and life is often composed of simple issues. Wonder at Pubah, an electrician—a female in a male-dominated profession, a woman with ever so much to do. Smile at Lazy, who writes and thinks wide thoughts and finally decides to write about the woman she loves. And wait, as their whimsical, beautiful life sneaks into yours.

E.B.

The Samaritan Treasure, Marianne Luban, *1990, United States,* SHORT STORIES

With rich imagery and insight, these five stories by Marianne Luban give perspective on Jewish life throughout the ages. A survivor of the Nazi camps, now living in the United States, tells a young American: "Those with courage were killed off almost immediately. Brave people are not survivors." Then she admits to him, "I was a *Kurveh* . . . a whore." That was how she "survived"; now, she deals with the personal consequences. "Professor Mondshane," a fifty-five-year-old voice teacher from Vienna, falls in love with a teenage student, who readily tells him: "I don't know any Jews—except you. Anyway, I guess Jews are human beings, no different from anybody else." A story in the form of a warmly written letter will leave the reader to wonder: Was the love of Jane Austen's life the Jew of Bath? The title story is a history of an area where there "seems to be a curse, but to whom it extends and what must be done to lift it, not even the wisest in Israel know." The final piece, which moves between Rome in the 1950s and England in the 1970s, is a story of a love lost for twenty years, of two lovers keeping from each other the fact that they are Jewish. Marianne Luban delights and amazes with her cast of characters, her movement through time, and the feelings she elicits with her words.

H.S.

A Small Country, Siân James, *1979, Wales,* NOVEL

When Rachel was young, her father wanted her to marry a man who could "unite two good farms." But Rachel's heart and hand went to handsome, black-eyed Josi Evans, a proud tenant farmer who, in both social status and age, was decidedly her junior. As the story opens, Catrin, Rachel and Josi's eighteen-year-old daughter, awaits the arrival of her elder brother Tom, home from Oxford for the summer. She is full of news: the hay is ready for cutting, their mother is very ill, and their father is gone, "off with one of his women. . . . A special one, perhaps. Anyway, he's set up house with her and their baby." Tom responds with predictable shock and determines to bring their father home just as soon as Edward, his Oxford roommate, finishes his imminent visit. The fact that Catrin flushes every time she hears Edward's name is only noticed by Nano, the family's lifelong servant. With the wild and beautiful landscape of Wales as a backdrop, the Evans family—along with their friends, foes, neighbors, and servants—struggle to understand and come to terms with personal pain and shame in the midst of an increasingly urgent and demanding national crisis—the onset of World War I.

J.L.

The Stillborn, Zaynab Alkali, *1988, Nigeria,* NOVEL

"It is well to dream . . . as long as we live, we shall continue to dream. But it is also important to remember that like babies dreams are conceived but not all dreams are born alive. Some are aborted. Others are stillborn." Zaynab Alkali's first novel, *The Stillborn,* follows the dreams of three Nigerian village women: Li, Awa, and Faku. All three wish to marry; each envisions her own satisfying future. Enchanted by tales of city life, Faku marries, moves to the city, and becomes the second wife of a polygamous husband. Awa marries the local school's headmaster and proclaims she will "not need to go to the city. The city will come to us." Progress does come to the village, but brings unexpected consequences for Awa. Li, the book's central character, marries her dashing lover but waits years in her village for him to come and collect her, only to discover that life with him is worse than without him. Each woman faces a changing world that presents both potential loss and a chance for freedom as traditions collapse and new ones form. *The Stillborn* sharply criticizes the sexism of traditional Nigerian society and the lack of roots in the new city-based culture, while at the same time it praises the strength and determination of three women who choose different paths into unhappiness and must find their own ways out.

E.B.

Stones for Ibarra, Harriet Doerr, *1985, Mexico (United States),* NOVEL

This is the story of an Anglo married couple, Richard and Sara Everton, who, in a burst of idealism, move from San Francisco to an old family home and abandoned mine in Mexico. Why, in the face of vociferous objections and concern from all their friends, would they move to a house they know has no electricity or water and aren't even sure is still standing? Richard and Sara go "in order to extend the family's Mexican history and patch the present onto the past. To find out if there was still copper underground and how much of the rest of it was true, the width of sky, the depth of stars, the air like new wine, the harsh noons and long, slow dusks. To weave chance and hope into a fabric that would clothe them as long as they lived." The story of their years as Ibarra's only foreigners—Richard's work, his illness, Sara's work, her care of Richard, their neighbors and friends, the constantly surprising landscape, the stones—is told with affectionate and patient wisdom. Perhaps it was a story a long time coming: Harriet Doerr got her B.A. at age sixty-seven and published this (her first) book a year later.

J.L.

The Tenant of Wildfell Hall, Anne Brontë, *1848, England,* NOVEL

Of the three Brontë sisters, Emily and Charlotte are better known, yet it is Anne's work that carries some of the strongest feminist themes. In *The Tenant of Wildfell Hall* a devout young woman named Helen falls in love with a man who is handsome, but whose values are questionable. Willing to believe she can alter his character, she marries him. Her marriage is one of misery she has no power to change until she devises a bold plan to take control. Her story comes through two voices —her own and that of Gilbert Markham, a man who falls in love with Helen later in her life—and is told through journals and letters written over a period of time. Because of the privacy and immediacy of these narratives, the reader sees personal changes and attitudes Helen and Gilbert are often unaware of at the time: we witness Helen's first naïve protestations of passion for her husband and follow her through her eventual disillusionment; we recognize Gilbert's early, unconscious egotism. While the plot continues and mysteries are unraveled, what Helen and Gilbert say—as well as what they don't say—provides another thread to follow, one which reinforces Anne Brontë's indictment of the sexual double standards of nineteenth-century Britain.

E.B.

Why Is There Salt in the Sea? Brigitte Schwaiger, *translated from German by Sieglinde Lug, 1977, Austria,* NOVEL

Why Is There Salt in the Sea? is the internal monologue of a young woman who marries the first boy who ever kissed her, only to find that she no longer loves the man he has grown into. Stuck in a marriage she doesn't want, the narrator observes her life in an almost deadpan stream-of-consciousness critique of patriarchy that is often painful and often humorous. Amidst ongoing commentary by her father, mother, husband, and lover concerning her stupidity and lack of preparedness for the real world, are her uncensored internal philosophical inquiries about the nature of men, or beautiful, provocative musings on her surroundings. On her honeymoon in Italy, in the midst of her husband Rolf's complaints about food and weather, she notes that Michelangelo may once have grasped the door latch she is now touching: "A small, secret happiness. I sneak fragments of pleasure out of Rolf's day." Yet for the most part this lovely, artistic personality is overwhelmed by the dogmatic opinions of her husband and relatives. Her monologue is a cry of frustration and a demand for freedom that many women will recognize.

E.B.

The Works of Alice Dunbar-Nelson, Volume I, Alice Dunbar-Nelson, *edited by Gloria T. Hull, 1895–1898, United States,* SHORT STORIES/POETRY

Blistering Bayou nights. Crowds of Creoles—laughing, dancing, loving, scheming. Voodoo queens, solemn cathedrals. Victorian gowns, greasy markets. Steamy streets of the French Quarter, angling away from moonlit Gulf lagoons. Boatmen languishing under the stars shimmering over swarmy Lake Pontchartrain. Seductive images so vivid and sensuous, they transport readers back to the Bayou country of southern Louisiana in the late nineteenth century. The author suspends time in the twenty-nine vignettes and poems of *Violets and Other Tales*, published in 1895, and the fourteen selections in *The Goodness of St. Rocque and Other Stories*, composed after her marriage to Negro Poet Laureate Paul Laurence Dunbar and published in 1898. While the stories in *The Goodness of St. Rocque* are especially well-crafted, all of her fiction demonstrates her early genius. Peppering her stories with a variety of dialects, she creates a chorus of voices that contrast with the sometimes romantic, sometimes ironical, always teasing voice of her narrator. Mostly, the stories are about love—unrequited, illicit, betrayed, avenged. And her lovers, like the author herself, are an ethnic mélange: immigrant grocers of the old countries—France, Italy, Greece; Camille, the beautiful, sequestered orphan; Annette, an accomplished, deceived songstress; the garrulous woman who sells pralines by the archbishop's chapel, endlessly waving a fan; an abused, distraught wife; M'sieu Fortier, Athanasia, Mr. Baptista, La Juanita, Titee. The characters and stories enchant with complex themes, pathos and beauty, color and wit.

J.M.

Wuthering Heights, Emily Brontë, *1847, England,* NOVEL

Wuthering Heights is a classic tale of possessive and thwarted passion, one of the forerunners of today's soap operas and romance novels. The tempestuous and mythic story of Catherine Earnshaw, the precocious daughter of the house, and the ruggedly handsome, uncultured foundling her father brings home and names Heathcliff, is played out against the backdrop of English moors no less wild and raw than the love they develop for one another. Brought together as children, Catherine and Heathcliff quickly become attached to each other. As they grow older, their companionship turns into obsession. Family, class, and fate work cruelly against them, as do their own jealous and volatile natures, and much of their lives is spent in revenge and frustration. Yet there is something magnificent about the depth and intensity of their love. Even as you condemn Catherine and Heathcliff for the pain they inflict upon themselves and others, it is hard not to listen in awe when Catherine cries out, "I *am* Heathcliff! He's always, always in my mind; not as a pleasure, any more than I am always a pleasure to myself, but as my own being."

E.B.

Work

At its best, work sustains and fulfills us. When we are held back by gender, class, or race, however, work can become soul-numbing, a theft of spirit and energy. The authors in this section show us the beauty, frustration, inspiration, boredom, challenge, and obstacles that make up women's work. Fanny Fern portrays one woman's struggle and eventual success as a writer in the nineteenth-century United States; *Rosie the Riveter Revisited* gives us the oral histories of women who worked in factories during World War II. Three "maids" teach us about work and class relations: Monica Dickens writes a humorous firsthand account of going from upstairs debutante to downstairs servant in early twentieth-century Britain. *Lady's Maid* presents a new perspective on Elizabeth Barrett Browning and the meaning of tragedy through its sensitive, fictional re-creation of the life of her maid. Set across an ocean and more than a century later, Alice Childress's vibrant and sharply pointed monologues let the reader know that a domestic worker is never "like one of the family." Passionately describing their experiences as migrant field workers are Toby Sonneman, a college graduate inspired by John Steinbeck, and María Elena Lucas, who began working as a farm laborer at age five. Margaret Mead and Alva Myrdal, and characters created by Natalya Baranskaya and Moa Martinson, focus on the added stresses and complexities of workers who are also mothers. Through the lives of five women, Mary Catherine Bateson plays out her theory that women "improvise" in their career paths in order to blend work with life. Penny Armstrong is a midwife among the Amish; Linda Hasselstrom is a cattle rancher; Anna Britt is a research scientist whose work becomes the object of observation in *An Imagined World.* A woman's work is never done—but these books show us that each woman's work is distinctly her own.

Alva Myrdal	Sissela Bok
Angie, I Says	Avra Wing
Blackberry Winter	Margaret Mead
Bobbin Up	Dorothy Hewett
A Bridge Through Time	Laila Abou-Saif
Call Home the Heart	Fielding Burke
Composing a Life	Mary Catherine Bateson
Daughter of Persia	Sattareh Farman Farmaian with Dona Munker
Doc Susie	Virginia Cornell
Forged Under the Sun	María Elena Lucas with Fran Leeper Buss
Fruit Fields in My Blood	Toby Sonneman
The Home-Maker	Dorothy Canfield
An Imagined World	June Goodfield
Lady's Maid	Margaret Forster
Like One of the Family	Alice Childress
A Midwife's Story	Penny Armstrong with Sheryl Feldman
A Midwife's Tale	Laurel Thatcher Ulrich
More Work for Mother	Ruth Schwartz Cowan
One Pair of Hands	Monica Dickens
Rosie the Riveter Revisited	Sherna Berger Gluck
Ruth Hall and Other Writings	Fanny Fern
Storm in the Village	Miss Read
A Week Like Any Other	Natalya Baranskaya
Windbreak	Linda Hasselstrom
Women and Appletrees	Moa Martinson

Alva Myrdal: A Daughter's Memoir, Sissela Bok, *1991, Sweden,* BIOGRAPHY

Constantly woven through Alva Myrdal's work on global problems was the intensely personal question of whether a rational balance is ever possible between work and marriage. Alva Myrdal's daughter, Sissela Bok, has written a multilayered chronicle of her mother's work and life that focuses on the achievements and on the emotional conundrum embodied in that question. On one level, this is a straight biography of Alva Myrdal—social reformer, educator, author, ambassador, cabinet minister, first recipient of the Albert Einstein Peace Prize, Nobel Prize winner. On another level, *Alva Myrdal* is a portrait of an older woman struggling for feminist rights, as viewed by a younger one who is ultimately the beneficiary of that battle. On yet another layer is Alva Myrdal as seen by her daughter. While Sissela Bok's love and respect for her mother are clear throughout, so is the anger, confusion, and estrangement felt by her and her siblings as a result of Alva Myrdal's public self and social activism. The unsettling news for readers who still hope that a magical balance between commitments can exist is that even the estimable Alva Myrdal did not succeed in "having it all." Hope and reaffirmation come in the wealth of her accomplishments and the strength of her spirit: "The greatness in being human lies in not giving up, in not accepting one's own limitation."

K.B.-B.

Angie, I Says, Avra Wing, *1992, United States,* NOVEL

Tina, the novel's narrator, and Angie, her best at-work friend, work as secretaries for a computer company in New York City. At just thirty, Tina counts as her priorities men, money, and clothes. And work, of course. Angie, the mother of three kids and wife of a mean husband, is the only person Tina can talk to, when there's time. Tina's no slouch when it comes to having opinions or knowing what she wants: "It's the ones in suits I like. The good suits. You can tell. Not like the jerks I see . . . I mean, Vinnie's got a suit, but it's green." She's also gentle enough to feel troubled by her own and others' pain. Told in Tina's raucously loving voice, *Angie, I Says* is full of surprises as it swings, rollicks, and rocks along with hilarious observations about terribly serious situations; it provides a welcome and sadly realistic perspective on the lives of one subset of that giant ageless category called "working girls."

J.L.

Blackberry Winter: My Earlier Years, Margaret Mead, *1972, United States,* AUTOBIOGRAPHY

During her lifetime, Margaret Mead (1901–1978) was the world's most famous anthropologist. In this insightful memoir, she recalls her childhood, her place in her family, and how the lessons learned and ideals instilled then shaped her life. Margaret Mead was the first child of a university professor father and a social activist mother; her paternal grandmother, who lived with the family, had been a school principal and taught the Mead children at home for much of their youth. In college, Margaret discovered anthropology, and as a graduate student went to Samoa to conduct the research on adolescent girls that resulted in her then-shocking study, *Coming of Age in Samoa.* In *Blackberry Winter*, she reflects on her life and work, through three marriages and groundbreaking field work in eight cultures. But perhaps her most fascinating revelations are the "gathered threads" of her own experiences of childhood, motherhood, and grandparenthood. In her observations of sex roles, childhood, and parenting styles in other cultures, in her appreciation of her own upbringing, and in her shift to single, working motherhood after the breakup of her third marriage, she anticipated and pioneered a new model for family life. "In my family I was treated as a person," she writes. "It was never suggested that because I was a child I could not understand the world around me and respond to it responsibly and meaningfully." Affirmed and valued for herself during her childhood, Margaret Mead was able to be herself throughout her life.

L.A.

Bobbin Up, Dorothy Hewett, *1959, Australia,* NOVEL

One night in 1958, Sputnik is visible in the Australian night sky. Throughout that night, *Bobbin Up* takes us into the lives of a group of women who work at the Jumbuck Woollen Mills in Sydney. We step into the deplorable working conditions of the factory and immediately feel the workers' frustration at the lack of time or energy or money to live beyond the bare necessities. At the mill, the "unspoken policy" is to create tension and resentment between the day and night shifts. If they're fighting each other they don't complain about the harsh conditions: no hot water, old machinery, no respect from the bosses. Betty has worked at the mill for eighteen years; she has her own routine and doesn't want to be bothered with the troubles of the others. Nell, an active communist, is awakened by her husband as Sputnik passes overhead. He's been fired and she wonders, Now what? The older of two sisters in the mill worries about the younger one: "How can she know right from wrong? I ought to have been a better mother to her." Overnight, workers' lives change. The next day, for "legitimate capitalist" reasons, some women are fired, some are given fewer hours—and none can afford less work. Will they rise together against yet another injustice thrust upon them? Based on the author's experience of working in textile mills, the story of these proud women resounds with the truths of life, friendship, and work.

H.S.

A Bridge Through Time, Laila Abou-Saif, *1985, Egypt,* AUTOBIOGRAPHY

The contrasts in Laila Abou-Saif's life are many. Born in 1941 and raised in Cairo, she grew up in a family that valued education for both men and women, and arranged marriages for their children. After her college graduation she endured a seven-year marriage to a man chosen by her family. An Arab woman raised in the Coptic church, a Christian minority in Egypt, she developed an awareness of all the citizens of her country and began to question the true costs of the ongoing religious war with Israel. During a performance for injured soldiers in Cairo, where she taught theater at the Academy of Arts, she realized that "in order to reach the masses, Egyptian theater must retain its indigenous roots, must remain visual, physical, and musical." Using this insight, she put herself at odds with the politicians in power by challenging the government's actions in her productions. During the forty days of mourning the death of a family member, in seclusion with other women, she was inspired to film a documentary on Egyptian women. When the finished film was shown in New York City, its feminist approach threatened and angered many Egyptian officials, who retaliated by denying her access to local theaters. Despite her experiences, Laila Abou-Saif's love of her homeland is consistently felt throughout her autobiography as we come to know this vulnerable yet determined woman, honest about her faults, and committed to her beliefs.

H.S.

Call Home the Heart, Fielding Burke (Olive Tilford Dargan), *1932, United States,* NOVEL

"Before she was seven, Ishma, the youngest child of Marshall and Laviny Waycaster, had joined the class of burden-bearers. By the time she was thirteen there was little rest for her except on Sunday." Ishma is the loving, spirited, and restless hero of this novel of the thirties. Sunday is her day to escape the drudgery of farming and helping her irascible mother with domestic work, a day she jealously protects to roam the hills of her beloved mountainous homeland and revel privately in its beauty. When Ishma is courted and encouraged to marry for economic advantage, she renews her decision never to be a wife; when she falls in love, her hesitations vanish. Money is scarce; the land does not always produce despite unending hard work and love. Her decision to follow her heart and move to the city so she can learn more about the world is nearly as painful as the inner death she fears if she does not. What she learns both bruises and builds her character. Written with breathtaking beauty and keenness of feeling, *Call Home the Heart* recalls a not-so-distant period of American working people's history that we can be both proud and pained to know.

J.L.

Composing a Life, Mary Catherine Bateson, *1989, United States,* NONFICTION

"It is time to explore the creative potential of interrupted and conflicted lives, where energies are not narrowly focused or permanently pointed toward a single ambition. These are not lives without commitment, but rather lives in which commitments are continually refocused and redefined." Utilizing the theme of improvisation, Mary

Catherine Bateson examines her own life and career, as well as those of five other women—an anthropologist and writer, a psychiatrist with special interests in the homeless, an educator and president of Spelman College, an engineer and owner of her own company, and a dancer, artisan, and writer—and weaves them into a fat braid of lost, discarded, and reworked strands that continually emerges with a new shape and texture. She carefully laces in the extraordinary with the ordinary of life, and portrays these exceptional women as human and understandable rather than superhuman and aloof. With the exception of the author's occasional tendency to vent her frustrations about her experience as dean of a prestigious Eastern college, this is an accessible and rich intermingling of the lives of wonderful, mature women. Mary Catherine Bateson quotes her mother, Margaret Mead, as saying that she believed women possess "post menopausal zest." If that is the case, this book should be an inspiration for the present and future "Age Wave" generation.

M.H.

Daughter of Persia, Sattareh Farman Farmaian with Dona Munker, *1992, Iran,* AUTOBIOGRAPHY

This wide-ranging autobiography begins with a history of the Persian people from ancient times through the rise of the Ayatollah Khomeini in 1979. Sattareh Farman Farmaian, born in the early 1920s, grew up in her father's compound, one of many children by one of his many wives. Her father, an ardent believer in education, supported Sattareh's determination to became the first female in her family to receive an advanced degree. In time, she realized her dream of opening the Teheran School of Social Work, and taught health and hygiene to hundreds of students over the years. Immersing herself totally in her work, she chose not to speak up about the abuse of power by the corrupt Iranian government or against the shah and his lust for material possessions. When the shah's government collapsed, she was accused of having supported his injustices. Despite her work of the previous twenty years, she was kidnapped, interrogated, and forced to leave Iran. *Daughter of Persia* is a phenomenal read; it offers a personal look at how both the shah and the United States government chose to see only what they wanted to see. Sattareh Farman Farmaian's is an important book, both for its history and its life story.

H.S.

Doc Susie: The True Story of a Country Physician in the Colorado Rockies, Virginia Cornell, *1991, United States,* BIOGRAPHY

In 1943, after reading about her in *Pic* magazine, Ethel Barrymore wrote to Susan Anderson and offered to buy the dramatic rights to her life story. "Doc Susie," then seventy-three, refused. But Ethel Barrymore had good instincts: Doc Susie's life was dramatic. Virginia Cornell's straightforward, accessible biography begins in 1907, when Susan Anderson, already a practicing physician, is dying of tuberculosis at the age of thirty-seven. She takes a death-defying train ride to the tiny, isolated high-altitude town of Fraser, Colorado, where she cures herself, then stays on for the next fifty-one years to treat the resident population of loggers, farmers, railroad personnel, and tunnel diggers. An opinionated woman, she is eager to lecture rural patients on the importance of vitamins, swing an axe at an illegal still, or tell off a farmer for treating his cows with more care than he shows his pregnant wife. She refuses to use or prescribe opiates, even painkillers. When telephones are installed, she tries one, then gets rid of it. She never buys a car; instead she hitches rides on horses, cars, and trains (sometimes on the cowcatcher if the ride is short). Virginia Cornell's years of research bring to life Susan Anderson and her time, informing the reader about an independent, strong-willed woman and about the human cost of the logging and railroad industries that are integral to the history of the northwestern United States.

E.B.

Forged Under the Sun/Forjada bajo el sol: The Life of María Elena Lucas, María Elena Lucas with Fran Leeper Buss, *1993, United States,* ORAL HISTORY

María Elena Lucas has the ability to "look way back into people's eyes and see their hearts and minds and tell what's there. It's a different way of loving life, of seeing life." The oldest of seventeen children, she was born in 1941 in southern Texas, where she and her family earn their living as migrant farm workers. Hers is a life full of hardships and poverty so pervasive that her telling of it can make for heart-wrenching reading. Married at sixteen, she defies family and religious traditions when, several years later, she leaves her husband, takes her seven children to Ohio, and works the farms there. In Ohio, she realizes her calling as an organizer for migrant workers. Initially, she sets up a social service agency with other women to ease burdens suffered by all; eventually, she becomes a spokesperson for the Farm Workers Organizing Committee. It is work done essentially without pay and often without thanks. Her vision for a greater good carries her through many trials—the constant harassments from landowners, the resentment of migrant males toward a woman who expresses opinions, and, on a hot, dry day in the fields, the glass of salt water given her to quench her thirst. Permanently disabled in 1988 by pesticide spray, María Elena Lucas continues to fight for the rights of poor, working women.

H.S.

Fruit Fields in My Blood: Okie Migrants in the West, Toby Sonneman, photographs by Rick Steigmeyer, *1992, United States,* NONFICTION

As a Chicago schoolgirl, Toby Sonneman got migrant fever from reading John Steinbeck's *The Grapes of Wrath.* Necessity as well as a desire for experience took her and her husband, Rick Steigmeyer, despite college educations, to work the fields and follow the migrant stream for fifteen years. With a journalistic eye, she writes lovingly and intimately of America's "Okie" migrant work force, created by the Depression 1930s and currently near demise. Her book depicts the "exhilaration" of hard work and fresh air, and the overwhelming beauty of a cherry orchard seen from the top of a ten-foot ladder. It tells of the "whir of Buick tires on the highway" that stirs the blood and locks the lifestyle into a people's heart into the third generation. Perhaps most importantly, it is about "choosing a way of life considered to be without merit by the rest of society," despite the label of "low down fruit tramp," the hardships of a capricious harvest, and the failure of unions and legislation—for if the people from the Great Plains love anything, it is their family, their freedom, and their sense of pride and dignity. Toby Sonneman's book, winner of the Western States Book Award, speaks plainly and honestly, with the wit and wisdom of her subjects.

N.C.

The Home-Maker, Dorothy Canfield, *1924, United States,* NOVEL

This is a book for every stay-at-home mother who has ever felt guilty for wanting a nine-to-five job, for every father who spends his workdays longing to be home with his children. Far ahead of its time in 1924, *The Home-Maker* can still bring light to many who will find their frustrations, passions, and dreams revealed in the lives of Evangeline and Lester Knapp. For fourteen years, Evangeline has been a full-time homemaker, pouring her considerable talent and energy into making a perfect house and perfect children—"forced, day after day, hour by hour, minute by minute, with no respite, into the life-and-death closeness of contact with the raw, unfinished personalities of the children, from which her own ripe maturity recoiled in ever-renewed impatience." Lester, on the other hand, is an absentminded poet, hopelessly ill-suited to his job as an accountant. When Lester takes a near-fatal fall from a roof, however, their roles are reversed. Evangeline becomes a saleswoman—happy, fulfilled, making far more money than Lester ever hoped to—while Lester's paralyzed legs ironically provide him with a socially acceptable reason to stay home and relish the imperfect unfolding of his children's lives. Dorothy Canfield follows the Knapp family's life before and after the accident; she shifts her focus from one character to the next, illuminates differences rather than failings, asks for tolerance in a world bound by tradition. Her conclusion is both triumphant and painful, and raises as many questions as it answers about individuals and society.

E.B.

An Imagined World: A Story of Scientific Discovery, June Goodfield, *1981, United States,* NONFICTION

An Imagined World follows the scientific research of Anna Britt as she explores the connections between cancer and iron (among many other things). June Goodfield, a philosopher of science, weaves together the bits and pieces of science—the euphoria of insight, the dynamics of an international laboratory, the problem of obtaining funding, the need for exact experiments and an open mind—and creates a mystery that is both suspenseful and comprehensible. Those without a scientific background will need real concentration when it comes to the discussions of Anna Britt's research, but June Goodfield makes sure the technical aspects of the work are both fully explained and well paced as she intersperses scientific explanations with explorations of interpersonal relationships and biographical information. Particularly striking are Anna Britt's own poetic discussions of her work. Describing the feeling of being alone with her idea, knowing she is one of few who truly understand and believe it, she comments, "It's like walking literally into one of those landscapes of Dali; where the clocks just drip like hanging linen so that you don't even feel the touch of the wind. Everything is still: time is still, the landscape is still; and one feels very alone." In the end, this is a story about people and a process. Through June Goodfield's commentary and Anna Britt's interpretations, science becomes something that is electrifying, consuming, beautiful—and ultimately lonely: "Love is light, warmth and comfort. Understanding is just light."

E.B.

Lady's Maid, Margaret Forster, *1990, England* (*United States*), NOVEL

When history is retold from the viewpoint of a "peripheral" character, the legendary aspects of events may be rendered ironic by intimacy. So, too, "great works" of the leisure class can be seen in another light when looked at from the perspective of the servants whose shadowed lives sustained them. *Lady's Maid*, written from the fictional perspective of Elizabeth Barrett Browning's personal maid, is a subtle and disturbing record of the relationship between the social classes in nineteenth-century England. On the surface, Wilson has a good situation and a kind mistress, but as her service stretches over decades it becomes apparent that the "friendship" between mistress and servant is distorted by a dramatic imbalance of power. Margaret Forster's fictional account is gracefully understated; the ramifications of this imbalance develop only gradually, as Wilson's life is consumed by the priorities of the family she serves. The personal tragedies suffered by Elizabeth Barrett and Robert Browning seem melodramatic compared to Wilson's quieter tragedy. *Lady's Maid* leaves one thinking hard about the role that personal choice plays in a definition of happiness. By the end of the book, a woman's entire life has been spent in service to circumstances beyond her control; this is a powerful and significant story in itself.

K.B.

Like One of the Family: Conversations from a Domestic's Life, Alice Childress, *1956, United States,* SHORT STORIES

In a series of one-way conversations with her friend Marge, Mildred examines life from the perspective of an African-American—"Negro"—domestic worker in New York City in the 1950s. These monologues were originally published as a weekly series called "Conversations from Life" in Paul Robeson's newspaper *Freedom* and continued as "Here's Mildred" in the *Baltimore Afro-American.* Mildred pulls no punches about the nonsense she sees on every level of life. When her employer tells her—with affectionate, if arrogantly ill-informed, intention—that she is "like one of their family," Mildred graphically points out the critical life differences that exist between a servant/employee and the boss. The confines of traditional literary boundaries don't always fit an oral tradition. In Mildred's after-work and weekend conversations with Marge—interrupted by kids and endless meal-related work—there is a profusion of immediate, repetitive detail: "Here Marge, want some coffee?" "Let's talk while I do up these dishes." "Let me get you some more coffee." But Mildred's social insight, wisdom, and powerful belief in people are inspiring and contagious and make this a compelling read.

J.L.

A Midwife's Story, Penny Armstrong with Sheryl Feldman, *1986, United States,* NONFICTION

A Midwife's Story begins with Penny Armstrong's middle-of-the-night realization that she wants to be a midwife; by the time the book is over, Penny Armstrong has delivered more than one thousand babies and experienced a dramatic change in both her daily life and her beliefs. Her midwifery training begins in Glasgow, Scotland, and is as far from ideal as she can imagine. She is shocked by the noisy, bureaucratic environment; by angry, impoverished mothers who try to shove their babies back into the womb to avoid birth; and by inflexible hospital regulations that can endanger the lives of baby and mother. Back in the United States, she works as a midwife among the Amish in rural Lancaster, Pennsylvania. Over the years she finds herself absorbing their values of communal living, love, and assistance, and becomes convinced that birthing is an experience that can and should occur in the home. Ultimately, it is her glorious descriptions of childbirth (and even one death), contrasted with her portrayals of sterile and unsympathetic hospital experiences, that are most persuasive. In their collaboration, Penny Armstrong and Sheryl Feldman have created a loving and generous book that speaks to many people on many issues: childbirth, families, the Amish, marriage, deformity, death, commitment, technology, and respect for the land.

E.B.

A Midwife's Tale: The Life of Martha Ballard, Based on Her Diary 1785–1812, Laurel Thatcher Ulrich, *1990, United States,* HISTORY

After raising nine children between 1756 and 1779, Martha Ballard spent the last twenty-seven years of her life as a midwife. Her work involved not only the delivery of 816 babies, but also responsibility for a spectrum of essential medical services in the town of Hallowell, Maine. Her diary entries are the resource and catalyst for Laurel Thatcher Ulrich's essays on the social history of late eighteenth- and early nineteenth-century New England. The diary itself is a straightforward daybook filled with notes on the weather, miscellaneous household tasks, regional politics and economics, births, deaths, marriages, illnesses, and other incidents that represent the concerns of a typical woman of Martha Ballard's time and place. Yet the indomitable personality of Martha Ballard herself is the guiding force behind this history. Laurel Ulrich writes, "It is in the very dailiness, the exhaustive repetitious dailiness, that the real power of Martha Ballard's book lies. . . . For her, living was to be measured in doing.

Nothing was trivial." Each chapter of *A Midwife's Tale* combines diary entries and editorial discussion; Martha Ballard describes how she gathers and administers herbal remedies, delivers babies, and prepares bodies for burial, and Laurel Ulrich places these tasks in a larger social context, exploring the often conflicting roles of male medical practitioners and local female healers. *A Midwife's Tale*, winner of the 1990 Pulitzer Prize for nonfiction, is an innovative approach to history, a book to be studied and savored.

K.B.

More Work for Mother: The Ironies of Household Technology from the Open Hearth to the Microwave, Ruth Schwartz Cowan, *1983, United States,* NONFICTION

Why is it that "a man works from sun to sun but a woman's work is never done"? It hasn't always been this way, and Ruth Cowan's meticulously researched and engagingly readable book shows the transformation. *More Work for Mother* describes the change not in terms of a capitalist or patriarchal conspiracy, but rather as the result of a series of small steps away from the traditional farming family, with its gender-specific but equally time-consuming tasks, toward completely "separate spheres" for the sexes, and toward households as units of consumption rather than production. Inventions such as washing machines, cotton cloth, and even white flour acted as catalysts by giving the less well-off a chance at the comforts the prosperous already possessed—but in general it was men and children whose chores were relieved by these innovations. Needing money to buy the things they could not produce, men left farming to become wage earners, while children went to school, leaving Mother at home alone with "labor-saving" devices, no help, and raised expectations for yeast bread and clean clothes. Unfortunately, women's roles did not change as dramatically as the technology, and our current housework rules and habits have their basis in issues of personal control more appropriate to times long gone. Even today, despite a grand array of high-tech gizmos, women still spend as much time on home maintenance as they did eighty years ago. We can't go back to our agricultural past, even if we'd like to, but historian Ruth Cowan shows us new ways to envision and direct our future.

J.K.

One Pair of Hands, Monica Dickens, *1939, England,* MEMOIR

What does a young, well-off Englishwoman do with herself when she's thrown out of acting school and is tired of being a debutante? Well, if you're Monica Dickens, you become a cook. She makes the plunge to a life "below the stairs," confident in her abilities to be a cook because she once took a course in French cuisine. She quickly learns the difference between school learning and real life. Scalded milk, dropped roasts, and fallen soufflés plague her in her domestic career, but she perseveres. What makes this book so delightful is the sense of humor and drama Monica Dickens brings to her work. From dressing up for job interviews in a "supporting-a-widowed-mum look" to eavesdropping on dinner guests, she tackles her work with an enthusiasm for discovery. To her descriptions of battles with crazy scullery maids, abusive employers, and unwieldy custards, she brings a humorous and pointed commentary about the delicate ongoing war between the wealthy and their servants. This true-life account reveals a writer who wasted no opportunity to observe daily lives and dramas. Her keen eye for detail, youthful resilience, and sense of the absurd make *One Pair of Hands* a delicious inside look at the households of the British upper class.

S.L.

Rosie the Riveter Revisited, Sherna Berger Gluck, *1987, United States,* ORAL HISTORY

When the United States entered World War II, the government put out a call for women to serve their country by going to work in the defense industry, a call that changed the lives of many American women. *Rosie the Riveter Revisited* comprises oral histories of ten women who worked in defense factories in southern California. Though patriotic duty was a rationalization for some, they all worked for economic reasons. Single, married, and divorced; African-American, Chicana, and Caucasian; teenage to middle-aged, these women incorporate family histories with personal opinions about their work, the war, and the societal attitudes of the time. These warm, spirited women were all affected by their war jobs, and, though some were reluctant to acknowledge it, experienced personal transformation. For many it was the first time they worked on an equal basis with someone from a different ethnic background, or the first time they were financially independent. For one woman, this book is her only chance to talk about this chapter in her life; another wants to make sure the housewife's story is heard. The wartime jobs provided an opportunity, supported by society, for these women to broaden their roles and their images of themselves, even though the majority of them had to give up their jobs to men when the war ended. *Rosie the Riveter Revisited* sheds light on women whose lives and contributions have been barely acknowledged in history books.

H.S.

Ruth Hall and Other Writings, Fanny Fern (Sara Payson Willis Parton), *1855, United States,* NOVEL

In 1852, Fanny Fern became the first woman to be a regular newspaper columnist in the United States; by 1855 she was the most highly paid newspaper writer in the country, male or female. While she was capable of producing the tearjerking prose popular in her time, she was most famous for her biting, satirical commentary on everything from the weather to marriage to a woman's right to her own children. *Ruth Hall,* her first novel, is largely autobiographical and contains scathing portraits of her father, in-laws, and brother (the poet Nathaniel P. Willis), which earned her much criticism for her "unfeminine" attitude. The book concerns a young, happily married woman whose husband dies suddenly, leaving her with two children and no money. Neither set of parents is forthcoming with financial assistance, and Ruth is left to fend for herself—which, after much trial, she does admirably, and eventually establishes a name for herself as a writer. Hers is a female version of the American dream, and Fanny Fern is careful to note exactly why that dream is more difficult for women to attain. She is just as careful not to let her heroine's success and security lie in marriage: Ruth succeeds on her own, with her children, usually without the help of men. She is a wonderful character, and Fanny Fern's prose sparkles with a delightful viciousness. Revenge can be sweet, and for Fanny Fern it was highly profitable as well: in its first few years, *Ruth Hall* sold more than 70,000 copies.

E.B.

Storm in the Village, Miss Read (Dora Jessie Saint), *1958 (1987), England,* NOVEL

Storm in the Village is the third in a series of novels detailing the adventures of the Fairacre village school teacher, Miss Read (the pen name for retired English schoolteacher Dora Jessie Saint). The storm in the title is the government's proposal to buy Mr. Miller's Hundred Acre Field, just on the edge of Fairacre, to build a "worker's estate." As is natural in both major storms and small villages, minor squalls abound. Miss Jackson, Miss Read's assistant, is currently boarding with Miss Claire, who is getting on in years, but there are problems with this arrangement because Miss Jackson—whom "no one would call tidy"—seems determined to fall in love with the local scoundrel. When Joseph Coggs, Miss Read's twelve-year-old student, runs away from his drunken and abusive father and is discovered hiding in the school, the village is quick to respond. The storm swells as Mr. Miller vows he will die before he is forced to sell his land, while the vicar can't help but think how more people would increase the church's membership and prestige. Sometimes behind but more often in the midst of all this furor are Mrs. Pringle, the ever-prickly cleaning woman, and Miss Read, the happily single schoolteacher who observes, with witty generosity and "a spinster's straight aim," everything that goes on in Fairacre.

J.L.

A Week Like Any Other: Novellas and Stories, Natalya Baranskaya, *translated from Russian by Pieta Monks, 1969–1986, Russia,* SHORT STORIES

In the title story, Olga, a scientific researcher and mother of two, is asked to fill out a questionnaire about how her time is spent during an average week. The novella follows her through her week as she mends clothing; leaps onto an overcrowded bus in an effort not to be late, again, for work; sweet-talks laboratory technicians into doing her tests; does the communal shopping for the other "mums" in the laboratory; tucks in her children; fights and makes love with her husband; and tries to find time to fill out the questionnaire. This story provides a brilliant, evenhanded description of an employed mother's "full" life; there is frustration, love, and sheer exhaustion. Why, the questionnaire wonders, are Soviet women having fewer children? By following Olga's life, we learn both why they have children and why they might choose not to. Underlying it all is a condemnation of a system that expects women to be both comrades and baby-producers yet has done little to make it possible for these two roles to co-exist peacefully.

E.B.

Windbreak: A Woman Rancher on the Northern Plains,
Linda Hasselstrom, *1987, United States,* JOURNAL

South Dakota is a land where the only rule is "You can never tell what a bobtail cow will do." In the winter, the temperature can drop to minus fifty-six—if the wind only blows twenty-five miles an hour. Spring means getting up at ten p.m., midnight, and two a.m. to check on pregnant cows. Snowstorms at the end of April can decimate a vegetable garden. In the summer, you can spend fourteen hours a day haying, and the rest of the time watching for fires. Then there's canning, drying, and freezing to get ready for winter again. So why would anyone want to be a rancher in South Dakota? Not for money—Linda Hasselstrom's neighbors say they could make more selling their farms and living off the interest. Yet as she takes us, day by day, through one year, we become immersed in the details and moments that make up a rancher's life. Interspersed among the journal entries are Linda Hasselstrom's poems that have their roots in and draw their inspiration from her surroundings. The journal entries and poems combine to portray a life that is alternately harsh, lush, mind-numbing, and ultimately rewarding.

E.B.

Women and Appletrees, Moa Martinson, *translated by Margaret S. Lacy, 1933, Sweden,* NOVEL

"Tonight Mother bathes. It's a long time since Mother Sofi and Fredrika began their bathing. . . . Two middle-aged women, both of them nearly fifty . . . who bathe every week. Nobody ever heard of anything like that in the parish. . . . Hired men and maids, sons and daughters, once in the summer maybe, but married women? And year round?" Mother Sofi, the mother of fifteen children, and her friend Fredrika, childless, both married "up"—for money—from poor, landless parents to farmers with land, but improvements to their lives were short-lived. When Sally, mother Sofi's "illegitimate" and abandoned first child, and Ellen, Fredrika's niece, find each other as adults, their friendship grows fast and strong. Whether they work in ill-lit, crowded, dirty factories or attempt to plow overused soil, their lots in life are hard. Based on the author's experiences in the industrial slums of Stockholm and in nearby rural farming villages in the 1890s through the 1920s, *Women and Appletrees* portrays the life-sustaining importance of friendships among working-class Swedish women. Through her characters' struggles with economic, social, and religious proscriptions, Moa Martinson tells a powerful story of endurance and intimacy among heterosexual women living women-centered lives.

J.L.

Contributors

Lynne Auld is a photographer, writer, wife, and mother of two young daughters. She has an M.A. in art and anthropology and has lived and worked in Latin America, West Africa, and the Pacific. Her interests include ethnographic photography, and body decoration and dress as expressions of identity.

Kirsten Backstrom makes sculptural baskets, teaches writing classes, works in bookstores, and does odd jobs (sometimes very odd jobs) to support herself, but writing is her primary commitment. She has written essays, reviews, stories, poetry, and four novels, but has only begun to seek publication.

Gloria Attoun Bauermeister has a B.A. in communications studies. She has worked as a radio producer for the National Public Radio affiliate in Kansas City, and is currently enjoying motherhood, music, books, and art near the small town of Augusta, Missouri.

Kate Boris-Brown received her B.A. from San Francisco State University and attended graduate school in Russian language and literature at the University of Washington. Her career has centered around books—in retail sales, publishing, and libraries. She lives in Seattle, Washington, with her husband and two sons and steadfastly continues her one-woman campaign to keep Seattle's independent bookstores financially solvent.

Sharon Canning is a busy graduate student in Whole Systems Design at Antioch University, in Seattle, Washington. Currently, her goals include remembering how to read and write for the fun of it.

Cynthia Chin-Lee is a teacher, consultant, and author of *It's Who You Know* and the children's book *Almond Cookies and Dragon Well Tea.* She studied Chinese at Harvard University and the University of Hawaii and lives in Palo Alto, California, with her husband, Andy Pan, daughter, Vanessa, and two cats.

Dr. Nelle M. Christensen earned a B.A. in English at Southern Oregon State College (1968), and a master of social work from California State University at Sacramento (1975). A divorced mother of five, she received these degrees after the age of thirty-five and subsequently worked many years in social services, labor organizing, and counseling. In 1993, she became an ordained minister after earning a doctorate of divinity in Seattle, Washington, where she now lives.

Averill Curdy is a writer and technical editor living in Seattle, Washington. Reading is her vice.

Heather Downey holds a degree in women's studies and community development from Antioch University, Seattle, as well as a certificate in fiction writing from the University of Washington. She is currently co-authoring a book on reading groups. She likes to write and read experimental fiction, loves excessively loud punk rock music, and dreams of publishing her first novel sometime before the end of the century.

Martha H. O. Hagemeyer —"Bunny"—is a knowledge junkie and book addict with no regrets or remorse in either case. Her primary purpose is to age gracefully and have it said at the end (or is it the beginning?), "She was a warm, wise, and wonderful woman."

Prudence Hockley was born and raised in New Zealand. She has lived for the last fourteen years in the United States—in Denali Park, Alaska; upstate New York; and, most recently, in Seattle, Washington. She is a poet, a runner, an aspiring high school English teacher, and the mother of a son and a daughter.

Mary J. Rigor Kaplan was born in Astoria, Oregon, and spent most of her childhood living alternately in the United States and the Philippines. She is the mother of two girls, and most of her commitments involve activities and organizations that have to do with them. For the last three years she was the editor of a parent education newsletter for the Bellevue Community College's early childhood program. Presently she is developing plans for a children's museum for Seattle's Eastside.

Jane Keefer began reading science fiction at age twelve. Twenty years and one Ph.D. (chemistry) later, fiction shifted to fact. Shortly thereafter, her right brain rebelled and she spent nine years as a folk music teacher and performer. She still likes figuring things out, and now, through her work as a science librarian at Johns Hopkins University, she helps other people do this as well.

Chris Kellett has a Ph.D. in English and teaches literature and writing at Antioch University in Seattle. As a teacher of mainly older, adult women, Chris is particularly interested in the themes commonly addressed in women's literature and their connection to her students' lives.

Bharti Kirchner is the author of *The Healthy Cuisine of India: Recipes from the Bengal Region* and *Indian Inspired: A New Cuisine for the International Table.* She has written numerous articles, short stories, reviews, and essays for regional and national magazines. She teaches both writing and cooking classes in Seattle.

Sonja Larsen has lived in California, New York, and Montreal. In addition to holding down several jobs, she writes and reads as much as possible, hoping to learn for herself the secret of writing a great book.

Mary Hope Whitehead Lee writes poetry and creates collage. Her most recent project is an illustrated poetic biography of Mexican painter Frida Kahlo.

Phyl Levine's published writing is mostly confined to professional journals related to her Ph.D. in special education from the University of Washington, but her passions lean more toward esoteric poetry, limericks in bad taste, philosophical novels, and children's fantasy stories. She is currently writing a "chapter book" with her seven-year-old son. When she is not on the road with her husband and two sons, she can be found tackling research issues concerning youth with disabilities, seeking the perfect latte, jazz dancing, or baking challah with her kids.

Margaret Liddiard is a marketing communications professional and a passionate reader. At thirteen she set out to read the classics in one summer. She still hasn't finished, mostly because she has been happily sidetracked for a decade by short stories, essays, and novels written by women.

Nancy Cottrell Maryboy lives on the Navajo Reservation, working at Navajo Community College in Arizona in the area of Navajo philosophy and teacher education. She is of Cherokee and Navajo descent and has an M.F.A. in writing from Goddard College.

Colleen Marie McQueen is a copywriter, a gardener, a book lover, a singer, and a traveler. She is totally in love with her three-year-old son and her husband, and is impatiently waiting for a daughter.

Marilyn Meyer has taught in the Lake Washington School District in suburban Seattle for nineteen years. Her poetry, essays, literary reviews, and commentary have appeared in a number of Northwest periodicals. She is presently working on a collection of personal essays.

Joycelyn Moody teaches African-American literature and women's studies at the University of Washington in Seattle.

Donna Nichols-White is the mother of three children. She is the publisher and editor of *The Drinking Gourd*, a publication for home-schooling families.

Vickie Sears is a Cherokee/Spanish/English writer living in the Pacific Northwest. Her poetry, short stories, and essays have been anthologized in several works. She is the author of *Simple Songs: Stories by Vickie Sears*, and is currently working on a novel. Her pleasures include her partnership, teaching, engaging in Native American causes, being a therapist, writing, and being out-of-doors playing with her dog, Tsa-la-gi.

Suzanne Leslie Simmons has spent the last five years proving that the good life is lived in celebration of the poop that falls into the toilet. As a wife and a mother to four boys, she manages to carve from the daily tumult space sufficient to drink of life, and be touched by God.

Suzanne Sowinska lives in Seattle, where she is currently working on a book-length study, *American Women Writers and the Radical Agenda, 1925–1940*. Her list of great books written by women almost always begins with feminist writers who consciously adhere to the adage "The personal is political."

Rebecca Sullivan is a native of Butte, Montana. She studied architecture and American history at Vassar and did graduate work in Russian language and history at the University of Washington. She is a photographer and mother of two sons, Henry and Jackson.

Lesley Thompson-Scott is a doctoral candidate in English at the University of Tulsa. Her dissertation discusses the use of the engaging narrator in American slave narratives. She has published and delivered papers on American and British women writers including Sarah Fielding, Kate Chopin, and Gertrude Stein. She lives in Tulsa with her husband and two children.

Caren Town is an assistant professor of American literature at Georgia Southern University in Statesboro, Georgia. She has published essays on Sinclair Lewis, Theodore Dreiser, F. Scott Fitzgerald, William Faulkner, Anne Tyler, and teaching literary theory. Her most consuming project, however, is her daughter, Rosa, who is named for the uncompromising German feminist/socialist Rosa Luxemburg, and who usually lives up to her name.

Index of Titles

Index of Authors

Index of Books by Date

Note: If there is more than a ten-year difference between date written and date published, or if a collection was written over a period of time, refer to earliest date.

Index of Books by Genre

Autobiographies and Memoirs

Biographies

Diaries, Journals, and Letters

Essays

Interviews and Oral History

Nonfiction

Novels

Short Stories

Index of Books by Region and Country

Note: Based on book content; if author is not from that country, the author's country is listed in parentheses.

Middle East

North America

Oceania

South and Central America

Index of Books About People of Color in the United States

Index of Some Books About Lesbian and Gay People

FOR THE BEST IN PAPERBACKS, LOOK FOR THE 

In every corner of the world, on every subject under the sun, Penguin represents quality and variety—the very best in publishing today.

For complete information about books available from Penguin—including Puffins, Penguin Classics, and Arkana—and how to order them, write to us at the appropriate address below. Please note that for copyright reasons the selection of books varies from country to country.

In the United Kingdom: Please write to *Dept. JC, Penguin Books Ltd, FREEPOST, West Drayton, Middlesex UB7 0BR.*

If you have any difficulty in obtaining a title, please send your order with the correct money, plus ten percent for postage and packaging, to *P.O. Box No. 11, West Drayton, Middlesex UB7 0BR*

In the United States: Please write to *Consumer Sales, Penguin USA, P.O. Box 999, Dept. 17109, Bergenfield, New Jersey 07621-0120.* VISA and MasterCard holders call 1-800-253-6476 to order all Penguin titles

In Canada: Please write to *Penguin Books Canada Ltd, 10 Alcorn Avenue, Suite 300, Toronto, Ontario M4V 3B2*

In Australia: Please write to *Penguin Books Australia Ltd, P.O. Box 257, Ringwood, Victoria 3134*

In New Zealand: Please write to *Penguin Books (NZ) Ltd, Private Bag 102902, North Shore Mail Centre, Auckland 10*

In India: Please write to *Penguin Books India Pvt Ltd, 706 Eros Apartments, 56 Nehru Place, New Delhi 110 019*

In the Netherlands: Please write to *Penguin Books Netherlands bv, Postbus 3507, NL-1001 AH Amsterdam*

In Germany: Please write to *Penguin Books Deutschland GmbH, Metzlerstrasse 26, 60594 Frankfurt am Main*

In Spain: Please write to *Penguin Books S. A., Bravo Murillo 19, 1° B, 28015 Madrid*

In Italy: Please write to *Penguin Italia s.r.l., Via Felice Casati 20, I-20124 Milano*

In France: Please write to *Penguin France S. A., 17 rue Lejeune, F–31000 Toulouse*

In Japan: Please write to *Penguin Books Japan, Ishikiribashi Building, 2–5–4, Suido, Bunkyo-ku, Tokyo 112*

In Greece: Please write to *Penguin Hellas Ltd, Dimocritou 3, GR–106 71 Athens*

In South Africa: Please write to *Longman Penguin Southern Africa (Pty) Ltd, Private Bag X08, Bertsham 2013*